BLESSING
THE WORLD

BLESSING
THE WORLD

RITUAL AND LAY PIETY IN
MEDIEVAL RELIGION

DEREK A. RIVARD

THE CATHOLIC UNIVERSITY OF
AMERICA PRESS • Washington, D.C.

Copyright © 2009

The Catholic University of America Press

The paper used in this publication meets the minimum requirements of American National Standards for Information Science—Permanence of Paper for Printed Library Materials, ANSI Z39.48-1984.

∞

Library of Congress Cataloging-in-Publication Data
Rivard, Derek A.
Blessing the world : ritual and lay piety in medieval religion / Derek A. Rivard.
p. cm.
Includes bibliographical references and index.
ISBN 978-0-8132-1545-7 (pbk. : alk. paper)   1. Benediction.   2. Liturgics—History—Middle Ages, 600–1500.   3. Piety—History—Middle Ages, 600–1500.   I. Title.
BV197.B5R58 2009
264'.0200902—dc22
2008026818

For my family,

whose inestimable love, support, and generosity

made this project possible

and my dreams attainable

And in loving memory of my father,

Dr. William H. Rivard

CONTENTS

ACKNOWLEDGMENTS

This book would not have been possible without the invaluable assistance of many of my teachers, colleagues, friends, and family. Special thanks go first and foremost to my graduate mentor, Richard F. Gyug, who went above and beyond the call of duty time and time again, particularly in the effort and time he invested in helping me perfect my translations, improve my writing, and strengthen my powers of argument. For this and his excellent teaching I will always be deeply grateful.

I am also indebted to the advice, instruction, and kindness shown to me by Louis Pascoe, S.J., who gave his time and effort to help improve the manuscript and my own thinking over the course of many years. Thanks also go out to H. Wayne Storey, whose advice and assistance in applying for grants to fund my research were invaluable, as were his insights on my subject. I also owe a great debt to Maryanne Kowaleski, who pushed me in every way to become a better writer and historian. The advice and conversation of Daniel L. Smail were also of great value to me in laying the foundations for my use of anthropological theory, as were the comments and numerous suggestions for revision provided to me by Frederick Paxton. I would be remiss if I did not also express my great appreciation for my earliest mentors, Dean Ferguson, Patricia Ranft, and Diane Mockridge, for guiding, teaching, and preparing me for the path that has ultimately led me to this place and this work.

As well as these individuals, my friends and colleagues in Fordham's graduate program, most notably Louis Hamilton and Christopher Bellito, provided numerous helpful comments and suggestions in the course of my study of blessings. The reference librarians and staff of Fordham University, Central Michigan University, Michigan State University, and the University of Michigan's libraries also deserve thanks for their assistance to me throughout the composition of this work.

Special thanks, finally, to my family, William, Nancy, Elizabeth, and David Rivard, and to my friends Roy Drake, S.J., William Bulger, Dennis Thavenet, Sarah Purcell, and Daniel Herman, who all helped me survive the process of writing and revision with my wits and good humor intact. Blessings to you all.

ABBREVIATIONS

AB	*Analecta bollandiana*
AS	Johannes Bolland et al., eds., *Acta sanctorum quotquot toto orbe coluntur: Vel a catholicis scriptoribus celebrantur,* 68 vols. (Antwerp: Jacob Meursium et al., 1643–)
CAO	René-Jean Hesbert, ed., *Corpus antiphonalium officii III: Invitatoria et antiphonae* (Rome: Herder, 1968)
CB	Edmund Moeller, ed., *Corpus benedictionum pontificalium,* 3 vols. (Rome: Turnhout, 1971–73)
Clm	Codex latinus monacensis, Munich, Bayerische Staatsbibliothek
CSG	Codex sangallensis, Sankt Gallen, Stiftsbibliothek
CVP	Codex vindobonensis palatinus, Vienna, Österreichische Nationalbibliothek
DMA	Joseph R. Strayer, ed., *Dictionary of the Middle Ages,* 13 vols. (New York: Scribner, 1983–87)
Franz	Adolph Franz, ed., *Die kirchlichen Benediktionen des Mittelalter,* 2 vols. (Freiberg im Breisgau: M. Herder, 1909; reprint, Graz: Akademische Druck-Verlagsanstalt, 1961)
Ge	Antoine Dumas and Jean Deshusses, eds., *Liber sacramentorum gellonensis,* Corpus Christianorum Series Latina 159–159a (Turnhout: Brepols, 1981)

ABBREVIATIONS

MGH SRM Bruno Krusch and W. Levison, eds., Deutsches Institut für Erforschung des Mittelalters, *Monumenta germaniae historica: Scriptores rerum merovingicarum,* 7 vols. (Hanover: Impensis Bibliopoli Hahniani, 1885, 1913, 1920)

Mon. liturg. Monumenta Ecclesiae Liturgica

NCE *The New Catholic Encyclopedia,* 18 vols. (New York: McGraw-Hill, 1967)

PG Jacques-Paul Migne, ed., *Patrologiae cursus completus, series graeca,* 161 vols. (Paris: Parisiis, 1857–66)

PL Jacques-Paul Migne, ed., *Patrologiae cursus completus, series latina,* 222 vols. (Paris: Parisiis, 1844–64)

PRC Michel Andrieu, ed., *Le pontifical romain au Moyen Âge,* 4 vols., Studi e Testi 86–89, vol. 2, *Le pontifical de la curie romaine au XIIIe siècle* [The Thirteenth-Century Pontifical of the Roman Curia] (Vatican City: Biblioteca Apostolica Vaticana, 1940)

PWD Michel Andrieu, ed., *Le pontifical romaine au Moyen Âge,* 4 vols., Studi e Testi 86–89, vol. 3, *Le pontifical de Guillaume Durand* [The Pontifical of William Durandus] (Vatican City: Biblioteca Apostolica Vaticana, 1940)

RGP Cyrille Vogel and Reihard Elze, eds., *Le pontifical romano-germanique du dixième siècle* [The Romano-Germanic Pontifical of the Tenth Century], 2 vols., Studi e Testi 226–27 (Vatican City: Biblioteca Apostolica Vaticana, 1963)

RP12th M. Andrieu, *Le pontifical romain au Moyen Âge,* 4 vols., Studi e Testi 86–89, vol. 1, *Le pontifical romain du XIIe siècle* [The Roman Pontifical of the Twelfth Century] (Vatican City: Biblioteca Apostolica Vaticana, 1938)

INTRODUCTION

MEDIEVAL BLESSINGS AND RELIGIOUS RITUAL

The idea of a reality that lies beyond our understanding, a sacred being or power existing adjacent to yet distinct from the mundane world as we perceive it, is a common element of the religious belief of human cultures throughout recorded history. As a general student of religion, I have long been interested in this idea of the sacred, along with the rituals that implore its power and the cosmological beliefs that such rituals express. Numerous studies by archaeologists, anthropologists, and historians of the ancient and modern world have satisfied my interest with texts that I, an outsider to these disciplines, could nevertheless appreciate and that brought into focus for me both the fundamental characteristics of human religious belief and the peculiarities that distinguish one era's faith from another's. As a medievalist studying the liturgical ritual of the medieval church, however, these interests more often than not found little satisfaction in my professional reading. Concerned with tracing the uniquely Christian expression of belief in the theology and public worship of the medieval church, the historical and textual studies of traditional liturgists and medieval historians leave much unsaid regarding the more fundamental issues of how the human cultures of medieval Europe conceived of the otherworldly power of the sacred and its connection with their lives, and how ritual was used to express and reinforce this conception.[1]

1. Josef Jungmann, *The Mass of the Roman Rite,* 2 vols. (New York: Benziger, 1983), and Theodor Klauser, *A Short History of the Western Liturgy* (Oxford: Oxford University Press, 1979), are excellent representative syntheses of the historical approach. More recent works worth consideration are George Every, *The Mass* (Dublin: Gill and Macmillan, 1978), and Aimé-Georges Martimort, *The Church at Prayer: An Introduction to the Liturgy,* trans. Austin Flannery and Vincent Ryan (Collegeville, Minn.: Liturgical Press, 1988).

This lacuna was especially frustrating when I first became aware of a large body of rituals lacking both detailed contemporary commentaries and modern historical treatments, rituals the scope and variety of which nonetheless convinced me that they played an important role in medieval Christianity: liturgical blessings. Blessings range in complexity from simple Latin prayers spoken over the recipients to lengthy and complex rituals including prayers, alternate prayers, rubrics for actions and gestures by celebrants and participants, psalmody, litanies of saints, and scriptural quotation and allusion. These rituals served an exceptionally large number of purposes, often using similar formulas but frequently manifesting distinctive traits and qualities that hinted much about how medieval people understood both the divine and ritual, and how they used both to better their lives. Given the paucity of historical sources discussing these rituals, I have chosen to adopt a textual approach drawn more from religious studies than from history and focusing primarily on the broad ideas, beliefs, and trends found within the language of these texts themselves. Where sources exist to provide details about the historical context, usage, and reception of individual texts, I discuss these, but I always return to the rituals themselves to explore the fundamental questions they raise concerning the nature, meaning, uses, and perception of the sacred.

The necessary first step in my project, thus, is a working definition of the sacred by which to approach the medieval benedictions. I choose to define the sacred in the language of phenomenology, as something originating wholly outside the moral and rational order constructed by the human mind. This definition is drawn from the work of Rudolf Otto, whose terminology and study of this power, which he terms the *numen*, elegantly encapsulates the nature and evolution of human religious consciousness of the sacred and the divine; this definition will anchor my discussion of the holy and the sacred.[2] This understanding cannot stand on its own, for while it of-

2. Rudolf Otto, *The Idea of the Holy*, trans. John W. Harvey (Oxford: Oxford University Press, 1923), 1–30. According to this paradigm, the *numen* is not *irrational*, but *nonrational*, originating not in theological ideation but in a "daemonic dread" of the primitive human consciousness toward a nonrational experience, a moment that made the human mind aware of its "creature consciousness," a feeling of utter nothingness in the presence of undeniable Being (that is, ultimate reality or divinity), and its "dependence sense," a feeling of utter reliance on this present Being. The experience of this *numen*, its presence, and its effect on its observers, is encapsulated in Otto's concept of the *mysterium tremendum*, embracing dread, such as the holy awe of Job before the presence of God; wrathfulness, the interpretation of this divine awe

fers a useful frame in which to place the idea of sacredness, it does not address the subject of ritual or its meaning.[3] This is a vital subject for any liturgical study, but especially for this project, since it can help address and
answer a range of pertinent questions. What, for example, did ritual blessing
mean to its recipients and celebrants, how did this meaning fit into and explain Christian cosmology? What role did blessing play in social life? What
was it thought to accomplish, how did it do so; what needs did it fill or assuage? How was the divine conceived of in rituals, and how did blessings
contribute to the persistence and survival of medieval Christianity?

It thus seems prudent to add to Otto's definition of the sacred a fundamental definition of ritual that can delimit the central issues of the study of
medieval blessings while allowing room for interpretive creativity. In the anthropological literature on ritual, I found the most comprehensive and use-

---

by the overawed human mind; overpowering *majestas* derived from a plenitude of might and
being, such as was expressed in the Old Testament's understanding of Yahweh; and an urgent
energy, inspired in those in the presence of the *numen* by means of its vitality, passion, and
will. It is, Otto argues, the experience of this tremendous mystery and power that is the foundation of the human conception of the sacred and the origin of the idea of the holy in the religious consciousness.

3. Ritual and its purposes form the heart of the new and evolving discipline of ritual studies, a subdiscipline of anthropology. The literature on this subject is immense and too lengthy
to summarize here, nor can I make any claims to be fully versed in it. The theories of some anthropologists, however, can put medieval beliefs into the wider context of religious experience.
For an introduction to ritual studies and its leading scholars, an excellent starting place is Catherine Bell, *Ritual: Perspectives and Dimensions* (New York: Oxford University Press, 1997). The use
of such anthropological theory is not without its critics, however. In particular, Phillipe Buc's recent study of early medieval political ceremonials and solemnities convincingly demonstrates
that while specific rituals could be dangerous owing to their manipulation and subversion by
contemporaries, the social scientific idea of ritual itself holds real dangers for historians who accept political texts as descriptive and ignore their more subtle narrative and persuasive purposes. Buc argues that the concept of ritual is so dependent on postmedieval paradigms of religion
and society (especially the theologies of the Reformation and French revolutionary period) that
the very use of the term runs the risk of misapprehending both specific contexts and the larger
world vision of early medieval sources. While there is merit to Buc's position and his cautious
examination of early medieval political ceremonial, I disagree with his broader conclusion that
ritual should be rejected entirely as "too-often vague, and [too] essentially alien" a concept to
apply to medieval texts, especially texts that are emphatically ritualistic, as benedictions are.
Used judiciously, the models and concepts of social scientific theory can bring us closer to an
understanding of these laconic, often elliptical sources that lack the narrative or argumentative
purpose of the political rites Buc studies in *The Dangers of Ritual: Between Early Medieval Texts and
Social Scientific Theory* (Princeton: Princeton University Press, 2001).

ful formulation in Ronald Grimes's synthetic definition of ritual as a mixture of "ceremony" and "liturgy."[4] Ceremony consists of symbolic social drama, and helps define individuals and communities. It is also competitive, often dividing the world into us and them, acceptable and unacceptable, insiders and outsiders. Power is a central consideration of ceremony, and the actions of the ceremony often symbolize and embody power itself, power that ultimately can be used to control our shared social world. Finally, ceremony often masks social ambiguities or contradictions.[5] Liturgy, on the other hand, manifests itself as a combination of symbolic and apotropaic action, and consists of any formulaic action "with an ultimate frame of reference [i.e., a cosmology] and the doing of which is considered to be of cosmic necessity."[6] It is a ritual cultivation of true Being, a mode of tapping the way things flow, or of connecting with the order and reason things manifest in the world, the way in which a people becomes attuned to the way things really are.[7] Unlike ceremony, however, liturgy is interrogative, acting in order to be acted upon.[8] Liturgy makes events endure, preserving the memory of the past and preventing it from becoming mere artifact.[9] This two-part definition is useful for its breadth and for the fact that it is a happy marriage of many fundamental elements of ritual theory that are valuable in orienting the study of medieval blessings.[10] Throughout this study, these concepts will be used as

4. Ronald L. Grimes, *Beginnings in Ritual Studies,* rev. ed. (Columbia: University of South Carolina Press, 1995), 48.

5. Ibid. This interpretation of ceremony as imperative, "seizing" and holding power, implies control not simply of the social world but, I would argue, also of the natural world itself. While this is a fruitful understanding of ritual, it is certainly not the only understanding with merit. Ritual has also been viewed as an expression of the fact that the world *cannot* be compelled by humans; see Jonathan Z. Smith, "The Bare Facts of Ritual," in his *Imagining Religion: From Babylon to Jonestown* (Chicago: University of Chicago Press, 1982), 53–65.

6. Grimes, *Beginnings in Ritual Studies,* 51. Liturgy, therefore, is not defined here as sacred ritual, as it frequently is.

7. Ibid.

8. Ibid., 51–52. Grimes is careful, however, to note in this definition that liturgy, like all the other categories he defines as "ritual sensibilities" (including, in addition to those selected here, ritualization, decorum, magic, and celebration), shares certain motifs with other modes of ritual and is not "purely" liturgical: "What is unique to liturgy is not that it communicates (decorum communicates), proclaims (ceremony proclaims), or exclaims (ritualization exclaims), but that it *asks* [emphasis added]. Liturgically, one approaches the sacred in a reverent, 'interrogative' mood, waits in 'passive voice,' and finally is 'declarative' of the way things really are."

9. Ibid.

10. In its definition of ceremony as social drama are included elements of Arnold van

needed to help illuminate the meaning of ritual benedictions, and to demonstrate their utility in helping scholars think about the medieval liturgy in new and productive ways.

THE BLESSINGS AND LAY PIETY

The scholar of religious life of the laity in medieval European culture is faced with a challenge, namely, how to reconstruct the outlook and mentality of an age that is tantalizingly familiar to our own, yet of which both subtle and substantial differences lie hidden in the shadows of enigmatic sources and incomplete records. Thus, while the disciplines of ecclesiastical, liturgical, and devotional history blossomed throughout the last century, in particular in the efflorescence of studies on the "popular piety" of the medieval world in the past two decades, much work remains to be done in understanding fundamental questions of how ordinary medieval believers envisioned their cosmology, their place within that cosmic order, and their relationship to the powers of that cosmos.

It is my belief that in this realm of unanswered questions, the most significant one is how the medieval laity understood the connections between the human world and the numinous world of the sacred. For it is in this understanding, most often expressed through complex ritualized action, in a world set apart from mundane reality, that medieval religion exhibits its fundamental connection to the religion of the modern world, and indeed to all expressions of the religious mind. Recent scholarship has begun to address this issue in studies of medieval ritual, and of the relationship between those ubiquitous medieval expressions of the sacred, the patron saints, and the use of ritual by their devoted communities.[11] Yet one essential element of medieval religious culture has gone relatively unexamined: the blessings dis-

Gennep's, Victor Turner's, and Mary Douglas's ritual theories on rites of passage, liminality, *communitas,* purity, and pollution. The definition of liturgy as a cosmological act of necessity that attributes being and meaning to its participants' lives and times draws on the work of Mircea Eliade and Clifford Geertz, among others. For further discussion of these theorists, and bibliographical references, see the following chapters.

11. This scholarship is too extensive to quote in full; for some especially pertinent works addressing the connections between the sacred and ordinary believers, see Mary Mansfield, *The Humiliation of Sinners: Public Penance in Thirteenth-Century France* (Ithaca: Cornell University Press, 1995); Megan McLaughlin, *Consorting with Saints: Prayers for the Dead in Early Medieval France* (Ithaca: Cornell University Press, 1994); and Sharon Farmer, *Communities of St. Martin: Legend and Ritual in Medieval Tours* (Ithaca: Cornell University Press, 1991).

tributed by the medieval church, outside of the formal sacraments, to the lay congregations that eagerly sought these benedictions. While commonly acknowledged as a crucial element in the life of medieval people, the function of blessings is overlooked by most liturgists and historians, who focus instead on the textual transmission and long-term changes in these blessings and the rituals that surround them.[12] The most important exception to this pattern, and the one on which much of this study depends, is that of Adolf Franz's *Die kirchlichen Benediktionen im Mittelalter.*[13] Franz's seminal study of blessing in the medieval liturgy is an invaluable resource: it is not simply an anthology of texts but also an excellent record of his interpretations of their historical development, and his discussions of the numerous sources he collected and studied, both individually and collectively, feature prominently in the present study.

The liturgical rituals of blessing present an excellent window through which to explore the relationship between the human and the divine in medieval religion, for it was through blessings, as much as through the sacraments marking liminal moments, that the clergy and laity brought the pow-

12. The essential earliest collection of this *corpus* of material is Edmond Martène, ed., *De antiquis Ecclesiae ritibus,* 3 vols. (Rouen: Sumtibus Guillemli Behourt, 1700–1702); see also the more recent work of Edmond Moeller, ed., *Corpus benedictionum pontificalium,* 3 vols. (Rome: Turnhout, 1971–73), hereafter *CB.* Other collections will be addressed in chapter 1's discussion of the liturgical genealogy of benedictions in the medieval church. While the religious significance of blessings has begun to be explored for early modern Europe, their content and meaning to medieval people have been studied less in recent decades, which can only hinder our understanding of this era's piety and its conception of the sacred. For examples of this scholarship, see R. W. Scribner, "Cosmic Order and Daily Life: Sacred and Secular in Preindustrial German Society," in *Popular Culture and Popular Movements in Reformation Germany,* ed. R. W. Scribner (London: Hambeldon Press, 1987), 1–16; Scribner, "Ritual and Popular Religion in Catholic Germany at the Time of the Reformation," *Journal of Ecclesiastical History* 35, no. 1 (1984): 47–77; Scribner, "Interpreting Religion in Early Modern Europe," *European Studies Review* 13 (1983): 89–105; Virginia Reinburg, "Liturgy and Laity in Late Medieval and Reformation France," *Sixteenth-Century Journal* 23, no. 3 (1992): 526–46; John Bossy, "The Mass as a Social Institution, 1200–1700," *Past and Present* 100 (1983): 29–61; and Jean-Pierre Delumeau, "Un dossier de bénédictions," in *Fêtes et liturgie: Actes du colloque tenu à la Casa de Velázquez, Madrid, 12–13–14 décembre 1985* (Madrid: Casa de Velázquez/Universidad Complutense, 1988), 291–98.

13. Adolph Franz, *Die kircklichen Benediktionen des Mittelalter,* 2 vols. (Freiburg im Breisgau: Herder, 1909; reprint, Graz: Akademische Druck-Verlagsanstalt, 1961) (hereafter Franz). With Martène, Franz's two-volume study forms the early essential work on medieval benedictions to which this study is deeply indebted.

er of the sacred into direct contact with the elements of daily human life. These rituals acted to bridge a perceived gap between the holy and the humdrum. In their language and rich borrowings from scripture, they also served as a form of encapsulated belief that provides the historian an example of the practical implementation of ethical and religious values through the performance of ritual. As an action, every form of blessing includes three fundamental elements: the establishment of a relationship with the realm of the "wholly other," the source of the desired beneficial effect; a transfer, to a being or an object, of an efficacious quality emanating from that realm, through some form of mediation; and the enhancement of the existence of the being or object that receives this quality.[14] The ritual mediation of a blessing typically requires special gestures, since the body is the instrument with which the intermediary expresses the emotion, intelligence, and will necessary to tap into the mystical power of words, which are often associated with the power of creation and being.[15]

For the purposes of this project, medieval Christian blessings are further defined as an active process, a process of negotiation between the human world and the divine, involving three factors: veneration of the divine (provided by the prayers of the blessing uttered by the clergy), human behavior conditioned by that veneration (involving the promise of moral propriety on the part of the congregation), and the self-interest (perceived and actual) of human life and sacred being. Through the spoken and acted reverence paid to the power of God, the clerical actor and lay recipients or audience of these blessings promised virtuous behavior and thanksgiving in exchange for access to the power of the sacred world to transform and manipulate the mundane world. This exchange was often contextualized by allusion to the paradigms of sacred scripture, which provided a means by which to position the lives of the blessing's participants in closer rapport with the sacred history of the Christian world. Ritual blessings thus both expressed and reinforced the religious values of the participants and the continuity of these values (and their possessors' lives) within the larger reality of Christian history, and as such should be thoroughly explored as a source for understanding medieval popular piety and its connection to the historic liturgy and ritual of the me-

14. Julien Ries, "Blessing," in *The Encyclopedia of Religion*, ed. Mircea Eliade, 16 vols. (New York: Macmillan, 1987), 2:247. Note that Ries himself is employing language borrowed from Rudolf Otto's theory of the *numen*.

15. Ibid., 248.

dieval church. This exploration is the objective of this project, which aims to move beyond the genetic study of these texts of blessing and offer instead a reading of the meaning of these rituals in the medieval religious *mentalité*. The approach to this meaning is constrained by the relative paucity of discussion concerning the historical role of ritual and the sacred in traditional liturgical and ecclesiastical studies; for this reason I will occasionally make use of some of the abundant literature of the anthropological study of religion, ritual, and the place of the sacred within religious cultures of the modern world.[16]

As well as representing an untapped source for the exploration of issues of ritual and sacrality in medieval religion, blessings offer an excellent opportunity to further attack the flawed model of medieval religion as divided into two foreign and opposed camps, on the one side an intellectual religion of theological and liturgical sophistication embraced by the clergy, and on the other a popular religion of emotive, irrational ritualism and superstition.[17] This simplistic bipolarity has rightly been challenged by the work of medievalists such as André Vauchez, Richard Trexler, and R. N. Swanson, and by liturgists such as Pierre-Marie Gy, but it still lingers within

16. This literature offers several useful interpretive strategies by which to approach the historical study of ritual, which can be divided into four essential groups: those that describe rituals' phenomenology (analyzing their themes, processes, and types); those that identify a ritual's underlying structure as a symbolic system employing performative utterance (or active speech); those that consider its social functions, covariants, and processes; and those that examine its relationship to individual and group psychology (in particular, investigating the validity of the archetype in discussing ritual). This schema of interpretive strategies is drawn from Grimes, *Beginnings in Ritual Studies*, 38–39. For a comprehensive discussion of the evolution and structure of ritual studies, see Bell, *Ritual*, 1–90.

17. The origins of this view date back centuries, but it was most persuasively put forth in David Hume's *Natural History of Religion*, which is summarized in Peter Brown's critique of this interpretation of human religious experience; see Peter Brown, *The Cult of the Saints: Its Rise and Function in Latin Christianity* (Chicago: University of Chicago Press, 1981), 12–22. As Brown points out, this view involved historians' adopting a "two-tiered model" of religious history, wherein the enlightened, elite religion was seen as constantly threatened with destruction by the attitudes and beliefs of the vulgar, who always greatly outnumber the elites. Though this bipolar model has been largely discredited by recent historical research, the simplicity of the model has guaranteed its survival in circles outside academic history. For early discussions of the supposed differences between popular and elite religion, see Natalie Zemon Davis, "From 'Popular Religion' to Religious Cultures," in *Reformation Europe: A Guide to Research*, ed. Stephen Ozment (St. Louis, Mo.: Center for Reformation Research, 1982), 321–41, esp. 321–24; and Don Yoder, "Toward a Definition of Folk Religion," *Western Folklore* 33 (1974): 7–14.

the collective consciousness of historians who isolate liturgical ritual as a field more properly left to liturgists, without considering its relationship to the religious needs and desires of the laity.[18] As a corrective to this lingering misconception, this study of nonsacramental blessings' content proposes that these rituals were, at least in part, composed to meet the expressed needs and desires of the laity in their daily lives. The exact nature of the relationship between clerical ritual and congregation will be explored in the following chapters, and that exploration will be guided by a dynamic definition of popular religion as a belief system embracing both "official" and "unofficial" elements in a constantly evolving relationship of mutual influence.[19] The relationship between laity and liturgy, which I will term *responsiveness*, forms the central issue of a debate within the historiography of early modern blessings, the major contributions of which include the works of two scholars, R. W. Scribner and Virginia Reinburg.[20] The crux of this debate is the degree to which liturgy is a coercive means for an elite stratum of clergy to control "popular" piety or a response to the demands of that piety. Reinburg answers the question of the degree of coercion and responsiveness by asserting, through a careful study of vernacular treatments of the Mass by both clerical and lay authors, that the laity were encouraged to value different moments and elements in the Mass from those valued by the clergy, a difference expected by the clergy themselves, who were fully aware they were

18. André Vauchez, *The Laity in the Middle Ages: Religious Beliefs and Devotional Practices*, trans. Margery J. Schneider, ed. Daniel Bornstein (Notre Dame: Notre Dame University Press, 1993); Richard C. Trexler, *Public Life in Renaissance Florence* (New York: Academic Press, 1980); R. N. Swanson, *Religion and Devotion in Europe, c. 1215–c. 1515,* (Cambridge: Cambridge University Press, 1995); and Pierre-Marie Gy, *La liturgie dans l'histoire* (Paris: Editions Saint-Paul, Editions du Cerf, 1990). This historiographical disjuncture has in places been bridged: thus, in recent years the Mass and popular paraliturgical practices associated with the Eucharist have been examined by such medievalists as Miri Rubin, *Corpus Christi: The Eucharist in Late Medieval Culture* (Cambridge: Cambridge University Press, 1991); Charles Zika, "Hosts, Processions and Pilgrimages: Controlling the Sacred in Fifteenth-Century Germany," *Past and Present* 118 (1988); and Caroline Walker Bynum, *Holy Feast, Holy Fast: The Religious Significance of Food to Medieval Women* (Berkeley and Los Angeles: University of California Press, 1987). Other rituals in the liturgies of the medieval church have also begun to attract the attention of historians: see Frederick Paxton, *Christianizing Death: The Creation of a Ritual Process in Early Medieval Europe* (Ithaca: Cornell University Press, 1990).

19. This definition is drawn from the work of several scholars, notably Swanson, *Religion and Devotion in Europe*, 185–88, and Scribner, "Ritual and Popular Religion," 74–75.

20. See note 12, above.

promoting this disjuncture.[21] The Mass was perceived by the laity as being conducted in a ritual language of gestures and symbols drawn from secular life (for example, the decorum of the Mass closely resembled the decorum of the royal court), a ritual affair in which the laity and the clergy had distinct parts to play. In particular, Reinburg argues that the laity saw the Mass less as a sacrifice and sacrament than as a communal rite of greeting, sharing, giving, receiving and making peace, with many of these associated with seigniorial rites of justice, administration, and peacekeeping gestures. This interpretation perceives the late medieval and early modern liturgy as establishing a social and spiritual solidarity that linked God, the church, and the lay community. The implication for medieval blessings, like the Mass, is that in the eyes of the laity they were a means and process to obligate God to assist the human community.

The emphasis on ritual as the bonding of God, the ultimate source of order, to the human community is also reflected in the seminal work of R. W. Scribner on ritual in early modern religion, which sees a close connection between rituals of blessing and exorcism, as both are central elements in popular religion that help establish cosmic order in daily life. Such religion is popular, argues Scribner, precisely because it often develops through lay initiative.[22] Scribner divides ritual within popular religion into two distinct categories: "folklorised ritual," with dramatic liturgical functions such as the processions of Palm Sunday, which involve lay participation in the liturgy; and "magical ritual," such as the blessing of palms and exorcism of commingled salt and water, activities that are mainly apotropaic.[23] Magical ritual is close to animism, the belief that spirits are inherent in inanimate objects and must be driven out or pacified for the spiritual and bodily well-being of the humans who use them. A belief in an inherent physical power imparted by blessing was common in the early modern German states (the focus of Scribner's research), the natural consequence of the late medieval and early modern understanding of the world as functioning in terms of divine agency. Scribner argues that the ritual of blessing was "seen to provide spiritual order in the

21. Reinburg, "Liturgy and Laity," 529, 532, 541.
22. Scribner, "Ritual and Popular Religion," 74, 52–53.
23. Ibid., 53, 66–67, 70. The later activity plays a major role in many of the blessings to be examined in this study. Scribner associates such magical rituals with the sacramentals of the high and later Middle Ages, all of which were dependent on the disposition of the user and were popularly thought to function in the same manner as grace. For a fuller discussion of sacramentals and blessings, see chapter 1.

world through its liturgical function of making spiritually efficacious what was indicated corporeally."[24] Blessings also provide natural order by their apotropaic power of banishing the demonic spirits who provoke disorder in the medieval world. Thus, for Scribner, liturgy is both salvific and instrumental, a duality that is reflected in Scribner's understanding of popular religion not as a group of fixed categories or sets of practices, but as a continuing dynamic as it develops and relates to the institutional church. The boundaries and forms of popular devotion are constantly being crossed and redefined by the laity, while continually being assessed and reassessed by the ecclesiastical establishment; thus popular religion embraces both official and unofficial elements, and such rituals as the blessings studied in this work represent a mingling of responsiveness, official influence, and coercion.

These interpretations of early modern blessings and responsiveness are similar to those in Megan McLaughlin's investigation of early medieval prayer for the dead. McLaughlin has revealed that such prayers follow a distinctive pattern that reflects the distinctive social, economic, and cultural structures that existed at the time of its composition.[25] This responsiveness of prayer to the lay culture of its age is evident in the nature of prayers for the dead, which McLaughlin argues convincingly are primarily "associative," that is, full of social and ecclesiological symbolism designed to emphasize the complex networks binding the intercessor and the divine.[26] Prayer may, she suggests, be better seen then more as a symbol of identity than as an object.[27] This interpretation is appealing, as I see the prayers of blessings as connected to, reflecting, and being similarly shaped by their audience, expressing symbolically and concretely the needs, desires, and sense of identity of the laity who petitioned the clergy for divine power.

While blessings can be read primarily as the product of established religion and its orthodoxy, it is also valid to see these texts as an expression of the influence of magical thinking upon medieval religious practice. The power of blessing as a quasi-magical act is a secondary issue in the historiographical debate on the rise and role of magic and magical practices in the early Middle Ages. The scholarship on this subject, when it addresses the subject of blessings and their origins, minimizes the Christian origins and influences of blessing, and instead points primarily to the culture and religion of Germanic society before its assimilation into the Christian world by

24. Ibid.
26. Ibid.

25. McLaughlin, *Consorting with Saints*, 2.
27. Ibid., 248.

the missionaries of the Carolingian era.[28] The reconstruction of the pagan beliefs of this mainly oral culture comes from archaeological sources (particularly runes and burial practices) and Christian written sources from the Celtic, Anglo-Saxon, and Scandinavian peoples.[29] Such written sources can be problematical, however, owing to their removal in time from the culture they claim to depict and the possible influence of later Christian thought (a principal example being the ambiguities of the northern epic *Beowulf*).[30] What clearly emerges from the available sources is that the Germans were polytheists, with a strong animistic element in their religious beliefs. All of nature was alive with spiritual entities, a very holistic view of the world that focused on nature as the source of both food and healing.[31] All life was implicitly thought to be both connected in the macrocosm and to reflect within itself that relationship in the microcosm; signs had actual, physical relationship to meaning, and words (for example, in the image of runes in Anglo-Saxon and Scandinavian folklore) had a real power over objects and the forces of the world.[32] Little distinction was made between natural and supernatural forces, and a whole host of supernatural entities caused illness and misfortune.[33] The divinities of the Germanic pantheon were somewhat more beneficent than the mischievous or malevolent nature spirits, and they included gods who were both fathers and protectors of their people, while their spouses assured the fertility of the earth and cattle. If properly

28. For a discussion of this issue, see Pierre Riché, "Spirituality in Celtic and Germanic Society," in *Christian Spirituality: Origins to the Twelfth Century*, ed. Bernard McGinn and John Meyendorff (New York: Crossroad, 1985), 163–76; Karen Louise Jolly, *Popular Religion in Late Saxon England: Elf Charms in Context* (Chapel Hill: University of North Carolina Press, 1996); and James C. Russell, *The Germanization of Early Medieval Christianity: A Sociohistorical Approach to Religious Transformation* (New York: Oxford University Press, 1994).

29. Jolly, *Popular Religion*, 181.

30. Ibid., 181–82. The richest sources include this epic as well as the Old Icelandic Eddas and the work of Snorri Sturluson.

31. Ibid., 27. This worldview regarded animals with a particular reverence, as is revealed by Tacitus's commentary on how the Germans of his day believed that beasts possessed a closer relationship than humans did to the powers of the universe. See Paul C. Bauschatz, *The Well and the Tree: World and Time in Early Germanic Culture* (Amherst: University of Massachusetts Press, 1982), 66.

32. Jolly, *Popular Religion*, 99, 110. Indeed, evidence from written charms indicates that even the manner of speaking could influence the power of the word: singing and chanting seemed even more efficacious than merely speaking the word aloud, a commonality between these polytheistic cults and Christianity.

33. Ibid.

reconciled through the prayers and magical formulas of human collaboration, these deities preserved the cosmic order until the inevitable death of the world in a cataclysmic conflict of gods and men.[34] With the arrival of Christian missionaries, these gods' temples were converted to churches, and the animistic landscape of holy trees, wells, and stones was Christianized through the agency of the cult of saints, whose calendar of feasts replaced the pagan celebrations and ritual calendar of sacrifice.[35]

Besides supplanting the pagan landscape and calendar, the missionaries to the Germanic and Celtic tribes brought to northern Europe a distinct, Christian understanding of the natural world. Whereas the early Germanic universe was open and in constant flux, the Christian universe was perceived as fixed and closed, emphasizing permanence over transience.[36] This "Augustinian worldview," a product of Mediterranean and antique Christian culture, had a method of assessing the validity of knowledge different from that of the modern world, in which knowledge gained via human observation and reason is distinguished from knowledge acquired directly or indirectly through the revelation of scripture, miracles, and tradition.[37] Early medieval thinkers made little effort to separate natural from supernatural phenomenon; rather, *natura* was understood to be equivalent to a form of revelation, so that the miraculous was considered merely to be God "raising his voice."[38] In this view, magic differed from miracle only in its source: while miracles are unusual events in the physical realm that proceed from God and are intended to provoke wonder and the glorification of God in human hearts, magic proceeds from the Devil and is an illusionary decep-

34. Riché, "Spirituality in Celtic and Germanic Society," 163, 165. Germanic spirituality was, as a whole, heavily influenced by the warlike tendencies of its culture, and this emphasis on war was transmuted in the Christian era into a belief in war as the judgment of God and a vision of God as protector and helper of true Christian warriors in battle (ibid., 173). In a similar fashion, the personal and reciprocal lord-vassal relationship within the Germanic *comitatus* was adapted as a model for the personal relationship between God and the believer; the Germanic concept of the lord as the giver of life and sustenance to faithful retainers, as well as the one to whom allegiance was rightly owed, was also easily transmuted into the concept of Christ as Lord, the giver of the greatest bread of all, his body (ibid., 28). For more on these subjects, see the discussion of the blessing of warriors and weapons in chapter 3.

35. Jolly, *Popular Religion*, 28.

36. Bauschatz, *Well and the Tree*, xii.

37. Ibid., 73. For a fuller discussion of this perspective, see Benedicta Ward, *Miracles and the Medieval Mind* (Philadelphia: University of Pennsylvania Press, 1982), 3–19.

38. Jolly, *Popular Religion*, 73.

tion designed to entrap gullible souls.[39] The recounting of stories of miracles by Christian authors thus continually reinforced the related Augustinian notion that God is active in the world of his creation, and fostered belief that humanity could tap this divine source for its own ends.[40] In addition to this notion, Augustine's doctrine of the "two books" deeply influenced the medieval Christian's perception of the world. According to Augustine, there are two books from which one can come to know God: the Book of Nature and the Book of Scripture. God has revealed himself in both. In the cosmos, Augustine wrote in his *De cura pro mortuis gerenda*, "some things happen naturally, others miraculously; God works in whatever is natural and he is not apart from the wonders of nature."[41] Nature thus has some value but, for Augustine, the first book (Nature) was only truly valuable in so far as it referred to the second (Scripture).[42] This attitude was much cherished by medieval theologians, who embraced it and Augustine's cosmology, which divided the world into three parts: God (the upper part), souls (the middle part), and material things (the lower part). While Augustine did echo earlier thinkers in believing that the cosmic order is reflected in human souls and moral conduct—that is, that the microcosm and the macrocosm are closely attuned—he preferred to focus on God and souls, the first two parts of this cosmological trinity, without assigning great significance or worth to the material world.[43]

39. Ibid. The main difference between liturgical and magical formulas is the brutality of the force applied to spiritual entities to make them to act in the desired fashion; see Elizabeth M. Butler, *Ritual Magic* (University Park: Pennsylvania State University Press, 1998), 202.

40. Jolly *Popular Religion*, 85.

41. Augustine, *De cura pro mortuis Gerenda*, PL 40:606–7, quoted in Ward, *Miracles and the Medieval Mind*, 4.

42. N. Max Wildiers, *The Theologian and His Universe: Theology and Cosmology from the Middle Ages to the Present* (New York: Seabury Press, 1982), 34; see St. Augustine, *De actis cum Felice Manichaeo libri duo*, 1:10 (PL 42:525–26). Augustine also commented on this in his discourse on the differences between the Catholic and the Manichaean life: "But we [Catholics] are forbidden to look to the things that are seen. He who wishes to offer to God that incorruptible love, therefore, must not love such things either. ... God alone is to be loved, then, and this entire world, that is, all sensible things, are to be condemned, although they must be made use of for the necessities of life." St. Augustine, *The Catholic and Manichaean Ways of Life* (*De moribus ecclesiae Catholicae et de moribus Manichaeorum*), The Fathers of the Church: A New Translation, vol. 56, trans. Donald A. Gallagher and Idella Gallagher (Washington, D.C.: The Catholic University of America Press, 1966), 32.

43. Wildiers, *Theologian and His Universe*, 35; see St. Augustine, *De ordine libri duo*, PL 32:977–1020; Augustine, *De civitate dei*, PL 41:637–42. Maximus the Confessor (580–662) greatly elaborated this theme in his own writings; see Wildiers, *Theologian and His Universe*, 35.

Examples of the influence of this view, whose origins can easily be traced back to Christian scripture, are abundant, but one story is particularly instructive: the German monk Caesarius of Heistrerbach, in his *Dialogus miraculorum* (c. 1219 to 1223), relates the story of a nun who, tormented by lust, prays for relief and is answered by an angel, who suggests recitation of a psalm verse as a cure. She recites the verse and the lust vanishes, but then a demon appears who compels her to blaspheme. At this the angel returns and suggests that the nun recite a different psalm verse to end the blaspheming, but warns her that if she says this she will once again be afflicted by lust. The nun chooses to recite the verse, for (as the author tells us) it is better for a body to suffer than a soul to be damned.[44] Considering the influence that this "Augustinian perspective," or relative ranking of the spiritual and material, had on ecclesiastical authors who moralized frequently on the need to disregard worldly and material concerns in favor of spiritual ones, the fact that the piety of medieval blessings often diverges from this hierarchy of values is significant, as we shall see below.

A belief in the accessibility of divine power fit well into the minds of converted Germanic peoples, for (as discussed above) both Christian theology and pre-Christian Germanic belief perceived power as residing in material objects, and held that both objects and words could be a means to access this God-given power, at least for those specifically qualified to access this *manna*.[45] To replace the magical incantations of pagan Germans, Christian clerics introduced a variety of Christian liturgies and "incantations"; these early medieval votive masses, prayers, and blessings (such as the *loricae*, or "breastplate" litanies of early Celtic Christians) functioned, as do some of the charms of the magical traditions of the Mediterranean world inherited by the Christian society, in a way fundamentally similar to the verbal, pre-Christian charms of the Germanic pagans, that is, to protect and serve the human community.[46]

44. Caesarius of Heisterbach, *Dialogus miraculorum*, book 5, chap. 44, cited in Norman Cohn, *Europe's Inner Demons: The Demonization of Christians in Medieval Christendom,* rev. ed. (Chicago: University of Chicago Press, 2001), 26.

45. Jolly, *Popular Religion*, 116.

46. Riché, "Spirituality in Celtic and Germanic Society," 167, 172; Jolly, *Popular Religion*, 117. The belief in the essential efficacy of words to reshape reality thus made understanding the language an issue of only secondary importance to believers: the mere act of forming the holy words would prove sufficient, even if their meaning was not understood. For a brief discussion of the history of charms, see Richard Kieckhefer, *Magic in the Middle Ages* (New York: Cambridge University Press, 1993), 69–75.

While a Germanic influence within the host of early medieval blessings seems readily apparent, the reasons for the inclusion of these quasi-magical prayers in the church's liturgical tradition remain hotly contested. The prevailing view for much of the last century was that the early medieval church, out of moral weakness or unwise compromise, lacked the power to keep these pseudo-Christian practices out of the church.[47] This view of magic was challenged in the early 1980s by Valerie Flint, who argued that Christian leaders actively invited non-Christian magic of certain sorts into the medieval Christian community, both because they knew that the elimination of magic would not help Christianity take root in the converted peoples and because they wisely recognized that magic gave consolation and encouraged loyalty where both were badly needed.[48] Because the leaders of the church valued established devotional habit and spiritual aspiration (both of which, Flint argues, were essential features of involvement with magical practices) over rationality, and because they so urgently needed devotion, Christians struck active bargains in some localities in exchange for the acceptance of their own leadership and the transfer of loyalties to the Christian faith; thus magic, apotropaic rituals, and prayers were allowed to enter the church as result of profound and careful thought, and not because of ineptitude or moral weakness on the part of the church.[49] While critics of Flint's interpretation have quarreled with her definition of magic and elements of her argument, Flint's emphasis on magic's ability to soothe medieval people's emotions and satisfy their desperate hope for healing fits well with my own interpretation of blessings' power to comfort and fulfill the needs of the laity in dealing with a seemingly chaotic world filled with capricious and malicious entities of greater power than they themselves possessed.[50]

Flint's thesis also offers the valuable insight that some of the non-Christian magic that entered the church was allowed because it served to eliminate other, less acceptable kinds. The borrowing and benevolent use

47. Keith Thomas, *Religion and the Decline of Magic* (New York: Scribner, 1971). This interpretation fit well with the view, inherited from nineteenth-century folklorists such as Frazer, that magic and magical practices represented a less sophisticated form of religion that was inevitably replaced by the intellectually sophisticated and inward-orientated religion of the Reformation and the modern era.

48. Valerie J. Flint, *The Rise of Magic in Early Medieval Europe* (Princeton: Princeton University Press, 1991), 397.

49. Ibid.

50. Ibid., 171.

of non-Christian specifics and aids to health must have helped to make the Christian God look more kindly than his competitors, at least when death threatened the believer.[51] I would argue that blessings of all sorts can be examined fruitfully from this perspective, as a potent means to generate the "wondering hope" and "barriers against terror of an overwhelming kind" that plagued life in an uncertain world.[52] This hope was needed even more when one considers the universal belief in maleficent demonic powers, inherited from the world of antiquity and Germanic culture but retained by the church as a useful way to isolate persons and practices that Christian authorities particularly wanted to proscribe or protect.[53] Humans, as lesser creatures, were thought to be vulnerable to both angels and demons in their relations with the supernatural, and demons' power to curse was feared enough to warrant turning to angels and other instruments of divine power to counteract this ill will.[54] Direct divine intervention sought through prayer, visible gestures like the sign of the cross, prayers to patron saints, and the use of their relics as talismans of power are well-known examples of the means by which divine aid was sought. The use of relics as talismans was believed to be so efficacious, in fact, that one scholar has argued cogently that relics of the saints, especially in post-Carolingian Europe, were "the only recourse against the myriad ills, physical, material and psychic, of a population defenseless before an incomprehensible and terrifying universe."[55] While this is true in general, it ignores the importance of blessings as a complementary force that used divine power to protect the human community, one whose similarities to magic may have been overlooked owing to the urgent felt need for such protection.

51. Ibid., 400.   52. Ibid., 403.

53. The fear of demons is ubiquitous in medieval Christian devotion, one example being the writings of Richalmus, the abbot of Schönthal, who in the *Liber revelationum de insidiis et versutiis daemonum adversus homines* asserted that, "Just as a man who plunges into the sea is wholly surrounded by water, so demons too flow around a man from all sides." Quoted in Cohn, *Europe's Inner Demons*, 27.

54. Flint, *Rise of Magic*, 107, 159, citing Hincmar of Rheims's *De divortio lotharii regis et tetbergae reginae*, *PL* 125:726. A particularly important conveyor of classical culture's ideas on angels and demons was John Cassian. See Eugène Pichéry, *Jean Cassien Conferences, Volume I, i–vii* (Paris: Editiones du Cerf, 1955), 257–58; St. Caesarius of Arles, "Sermon 113," in *Saint Caesarius of Arles, Sermons*, ed. M. M. Mueller, 3 vols. (Washington, D.C.: The Catholic University of America Press, 1956–73), 2:156, 158.

55. Patrick J. Geary, *Furta sacra: Thefts of Relics in the Central Middle Ages* (Princeton: Princeton University Press, 1978), 22.

INTRODUCTION

To illustrate that importance, it is worth taking a moment here to examine a blessing of a most sacred Christian object and its uses in protecting a Christian community. The Cross's importance in blessings, and its ability to enhance the power of such rituals, is seen in the practice of blessing crosses to be placed on the roadside and in the fields to protect the community and its agricultural produce from harm. A "Blessing of a Cross on the Road or Standing above a Crop," taken from an eleventh-century collection of rituals from Prüm, calls for a prepared cross to be placed before the doors of a church on Friday, and for a Mass to be sung concerning the Cross, no doubt to enhance its efficacy by reminding God of the human devotion to the Cross's significance and past prowess, but also to actualize the Christian ethos through this, its most powerful symbol.[56] The priest is then to come to the cross with a blessed candle and incense, and a litany is sung there with several psalms and an antiphon: Psalm 67, *Deus miseratur;* Psalm 46, *Deus noster;* Psalm 21, *Domine in virtute;* Psalm 76, *Notus in* and the antiphon *Signum salutis.* Litanies of saints are present in some agricultural blessings as early as the eleventh century but become more common in the fifteenth and sixteenth centuries.[57] In this they parallel many other kinds of blessings that evolved into more and more elaborate rituals over time, which seems to be a universal in the evolution of ritual. Beyond this generality, however, we are unable to point to any one particular cause for this change. There is a strong temptation to describe ritual sophistication and elaboration as a natural response to the increasingly sophisticated theology and doctrine of the medieval church, but this impulse must be resisted here, because a litany in no way suggests a complication of a ritual, only an elaboration or expansion.[58]

Returning to the litany of this particular blessing, Psalm 67 seems espe-

56. Franz, 2:13 (from Clm 100). For a further discussion of ritual's uses in making real the symbols of a religious culture, see Clifford Geertz, "Religion as a Cultural System," in *Anthropological Approaches to the Study of Religion,* ed. Michael Banton, 1–46 (London: Tavistock Publications, 1966).

57. See Prüm's "Blessing of a Cross," Lausanne's "Exorcism of Water," and the Ordinarium of Valencia's "Against Locusts." All Psalm citations are from the NRSV. With this blessing, and throughout this study, all translations of liturgical Latin are my own unless otherwise noted. English translations of Latin and other medieval and modern sources are, unless otherwise indicated, those of the scholars and works consulted in my research.

58. On the other hand, we can identify certain trends in the appearance of saints in agricultural blessings. Saints most often appear in adjurations and exorcisms, lending credence to the idea that saints were deemed good channels of divine power for purifying the profane landscape.

cially appropriate, as it is a song composed probably for use during the feast of Pentecost, after the harvest was gathered in ancient Israel, and is both a thanksgiving for a plentiful harvest and a recollection of deliverance: "May God be gracious to us and bless us and make his face to shine upon us, that your way may be known upon earth, your saving power among all nations. . . . The earth has yielded its increase; God, our God, has blessed us. May God continue to bless us; let all the ends of the earth revere him."[59] This psalm echoes an idea common to blessings: benediction in exchange for praise and worship. Blessing is implored so "that your way may be known upon earth," so the power of God's protection will be told to "all the ends of the earth." Deliverance from danger and the bestowal of domestic prosperity serve in the psalm as evidence of Jehovah's true beneficent nature, a nature reaffirmed by this medieval ritual, which seeks the same fruits of devotion. Blessing is here equated with the natural progress of the harvest, an equation that connects the medieval farmers who heard this psalm sung over their fields with the divine words spoken over ancient Israel, weaving the sacred past into the fabric of daily life.

The second psalm, *Deus noster,* also invokes the power of the divine to protect the roads and fields of the community. The psalm is part of a trilogy of praise, wherein the deliverance of Jerusalem from foreign enemies is praised and celebrated, the leading idea being that the presence of Jehovah in the midst of his city and people is the ground of Israel's faith: "God is our refuge and strength, a very present help in trouble. Therefore we will not fear, though the earth should change, though the mountains shake in the heart of the sea; though its waters roar and foam, though the mountains tremble with its tumult. . . . God is in the midst of the city; it shall not be moved; God will help it when the morning dawns."[60] This affirmation of faith in the

59. A. F. Kirkpatrick, *The Book of Psalms* (Grand Rapids: Baker Book House, 1982), 372 (Ps 67:1–2, 6–7). Throughout this study, commentary on the psalms' origins and meanings accompanies the analysis of the verses that appear within various blessings, even in cases where the psalm may not have been sung in its entirety. While it is possible that celebrant and congregation may have understood the verses they heard in a blessing to have a distinct meaning outside the context of the entire psalm, it seems reasonable that the author would also have drawn on his knowledge of the Psalter to choose psalms most suited to the subject and intent of his ritual. Thus the history and theology of each psalm can provide assistance in understanding the thinking that underlay the creation of blessings.

60. Ibid., 253 (Ps 46). This psalm probably originated in the miraculous deliverance of Jerusalem from the army of Sennacherib in 701 BCE.

divine evokes the instability of the natural world, a concern of great consequence to the agricultural communities that typified medieval civilization, but it refutes the power of that chaos and asserts instead the presence of the numinous within the community as a sure shield against any danger. This psalm thus reflects both the fears of the laity beseeching the blessing and the hope that the ritual blessing engendered in their minds. The third psalm, Psalm 21, continues to play up the hope of the faithful, for *Domine in virtute* is a psalm of thanksgiving for victory, one that anticipates the future victory of the heavenly king:

> In your strength the king rejoices, O Lord, and in your help how greatly he exults! You have given him his heart's desire and have not withheld the request of his lips. For you meet him with rich blessings; you set a crown of fine gold on his head. . . . Your hand will find out all your enemies; your right hand will find out those who hate you. You will make them like a fiery furnace when you appear. The Lord will swallow them up in his wrath, and fire will consume them.[61]

Through the earthly king this psalm looks forward to the heavenly king, and the blessings bestowed on the king echo the blessing sought by medieval celebrants, so that the desires of the people might be answered and their community be protected from all harm of the enemies, carnal and spiritual, that assaulted it.

Following these psalms, the celebrant continues, "Sanctify, Lord Jesus Christ, this symbol of your Passion, so that it may be an obstacle to your enemies, and for those believing in you it may be made an everlasting standard of victory."[62] The military image of an obstacle or barrier, visible in other blessings studied in the following chapters, is presented here by the blessing upon the Cross, marking out the sacred precinct and power of God from the surrounding forces of darkness and evil, and their human agents.[63] This de-

---

61. Ibid., 109–10 (Ps 21:1–3, 8–9). Psalm 21 also appears as one of the proper psalms of Ascension Day.

62. Franz, 2:13: Sanctifica, domine Iesu Christe, istud signaculum passionis tue, ut sit inimicis tuis obstaculum et credentibus in te perpetuum efficiatur victorie vexillum.

63. Such as the canon, cleric, and layman who in 1326, in the southwestern French town of Agen, were charged with invoking demons to create hail. See J. M. Vidal, *Bullaire de l'inquisition francaise au XIV siècle*, doc. 72 (Paris: Librairie Letouzey et Ané, 1913), 118–19. This belief was widespread in Europe, as can be seen in the belief in central Europe, namely, the former Yugoslavia and Hungary, in *kresniks*, spiritualists who were believed to battle witches and

marcation is enhanced by the sprinkling of blessed water and incensing, as well as by the addition of a talismanic inscription of the initials of the four evangelists.[64] These physical objects are finally enhanced by another appeal to the power of the Cross to limit the power of the demonic to wreak havoc on the human order of existence: "Let this sign of the holy Cross be sanctified in the name of the Father, Son and Holy Spirit, so that it may be the protection of the Christian people against the powers of the air and evil spirits, which are allowed to do harm upon the earth."[65] Thus is the pollution banished, the Christian worldview of a reality alive with invisible powers realized and reinforced, and the stability and continuity of the community preserved.

From this brief sampling of blessings, we can see how such liturgical rituals could provide comfort and solace in a hostile and threatening world, in a manner not far removed from magic according to Flint and other historians of magic in the Middle Ages. A similar perception of the Christian implementation of magical practices is provided in the recent work of Karen Louise Jolly, whose study of the adaptation of Christian elements in pagan Anglo-Saxon charms against the ill effects of "elf-shot" demonstrates that it was not the weakness of early medieval Christianity that allowed such "Christian magic" to be accepted. Rather its ability to succeed through accommodation of Anglo-Saxon culture is evidence of Christianity's success in conversion.[66] Both Flint's and Jolly's work thus opposes the dialectical model of Manselli and older scholarship on the relationship between "elite" and "popular" re-

---

protect against the hail summoned by the witches. See Gábor Klaniczay, *The Uses of Supernatural Power: The Transformation of Popular Religion in Medieval and Early Modern Europe*, trans. Susan Singerman, ed. Karen Margolis (Princeton: Princeton University Press, 1990), 134–36.

64. Franz, 2:14. A cross as a tool of demarcation had many uses in Christian society. For example, in the Italian communes crosses were erected over demolished churches to remind passersby that they walked on consecrated ground and thus should show respect. The supposed founder of communal independence for Bologna, St. Petronio, is said in his heavily dramatized *Vita* to have erected four monumental crosses to mark out the four quarters of the medieval city and called on Mary to bless them and protect the city. See Augustine Thompson, *Cities of God: The Religion of Italian Communes, 1125–1325* (University Park: Pennsylvania State University Press, 2005), 119 and 383; for the *Vita*, see Bologna, Biblioteca Universitaria MS 2060 (14th cent.), fols. 19r–20v.

65. Franz, 2:14: Sanctificetur istud sancte crucis signum in nomine patris et filii et spiritus sancti, ut sit protectio populi christiani contra potestates aereas et spiritales nequitas, quibus datum est nocere terre.

66. Jolly, *Popular Religion*, 173–74.

ligion, for Flint and Jolly treat both popular and formal religion as overlapping spheres of influence.[67] This is much the same conceptual model as that provided by Scribner's study of early modern blessing.[68] This model is predicated on the involvement of lay Christian culture in shaping religious ideology, and it seems eminently suited to understanding the complex relationships between liturgy and laity in medieval blessings. It is also supported by Augustine Thompson's recent groundbreaking study of the lay piety in the Italian communes, which goes much further in questioning the validity of the distinction between popular and elite piety. Thompson treats what has often been called "popular" piety as part of orthodox worship and belief as experienced by all its practitioners, from commons to the elite, and focuses on the same day-to-day realities of Christian life and liturgy that many of the blessings studied here address.[69]

After introducing the history of blessing within the Judeo-Christian tradition and the historiographical issues surrounding the blessings, the remaining chapters of this work examine blessings of places, people, items, and events outside the canonical sacraments proper. I chose these particular blessings because, by their very separateness from the central physical

67. For the two-part model of religion, see Raoul Manselli, *La religion populaire au Moyen Âge: Problèmes de méthode et d'histoire* (Montréal: Institut détudes médiévales Albert-le-Grand, 1975).

68. Ibid. Jolly does take issue, though, with Keith Thomas's and Flint's characterization of magic and magical practices as essentially irrational, arguing that this view is anachronistic in positing a distinction between magic and science (and religion) that developed only later (Jolly, *Popular Religion*, 16). For further criticisms of Thomas's and Flint's work, see Alexander Murray, "Missionaries and Magic in Dark Age Europe," *Past and Present* 36 (1992): 186–205, and Kieckhefer, "The Specific Rationality of Medieval Magic," in his *Magic in the Middle Ages*, 1–20. Both of these critiques reject the view that the masses are ignorant of what they should have known was magic and non-Christian, and of church leaders as knowingly perpetuating a fraud, purposely demeaning Christianity by compromising it with pagan magic. Both, like Jolly, suggest a different model that accommodates the mixture of apparent opposites without de-Christianizing medieval society.

69. Thompson, *Cities of God*, 2–8, 141. Thompson's understanding of liturgy, based as it is on the original Greek meaning "the work of the people," and his approach to the study of devotional practices and rituals that arose from it, is insightful and compelling, linking liturgy and believers in a way that supports many of the points made in the following chapters. His emphasis on ritual as a tool to make the city come alive, claim a place for itself in the world, and unite the citizens in an ordered society, as well as the copious examples he draws from a wide array of sources, make this work indispensable in understanding the piety of the medieval laity.

and spiritual domains of the clergy (i.e., the church structure and the sacraments), these were ceremonies that presumably the clergy could feel reasonably free to mold to fit the particular desires of the laity. In such ceremonies contextual expectations were more communal and vulgar, thus encouraging clerical experimentation without fear of doctrinal error. As such, they represent a way to explain the connection between the liturgy and the religious values of the laity, as well as an avenue for further developing our understanding of how medieval believers constructed and maintained their cosmology through ritual prayer and invocation. The guiding methodology of this study is traditional textual analysis supported by the occasional use of extradisciplinary theoretical models of ritual studies. As it is my desire to produce a syncretic study that will lay a foundation for future research into the subject of extrasacramental blessings, I have chosen to examine a broad sample of the texts available in edited collections rather than focus on a single liturgical book or group of similar works. This method carries the potential danger of making ahistorical judgments, a criticism often leveled at the phenomenologists and other theorists whose work supports my own, but I believe that the abundance of edited texts whose content has not been examined in such a way makes such a broad study worthwhile. My hope is that it will illuminate general patterns and themes that later researchers may develop through more narrowly focused studies.

The study is roughly framed by the tenth-century Romano-Germanic pontifical of Mainz and the thirteenth-century pontifical of William Durandus, bishop of Mende.[70] While this Roman tradition is vital to the development of blessings and will be studied in depth, it represents only a portion of the ritual corpus; selected earlier and later non-Roman traditions of blessings will also be examined, especially those of the Franco-Roman territories and liturgical books, with an occasional foray into insular and Iberian texts. The framing of this study by these chronological and geographical boundaries is deliberate. It begins with the Roman liturgical tradition after it had been heavily influenced by early medieval Frankish innovations during the Merovingian and Carolingian eras and had taken the forms that were to become influential in Rome itself. From this starting point, the development of the blessings may be traced throughout the pontificals and benedictionals of

70. This division is intended only as a useful guideline. There are some rituals, both earlier and later, that will be examined in order to present a more complete picture of individual blessing traditions. For a detailed discussion of these two pontificals, see the following chapter.

the high medieval era, taking into account the changes brought to the liturgy of blessing by reform movements, and to the theological status of blessing by the eleventh- and twelfth-century revolution in sacramentary theology, which sought to distance such blessings from the seven sacraments. Concluding the study with William Durandus both limits the already considerable chronological scope of the project and allows me to chart the impact of high medieval church council reforms on blessing and its liturgy. As Durandus's text is the culmination of the medieval pontifical tradition (and thus the standard text for the late medieval church), the conclusions drawn from a study of its blessings can reflect not only the thirteenth-century use of blessing rituals but also contribute to a better understanding of late medieval blessings. With these parameters set and the overarching interpretive framework established, let us turn now to the origins of medieval blessings in the religious tradition of the ancient Judeo-Christian world.

Chapter 1

THE HISTORY AND THEOLOGY OF
CHRISTIAN BLESSING

The origins of Christian blessing are to be found in the scriptural traditions of the ancient Israelites. The theology of the Old Testament does not primarily emphasize blessing and God's role in it, focusing its attention rather on God as one who saves, a God of deliverance.[1] This is not to say, however, that blessing is absent from Hebrew scripture. Rather, blessing (understood as actions of God that produce a condition of well-being) exists side by side with God's acts of deliverance. Deliverance is experienced in intercessory events, while blessing is a continuing activity of God present at God's will, but both are necessary to scripture's presentation of the sacred history of humanity's relationship with God.[2]

Blessing, or *berkhah,* in particular was understood to be both the inner vi-

1. Claus Westermann, *Blessing in the Bible and the Life of the Church,* trans. Keith Crim (Philadelphia: Fortress Press, 1968), 15 (for detailed treatment of blessing in each book of the Old Testament, see 29–34). For an important study of the significance of blessings in the Psalms, see Sigmund Mowinckel, *Psalmenstudien,* 6 vols. (Kristiana, Norway: J. Dybwad, 1921–24), esp. "Segen und Fluch in Israels Kult und Psalmendictung" in vol. 6. Also important is the work of Johannes Hempel, *Die israelischen Anschauunen von Segen und Fluch im Lichte altorientalischer Parallelen,* Zeitschrift der deutschen morgenländischen Gesellschaft 79 (Leipzig: F. A. Brockhaus, 1925).

2. Westermann, *Blessing in the Bible,* 3–4. Westermann argues that this distinction is of vital significance to the Israelites' conception of God: the God of deliverance is "one who comes" (for examples, see Ex 3:8, 15:21), while the God of blessing is "one who is present" and enthroned (see Is 6:1; 1 Kgs 22). These two conceptions of God are seen to have joined when the Israelites made the transition from nomadic to settled life, as the God who comes is united with the enthroned God in the ark of the temple (Westermann, *Blessing in the Bible,* 9).

tal power of the soul and the external good fortune that produces that pow-er.[3] Blessing manifests itself primarily as the power of fertility, both within the family and in the practice of farming, and as such represents a sharing in the life of God and the power to pass on that life by virtue of the bless-ing of creation.[4] While God's primal blessing was considered the gift of gen-eration to all living things on the fourth day, it could also be manifest as the bestowal of the power to defeat enemies, as when Rebecca's brother wishes, "May you, our sister, become thousands of myriads, may your offspring gain possession of the gates of their foes."[5] Jacob, Joseph, and Judah were espe-cially endowed with this power, Jacob and Joseph also possessing the pow-er to spread blessing around them as they traveled through foreign lands, as when Moses spoke to the Israelites before his death: "And this he said to Judah: O Lord, give heed to Judah, and bring him to his people; strengthen his hands for him, and be a help against his adversaries."[6] Blessing, an ac-tion in which the divine descends upon an individual or group, obviously had spiritual effects upon its recipients; it was apparent in the counsel a man gives, as when Isaiah prophesied concerning the messiah, "The spirit of the Lord shall rest on him, the spirit of wisdom and understanding, the spirit of counsel and might, the spirit of knowledge and fear of the Lord."[7] Blessing, then, is at times considered a form of wisdom, and like wisdom it is consid-ered to be the power to accomplish and succeed.[8]

The act of blessing, *barakh,* was understood as the imparting of vital power to another person, thus giving another a part of the blessing of one's soul originally bestowed by God. The handing on of blessings from father to son, as related in the story of Jacob's deception of Isaac through the theft of Esau's blessing, was thus seen as means to continue the "soul" of the fami-

3. Westermann, *Blessing in the Bible,* 18. This analysis is drawn largely from Johannes Ped-ersen, *Israel: Its Life and Culture,* 2 vols. (London: Oxford University Press, 1926), 162–212.

4. Irene Nowell, "The Narrative Context of Blessing in the Old Testament," in *Blessing and Power,* ed. Mary Collins and David Power (Edinburgh: T. and T. Clark, 1985), 3.

5. Gn 24:60; Westermann, *Blessing in the Bible,* 19. Similar invocations are to be found in Gn 27:29 and Nm 24:17–18. For a survey of the power of blessing in the physical world as un-derstood in scriptural times, see Rinaldo Fabris, "Blessings, Curses and Exorcism in the Bibli-cal Tradition," in Collins and Power, *Blessing and Power,* 13–23.

6. Dt 33:7, Gn 42:22–26; Westermann, *Blessing in the Bible,* 18–19.

7. Is 11:2; Westermann, *Blessing in the Bible,* 19. For other examples of this principle, see Is 9:5; 2 Sm 15:34.

8. Westermann, *Blessing in the Bible,* 19.

ly.[9] While blessings could be thus transferred by a human father, all blessings were understood to derive ultimately from Yahweh. The loyal Israelite sensed a total dependence upon the Lord as the source of all blessedness, as reflected in the traditional Hebrew greeting "The Lord be with you. [Response] The Lord bless you."[10] Interpersonal relationships were impossible without the blessing of God, the source of all well-being within the human community.[11] The blessings that God had imparted through fertility and generation in Genesis were reaffirmed for the chosen Israelites in God's words to Abraham: "I will make of you a great nation, and I will bless you and make your name great, so that you will be a blessing. I will bless those who bless you, and those who curse you I will curse; and in you all the families of the earth shall be blessed."[12] Thus blessings were seen to proceed from God through Abraham, from Father to father, as it were. This paternal blessing was transmitted into the society of ancient Israel in the form of a conception that certain individuals had special authority to call down blessings upon the human community: fathers upon their children, the paradigmatic example from the Old Testament being the deceptive blessing of Jacob by Isaac; kings upon their subjects, as when David blesses his people following the burnt offerings before the ark of the covenant, and Solomon's blessing following the dedication of the temple in Jerusalem; and priests upon the people, as recounted in the priestly blessing in the book of Numbers: "the Lord bless you and keep you, the Lord make his face to shine upon you, and be gracious to you; the Lord lift up his countenance upon you, and give you peace."[13]

9. Ibid., 19–20.

10. J. V. Morris, "Blessing," *NCE* 2:612; Ru 2:4. This greeting also is suggested earlier by the words of Rebecca's sister Laban to Isaac (Gn 24:31). This conception of God as the source of all blessings is the achievement principally of the Yahwist author (Westermann, *Blessing in the Bible*, 65).

11. Westermann, *Blessing in the Bible*, 19–20.

12. Gn 12:2–3.

13. Morris, "Blessing," 612; Gn 27:28, 49:25–26, 28; 2 Sm 6:18; 1 Kgs 8:14, 55–61; Nm 6:22–26. Isaac's blessing of Jacob was a subject of some interest in the patristic era, when Augustine based several sermon cycles on the craftily acquired blessing as a metaphor for the younger faith of Christianity receiving God's blessing, while the elder "brother," Judaism, was denied a freely granted, and thus efficacious, blessing. The one blessing of Jacob is also taken as a sign of the unity of the church, and Augustine adds that this blessing would not be received unless Christians, cleansed of sin by grace, bore the sins of others out of charity. See Augustine, *Sermons: Volume I on the Old Testament*, ed. Edmund Hill, vol. 1 of *The Works of*

Incidents of blessing in the Old Testament reveal essential qualities of scriptural blessings, namely, that they are prayers in which the supplicant blesses God himself (in this case, a form of praise and grateful worship) and simultaneously appeals for God's blessing upon humanity, a gift that scriptural authors were careful always to stress came freely from the goodness of the Lord.[14] By blessing Yahweh, the Israelite solemnly acknowledges him as lord, king, and source of all blessings.[15] Yet there is also evidence of an earlier conception of the power of blessing in the narrative of Jacob's wrestling with the angel of the Lord at Peniel, wherein Jacob wins from his mysterious opponent (the angel) his blessing, who declares to Jacob, "you shall no longer be called Jacob, but Israel, for you have striven with divine and human beings, and have prevailed. . . . And then he [the angel] blessed him."[16] Thus it would seem that a blessing could, at least in a superficial fashion, be compelled from a numinous being.[17] Nevertheless, the dominant view of blessings in the Old Testament perceives them as freely given gifts of God to the people of the covenant, accessible to all through the mediation of figures of authority within Israelite society. This conception deeply colored the medieval perception of blessings, but before moving to a discussion of that era we must examine the conception of blessing in the new covenant that Jesus and Christianity offered to the world.

Blessing in the New Testament is spoken of without any serious reflection or explicit discussion of its meaning, most probably because it was a known and accepted reality of the Israelite cosmology.[18] Blessings in the four Gospels seem to function in precisely the same way as they did in the Old Testament, as seen in Christ's blessings of the little children, the loaves, and the fishes.[19] In the later books, the concept of blessing seems to have been

---

St. Augustine: A Translation for the 21st Century, ed. John E. Rotelle (New York: New City Press, 1979), 193, 201.

14. Morris, "Blessing," 612; see also Pierre Gy, "Benedictions," *DMA* 2:177–78.

15. Morris, "Blessing," 612. For examples of this process, see Gn 24:48, Dt 8:10, Ps 66:8, and Ps 103:1–2.

16. Gn 32:28–30.

17. Morris ("Blessing," 612) points out that this passage may have been based on an older narrative, before the Israelites turned to monotheism, but the scriptural author made sure to leave no explicit sense of God being compelled: Jacob asks the angel to reveal his name—he does not demand it—and the bestowal of the blessing is phrased in a neutral mood (Gn 32:29).

18. Westermann, *Blessing in the Bible*, 24.

19. Mk 10:13–16, 6:41, 8:6–7, and their parallel passages in the other synoptic Gospels.

modified to mean generally God's salvific acts through Christ, thus incorporating the concept into the "Christ-event."[20] Perhaps the most typical incident of blessing in the New Testament is to be found within the account of Christ's ascension in Luke's Gospel. "Then he led them out as far as Bethany, and, lifting up his hands, he blessed them. While he was blessing them, he withdrew from them and was carried up into heaven. And they worshipped him, and returned to Jerusalem with great joy; and they were continually in the temple blessing God."[21] With its blessing by God and of God, this benediction is clearly derived from the tradition of the Old Testament. These two aspects of Israelite blessing found their ultimate realization in the body of the Eucharist, in Christ's benediction at the Last Supper, which combined a prayer of thanksgiving with a calling down of the sanctifying power of God to consecrate the bread and wine shared by Jesus and his apostles.[22] Thus the most holy act of the Christian faith is a constant reminder of the blessings God imparts to his creation and his people. But the blessing of the Eucharist was, in the developmental era of the Church's liturgy, to be paralleled by other acts of blessing within the liturgy.

Blessings are present in the earliest liturgical documents surviving from the postapostolic era of the church's history. Benedictions of honey, milk and water, light, new fruits, and oil for anointing the sick are found in the antipope Hippolytus's *Apostolic Tradition,* composed around the year 220, the first text that gives a clear view of the entire liturgy during the age of the martyrs.[23] These blessings were probably performed during the Mass itself to highlight the relationship of such blessings to the greatest blessing of all, Christ and his work of redemption.[24] Blessing was also present in the early liturgy by means of the canon, the heart of the Mass, which corresponded to the central action of the Jewish paschal meal, namely, the blessing of the meal itself.[25]

20. Gal 3:8–9, 14; Acts 3:25–26; Eph 1:3, Westermann, *Blessing in the Bible,* 24, 26, 65.

21. Lk 24:50–53.

22. Morris, "Blessing," 613; Mt 26:26, Lk 24:30.

23. J. R. Quinn, "Blessings, Liturgical," *NCE* 2:613. For a full discussion of this document and the early era of church liturgy, see Klauser, *Short History of the Western Liturgy,* 1–44, esp. 10–18; and, more recently, Gregory Dix, ed., *The Treatise on the Apostolic Tradition of St. Hippolytus of Rome* (London: S.P.C.K., 1937; reprinted with supplement, London: Henry Chadwick, 1968).

24. John H. Miller, *Signs of Transformation in Christ* (Englewood Cliffs, N.J.: Prentice-Hall, 1963), 282–83.

25. Ibid., 87. In his sermons Augustine incorporates these blessings called down during

The earliest texts of liturgical blessings from the medieval era are contained in the sacramentaries, books compiled for the use of those presiding over the Mass and containing all the prayer texts needed for the celebration of the Eucharist, the administration of the sacraments, and a variety of other liturgical events, notably episcopal and sacerdotal blessings and consecrations.[26] These benedictions are directly related to the sacraments; for example, they sanctify the holy oils (used on Holy Thursday) and the baptismal water (used during the Easter vigil).[27] The oldest identifiable sacramentary, the Old Gelasian, originated in the diocese of Rome, and was most probably made up of *libelli* used at Rome between 628 and 715.[28] It was brought to Gaul during this period probably by pious pilgrims and admirers of the Roman liturgy.[29] There was also a Gallican benedictional of the eighth century, now surviving only in fragments.[30] Many of its benedictions were com-

---

into his overall arguments against the "folly" of the Pelagian heresy; *CB* 1:x. The *Apostolic Constitutions* know only one prayer (verse 400, 8:13–15), while St. Gregory of Nazianze (c. between 329 and 389–90) mentions a blessing of the people that concludes the Anaphor. In the Coptic and Ethiopian versions of the *Apostolic Tradition,* Hippolytus divided the blessing into two parts: a postfraction prayer and a prayer (with imposition of hands) following the thanksgiving prayer after Communion.

26. For a concordance to the major sacramentaries of the medieval era, see Jean Deshusses and Benolt Darragon, *Concordances et tableaux pour l'étude des grands sacramentaires,* Spicilegii Fiburgensis Subsida, vols. 9–14 (Fribourg: Éditiones Universitaires Fribourg Suisse, 1982–83). For a discussion of the sacramentaries and a bibliography, see Cyrille Vogel, *Medieval Liturgy: An Introduction to the Sources,* trans. William G. Storey and Neils Krogh Rasmussen (Washington, D.C.: Pastoral Press, 1986), 61–110.

27. Gy, "Benedictions," 177, also listing other blessings such as those for the candles used on the Feast of the Presentation, the blessing of ashes for use on Ash Wednesday, blessings of palms on Palm Sunday, of the paschal candle on Holy Saturday, and Easter blessings for food.

28. For a critical study of this text, see Antoine Chavasse, *Le sacramentaire gélasien* (Tournai: Desclée, 1958). For a discussion of its origins and surviving manuscripts, see Vogel, *Medieval Liturgy,* 67–70. The Verona sacramentary, another early sacramentary, completely omitted blessings and is therefore excluded from this study. See Leo Cunibert Mohlberg, ed., *Sacramentarium Veronense* (Rome: Casa Editrice Herder, 1956).

29. The Old Gelasian sacramentary is edited in Leo Cunibert Mohlberg, Leo Eizenhöfer, and Peter Siffrin, eds., *Liber sacramentorum Romanae Aeclesiae ordinis anni circuli,* Rerum Ecclesiasticarum Documenta, Series Maior Fontes 4 (Rome: Casa Editrice Herder, 1960). For an excellent study of the eighth-century Gelasian sacramentaries, see Bernard Moreton, *The Eighth-Century Gelasian Sacramentary: A Study in Tradition* (Oxford: Oxford University Press, 1976).

30. The genealogy of this unedited benedictional is a subject of some dispute. While M. Manz argues that the short anthology known today is the oldest form of this benedictional, J. Deshusses and Edmond Moeller argue persuasively that a long anthology of bless

posed on the model of the sacerdotal blessing of the book of Numbers, discussed above, and its style hearkens back to the ancient blessings of the late seventh-century *Missale gothicum*.[31] The Old Gelasian sacramentary, with its blessings for many occasions (for example, the blessing of houses, blessings against pestilence afflicting humans and animals, against drought and storm, for trees and fruits, for peace, and for kings in time of war), in turn gave birth to a hybrid text, the Frankish-Gelasian sacramentary of the eighth century, the prototype of which was most probably created at the Benedictine monastery of Flavigny, in Burgundy.[32]

---

ings, composed in early eighth-century Autun, was abridged at Flavigny around 770, concurrent with the composition of Flavigny's Frankish-Gelasian sacramentary. See *CB* 1:xxiv. Elements of this text may be found in the sacramentaries of Berlin (Berlin, MS Phillipps 1667, fols. 106r–111r); of Fribourg (Fribourg i. Br. Univ. Bibl MS 363); of Donaueschingen (Fürstl. Fürstenberg Bibl. Codex 192), and in the first benedictional of Freising (Clm 6430, fols. 1–14v and 15–75; for a criticial edition of this manuscript, see Robert Amiet, ed., *The Benedictionals of Freising* [*Munich Bayerische Staatsbibliothek codex lat. 6430*], Henry Bradshaw Society 88 [Maidstone, Kent: Henry Bradshaw Society, 1974]). Parallel to the origin of the abridged anthology is another family of texts representing a new expansion and profound elaboration of the abridged anthology, principally the late ninth-century pontifical of Cahors, the pontifical of Angoulême, and the ninth- or tenth-century Augsburg benedictional.

31. CB 1:xxvi–xxvii. Moeller notes two distinct families of blessings before communion dating to after the period of the ancient Gallo-Roman and primitive Spanish liturgies: the Gallican and the Visigothic. M. G. Manz asserts the priority of the Visigothic (a position Moeller agrees with), the influence of which was felt in early Gallican benedictionals of the seventh century, the Gallican benedictional of the eighth century, in the supplement to the *Hadrianum*, and in later Gallican anthologies. The style is characterized by median and final assonance within each of the three members (parts) (ibid., xxi–xxii). By a study of the older *Missale gothicum* (c. 680, from the diocese of Autun), MS Vatican City, Reg. lat. 317, and the *Missale gallicanum vetus* (early eighth century, possibly from the school of Luxeuil), MS Vatican City, Biblioteca Apostolica Vaticana Palatinus latrina (hereafter BAV Pal. lat.) 493, Moeller shows a continuous line of transmission between the oldest Gallican benedictionals and the revised Gallican benedictional of the eighth century, which is clearly influenced by the Visigothic style of blessing (ibid., xxvi–xxvii). This evident relation of the *Gothicum* to the eighth-century Gallican benedictional supports Deshusses's assertion that "the matter of the benedictional of the eighth century dates back, in its body, at least to the middle of the seventh century" (*CB* 1:xxii–xxiii). Moeller believes that the similarity of these blessings to Visigothic blessings suggests that there was a literary renaissance, influenced by the Visigothic milieu, long before the Carolingian renaissance of the ninth century. For a critical edition of the *Missale gothicum*, see H. M. Bannister, ed., *Missale gothicum*, Henry Bradshaw Society 52 and 54 (London: Henry Bradshaw Society, 1917–19).

32. For the most representative surviving example of this family of sacramentaries, see A. Dumas and Jean Deshusses, eds., *Liber sacramentorum gellonensis*, Corpus Christianorum Series

The Frankish-Gelasian sacramentary mixed Romano-Gelasian prayers with many specifically Gallican practices: rogation days, mixed Romano-Frankish rites for ordinations and the consecration of churches, numerous votive masses (for kings, queens, sterile women, in time of war, for travelers and sailors, among others), and numerous episcopal blessings to be performed in the Mass before communion (such as blessings against plagues, blessings of salt and water for houses, trees and fruit, against war, for travelers departing and returning, and for tombs and graves), as well as a selection of blessings *super populum* at the close of the Mass.[33] The former blessings continued throughout the medieval era to maintain their position in the Mass, their use being inspired by the vetero-testamentary benediction from the book of Numbers.[34] The Frankish-Gelasian sacramentary seems to have been compiled to meet the needs of Frankish bishops and abbots sometime between 751 and 768, and enjoyed widespread use in the Frankish territories.[35] Its liturgical blessings are the first nonsacramental benedictions to incorporate a significant apotropaic element, invoking protection against the powers of Satan and his minions as well as calling for the goodwill of the divine. This apotropaic emphasis, however, was already familiar to liturgists through the blessings and exorcisms associated with baptism, which in the third century had quickly developed into an elaborate ritual in which the real life drama of the Christian's struggle with Satan became ritualized and liturgized.[36] Its appearance in nonsacramental blessings may

---

Latina 159–159A (Turnhout: Brepols, 1981). Also noteworthy is P. Cagin, ed., *Le sacramentaire gélasien d'Angoulême* (Angoulême: Societe Historique et Archéologique de la Charente, 1919).

33. Vogel, *Medieval Liturgy*, 74. For the placement before Communion, see the Roman *ordines* discussed below. These Gallican blessings often have a triple-optative structure, inspired by the three-tiered Visigothic style modeled after the benediction of the Book of Numbers (*CB* 1:xvi). Moeller concludes that this was a source common to both Gallican and Visigothic benedictions (*CB* 1:xxxiii).

34. Gy, "Benedictions," 178; Nm 6:22–26. This blessing tradition also found its way into the ancient Hispanic liturgy, which I intend to address in a future work.

35. Vogel, *Medieval Liturgy*, 74–76.

36. Henry Ansgar Kelly, *The Devil at Baptism: Ritual, Theology and Drama* (Ithaca: Cornell University Press, 1985), 1–12. Kelly's excellent study discusses how early followers of Jesus developed three basic processes for dealing with evil spirits: expulsion, usually through exorcism, with commands uttered against the spirits to depart; renunciation, a voluntary rejection of allegiance to evil spirits; and repulsion, by use of apotropaism, i.e., the use of spiritual aids against evil, whose descriptions and invocations were based on the language of Eph 6:10–18. The use of apotropaic actions and prayers developed in the prebaptismal exorcism is probably

possibly have been inspired by continued conversion efforts and the need to substitute Christian magic for the supernatural protections of displaced native religions.[37]

In the later eighth century, the Old Gelasian and Frankish-Gelasian texts were joined in the north by the textual tradition of the Gregorian sacramentaries. These books were composed for the use of the pope in the Lateran and throughout the stational churches in the city of Rome.[38] The most important of these sacramentaries was the *Hadrianum*, a text sent by Pope Hadrian I in 784–5 to the court of Charlemagne in answer to a request for a "pure" sacramentary in accord with Roman liturgical practice.[39] This book was placed in the royal library at Aachen and became a standard from which copies were made and distributed throughout Charles's realm. A supplement to this text was composed in Septimania sometime between 810 and 815 by the monastic reformer St. Benedict of Aniane (d. 821), who composed it as part of a new, corrected version of the *Hadrianum* for use in his abbeys. The

founded on the belief in indwelling "sin-demons," a doctrine that failed to win the support of most church scholars (ibid., 21–23, 45–55). Hippolytus in Rome and Tertullian in Carthage are the first authors to provide initiatory rituals directed against evil spirits, in which renunciation of the Devil and all his works figures heavily and clearly had a deep impact on the Christian community, as evidenced by the many references to the renunciation of Satan in the writings of the fathers. The many forms this renunciation took show that the formulas and services were constantly adapted to make the repudiation (of the things of the world and its ruler) more meaningful to the Christian community (ibid., 81–90, 104).

37. Gy, "Benedictions," 177. On the origin of this apotropaism, it may be useful to note Kelly's observation that, for the rites associated with baptism, seeing Satan as the "ruler of this world," a power to be feared and warded off by ritual action, corresponds with the dualistic tendencies of the Celtic and Germanic peoples among whom the Gallican liturgy originated, but since the Romans also believed in the indwelling of spirits in material objects, it could also have come from them (Kelly, *Devil at Baptism*, 212). The ultimate origin of these earliest blessings' apotropaic elements is likely to remain uncertain.

38. Vogel, *Medieval Liturgy*, 79.

39. The best critical edition of this text and its supplement is Jean Deshusses, ed., *Le sacramentaire grégorien, ses principales formes d'après les plus anciens manuscrits*, Spicilegium Friburgense 16, 24, 28 (Fribourg: Editones Universitaires, 1971, 1979, 1982). Other manuscripts and studies of note include Joseph Decréaux, ed., *Le sacramentaire de Marmoutier dans l'histoire des sacramentaires Carolingiens du IXe siècle*, 2 vols. (Vatican City: Pontifical Institute of Christian Archaeology, 1985), the first supplement of which considerably expands the number and variety of blessings in the original sacramentary (see note 37); and the "mixed sacramentary" reproduced in Gregor Richter and Albert Schönfelder, eds., *Sacramentarium Fuldense: Saeculi X*, Henry Bradshaw Society 101 (Fulda: Druck der Fulder Actiendruckerei, 1912; reprint, 1980); see also Vogel, *Medieval Liturgy*, 80, 85–86.

lengthy appendices of this sacramentary incorporated many votive masses and blessings that became a standard element in Frankish liturgies throughout the empire.[40]

The *Hadrianum* would eventually fuse with Frankish-Gelasian sacramentaries to produce the final expressions of this form of liturgical collection, the Mixed-Gregorian sacramentaries of the tenth and eleventh centuries.[41] Under the aegis of the Ottonian dynasty, these hybrids would be imported during the later tenth and eleventh centuries to Rome (where the reformers claimed the liturgy was in a notorious state of decay) and adopted as a standard Roman Mass book, whence they would be exported throughout Latin Christendom by the Mendicants, who adopted it as their own.[42] These Romano-Frankish blessings were thus widely disseminated and assured a continued place in the liturgical practice of the Western church.

Our comprehension of how the laity of the early Middle Ages understood these blessings is hampered by the lack of sources explicitly dealing with this form of ritual, which seems to have fallen into that rather paradoxical category of things so common as to be unworthy of mention. What does appear clearly, though, is that owing to ambiguities in thinking on penance

40. Moeller notes that the Visigothic structure, described above, is evident in the supplement. This point was first made by Deshusses in his study of the supplement's new episcopal blessings, in which he successfully argued that the rhythmed prose, median, and final assonance in two of the three members of the blessings indicates that Benedict of Aniane, and not the previously credited Alcuin, was the author of the supplement. *CB* 1:xxix; see Vogel, *Medieval Liturgy*, 85–92, for a full discussion of this issue and source.

41. Vogel, *Medieval Liturgy*, 102–3. The Fulda sacramentary is an example, and such sacramentaries are the basis for Latin sources such as the thirteenth-century missal of the Roman Curia, found in Martin Rule, ed., *The Missal of St. Augustine's Abbey, Canterbury* (Cambridge: Cambridge University Press, 1896). After Benedict's supplement, all new composite blessing texts for later Gallo-Roman sacramentaries are of the Visigothic type. These new compositions allowed diversification into several families: German, with subfamilies represented by Cologne MS 137 (blessings drawn from a pontifical in use by the bishop of Cologne), and St. Gall MS 398 (from the abbacy of Burchard, 1001 to 1022, containing three benedictionals) of the first subfamily, and Wolfenbüttel, Landes-Hauptarchiv MS 213 (of St. Blaise of the diocese of Braunschweig) of the second, among others; Anglo-Norman, such as the benedictional of St. Aethelwold, bishop of Winchester (963–984), the Canterbury benedictional (eleventh century), the pontifical of Egbert, archbishop of York (732–736), the Lanalet pontifical (tenth century), the Leofric missal (between 1050 and 1072), and others; and French, represented by the Gellone sacramentary (see above), plus, according to dom. Laporte, three other subfamilies; see *CB* 1:xxxv–xxxix.

42. Vogel, *Medieval Liturgy*, 104.

and postbaptismal error, the great majority of early medieval Christians felt a strong and very real need for frequent blessings in order to eradicate the evil power of postbaptismal sin.[43] For early medieval Christians, no middle ground existed between blessedness and vulnerability to the powers of the demonic; thus, driven by anxiety over that vulnerability, the laity demanded blessings from their clergy, basing their demand indirectly on scripture's commission of Aaron and his sons and on the assumption that the spiritual authority to bless arose from the voluntary assumption of a religious life.[44] An instructive example of the importance of nonsacramental blessings can be added to the better known practice of blessing candles and bread before, during, or after the Mass. One of the earliest is provided by Gregory of Tours, who relates in his *Liber in gloria confessorum* (c. 587) how the nuns of Poitiers considered it unthinkable to bury their patron, Queen Radegunda, without a blessing of her sepulcher. As the local bishop was absent at the time, the crowd that had assembled pressed Gregory into service to perform the blessing himself, which he dutifully did.[45] Another comes from the court of William Rufus, where, in 1104, St. Anselm exercised his control over the highly valued power to bless by denying his blessing to the fashionable young men of court who wore their hair long. Anselm had earlier had the hair of certain young men cut, as he considered it lewd, and he granted his blessing only to those "whose hair was cut in a manly fashion," which did not at all please those who chose fashion over faithfulness to clerical tastes.[46] Their

43. Lester K. Little, *Benedictine Maledictions: Liturgical Cursing in Romanesque France* (Ithaca: Cornell University Press, 1993), 187. In the Celtic tradition, popular prayers complemented these blessings, such as the poem "The Saint's Calendar of Adamnán": ("The saints of the four seasons, / I long to pray to them, / May they save me from torments, / The Saints of the whole year"), and "A Prayer to the Archangels for Every Day of the Week" ("May the Trinity protect me! May the Trinity defend me! May the Trinity save me from every hurt, from every danger"), in Oliver Davies, ed., *Celtic Spirituality*, Classics of Western Spirituality (New York: Paulist Press, 1999), 263, 265.

44. Little, *Benedictine Maledictions*, 189–90, 192. This lack of a middle state between safety and peril is a central argument in Jacques LeGoff, *The Birth of Purgatory*, trans. Arthur Goldhammer (Aldershot: Scholar Press, 1990). It is doubtful that many members of the laity would be directly familiar with this scriptural passage; it is more likely that they would have based their claim on the respect, inherited from antiquity, for the figure of the holy man and priest, who existed on a more rarified plane and thus was closer to the ear of God.

45. Gregory of Tours, *Glory of the Confessors*, trans. Raymond van Dam (Liverpool: Liverpool University Press, 1988), 104–6.

46. See Geoffrey Bosanquet, ed., *Eadmer's History of Recent Events in England* (London:

outrage is understandable in light of the examples given above of blessings' importance, even more so when one considers that some clearly regarded the divine protection of a blessing as a literal shield that could render one invincible and even invisible, as was done for St. Columban.[47] While Celtic spirituality offered continental Christians its *loricae*, "breast-plate poems" such as St. Patrick's Breastplate, which promised its speaker the power of Christ and a protective screen against evil, such stories and prayers were exceptional; more common was the conception of blessing as metaphorical, spiritual layers of protection against temptation, as recounted in the life of St. Anthony.[48]

While sacramentaries declined in use by the beginning of the twelfth century, when the collects were often incorporated with the lectionary and gradual to form the new plenary missal, the blessings of the sacramentaries continued to be copied in two kinds of books that developed contemporaneously: the pontifical and the benedictional.[49] Pontificals were the result of a long process of experimentation undertaken to simplify the bishop's task by incorporating both the noneucharistic *ordines* and the corresponding prayers

---

Cresset Press, 1964), 47–49. Benedictine monks turned the cutting of hair and beard into a ritual event accompanied by benedictions. Those who cut their hair "rid the body and soul of sin, when removing the curls growing on their heads." For the subject of haircuts and blessings, see Franz, 2:254–56, and Gábor Klaniczay, "Fashionable Beards and Heretic Rags," in his *Uses of Supernatural Power*, 51–58.

47. Little, *Benedictine Maledictions*, 188. For the primary sources, see Jonas, *Vita Columbani abbatis discipulorumque eius*, MGH SRM 4:90.

48. Little, *Benedictine Maledictions*, 188–90; Whitley Stokes, ed., *The Tripartite Life of Patrick with Other Documents Relating to the Saint*, 2 vols. (London: Eyre and Spottiswoode, 1887), 2:381 and 1:49–53; and Athanasius, *Vita Sancti Anthony*, chapter 5, PG 26:358. The origins of *Loricae* remain unclear: they appear first in the late eighth century in collections of prayers intended for private devotional use, although some may have had paraliturgical functions. They may have first developed as morning prayers to consecrate the whole of human life; see Davies, *Celtic Spirituality*, 46. Davies's translation of Patrick's Breastplate richly conveys the versatility attributed to these potent prayers, echoing later blessings: "Around me today I gather all these powers: / against every cruel and merciless force / to attack my body and soul, / against the charms of false prophets, / the black laws of paganism, / the false laws of heretics, / the deceptions of idolatry, / against spells cast by women, smiths and druids, / and all unlawful knowledge / that harms the body and soul.... May Christ protect me today: / against poison and burning, / against drowning and wounding, / so that I may have abundant reward" (119–20). These prayers bear the greatest similarity to the adjurations studied in chapter 4's discussion of ordeals, wells, and vessels.

49. Vogel, *Medieval Liturgy*, 105–6.

from the sacramentaries into a single book.[50] Although there were earlier attempts, the first expression of this idea with more than local significance is in what Michel Andrieu termed the Romano-Germanic pontifical (RGP), a tenth-century fusion of *ordines*, juridico- and theologico-liturgical texts, and excerpts from sacramentaries.[51] This text was composed in the German city of Mainz, in the Benedictine monastery of St. Alban, between 950 and 962.[52] A product of the *Renovatio imperii* of the Ottonians, the establishment of this text in Rome marked the beginning of the second great stage in the liturgical growth of the Western church.[53] It was soon copied in many Western *scriptoria*, taking with it the numerous and textually rich blessings adopted from the Frankish liturgical tradition. The Romano-Germanic pontifical remained the source common to all the subsequent Roman episcopal books of the twelfth century, which sought to trim down the Mainz pontifical's materials that were unnecessary for Rome and its suffragans, cutting (among other things) the number of blessings to fit the needs of the papacy while still retaining many of the rites inherited from its German neighbors.[54] From this effort was born the twelfth-century Roman pontifical, which the popes carried with them throughout their travels, spreading the influence of this book and its blessings far beyond the diocese of Rome.[55]

While the twelfth-century Roman pontifical (RP12th) exerted a strong influence on liturgical practice in the West, it was soon replaced by the pontifical associated with the liturgical reforms of Pope Innocent III: the pontifical of the Roman Curia of the thirteenth century (PRC).[56] While the essence of the twelfth-century Roman pontifical survives in this work, many of the rich texts of blessings inherited from the RGP were excised, proba-

50. Ibid., 225.

51. Ibid., 230–32. Cyrille Vogel and Reinhard Elze, eds., *Le pontifical romano-germanique du dixième siècle*, 3 vols. (Vatican City: Biblioteca Apostolica Vaticana, 1963–72).

52. Vogel, *Medieval Liturgy*, 232–33.

53. Ibid., 238.

54. Ibid., 249–51.

55. Ibid., 251. The standard edition is Michel Andrieu, ed., *Le pontifical romain au Moyen Âge, sacramentaire de Marmoutier*, vol. 1, *Le pontifical romain du XIIe siècle* (Vatican City: Biblioteca Apostolica Vaticana, 1938). For a more detailed introduction to this text's history, see pp. 3–19 of this work.

56. Vogel, *Medieval Liturgy*, 251–52. The standard edition is Andrieu, *Pontifical romain au Moyen Âge*, vol. 2, *Le pontifical de la Curie romaine au XIIIe siècle* (Vatican City: Biblioteca Apostolica Vaticana, 1940). For a survey of the text's history and forms, see pp. 229–323 of this work.

bly because they were deemed inappropriate to its intended churches of use, namely, the Lateran and the Italian churches immediately subject to the Holy See of Rome.[57] This pontifical of the Curia would be the prime competitor for the last major liturgical monument to fall within the chronological scope of this project: the pontifical of William Durandus (PWD), bishop of Mende in southern France.[58] Composed between 1293 and 1295, this pontifical was designed for universal use in the Western church, a more comprehensive goal than the pontifical of the Curia, and one that it achieved with papal support.[59] The core of this book's rituals are Roman in origin, drawing from the Roman pontifical of the twelfth century and the pontifical of the Roman Curia, as well as the Romano-Germanic pontifical and local pontifical ceremonies, but it is unique in that the author removed all nonepiscopal materials, making it the first true pontifical of the medieval era.[60] Many blessings were left within this version, and we will examine Durandus's impact on the blessing tradition in later chapters.

While the importance of blessings and the pattern of their textual dissemination changed throughout the high medieval era, significant developments within sacramental theology transformed the church's conception of these blessings' role within the larger Christian culture. In the early liturgy outside of Rome, the sacraments were thought of, first, as consecrated physical matter, a conception that gave birth in the early Middle Ages to the view that the elements used in the sacraments were themselves a means of grace, worthy of veneration.[61] This in turn promoted widespread Christian acceptance of a belief in the existence of sacred, blessed objects, a belief that

---

57. Vogel, *Medieval Liturgy*, 252.

58. The standard edition is Andrieu, *Pontifical romain au Moyen Âge*, vol. 3, *Le pontifical de Guillaume Durand* (Vatican City: Biblioteca Apostolica Vaticana, 1940). For a more detailed introduction to this text's history, see pp. 3–22 of this work.

59. Vogel, *Medieval Liturgy*, 253.

60. Ibid., 254. The composition of Durandus's pontifical coincided with a totally different late thirteenth-century collection, the benedictional of John Peckham, archbishop of Canterbury (1279 to 1282). The latter is preserved in the benedictional of John Longlonde, bishop of Lincoln (between 1521 and 1532?), and the pontifical of Lacy, bishop of Exeter, and partially in the benedictional of Anianus, bishop of Bangor (1279). Moeller states that Peckham's benedictional, which never achieved popularity, was very heavily influenced by the Scholastic thought of its time, and this novelty is probably the reason for its obscurity. I intend to address this assertion in a later work.

61. Herbert Vorgrimler, *Sacramental Theology*, trans. Linda M. Maloney (Collegeville, Minn.: Liturgical Press, 1992), 50–51.

formed the foundation for the use of the high medieval blessings studied in this project.[62] Throughout the eleventh and twelfth centuries, theologians and philosophers within the church struggled to produce a new, coherent, and mutually agreeable vision of what constituted a true sacrament.[63]

An issue of great interest to the first sacramentary theologians of the high medieval era was the number of actual sacraments. Early medieval theologians tended to expand the number of sacraments, thus extending the church's competence over the affairs of the world: St. Augustine counted the font of baptism, the giving of salt during baptism, the ashes at baptism, the Lord's Prayer, and Easter Sunday itself as sacraments.[64] Peter Damian (d. 1072) counted a total of twelve sacraments, including monastic vows and the consecration of kings.[65] Other theologians, notably Hugh of St. Victor, in his *De sacramentis,* included the dedication of churches and the making of the sign of the cross in the list of sacramental acts as late as the twelfth century.[66] Such blessings, along with the blessing of Easter candles, belonged among the sacraments (according to Hugh) as "those sacraments in the Church from which, even though salvation does not actually consist in them, salvation is enhanced in so far as devotion is exercised."[67] But by that time the scope of

62. Ibid., 51. Early medieval theology was very concerned with the qualifications of persons performing consecrations, and with the correct utterance of the words believed to be instituted by the living God himself. These legalistic and ritualized notions continued to dominate sacramental theology well into the high Scholastic age.

63. The early struggle for reform began with the controversy over Christ's presence in the sacrament; see Allan John Macdonald, *Berengar and the Reform of Sacramental Doctrine* (New York: Longmans and Green, 1930).

64. Vorgrimler, *Sacramental Theology,* 51; Laurence F. X. Brett, *Redeemed Creation: Sacramentals Today* (Wilmington, Del.: Michael Glazier, 1984), 38.

65. Vorgrimler, *Sacramental Theology,* 51; Jaroslav Pelikan, *The Christian Tradition III: The Growth of Medieval Theology (600–1300)* (Chicago: University of Chicago Press, 1978), 213. For the primary sources, see Peter Damian, "De perfectione monachorum," in *De divina omnipotentia, e altri opuscoli,* ed. Paolo Brezzi (Florence: Vallechi, 1943), 232; Damian, *Opuscula* 16.8 (*PL* 145:376); and Damian, *Sermon* 69 (*PL* 144:901).

66. Vorgrimler, *Sacramental Theology,* 51. For the primary sources, see Bruno of Segni, *De sacramentis ecclesiae* (*PL* 165:1090); Hugh of St. Victor, *De sacramentis* 2.5.1 (*PL* 176:439); for a translation of this last work, see Roy J. Deferrari, ed., *Hugh of St. Victor: On the Sacraments of the Christian Faith (De sacramentis)* (Cambridge, Mass.: Medieval Academy of America, 1951).

67. Bruno of Segni, *De sacramentis* (*PL* 176:471); Deferrari, *Hugh of St. Victor,* 315; Pelikan, *Christian Tradition III,* 213. Hugh calls these devotional sacraments "sacraments instituted for practice," sanctified by the word of God. They are classed into three categories: things (the water of aspersion, the reception of ashes, the blessings of branches and candles, etc.); deeds

sacraments was shrinking in the face of recent events. The investiture controversy raging between the papacy and Holy Roman Empire encouraged the Roman church to take a stronger view on the sharp separation of the world and the church. As the church struggled to assert the supremacy of the clergy over secular authorities, the church itself became steadily more clericalized, and the consecration of such vocations as hermits, nuns, and kings was no longer counted among the formal sacraments: the realm of the sacraments was becoming, in the words of one commentator, "a world unto itself."[68]

By the mid-twelfth century, under the influence of the theologian Peter Lombard, the tally of seven sacraments had achieved acceptance throughout the Latin church.[69] From the impetus of the Lombard's writings, sacramental theology became driven by the desire to distinguish between the sacraments of the new covenant and the broad, sacramental realm of natural sacraments, the Old Testament's sacraments, consecrations resembling sacraments, and the benedictions given by bishops and abbots since the Carolingian era.[70] A higher dignity was now to be given to the new covenant sacraments, as they were seen to be elevated by reason of having been instituted by Jesus himself.[71] Theologians thereafter sought to distinguish between es-

---

(making the sign of the cross, the blowing of exorcism, the spreading of hands, kneeling, etc.); and words (the invocation of the Trinity and other invocations). See Deferrari, *Hugh of St. Victor*, 315–20.

68. Vorgrimler, *Sacramental Theology*, 51.

69. For a full discussion of Peter Lombard's role in rethinking sacramental theology, see Elizabeth Frances Rogers, *Peter Lombard and the Sacramental System* (Merrick, N.Y.: Richmond Publishing, 1976). In particular, Lombard was the first to verbalize the doctrine that the sacrament is a cause (*causa*) of grace, a central issue in high Scholastic sacramental theology; see Vorgrimler, *Sacramental Theology*, 53–54.

70. Vorgrimler, *Sacramental Theology*, 52; Gy, "Benedictions," 177. The custom of abbots giving blessings was widely adopted in Benedictine houses from the ninth century onward, and the Gregorian reform of the eleventh century granted the abbots the right to perform such blessings by means of papal concession.

71. Vorgrimler, *Sacramental Theology*, 52. It is also worth noting that, following the theologians' efforts to redraw the line between sacrament and sacramental, the laity (at least in the Italian communes) in the thirteenth century become more and more sensitive to the division of sacred and profane space, and more eager to participate in the sacred space of the communal church. Thompson notes numerous measures the laity took to make the nave of the cathedral, their part of the church, as sacred as that of the choir reserved for the clergy (Thompson, *Cities of God*, 238). This lends some support to the real connection of the laity not only to the outward observance of doctrine and liturgy but also to some of the most central beliefs on which the blessings, especially those of space presented in the next chapter, rest.

sential prayers concerning the sacraments and nonessential prayers, notably the benedictions.[72] Sacramental theology was clarified to distinguish between the objective effectiveness of a sacrament (*opus operatum*, the work of God in the sacrament in regard to the minister and recipient, and the sole source of grace) and the human, subjective action in carrying out a sacrament (*opus operantis*, the condition that permits grace to be present).[73] The principle that each of the sacraments contained and conveyed a special grace, along with a more precise definition of what a sacrament was, helped establish the normative list of sacraments for the remainder of the medieval era.[74] This list excluded many sacred acts mentioned above, most notably benedictions, and demoted them to the rank of "sacramentals."[75] These can be divided into three main types: blessed objects that were widely distributed for use by the recipients, some for use on specific days of the liturgical calendar (for example, the candles blessed for Candlemass and the palms for Palm Sunday); rites and benedictions performed by priests to ensure a beneficent natural order, similar to votive masses; and prayers and incantations used to gain protection of various sorts.[76]

The issue of sacramental protection from the natural world lies at the heart of the blessings' meaning to medieval people and their piety. Sacra-

72. Gy, "Benedictions," 177. The distinction between a benediction and a consecration (the act of making someone or something sacred), previously poorly defined, was a subject of special interest.

73. Vorgrimler, *Sacramental Theology*, 52. This distinction was added to in the thirteenth century, when the rediscovered works of Aristotle fueled an effort to achieve intellectual clarity on the nature and meaning of *signum* in the sacraments, leading to a full schematization of all the sacraments (ibid., 52–53). Thomas Aquinas first presented the idea that the sacraments served to sanctify the most important moments in human development (birth, becoming an adult, and receiving nourishment, through baptism, confirmation, and the Eucharist), transformed the things that threaten and make ill (through reconciliation and the anointing of the sick), and made human social existence fruitful before God (through holy orders and marriage; see ibid., 54).

74. Pelikan, *Christian Tradition III*, 213–14.

75. For a history of this term, see Magnus Löhrer, "Sakramentalien," *Sacramentum Mundi* 4 (1969): 341–47.

76. Swanson, *Religion and Devotion in Europe*, 182–84. Of these, only the blessed objects were officially recognized as sacramentals by the church, and these objects not only were ascribed protective power but also served devotional purposes throughout the year. Only after the era in question did the idea of sacramentals fully evolve to include such consecrations as those of kings and bishops; see Pelikan, *Christian Tradition III*, 213. For a current theological understanding of sacramentals, see J. R. Quinn, "Sacramentals," *NCE* 12:790–92.

mentals reflect a rather utilitarian approach to divinity by medieval religion, where blessings, incantations, and objects could serve to harness God to (in one historian's words) "make the master the servant."[77] The blessings were a source of power to medieval Christians, power to control their world, their God, and ultimately their own lives.[78] Their integration into daily life shows a widespread appreciation of a "magical" aspect of religion, as the claims made for sacramentals' powers were the mirror image of magic, and often it seems as if only the status of the practitioner distinguished the blessing from the spell.[79] The laity were especially desirous of a clerical presence to ensure that sacramentals were available, and could even be forceful in compelling blessings from the clergy when need arose; as keepers of the keys of heaven, the clergy were indispensable to the life of the small communities to which they ministered, for both sacrament and sacramental salvation.[80] Church court records from early fifteenth-century England reveal how priests who neglected their duties to provide spiritual relief could evoke the wrath of their parishioners, while contemporary French records from Narbonne show the laity praising the rector of Saint-Pierre-des-Champs, since he "was and is an honest and knowledgeable man, and has and does serve the church well, instructs people, ministers the ecclesiastical sacraments, and maintains due hospitality."[81]

Demand for blessings remained in this time as intense as it had been in earlier centuries, as illustrated by several incidents. Centuries later than, and south of, Gregory of Tours' example discussed above, Emperor Frederick Barbarossa was besieging the communal Italian city of Gubbio when its saintly bishop, Ubaldo, "went out, confronted the emperor, and gave him a stern lecture."[82] Frederick promptly ended his attack and departed. In the

77. Swanson, *Religion and Devotion in Europe*, 182.

78. Ibid., 183. For further examples of such a conception, see Vauchez, *Laity in the Middle Ages*, 3–26, 129–39.

79. Swanson, *Religion and Devotion in Europe*, 189.

80. Ibid., 242–48.

81. Ibid., 242, as translated from V. Chomel, "Droit de patronage et practique religieuse dans l'archevêché de Narbonne au début du XVe siècle," *Bibliothèque de l'École des Chartes* 115 (1957): 93n6.

82. Thompson, *Cities of God*, 44–45, citing Giordano di Città di Castello, *Vita beati Ubaldi Eugubini episcopi*, ed. François Bolbeau, 15.1–4, in "La vita di sant'Ubaldo, vescovo di Gubbio, attribuita a Giordano di Città di Castello," *Bolletino della Deputazione di Storia Patria per l'Umbria* 74 (1977): 102.

Italian communes of the twelfth and thirteenth centuries, priests were expected to chant solemn blessings over the unusually sumptuous fish dishes served on Christmas Eve, and in the communal courts bishops were required to bless the hot iron or cold water used in ordeals imposed by the court, at least until clerical participation in ordeals was banned by the Fourth Lateran Council of 1215.[83] Another incident from the same period reveals how the laity themselves might be more flexible in defining a blessing than the clergy who dispensed it. Citing the sainted bishop's *Vita*, Augustine Thompson relates how, "while Bishop Lanfranco of Pavia lay on his bier in the cathedral, a pious old woman hobbled in through the screen, took his hand, and blessed herself. His relics healed her of a two year paralysis of her feet."[84] Though no formal blessing by the bishop was possible, of course, the determination and effort of this elderly woman speaks clearly of the value the laity placed upon the sacred power of blessings, especially those imparted by the sainted, living or dead.

To conclude this brief survey of the history of blessings, the quasi-magical approach to blessings and their administrators can also be clearly seen in developments within eucharistic piety at the close of our era of study, when the host was used in processions to bless fields and protect crops and communities from natural evils and disorder.[85] As an embodiment of the ultimate blessing of God, the corpus Christi assumed tremendous power within the imagination of lay Christians, overshadowing but never eliminating the need for blessings that permeated the piety of the medieval world. Indeed, this devotion may arguably be seen as merely a further expression of the medieval belief in the power of meaningful words to affect the natural order of existence. This belief is evident throughout the ritual blessings to which we may now turn our attention.

83. Thompson, *Cities of God*, 275, 105; for the blessing of dishes, see Giovanni Crisotomo Tombelli, ed., *Ordo officiorum ecclesiae canonico anno MCCXIII compositus* (Bologna: Longi, 1766).

84. Thompson, *Cities of God*, 406; for this story, see Bernardo Balbi, *Vita S. Lanfranci*, 3.22, *AS* 25 (June 5), 537.

85. Thompson, *Cities of God*, 182. For a full discussion of eucharistic piety in the high and late medieval world, see Rubin, *Corpus Christi*. For the use of the Eucharist as a ritual object of power, see the same work, 334–42. See also Zika, "Hosts, Processions, and Pilgrimages," 25–64.

Chapter 2

SACRED PLACES AND SACRED SPACE

SACRED SPACE: A BRIEF SURVEY

The human experience of our environment has always been subjected to the drive to order the cosmos in such a way as to make it comprehensible. This process has been particularly evident in the development of human religious systems and cultures, which often seek to establish as unquestionable the existence of a reality hidden behind the sensual one. This hidden reality is usually considered to be of a higher order than mere visible reality, and human beings have always looked to it for the deepest meaning of human existence and have linked it with the divine origins of creation itself.[1] The process of discovering this conceived hidden and sacred dimension of reality is rarely considered easy; by its very nature, sublime reality transcends common experience, and thus human beings must discover or create a way to isolate this deeper reality from ordinary life. In medieval Europe, as in many religious cultures, one means of distinguishing the sacred from the profane was through the ceremonial consecration or blessing of a locale. Before investigating this method of creating sacred space, however, we must first lay out an interpretive model for understanding the nature and function of sacred space within human religious culture, and then examine the historical evolution of medieval methods of creating sacred space, the blessing and consecration.

Sacred space is essentially conceived of as significant space, a place where the barriers between visible and hidden reality are believed to have

1. For example, see Otto's discussion of the *numen* in the development of human religion: Otto, *Idea of Holy*, 1–11, 72–135.

weakened sufficiently that human beings may experience both worlds within its confines. Sacred space is thus perceived to be full of potential, a place where nothing is accidental and everything is potentially significant, where humans and gods "are held to be transparent to one another" and may commune freely without the interference of mundane reality.[2] While scholarship on the role and nature of the sacred in human religion disagrees over the origin of this concept of sacred space, it is unanimous in acknowledging that it is perceived to differ significantly from the world outside its boundaries.[3] Rituals for creating sacred space often include explicit acts or words that delimit the territory where the power of divinity is thought to operate.

The idea of sacred space not only provides its adherents with a comprehensible and reliable locale in which to gain access to hidden reality; it also serves the crucial function of grounding the human within the cosmos. Where the sacred is conceived to manifest itself is a point from which to acquire a kind of orientation, to position the individual and community in a meaningful portion of the world, most typically at its imagined center.[4] Such a positioning speaks to the human need for order in this world, but it also marks such space as a threshold or place of passage into another world, the realm of the gods or divinity. Sanctified space, be it made such by either human or divine agency, thus "breaches the veil" between realities, allowing passage of knowledge and power between the divine and the human for the benefit of both.[5] One such benefit is the identification of the human community with

2. Smith, *Imagining Religion*, 54.

3. There are significant differences in the scholarship on the sacred on the question of exactly why and how a place becomes sacred. For example, while Mircea Eliade and phenomonologist scholars such as Rudolf Otto take as a given the existence of the sacred as an active force that manifests itself in the world (e.g., in Eliade's notion of the hierophany), Jonathan Smith argues that ordinary places become sacred by having human attention directed toward them in a special way (thus implying that nothing is sacred in itself but only in relation). See Mircea Eliade, *The Sacred and the Profane: The Nature of Religion,* trans. Willard Trask (New York: Harcourt Brace, 1959), 11–12, 20–24; Smith, *Imagining Religion,* 54–55.

4. This belief can be seen not only in native cultures throughout the world (for example, in the ceremonial male houses of Waropen, New Guinea) but also in the origins of European religion in the religion of the Israelites, who placed the sanctuary of the temple in Jerusalem at the center of the world, an idea inherited by Christians of medieval Europe who located Jerusalem itself as the center of the world, as can be seen by even a cursory examination of medieval cartography. See Eliade, *Sacred and Profane,* 42–47.

5. Marion J. Hatchett, *Sanctifying Life, Time and Space: An Introduction to Liturgical Study* (New York: Seabury Press, 1976), 10.

not only a hidden world but a world singularly imbued with being, reality, and permanence, a world not subject to the vagaries and transitory nature of the visible, natural world.[6] Thus human life takes some of the divine world's essence into itself when it dwells in proximity to divinity, ensuring continuity and stability for both the community and its constituent individuals.

The idea of sacred space plays an important role within religious culture as a source for satisfying and assuaging emotional and psychological needs. A sacred space, such as a shrine or a holy well to which powers of healing are attributed, can serve as a "focal point of reverent expectation," where anxiety and distress may be relieved and the terror of uncertainty alleviated in those suffering from mental and physical ills.[7] Sacred space provides the context for this relief, a place of potency and access to a brighter future. The creation of such spaces by the blessings of the medieval church brought the power of the divine into contact with humanity, and helped to stabilize the community in the face of the human misery and despair that could infect and diminish the ability of the community to deal with everyday life.

While an understanding of the sacred is essential to understanding the power of blessings, it is also necessary to understand the evolution of the concept of sacred space and how this evolution affected medieval people's understanding of consecrated ground. It would seem that the earliest conception of sacred space in Western culture was that the sacredness of a place came from the presence of something sacred in that place.[8] We know from archaeological evidence of prehistoric Europe that geographical features, especially chthonic and evocative ones, were also perceived by primitive humans as sacred: an example par excellence would be a mountain, a place closest to heav-

6. Eliade, *Sacred and Profane*, 64–65.

7. Flint, *Rise of Magic*, 206. For example, concerns over fertility and prosperity may be seen in popular beliefs in early medieval Europe concerning the powers of springs and fountains; see Alcuin, *Vita Willibrordi archiepiscopi Traiectensis*, MGH SRM 7:124–25. Space itself, its definition, meaning, and uses, has attracted significant scholarly attention in recent years. One scholar has argued cogently that space itself can be gendered, so that when examining structures and open places, "entrances and interiors are females, especially churches, and even whole cities," both of which could also be recipients of ritual blessings. See Peter Stallybrass, "Patriarchal Territories: The Body Enclosed," in *Rewriting the Renaissance: The Discovery of Sexual Difference in Early Modern Europe*, ed. Margaret W. Ferguson et al. (Chicago: University of Chicago Press, 1986), 126.

8. Louis Bouyer, *Rite and Man: Natural Sacredness and Christian Liturgy*, trans. M. Joseph Costelloe (Notre Dame: University of Notre Dame Press, 1963), 151–52.

en, uninhabitable by men, a place of silence, solitude, and storms, evocative of mighty powers. Other chthonic sites, such as grottos and forests, also seem to have often been regarded as holy, as a womb of mother earth or a place where life springs up from the earth and reaches toward the light of the sun, evocative perhaps of the human spirit reaching toward the divine.[9]

This connection of the sacred with the natural world, while never completely supplanted, came to be overshadowed by the development of constructed sanctuaries where either the shape, the orientation in space, or the location of the sanctuary determined what constituted sacred space.[10] In particular, the shape of sanctuaries evolved into a powerful agent for sanctifying a place in Western religious culture, as long as the shape chosen could be taken as a cosmic image, a late example of which may be seen in the construction of Christian churches in late antiquity in the form of a cross.[11] A building whose shape was in tune with the rhythms of the universe acted as a "resonator of the sacred" and was sought out by the religious mind for this connection with the numinous world. But shape was not the only determinant of sacred space: ground could be made holy if an event or happening occurred there that could be taken as a manifestation of the divine.[12] The cave that, according to one tradition, served as the tomb of Jesus and the site of his resurrection, and around which was built the Church of the Holy Sepulchre, is one such place of special distinction in the Christian tradition.

Finally, Western religious culture developed the conception that space could be made sacred by a deliberate act of consecration by a human agent, acting on behalf of both the human and divine worlds. By this means humans could localize the sacred and control it to some extent. Examples from the pre-Christian cultures of Europe can be found within the temples of the Greco-Roman world or within some of the elaborate pagan shrines of southern Gaul during late antiquity.[13] This reverence for structures and geo-

9. Ibid., 153. One such example of reverence for natural features in Western culture may be seen in Genesis 18:1, where God appears to Abraham as he encamped in a grove of oaks at Mamre.

10. Ibid., 154–55. For example, the orientation of solar cult temples toward the east and the rising sun, or the location of the temple at Delphi, situated over the crack in the earth by which the oracle obtained her prophetic visions.

11. Ibid.   12. Ibid., 156.

13. Ibid. Bouyer himself argues that the earliest rites of consecration were the result of man, fearful of the sacred, trying to preserve something he would like to make his own (for example, a home or field) by separating it from the power of sacred and potentially hostile

graphical centers can be seen to both parallel and diverge from the evolution of the scriptural and Christian conception of sacred space. While the theology and history of the Old Testament is geographically centered in Canaan and Israel, the prophets of nomadic Israel saw the native Canaanite cultic centers as "an idolatrous and magical attempt to lay hands on the sacred," and out of opposition to rooted shrines employed a moveable tabernacle as the center of sacred space, wherein God could live with his people but not be bound to any one place. This opposition to rooting the divine in one locale persisted even after the construction of the temple in Jerusalem, for the holy of holies at the center of the temple was left empty, as a place for God's presence rather than as an objectification of the divine.[14]

The theology of the New Testament is even more detached from specific and concrete space and objects than the Old Testament. While the book of Genesis portrayed the covenant of God with his chosen people as intimately bound up with God's granting of possession of the land that would become Israel to the descendants of Abraham, a disposition that made this land holy, the new covenant is explicitly divorced from such geographical connections. This is evident in Jesus' reply to Pilate: "My kingdom is not from this world. If my kingdom were from this world, my followers would be fighting to keep me from being handed over to the Jews. But as it is, my kingdom is not from here."[15] This may also be seen in Jesus' dialogue with the Samaritan woman:

> The woman said to him, "Sir, I see that you are a prophet. Our ancestors worshipped on this mountain, but you say the place where people must worship is in Jerusalem." Jesus said to her, "Woman, believe me, the hour is coming when you will worship the Father neither on this mountain nor in Jerusalem. . . . But the hour is coming, and is now here, when the true worshippers will worship the father in spirit and truth, for the Father seeks such as these to worship him. God is spirit, and those who worship him must worship in spirit and truth."[16]

The message of Jesus is portrayed here as transcending not only the boundaries of sacred space as delimited in the temple and within the land and peo-

---

powers. Only later, Bouyer contends, when the practice of magic was adopted, did humans intend to shut up the sacred in order to have it at their disposal (157). Yet magic could also serve to exclude things, as in the case of pentagrams barring the entry of demonic forces. See H. R. Ellis Davidson, *Myths and Symbols in Pagan Europe: Early Scandinavian and Celtic Religions* (Syracuse: Syracuse University Press, 1988), 31.

14. Bouyer, *Rite and Man*, 159, 161–62.   15. Jn 18:36.
16. Jn 4:21, 23–24.

ple of Israel, but also the very manifestations of physical space and the geography of the created world. This is a relationship within the divine that is predicated on an internal geography, not an external one.

This deemphasizing of the importance of sacred space lies at the heart of the universalism of Christianity as a faith of many nations, but this minimization of geography in worship did not long endure contact with the Greco-Roman world and the Germanic cultures that melded to create early medieval civilization. Christianity encountered and embraced not only the embedded use of temples as it converted the Roman world, but also accepted a degree of reverence for natural places inherited from Germanic and Celtic cultures.[17] The pagan cultures and their religious beliefs came into close contact and interaction with Christianity as Christian missions to northern peoples accelerated during and after the pontificate of St. Gregory the Great (d. 604).[18] Scholars have argued that the pagan religions of the north rooted much of their faith in the natural and harsh geography in which they struggled to eke out a secure existence, and the severity of the wilderness and climate (particularly for the northern Germanic and Scandinavian peoples) often lent both a violent and a naturalistic cast to pagan devotions.[19] If archaeological evidence is any indication, pagan Celts and Germans built few

17. For an excellent survey of the idea of sacred space in pre-Christian tribal culture, see Davidson, *Myths and Symbols in Pagan Europe*, 13–31. The idea of natural or supernatural sanctification without human agency seems to have been readily incorporated into Christian belief. An early medieval example may be seen in the Anglo-Saxon *Blickling Homily XVII: The Dedication of Saint Michael's Church*, which tells of the consecration of Monte Gargano in southern Italy by the archangel Michael, wherein the archangel addresses the local people thus about a special cave they later desire to consecrate in his name: "I am the archangel of the King of Heaven, and I always stand in his sight. I tell you now also that I especially love this place here on earth and I have chosen it over all others and also will make known in many signs that take place here that I am the creator and herdsman of this place in all ways.... There is no need for you with respect to this matter to consecrate the church, because I have already fashioned it and consecrated it. You must now go inside and wait for me, and devoutly believe in the protector of that place and draw near to it in your prayers." See Robert Boenig, trans., *Anglo-Saxon Spirituality: Selected Writings*, Classics of Western Spirituality (New York: Pastoral Press, 2000), 73, 75–76.

18. David Hugh Farmer, *The Oxford Dictionary of the Saints*, 3d ed. (Oxford: Oxford University Press, 1992), 211–15. Evidence of the lingering presence of pre-Christian notions of nature in early medieval culture may be seen in the devotional literature, art, and poetry of the Celtic world, where strong images of nature as an autonomous realm touched by grace predominate, and the body is the focus of human existence, to be transformed by the reception of new life into glory (Davies, *Celtic Spirituality*, 24).

19. Davidson, *Myths and Symbols in Pagan Europe*, 13.

shrines, preferring instead to locate their sites of contact with supernatural powers outside and in the open air.[20] Despite this proclivity, these cultures did add human construction to the work of nature when establishing their sacred spaces, burial mounds of honored ancestors and kings being one common situating of sacred power. Such sites could serve as both important symbols of the tribe's heritage and as a possible means of communication with the other world, where visions, inspiration, and guidance could be bestowed upon the respectful supplicant.[21]

With this outline of the evolution and importance of the notion of sacred space, we may now turn to medieval liturgical blessings of space and the sacred instruments used to consecrate it. In the following analysis, we will examine how these rituals share four common themes that appear in all sorts of blessings: an emphatic presentation of God's perceived nature; a concern over pollution caused by human, natural, and demonic agency; expression of belief in a profound connection between divinity and the natural world; and an understanding of the relationship between humanity and divinity as a contractual bond. Spatial blessings additionally manifest their own distinctive themes, which will be elaborated as we examine each category of blessings in turn.

FIELDS, GARDENS, AND THE AGRICULTURAL WORLD

The blessing of fields and their harvests predates Christianity by centuries. The pagan religions of antiquity practiced the sacrifice of fruits as a means to ward off danger, an act that assumed particular importance in the Israelite faith. This religion attributed a higher meaning to sacrifice of first fruits, since the whole country of Israel was considered a gift from God, who had explicitly commanded the offering and sacrifice of the firstborn. Christianity later limited the Old Testament sacrifice of the firstborn to the harvested products of field and garden, which were delivered as voluntary gifts to the priests and bishop and consecrated in the local church, with a prayer of thanksgiving for God's gifts.[22] In the early medieval Roman church, this

20. Ibid. One example of such a locale is the Helgafell in Iceland (ibid., 13–16).

21. Ibid., 19. At such places, poets were often the recipients of such visions and inspiration, and Celtic poetry is filled with notions of supernatural power and divine inspiration. Davies, *Celtic Spirituality*, 41.

22. Franz, 1:361–62. All first fruits were at first placed on the altar, a practice that aroused concern over corruption of the altar and ultimately led the apostolic canons to command a

harvest thanksgiving was at first connected with the Ember Day fasts, which attempted to replace the August and December harvest festivals of pagan Rome with a more ascetic praxis of fasting and penitence in this time of thanksgiving.[23] But this connection slowly vanished from popular Roman consciousness, and it failed to spread beyond Rome, owing to differences in harvest times and customary practice among the peoples of the Latin West.[24]

The first consecration ritual for first fruit is found in the Roman church, in the *Liber Pontificalis* entry for Pope Eutychianus (reigned from 275 to 283). This text ordered fruits and eggs to be consecrated upon the altar, and beans later came to be included in this category.[25] The consecration of grapes and beans is not found in the Verona sacramentary, whereas the old Gelasian sacramentary has a consecration of new beans included in the Mass of the Ascension of the Lord.[26] The Gregorian sacramentary contains a consecra-

---

ritual purification for the altar in question, but in later centuries only wheat and grapes were permitted on the altar, while the other fruits would be taken to the bishop's house (ibid., 363). Franz cites an example of this type of custom in the vita of the early medieval St. Tychon of Amathus (written by Patriarch John Eleemon of Alexandria [d. 617]), which tells how the bishop ordered the planting of a withered branch at the death of the saint, which led (on 6 June, the anniversary of the saint's passing) to the branch's flowering and bearing sweet grapes before other grapes were mature. Grapes were placed on the altar on the feastday of Tychon in honor of this miracle, remaining there during the Mass and receiving the consecration of the Holy Spirit, and were then distributed among the people. The juice of these grapes was also dribbled into the Mass chalice every time this feast was celebrated; legend had it that, even if they were unripe when placed on the altar, the grapes sweetened on the altar or in the hands of the faithful. Franz dismisses attempts to connect this story to pagan myth, seeing it instead as a recognition of the gift of the bishop, or as an attempt to honor the saint (1:364–66).

23. Ibid., 1:367–69. The pagan festivals honored the gods Consualia and Opalia on 21 and 25 August and 15 and 19 December. The festivals of Volcanalia (27 August) and Volturnalia (23 August) were also held to protect the gathered harvest from fire and flood. Pope Leo's *Homilies* for the days of these feasts speak of sowing and the harvest and admonish the congregation to add thanksgiving to the traditional mortification and giving of alms.

24. Ibid., 1:369. Medieval liturgists outside Rome, ignorant of the Romans' intentions, found explanation for the introduction of Ember Day fasts in allegory and mystical interpretations.

25. Ibid. This order probably comes from some later date, in that it parallels canon 3 of the apostolic canons, which permitted only wheat and grapes on the altar. In Rome, beans came to replace wheat, in accord with ancient popular attitudes that saw the bean as a holy fruit (ibid., 1:369–70).

26. Ibid., 1:370. Another prayer for grapes or beans is also included in the sacramentary, although Franz is unsure of the date on which it was performed.

tion of grapes during the canon on 6 August (the Feast of the Pope St. Six-tus II [reigned from 257 to 258]), which corresponds in time with the grape harvest in Rome, if not in other localities.[27] The consecration of first fruit had both general and special formulas during the Middle Ages.[28]

The prayers and blessings spoken over fields, crops, and the harvest form some of the most numerous blessings that have come down to us from the medieval period. While some scholarship has perceived such blessings as primarily a means to ensure a beneficent natural order and exclude the forc-es of chaos from the agricultural world that formed the foundation of medi-eval civilization, these blessings can also tell us a great deal about what me-dieval people believed about both divinity and the natural world.[29] Prayers

27. Ibid. Nothing in the legend of the saint deals with grapes; it was probably chosen simply for its convenient timing. This custom of consecrating beans and grapes must have been entrenched in Rome by the fifth century, as the *Liber pontificalis* mentions it. Franz sees this linking as an example of the tendency to connect agrarian celebrations with the feasts of saints, both of which are communal events (1:372). The date for this consecration varied in different regions: in Germany the date was often pushed later into the year to accommo-date the growing season (a good example of the general custom may be found in the *Anti-quores consuetudines cluniacensis monasterii* of St. Urich, which prescribed the blessing and distri-bution of grapes on Sixtus's feast day, or when they were ripe [book 1, chap. 35; *PL* 149:682]); in Spain, Sixtus's feast was celebrated on 10 August, without a Roman consecration of grapes, but the ritual for grapes was nevertheless well known, as can be seen in the *Liber ordinum* of Si-los (Franz, 1:375–76). Other localities in the Latin church celebrated the feast of the Transfigu-ratio Domini on 6 August. This feast came to be celebrated in southern Italy in the eleventh century, in France in the twelfth century, and in Germany in the fourteenth century (Franz, 1:374–75).

28. Of the special formulas, those for particular fruits and for herbs stand out. For exam-ple, apples received a special consecration, probably on the feast of St. Jacobus, the ritual for which is found first in the Old Gelasian sacramentary (see the *Benedictio arboris* in Mohlberg, Eizenhöfer, and Siffrin, *Liber sacramentorum,* 234, *ordo* 90). The strong belief of medieval cul-tures in the healing power of "words, herbs and stones" to animate, heal, protect, and defend explains the concern of medieval liturgists to enhance the power of herbs and garden fruits with the power of the holy words of blessing. Liturgical authors such as Konrad of Megen-berger claimed that herbs obtained their healing power both from their natural state and from adjuration and blessing, which could include liturgical rituals as well as charms and incan-tations of *magi* and ritual methods of harvesting the plants. Within the church, the feast of Mary's Ascension (in August, during the harvesttime for field and garden) was chosen as the consecration day for herbs. For further discussion of such beliefs and their commentators, see Franz, 1:376, 393–98. The Mozarabic liturgy contains the most and the longest rituals, as found in the *Liber ordinum* of Silos and in other sources (Franz, 1:387–88).

29. Scribner, "Cosmic Order and Daily Life," 1–16. Scribner's work focuses mainly on blessings of fields against thunderstorms and other natural disasters.

and exorcisms were used to protect the farmers and their produce from natural dangers, such as storms or destructive animals, and also from supernatural hazards, such as the malicious action of Satan and his minions.[30] For example, Anglo-Saxon penitentials of the eighth century refer familiarly to the activities of *tempestarii* (storm callers) as one dangerous kind of Satanic minion. This fear of demons' attacking agriculture through disease, blight, and hail was rooted in long tradition, with Christian scholars as early as Tertullian asserting demons' responsibility for collective disasters such as drought, bad harvests, and epidemics.[31] To counter these threats, the authors of blessings called upon the divine in many forms and guises.[32]

Let us examine eight ritual blessings that provide a representative sample of the themes of piety in this genre of ritual: a "Blessing of New Fruits," from the Romano-Germanic pontifical (hereafter RGP);[33] a "Blessing of Veg-

30. In agricultural blessings the fear of demonic malice was often accompanied by fear of generalized dangers. This fear always manifests itself in rituals specifically aimed at driving out enemies and destructive entities. This concern appears in rites as early as the tenth and as late as the sixteenth century, originating in German, Swiss, and Spanish texts, indicating that general fear of hostile powers was a significant driving force behind many blessings. For examples, see the *RGP*'s "Blessing of Water for Crops against Vermin," "Blessing of Water for Crops," Lausanne's "Exorcism of Water," and the Ordinarium of Valencia's "Against Locusts," all discussed below.

31. Tertullian, *Apologeticum*, chap. 22, cited in Cohn, *Europe's Inner Demons*, 212, 22. Of course, the appearance of such natural terrors could have a divine origin as well, as when "lightning flew like arrows toward the pagan people so that they by no means could look towards it" during a battle of Christians and pagans recounted in the Anglo-Saxon account of the dedication of St. Michael's church (Boenig, *Anglo-Saxon Spirituality*, 74).

32. Blessing rituals frequently create an image of the divine that illuminates popular notions about God's nature. While all the categories of spatial blessings manifest this theme, it is always tailored to the particular need of the community or individual seeking the blessing. Blessings of fields and crops, for example, portray divinity as a cultivator and farmer, but only in rites that specifically bless agricultural produce, and only in German and Austrian rituals of the tenth to the twelfth century. The statements made here rely on analysis of numerous manuscripts, not all of which appear directly in the main body of this work; such manuscripts are discussed, however, in the notes to each chapter and are referenced in the index. The specific rituals cited here are the *RGP*'s "Blessing of Vegetables," the St. Florian "Blessing of Crops," and Clm 22040's "Prayer in a Vineyard."

33. *RGP* 2:370 (*ordo* 223). The ritual appears in the manuscripts Bamberg, Staatsbibliothek *cod. lit.* 53, and Eichstätt, Diözesanarchiv (also called Bistumsarchiv), pontifical of Gondekar II. This rite is reproduced in Franz, 1:248; in Adolph Franz, *Das Rituale von St Florian aus dem 12. Jahrhundert* (Freiberg: Herder, 1904), 104; and in H. A. Wilson, ed., *The Gregorian Sacramentary under Charles the Great*, Henry Bradshaw Society 49 (London: Henry Bradshaw Society, 1915), 221–22.

etables," from the same manuscripts in the RGP;[34] a "Blessing of Seed," from the *Liber ordinum* of Silos in Spain;[35] a "Blessing of Water against Vermin in the Crops," from the RGP;[36] a "Blessing of a Cross on the Road or Standing above a Crop," from an eleventh-century *rituale*, possibly from Prüm;[37] a "Blessing of Crops," from the twelfth-century *rituale* of St. Florian;[38] a "Blessing against the Worms Which Afflict Vegetables," from a fourteenth-century manuscript;[39] an "Exorcism of Blessed Water Versus Whatever Worms and against Whatever Animal Is Destroying the Fruit of the Earth," from the *manuale* of Lausanne of 1451;[40] and the "*Ordo* for the Blessing and Exorcising of Fruits against Locusts, Grasshoppers, and Other Corrosive Animals," from the *Ordinarium* of Valencia (c. 1514).[41] Other rituals will provide supporting evidence for my conclusions; these, and all such rituals not directly analyzed in each chapter, can be found in the detailed index at the end of this work.

In the case of blessings for agriculture, its products, and the implements employed, God is most often appealed to and understood as a cultivator and creator. This is first evident in the "Blessing of New Fruits," which embraces all grown products. Appearing first in the supplement to the Gregorian sacramentary, this blessing emphasizes God's being as a creator: "Lord, Holy Father, Omnipotent eternal God, who created heaven and earth, the sea and all living things . . ."[42] The vast expanse of creation is invoked by this prayer, as a testament to the capacity of God to affect the natural order. This nature is not only stated here, however; it also is affirmed to assist the growing of natural crops when, following the invocation of God's nature as creator, the supplicant continues:

---

34. *RGP* 2:368 (*ordo* 218); see also Franz, 1:415.

35. Franz, 1:10; see also M. Férotin, ed., *Le liber ordinum en usage dans l'église wisigothique et mozarabe d'Espagne du cinquième au onzième siècle,* Monumenta Ecclesiae Liturgica 5 (Paris: Firmin-Didot, 1904), 166.

36. *RGP* 2:363–67 (*ordo* 214b).

37. Franz, 2:13–14. This rite is examined in the introduction.

38. Ibid., 2:12. See also Franz, *Das Rituale von St Florian aus dem 12. Jahrhundert* (Freiberg: Herder, 1904), 105.

39. Franz, 2:168 (from Clm 7021).

40. Ibid., 2:163.

41. Ibid., 2:167; the ritual occurs on fols. 146v–148 of the *Ordinarium.*

42. *RGP* 2:370 (*ordo* 223): Domine, sancte pater, omnipotens aeterne Deus, qui caelum et terram, mare et omnia creasti . . . See also Wilson, *Gregorian Sacramentary,* 221–22. This rite also appears in the St. Florian *rituale,* from Austria (see also Franz, *Rituale von St. Florian,* 104).

we supplicants beseech you so that you may deign to bless and sanctify this new fruit and multiply it abundantly for those offering it to you. Replenish their pantries with the power of grain, wine and olive oil, so that rejoicing in these things they may yield praises and thanks to you, almighty God.[43]

In this entreaty we observe one of the fundamental elements of medieval blessings at work, namely, the promise of praise and adoration for divinity in exchange for material prosperity. Both the understood interest of the divine (i.e., the need or desire for worship) and the human world's interest are satisfied by this ritual, which infuses power into the natural world for the benefit of humanity through a ritual negotiation similar to a contract.[44]

God's role in the creation of growing food manifested to the author of this blessing a power that could be accessed, even millennia after the creation of the world, to support and sustain the present human community. This power is conceived of as deriving from God's intimate connection with the origins of the world, as may be seen in the blessing of vegetables:

Omnipotent God, author of all human health and salvation, doctor of bodies and souls, who through ineffable wisdom appointed an abundance of herbs as health-giving medicine, for the uses of those languishing, grant, we beseech [you], that you may refresh this creation of vegetable with your health-giving blessing, so that they may be medicine of the body and strength of the spirit for whoever being sick uses them.[45]

The power imbued by God into the ancestors of the herbs and vegetables grown in medieval gardens is here invoked to ensure the potency of medic-

43. *RGP* 2:370: te supplices quesumus, ut hunc fructum novum benedicere et sanctificare digneris et multiplicare abundanter offerentibus tibi. Repleas eorum cellaria cum fortitudine frumenti, vini et olei, ut laetantes in eis referant tibi Deo omnipotenti laudes et gratias.

44. The implicit and explicit statement of this relationship is predominant in agricultural blessings. Blessings of fields and crops invoking a contractual relationship appear in the high and late Middle Ages, although fully half of these eight rites date to the tenth century, most appearing first in the *RGP,* though some are older. Accordingly, while this theme is present in Swiss and Spanish agricultural blessings, it appears mainly in German liturgical books and manuscripts; see the *RGP*'s "Blessing of New Fruits," "Blessing of Water for Crops," and "Blessing on a Plain," St. Thierry of Rheim's "Blessing of New Fruit," Lausanne's "Exorcism of Water," and the Ordinarium of Valencia's "Against Locusts."

45. *RGP* 2:368: Omnipotens Deus, totius humanae salutis et sanitatis auctor, animarum et corporum medicus, qui copiam herbarum ad usus languentium salubri medicina per ineffabilem sapientiam condidisti, presta, quesumus, ut salutari tua benedictione hanc holerum creaturam repleas, ut, quicumque infirmus eis usus fuerit, sint ei corporis medicina et animae fortitudo.

inal plants. Interestingly, God himself is defined by this prayer as both the source of all good health and a kind of prescriber of natural medicines, suggesting the depth of the imagined connection between creator and creature in medieval people's minds, a connection that could be recalled to the mind of God in order to ensure God's intervention.[46] That this attribution appears in German and Spanish rituals, both early (tenth century) and late (sixteenth century), that ask that health and healing be bestowed through blessed produce suggests that it was a powerful and persistent image of the divine.[47]

God's nature as a creator and therefore as a sustainer of life and growing things is evident in a Spanish prayer similar to the blessings of the RGP. In a "Blessing of Seed," from the *Liber ordinum* of Silos, the third of three prayers begins thus: "Creator of all creatures, omnipotent God, who gave seeds their condition of bringing forth and sowing and fructifying, we entreat you so that you may look kindly upon our prayer and thus at length may you yield enlarged grace in sowing seeds."[48] Here God's nature as a creator is highlighted through a reminder of his role in spreading all living things on the face of the earth in the beginning times of Christian sacred history, intimately associating the sacred and divine with motion and life.[49] This idea appears only in high medieval blessings of the tenth to twelfth century but is common to both Germanic and Spanish rituals of this period.[50] Thus this blessing keeps

46. Similar invocations of God's nature appear in later blessings: see Clm 22040, fol. 86, and Clm 22040, fols. 87 and 89 (and also Clm 17027, fol. 116; see Franz, 2:14–16), in the index.

47. See the *RGP*'s "Blessing of Vegetables" and "Blessing of New Fruits," and the Ordinarium of Valencia's "Against Locusts."

48. Franz, 1:10: Creator omnium creaturam, omnipotens deus, qui omnium seminum gignendi serendique atque fructificandi conditionem dedisti: te deprecamur, ut pius ad precem nostram respicias et ita demum in serendis seminibus amplificatem gratiam tribuas. The first prayer of this ritual is identical to the "Blessing of Seed" from the *RGP* (*ordo* 213).

49. A similar emphasis on God as creator appears in German, Austrian, and Spanish rites from the tenth to the sixteenth century: see the *RGP*'s "Blessing of New Fruits," the Ordinarium of Valencia's "Against Locusts," and Clm 22040's prayer "In the Early Morning."

50. See the *RGP*'s "Blessing of Vegetables" and "Blessing of Water for Crops," the Old Spanish "Blessing of Seed," and Clm 22040's "Prayer in a Vineyard." The divine is also associated with the element of water by agricultural blessings, a natural connection given the necessity of water in farming. This connection is probably regional, as it appears only in German and Austrian texts, but it may have been a constant, for it is present in both tenth- and fifteenth-century rituals. Or it may simply be determined by the centrality of water to these two rituals; see the *RGP*'s "Blessing of Water for Crops against Vermin," and Lausanne's "Exorcism of Water."

alive that memory in the mind of the community as it helps to entreat the divine for power to ensure a good harvest in the coming autumn.

This recalling of the original creation and God's role in it raises an important issue in the analysis of blessings, namely, the apparent uncertainty of the medieval clergy and laity about the consistency and reliability of God's nature and approach to the human community. The writings of Boethius at the beginning of the early Middle Ages demonstrate how pre-Christian classical notions about the nature of the world and the capriciousness of life lingered in the *mentalité* of medieval Europe after the decline of the religions that had shaped them. In his famous work *The Consolation of Philosophy*, Boethius, imprisoned and awaiting execution, engages in a dialogue with Fortuna, the divine embodiment of fate familiar to the classical mind, who points out how the divine exercises itself through both good and evil: "When you were a little boy," she tells Boethius, "surely you must have heard Homer's story about the two jars standing in God's house, the one full of evil and the other of good."[51] This classical image of a deity who doles out both good and ill would fit well with the Christian conception of a God who could both provide the salvation of the new covenant and at the same time be the God of wrath and destruction recounted in the Old Testament. This ambiguity in God's nature could only have been enhanced in the mind of the reader of Boethius's discussion of the nature of Fortuna, one of the manifestations of divinity from the classical world that most often interacted and worked upon the lives of human beings: "Change is her normal behavior, her true nature. In the very act of changing she has presented her own particular kind of constancy towards you."[52] Boethius also attributes this capriciousness to the divinely created natural world:

> In shimmering waves at rest,
> And often the north wind churns the deep
> With raging storms and mad unrest.
> The world stays rarely long the same,
> So great its instability . . .
> In law eternal it lies decreed
> That naught from change is ever freed.[53]

51. Boethius, *The Consolation of Philosophy*, trans. V. E. Watts (New York: Penguin, 1969), 58.
52. Ibid., 55.
53. Ibid., 61.

The created world was seen as afflicted with never-ending change, turbulence, and chaos. As part of this instability, human life was perceived by Boethius and his readers as suffering from this condition: "It is the nature of human affairs to be fraught with anxiety; they never prosper perfectly and they never remain constant."[54] From this viewpoint chaos and imperfection ruled the existence of humanity, a perspective that, in the absence of science and effective medicine to provide explanations and comfort, could easily dismiss as an unjustifiable fantasy the notion of progress so beloved by modern peoples, if it could even have contemplated such a thing.

While Boethius could express a profoundly classical understanding of the capriciousness of the world and the relationship between divinity and humanity, as a Christian he held out hope that the power of the divine can and does prevent the instability and uncertainty of the world from devolving into complete chaos:

> The world in constant change
> Maintains a harmony,
> And elements keep peace
> Whose nature is to clash.
> The sun in car of gold
> Draws forth the rosy day,
> And evening brings the night
> When Luna holds her sway.
> The tides in limits fixed
> Confine the greedy sea . . .
> And all these chain of things
> In Earth and Sea and Sky
> One ruler holds:
> If Love relaxed the reins
> All things that now keep peace
> Would wage continual war.[55]

Christian faith here envisions a desire on the part of divinity to prevent an imbalance in the natural world, so that divine love works constantly to prevent utter chaos from triumphing in the natural world, and implicitly in the lives of humans. Thus at the heart of this, one of the most widely read and respected Christian philosophical works of the medieval period, lies the am-

54. Ibid., 62.   55. Ibid., 77.

biguity of a divinity that in the blessings acts with both reason and caprice, dispensing good and evil, order and chaos, to humans seemingly on the sole basis of whether proper rituals have been carried out. Ambiguity in fundamental beliefs about the divine almost always produces some form of anxiety in the human consciousness, and it is precisely this anxiety, I would argue, that we see in the blessings of the medieval church.

Such anxiety, particularly about individual salvation, may be seen in other medieval sources, such as numerous pieces of early medieval visionary literature, where there often seems to be no assurance that the visionaries lying at death's door will be assured salvation by merit of their deeds alone. Rather, these texts more often contain the assumption that without protective prayer and the intervention of the angels and saints (such as are offered by the blessings), the demons that assail the human soul will prevail and drag the soul down to damnation.[56] Even the saints cannot necessarily be relied upon, but must be placated and petitioned for their aid.[57] A divinity that is understood to allow this cannot be seen as being anything other than somewhat capricious, and it is this capriciousness that the blessings' invocations of God's past good deeds seek to convert to assured beneficence.

Agricultural blessings emphasize the power of the divine as a force in the cultivation of growing plants. In a short "Blessing for Crops," from St. Florian, God becomes a farmer not only of crops but of the spirit: "Omnipotent eternal God, sower and cultivator of the heavenly word, who furrows the field of our hearts by means of spiritual plows, deign to be present through our prayers and over this field carrying seeds for human food pour forth a great blessing."[58] In this beautiful prayer, the power of the sacred, of the *numen*, to spark life in growing things is implicitly understood to be intimately linked to the internal life of members of the community. The life of the spirit experienced in the hearts of the congregation receiving the blessing is nurtured in the same manner as crops are nurtured by a farmer. The divine thus participates in all dimensions of the community's life, collective and particular, external and internal, earthly and spiritual. This is an important point, for it re-

56. McLaughlin, *Consorting with Saints*, 202.

57. Saints such as Firminius, for example, could be capricious and were thought of as such, choosing to help or ignore the petitions of their devotees at whim (Geary, *Furta sacra*, 33).

58. Franz, 2:12 (Franz, *Rituale von St. Florian*, 105): Omnipotens sempiterne deus, celestis verbi seminator et cultor, qui nostri cordis aream spiritalibus rostris exerces: adesse propicius precibus nostris dignare et super hunc agrum segetes victui humano gestantem benedictionem largam diffunde.

veals how blessings could be seen as a means by which the medieval religious mentality sought to inject divine and human meaning into the seemingly chaotic natural order, to relate the inner struggle for salvation to the natural world outside. For the medieval Christian author of this benediction, God could fill both the exalted role of creator and the humble place of the farmer and field hand, suggesting that versatility was one fundamental trait of divinity and its power.

A rich source of blessings that reveal such close connections between God and creation can be found in benedictions for the protection of crops through the use of holy water. Holy water, along with prayer, adjuration, and exorcism, formed the principal ritual means employed by the church to defend farmers from infestations of destructive animals and insects.[59] In the "Blessing of Water against Vermin in the Crops," found within the RGP, God is closely associated with the waters, both of the original creation and of this particular blessing. The second prayer of this blessing begins with the sign of the cross being made thrice by blowing on the water to be used, followed by a standard invocation for the creation of such sacred water: "Let this commingling of this salt and water be made salutary through the power of the undivided trinity and through the power of its cross."[60] The cross and act of crossing are here presented as a symbol imbued with the intensity and the power of the divine to affect the world.[61] The water and sacred power joined, an antiphon closely associating God with the chthonic waters of the creation is sung: *Vox domini super aquas. Deus maiestatis intonuit. Dominus super aquas multas.*[62] God is further associated with the element of water in the first

59. Franz, 1:165–66 (*ordo* 214B.2–3). Popular formulas for adjurations against animals also existed, such as used in northwest Switzerland and southwest Germany in the sixteenth century, where the rod and relics of St. Magnus were carried out in pedestals on foot to communities threatened with infestations (ibid., 1:169).

60. *RGP* 2:363–64: Hic suffla ter in aquam in modum crucis et commisce sal et aquam dicendo: Haec commixtio salis et aquae per virtutem individuae trinitatis et per virtutem suae crucis salutifera efficiatur. This rubric also appears in the "Incipit benedictio salis et aquae ad omnia valde necessaria et maxime pro peste animalium" (Franz, 1:168n17), found in Clm 17027, and CSG MS 339.

61. The sign of the cross, made on the forehead, first appears in initiation rites in the beginning of the third century in the African and Roman liturgies. It was used "to imprint, as it were, an invisible seal," and later was extended to the sense organs and became an exorcism. See Martimort, *Church at Prayer*, 154–55.

62. *RGP* 2:363–67 (*ordo* 214B.5). The manuscripts in which this ritual is found are Bamberg, Staatsbibliothek, *cod. lit.* 53, and Eichstätt, Diözesanarchiv (also called Bistumsarchiv), pontifical of Gondekar II.

alternate prayer for the *oratio post commixtionem,* when the deity is invoked as "God, to whom, residing on the sublime throne above the Cherubim, all the profundity of the abyss and the sea and the breadth of the earth is evident."[63] The close connection of the divine realm with the created world adds evocative resonance to this prayer and reaffirms the connection of the sacred and its power with the natural element of water to be used in the ritual.

The sprinkling of water was a common element of medieval blessings, and an element that finds its origins in the most ancient of religious practices. Greco-Roman cults often believed that rivers, streams, and springs held sacred, and especially purifying, power. Water was used to purify oneself (through bathing), in libations, and in sacrifices offered to the deities, as well as in rites of birth, marriage, and death.[64] As early as the first century of the common era we find Ovid's *Fasti* relating how the goddess of the same name uses the sprinkling of water to protect a child from a malicious magical attack, while the use of water in medieval Christian blessings echoes the Germanic belief in the magical power of fountains and streams and the spirits of water that dwelt therein. A much clearer connection, of course, can be found in the Christian ritual of baptism, which uses water as a means to liberate the soul of the newborn from the powers of the demonic. In the early Middle Ages baptism served as an attractive method of invoking the supernatural in the context of water and expressed the pre-Christian Germanic reverence for this element.[65] The early medieval church allowed this practice to spread, as witnessed by Hincmar of Reims (d. 882) in his *Capitula Synodica:*

63. Ibid.: Deus, cui super Cherubim sublimi throno residenti omnis profunditas abyssi et maris terraeque latitudo perspicua est.

64. Johan Harm Croon, "Water," in *The Oxford Classical Encyclopedia,* ed. Simon Hornblower and Antony Spawforth (Oxford: Oxford University Press, 1996), 1619. Water was also offered to the dead, who were believed to thirst for it. Water's supernatural powers were shown in mythology and legend, such as in the story of Glaucus, who was bathed and thus purified in a sacred pool in preparation for the deification that was his fate, and that of Pherecydes, who used water as an instrument of prophecy and divination. See Jean Rudhardt and Erica Meltzer, "Water," in Eliade, *Encyclopedia of Religion,* 15:357. Greek practice also commonly prescribed bathing in rivers following any expiatory sacrifice as a necessary purification. See Diana L. Eck, "Rivers," in Eliade, *Encyclopedia of Religion,* 12:427.

65. Flint, *Rise of Magic,* 26, 90, 263. The central element of the sacrament of baptism that evokes this concern is the renunciation of Satan and his works. As early as the composition of the Gelasian rite for the catechumenate in early medieval Rome, we find abjurations of the diabolic and its ways as an essential part of the sacrament of baptism: the ears of the

Every Sunday, before the celebration of the Mass, the priest shall bless the water in his Church; and, for this holy purpose, he shall use a clean and suitable
vessel. The people, when entering the Church, are to be sprinkled with this water; and those who desire may carry some away in clean vessels so as to sprinkle their houses, fields, vineyards and cattle, and the provender with which
these last are fed, and also to throw over their own food.[66]

In later times, the origin of aspersion was ascribed by theologians such as
Hugh of St. Victor to Pope Alexander, the fifth successor of St. Peter, for the
blessing of the people and their habitations, "following Elisaeus the prophet
putting salt into the bitter springs to turn them sweet."[67] Aspersion frequently occurs in our agricultural blessings, playing a role in six of them.[68] But the
manner in which this sacramental action was carried beyond the walls of baptistery and church into the natural world may mean that the Christian be-

---

catechumen in preparation for baptism were anointed with holy oil, "so that, the ears being
as it were fortified by a kind of wall of sanctification, may permit entrance to nothing harmful, nothing which may entice them back [into the service of the Devil]." A. Wilmart, *Analecta
Reginensia*, Studi e Testi 59 (Vatican City, 1933), quoted in J. D. C. Fisher, *Christian Initiation:
Baptism in the Medieval West* (London: S.P.C.K., 1965), 8, 12, 89. This emphasis on protection
from the Devil's power may also be seen in Isidore of Seville's commentary on Christian initiation in the early seventh century, where he discusses the exorcism that was given to catechu-
mens (with parents answering for infant baptismal candidates) as "a rebuke against the unclean spirit . . . by means of which the abominable power of the devil, his age-long malice and
violent assault, may be cast out of them and put to flight," so that they might renounce Satan and be delivered from the power of darkness (Isidore of Seville, *De ecclesiasticis officis* 2:21,
quoted in Fisher, *Christian Initiation*, 89). This interpretation of baptism is also supported by
Hincmar of Rheims, who, Flint notes, compared the waters of baptism to a shield for the righteous (in particular during ordeals involving water); see Hincmar of Rheims, *De divortio* 6 (*PL*
125:668–69). The sacrament of baptism was also often used to Christianize non-Christian
magical springs. See Gregory of Tours, *In gloria martyrum* 23, *MGH SRM* 1 (2):51–52. Many lay-
persons took such water and poured it over their crops and fields as a kind of "home remedy"
for their protection and prosperity. Flint, *Rise of Magic*, 268.

66. Hincmar of Rheims, *Capitula Synodica*, PL 125:774.

67. Hugh of St. Victor, *On the Sacraments*, 316. Martimort agrees with this attribution, noting that, in its origin and most common use, holy water is water of purification. Used for aspersion and combined with salt, holy water was in use since at least the sixth century for sprinkling
mundane places as a reminder to those present of baptism (Martimort, *Church at Prayer*, 160).

68. Aspersion also appears in a blessing of a house and all rites of reconciliation; see the
RGP's "Blessing of Water for Crops against Vermin" and "Blessing of Water for Crops," Prüm's
"Blessing of a Cross," Clm 7021's "Against Worms," Lausanne's "Exorcism of Water," the Ordinarium of Valencia's "Against Locusts," the *PWD*'s "Blessing of a New House," and all the
reconciliations of churches and cemeteries discussed below.

lief in the efficacy of water drew some support from pre-Christian convictions that the sprinkling of water could act as a guard and ward to all parts of creation.[69] What is certain is that by the later Middle Ages belief in the efficacy of holy water and aspersion had permeated the mentality of Christians in the Latin West, as may be seen in the writings of one fourteenth-century Italian author, who attributed to holy water many virtues in his collection of prayers: the water "cleansed venial sin, increased goodness, loosed the snares of the Devil, and protects against impure thoughts."[70] The powers of the blessed water were numerous and varied, protecting the exterior landscape from destructive forces.

This principle is most clearly demonstrated in the blessing of crops we have been examining. In the prayer after the commingling, grain itself indirectly receives the gift of baptism:

> You, therefore, Lord, we in the carrying out of our unworthy office ask that this holy mixture of salt and water may be sanctified in your name by the gift of your clemency, through which you mysteriously bestow ease to the baptized, enmity on the guilty savage, rightness on the wise, contrariness on the erroneous, and may you restore the blessed by the sanctity of your holy spirit, nor may it be re-infected by any contagion, which we believe to be made blessed by your majesty.[71]

While the author makes clear that it is the water and salt that are receiving the blessing of baptism, it seems apparent that what is happening in this ritual is that a human sacrament is being extended into the nonhuman world, so that the waters will be infused with the power of the sacred, and the grain to be protected will experience what might otherwise be considered contact with the divine restricted to human beings.

---

69. The sprinkling of blessed salt and water was often, as Flint points out, used to expel supernatural terror in the early Middle Ages (*Rise of Magic*, 154): see the *Vita Ursmari episcopi et abbatis Lobbiensis* 4, ed. Bruno Krusch and W. Levison, *MGH SRM* 6:458–59.

70. Thompson, *Cities of God*, 438, citing Bologna, Biblioteca Universitaria, MS 158, xiv c., fol. 45v.

71. *RGP* 2:364 (*ordo* 214B.4): Te igitur, domine, officii nostri funccione quesumus immeriti, ut haec salis et aquae in tuo nomine sacra permixtio, clementiae tuae dono sanctificetur, per quae misterialiter baptismo commodum, culpae truci inimicum, sapientiae aptum, errori prestas adversum, sancti spiritus sanctitate reddas sanctificatum, nec ullo contagio reddatur immundum, quod tua fieri credimus maiestate beatum. This prayer also appears in Franz, 1:152n6, the Mozarabic formula *Ordo quando sal ante altare ponitur, antequam exorcizetur,* from the *Liber ordinum* of Silos (Mon. Liturg. 5:11–15).

This ritual highlights another important theme within medieval blessings, the connection of the natural world to the virtues and vices of human nature. This theme first appears in the seventh prayer of this benediction, an alternate blessing:

> Lord, holy father, omnipotent restorer of your every creature, who in place of the ancient curses promised peace to men through your son our Lord Jesus Christ, grant your peace for this blessing so that, our iniquities removed, your holiness and blessing alone may abide in this creation of salt and water.[72]

In this prayer we see that a blessing can remove pollution and human iniquity, thus connecting the natural world to human virtue and shaping it by the interior moral landscape of humans.[73] This conclusion is supported by the commentary of Hugh of St. Victor, who declared when discussing aspersion that "the water signifies penance for past acts, salt discretion and caution regarding future acts, and, if these two are mixed together, bitter conscience is turned into sweetness and the illusions and disturbances of the demons no longer dominate it."[74] Virtues and vices in this cosmos, then, have some substantial existence that the power of the sacred can buttress or demolish in order to establish purity and keep out the pollution that could contaminate the human community.[75] This is further confirmed by the preface to the Mass that accompanies the blessing: "Hence as supplicants we pray that you may hearken to us and have pity on our cries, so that wherever the grace of aspersion and purification of this water shall have been spread, a house may have there peace, joy, faith, charity, hope and everlasting honor, so that all

---

72. *RGP* 2:365 (*ordo* 214B.7): Domine, sancte pater, omnipotens instaurator totius creaturae tuae, qui pro antiqua malediccione per Iesum Christum filium tuum domnium nostrum pacem hominibus promisisti, tuam huic pacem concede benediccioni, ut remotis iniquitatibus nostris, tua solummodo in hac creatura salis et aquae remaneat sanctificatio et benedictio.

73. This theme of pollution also appears in four other rites (see below, and the index). This pollution takes two forms, one being the presence of demons and the deceptions of Satan as the source of pollution, the other a general notion of ill will and threatening forces at large in the world. The connection between the elements and human morality made in tenth- and twelfth-century agricultural blessings may be a regional trait of central European benedictions: three out of four of the rituals with this theme derive from southern Germany and Austria, while the one French ritual is from nearby Rheims in eastern France.

74. Hugh of St. Victor, *On the Sacraments*, 316.

75. For the operation of similar notions in premodern cultures outside the West, see the work of Mary Douglas on taboo and pollution, especially *Purity and Danger: An Analysis of the Concepts of Pollution and Taboo* (London: Routledge, 1966).

the hatred of the malevolent enemy may be expelled and separated."[76] The grace of aspersion, the power of the divine within the commingled salt and water, can instill human virtues and good qualities while excluding the unclean impulses of the demonic world from the harmonious workings of the human community.

But this spiritual dimension is not limited to humans and insensible elements: it also applies to the animals that support the human world through their deaths. An alternate pre-blessing of the water and salt states: "May the blessing of God the Father, Son and Holy Spirit deign to descend upon this creature of salt and water, so that it may be made a salutary perfect medicine for souls and bodies and beasts."[77] Thus the entire visible world of the average medieval soul's experience is embraced by the power of the sacred. The sacred strengthens the spirit of human being, animal, and element, just as like effects like in thaumaturgical magic; but the act of blessing is required to open a causeway between the world of the numinous and the visible world, a causeway that may well have been regarded as in constant need of human maintenance, as is evidenced in the final prayer of this blessing, which begins: "Omnipotent and merciful God, who granted such great grace to your priests before others, so that whatever is made by them deserving and perfect in your name, may it be believed to have been done by you."[78] While there is no doubt that the author sought in this opening statement to remind the audience that priests had no power independent of God, there also

76. *RGP* 2:366 (*ordo* 214B.12): Proinde supplices exoramus, ut nos exaudias et miserearis precibus nostris, ut, ubicumque gratia aspersionis et purificationis huius aquae fuerit emissa, habeat ibi domus gaudium, pacem, fidem, caritatem, spem et honorem perpetuum, ut omnis malivoli inimici invidia expellatur et separetur.

77. Ibid., 2:367 (*ordo* 214B.18): Benediccio Dei patris et filii et spiritus sancti descendere dignetur super hanc creaturam salis et aquae, ut animabus et corporibus et iumentis salubris et perfecta medicina efficiatur. It may be that the animals' sacrifice entitled them, in the minds of medieval men and women, to a certain spiritual dignity: in the sixth prayer of this ritual, cattle are referred to with the phrase "which you [God] deigned to yield up for human needs," a reminder to the celebrant and congregation of what (to my mind) resembles nothing so much as the apology to slain beasts made by native hunting cultures that revere their source of livelihood as a divine gift to be respected even in death. This prayer also appears in the Freising formula of 1484 for the *Benedictio maior salis et aquae* (Franz, 1:191) and in the *Incipit maior benedictio salis et aque ad pecora*, also from Freising (Franz, 1:183n22 [Clm 6425]).

78. *RGP* 2:367, (*ordo* 214B.21): Omnipotens et misericors Deus, qui sacerdotibus tuis prae caeteris tantam gratiam contulisti, ut, quicquid in tuo nomine ab eis digne perfecteque agitur, a te fieri credatur.

seems to be some doubt or hesitancy in the author's approach to the divine; the sacred history of scriptural priests such as Samuel and Aaron was well known to the clergy, so why reiterate it here? It points out the perceived need of medieval believers to "remind" God of his nature and goodness, so as to ensure his consistency in guarding their own lives and well-being with the grace he could bestow on faithful servants. Such an invocation could also be taken to reaffirm the commitment of the Christian congregation to return praise and thanks for blessings, to fulfill the terms of the bargain represented by the faith in and practice of benedictions.

Blessings drawn from the close of the Middle Ages continue to manifest the theme of the connection of the natural world and the divine, as well as elaborating the perceived position of the blesser and blessed within the framework of sacred history. An "Exorcism of Blessed Water Versus Whatever Worms and against Whatever Animal Is Destroying the Fruit of the Earth," from the 1451 *manuale* of Lausanne, connects the power of the divine intimately to the water employed in the ritual:

> I adjure you through God, who in the beginning separated you from the dry land. I adjure you through the true God, who commanded you to flow from the font of paradise. I adjure you through him, who by his power in Cana, Galilee, converted you into wine, who walked with dry feet upon the sea, who imposed the name Syloam on you. I adjure you through him, who through you cured Naaman Syrum from his leprosy, who with an infusion of salt through the hand of the prophet Elias cleansed you, saying "holy water, purified water, water which washes away all the soiled, cleanses sin . . ."[79]

In this passage, the origin of water (as recounted in scriptural history) is reiterated as a means by which a human agent of the divine exerts control over a natural element, an element in the Christian cosmology that has always been linked with the power of purification and healing. In the same manner that God is reminded of his earlier works of goodness toward the Chris-

---

79. Franz, 2:163: Te adiuro per deum, qui te in principio seperavit ab arida. Adiuro te per deum verum, qui te de fonte paradisi manare precepit. Adiuro te per eum, qui te in Chana Galilee sua potentia convertit in vinum, qui super mare siccis pedibus ambulavit, qui tibi nomen imposuit Syloam. Adiuro te per eum, qui [per] te Naaman Syrum sua lepra curavit, qui immisso sale per manus Helysei prophete [te] mundavit dicens: aqua sancta, aqua munda, aqua, que lavat omnes sordices, mundat peccata . . . The blessings of fields and crops include such allusions in five rituals from German, Spanish, and Swiss manuscripts (the studied rites being Lausanne's "Exorcism of Water" and the Ordinarium of Valencia's "Against Locusts").

tian community, this invocation seeks to remind the element of water of its subservience to the human community through obedience to divine will as dictated by sacred history, an approach that is also found within the corpus of medieval charms and magical incantations.[80] That the cleansing power of water is emphasized, as in the mention of the healing of the leper, is only fitting in a ritual aimed at purifying a corrupted element of the human world, separating the dirty from the clean for the health of humanity. The invocation of Christ's interactions with water also helps to lend a sacred air to the use of water by the medieval priesthood, the spiritual descendants of Christ whose power flowed from the life and ministry of Jesus.[81]

80. For an example, see the "Lay of the Nine Herbs," in Jolly's excellent study, wherein the charm acts as a reminder to the herbs to act according to their created nature and purpose (Jolly, *Popular Religion*, 125). A view of the elements as bound by duties derived from their nature may also be seen in Scholastic philosophy; St. Thomas Aquinas argued for the "natural propensity" of elements, whereby each of the four elements strives after its proper place in the world order: for example, fire naturally reaches upward to the firmament. While Aquinas could be interpreted as speaking of mundane matters of physics, this argument may also be seen to reflect a conviction, in the presence of certain imperatives in "inanimate" nature, that could sometimes bind the elements to humanity in a relationship of service. This position is supported by evidence from Isidore of Seville's *Etymologiae*, wherein the author describes how, when a burning lamp is placed upon the surface of the Dead Sea, it will float; but when the flame is extinguished it will sink, since the sea pulls everything dead into it (Isidore, *Etymologiae* 13.19.3–4). This kind of attraction is also paralleled in many medieval sources that describe the operation of magic, most especially what James Frazer first called "sympathetic magic," magic that operates by a "secret sympathy" or symbolic likeness between cause and effect (see Sir James Frazer, *The Golden Bough: A Study in Magic and Religion*, 3d ed. [New York: Macmillan, 1951], vol. 1), which in medieval magic could manifest itself in beliefs about certain minerals, elements, and animal organs or flesh carrying the character attributed to them by popular belief, such as preferring a bull over a sow in creating a powerful healing concoction (see Kieckhefer, *Magic in the Middle Ages*, 12, 67). To return to the rather fabulous description of the Dead Sea, this passage indicates that it was perfectly plausible to Isidore that elements could recognize fundamental categories of human perception: dead versus alive, hot versus cold, and so on. This presupposes a certain intelligence on the part of the sea, and it is just this kind of awareness that I contend the blessings attribute to the elements, reminding and compelling them to fulfill their duties and obey. For the treatment of material elements in the modern liturgy and in the theology of ancient Israel, see Martimort, *Church at Prayer*, 148 and 157–58.

81. The blessings of fields and crops include such allusions in only five rituals, from German, Spanish, and Swiss manuscripts (among them Lausanne's "Exorcism of Water" and the Ordinarium of Valencia's "Against Locusts"). None of the allusions appear in more than one ritual, and they are drawn from the Old and New Testaments in nearly equal measure. The two rituals that contain the greatest number of allusions are both late, from the fifteenth and sixteenth centuries, which may indicate a gradual shift toward more elaborate blessings. The

This power infused into water by the blessing's invocation of the historical connection of the sacred and the elements was so great in the minds of
medieval authors that it was considered to have a universal potency to expel
evil from the human world. The blessing against worms displays this in a
common invocational form when addressing the water:

> that you might be a font exorcised and also the salvation of those believing in
> you, so that wherever you shall have been sprinkled, either on the crops, or on
> trees, or in granges and in the house, or in the corners of bed chambers, or in
> fields, on vegetables, on turnips, or in every hamlet, or on men and women, or
> on sheep and cattle and other domestic animals and profitable things, so that
> whoever shall have tasted or partaken of you [the water], it may be a defensive
> ward for them against all worms.[82]

Water empowered by the divine and the proper ritual became the vehicle for
maintaining the purity of the community and workplace, as well as ensuring
its collective survival in the face of pestilence sent against them by the forces
of chaos and evil, as represented by the malignant worms.

A similar invocation of scriptural history may be found in many other
blessings, including some for the products of the harvest. Blessings of fruit,
be they grapes or vegetables or even animal products, form a significant portion of the corpus of blessings. In particular, an "Ordo for the Blessing and
Exorcising of Ripe Grain against Locusts, Grasshoppers, and Other Corrosive Animals," from the *Ordinarium* of Valencia, dated to the very end of
the Middle Ages (c. 1514), uses incidents from scriptural history to bestow
on the invocations of the contemporary celebrant a power rivaling that of
the earliest years of Christianity: the insects in question are commanded,

---

reasons for this shift are unclear, but one possibility is that increasing criticism of the orthodox Christian belief in sacred ground, voiced among others by the Cathars of the twelfth and
thirteenth centuries, may have urged the authors of blessings to stress the scriptural precedent for the hallowing of ground through ritual and divine will. In keeping with rituals that
featured aspersion, five of these six blessings deal with scriptural incidents involving water:
the conversion of water to wine at the marriage of Cana, Moses' parting the Red Sea, Elijah's
cleansing of the waters, Christ's walking upon the Sea of Galilee, etc. The allusions are to
Jn 2:1–12, Ex 14:1–31, 2 Kgs 2:19–22, and Mt 14:22–33.

82. Franz, 2:163: sed efficiaris fons exorcisatus atque salus in te credentium: ut ubicunque
fueris aspersa sive in segitibus, sive in arboribus, sive in grangiis et in domibus, sive in angu-
lis cubiculorum, sive in agris, oleribus, rapis, sive in omni curtilagio, sive in homines et femi-
nas, sive in pecoribus et iumentis et aliis animalibus domesticis et utilibus, ut, quicquid ex te
gustaverit vel senserit, fiat ei defensaculum omnium vermium.

"through the mystery of the holy incarnation of Jesus Christ and through His nativity," to "withdraw from the boundaries or possessions of this village and make no evil for them."[83] This invocation thus makes the events of Christ's life endure, keeping them real and meaningful. That the very incidents of Christ's divine life have power to influence the natural world is a striking proposition, emphasizing Christ's divine origins and (as in many other religious cultures) asserting the power of that embodied divine to profoundly affect the created world. But this power is not limited to the events of the Christian era, for the events of the Old Testament are employed by the author of this ritual for a malediction, a relatively rare item within a blessing. The celebrant addresses the insects: "If you shall have not agreed to depart, may the curse of the Lord descend upon you and make you transfixed through his holy angel, just as he transfixed the army of Sennacherib, so that the people may perceive and fear the holy name of Him."[84] By this reference, the enemies of medieval farmers are equated with the enemy of the chosen people of Israel, elevating the daily struggles of the village community to a sacred level at the same time that it imbues the blessing with significant being and power to affect the natural world.[85] The connection of the medieval Christian community's struggle with sacred history is made complete in the final allusion of this benediction:

> Omnipotent everlasting God, who at the prayers of your servant Moses made the most vehement wind blow from the west and cast the seized locusts into the Red Sea and not one remained in any territories of Egypt, since you are He who scourges and saves: thus by the prayers of the people redeemed by the precious blood of your son, we entreat you to command locusts and other

83. Ibid., 2:167: Per mysterium sancte incarnationis Iesu Christi ac per eius navitatem precipio vobis, ut recedatis a terminis seu possessionibus huius ville et eis nihil mali faciatis. This *ordo* was widely distributed in Germany through the popularity of Gelasius de Cilia's *Thesaurus locupletissimus continens varias et selectissimas benedictiones, coniurationes, exorcismos . . redditus a Gelasio di Cilia,* 7th ed. (Paedeponti: State and City, 1750). Franz notes that native German texts do not contain such rituals, instead being content with the *Benedictio maior* of water to be used by farmers. Special formulas appear sporadically.

84. Ibid.: Si abire distuleritis, maledictio domini descendat super vos et percuti vos faciat per angelum sanctum suum, sicut percuti fecit exercitum Sennacherib, ut cognoscant gentes et timeant nomen sanctum eius. The event is drawn from Is 37:36.

85. A parallel to this address to insects may be found in the Exultet blessing of the Easter candle, wherein the bees that produced the honey are praised for their work (see Thompson, *Cities of God,* 328).

noxious animals which endeavor to infest us and to destroy the harvests, to be reduced to nothing and go to perdition though the power of the most holy cross.[86]

This allusion directs the potency of the sacred paradigms of scripture not only to the Christian community but also to the natural blight of insects, equating their destruction with the power of God to torment the Egyptians and deliver the Israelites from bondage. The daily life of the village receiving the blessing is thus woven into the events and stories of the sacred past that form a living part of the life of the community, focusing the attention of the community on its links with the past.

This selection manifests an important element of many blessings, the invocation of the power of the Cross to defeat natural forces threatening to bring chaos and want down on the Christian fellowship. The sign of the cross in the early Middle Ages became a means to expose and expel demons, to define and delimit the demonic and separate it from acceptable forms of supernatural power; and its invocation and presence could cause demons to vanish like smoke into thin air when the Cross was used to bar their paths.[87] This was an important power due to the malignant potency attributed to demons, whom medieval people considered real and powerful agents of human misfortune, possessing powers to cause plague, tempests, stormy seas, sickness, and death, among other calamities.[88] The popularity of this practice, and the belief in its efficacy, persisted to the end of the medieval period, and by the later Middle Ages the church accepted its efficacy for use by laypeople, so that "even a woman, like Umiltà of Faenza, might use the sign of the cross for imparting blessings," such as using it at table or over the knife that will cut the bread for the meal.[89]

---

86. Franz, 2:167: Omnipotens sempiterne deus, qui precibus servi tui Moysi flare ventum ab occidente vehementissimum fecisti et arreptam locustam proiecit in mare rubrum et non remansit una in cunctis finibus Egipti, quoniam tu es, qui flagellas et salvas: ita precibus populi pretioso filii tui sanguine redempti, quesumus locustas et alia noxia animalia, que nos infestare et messes destruere conantur, ad nihilum redigi et in perditionem ire iubeas per virtutem sanctissime crucis.

87. Flint, *Rise of Magic,* 176. For an example of such an exorcism, see Gregory of Tours, *De virtibus* [*virtute*] *Sancti Martini* 1:18, ed. Bruno Krusch, *MGH SRM* 1 (2):165.

88. Flint, *Rise of Magic,* 20; for ancient examples of this belief, see Origen, *Contra celsum,* ed. Henry Chadwick (New York: Cambridge University Press, 1965; reprint, 1980), 1:31, 8:27, 32, 30–31, 471, 474–75.

89. Thompson, *Cities of God,* 356, citing Bologna, Biblioteca Universitaria, MS 1552,

The presence of the Cross, either as a physical object or as a gesture by the ritual celebrant of the blessing, was one of the major Christian means for creating and defining the confines of sacred space.[90] This is evident in the blessing of fruit in the initial rubrics of the ritual: "First let the priest, who shall have celebrated a Mass for ending the devastating of crops and fruits, don the stole along with a cloak, and let the school master go before with a cross, and let the other clerics in procession draw near and in a place fitting or dedicated for blessings let the priest say the following prayer facing east."[91] Employing the Cross as a talisman to channel the sacred power of the divine, a powerful symbol of the intimate Christian connection between the human and divine worlds, the priest faces the direction of the rising sun and Jerusalem, aligning himself with the powers of light and divinity to complete his ritual blessing of the collective's produce.[92]

Filippo of Ferrara, *Liber de introductione loquendi*, 1.4, fol. 3r; and Bonvesin de la Riva, *Vita scholastica*, ed. Anezka Vidmanová-Schmidtová, in *Liber Quinque Clavium Sapientiae* (Leipzig: Teubner, 1969), 60, lines 303–4. For the story of Umiltà, see Biagio of Faenza, *Vita* [*S. Humilitatis Abbatissae*], *AS* 18 (May 5), 3.31, p. 213.

90. The Cross in blessings was principally used in rogation processions, which were specifically recommended by Carolingian synods for the protection of the harvest. André Vauchez in particular has made an interesting study of the rogation procession, arguing that it arose out of a desire to sacralize the earth and its fruits, bringing fertility and warding off the demonic (see Vauchez, *Laity in the Middle Ages*, 129–39). In the tenth century, the Feast of the Ascension was still considered a suitable occasion on which to promote this Christian weather-making procedure in opposition to the demonic and magical incantations that so infuriated commentators yet proved so appealing to the laity (Flint, *Rise of Magic*, 186; see also Ratherius of Verona, *Sermo VII: De ascensione domini, PL* 136:739). In the Italian communes of the twelfth and thirteenth centuries, the entire city, clergy and laity, would march in procession with crosses on the major litanies of the Feast of St. Mark the Apostle (25 April), and on the minor litanies (three days before Ascension Thursday). From the eighth century, the major litanies were linked to the pagan Robigalia, an ancient procession to ward off crop blight (see Thompson, *Cities of God*, 152, citing Sicard of Cremona, *Mitrale*, 7.6, col. 368). In a similar manner, when the Russian abbot Daniel, on pilgrimage to Cyprus, saw a cross erected by the empress Helena, he affirmed that it was "able to drive away evil spirits and heal all sorts of disease" ("The Pilgrimage of Abbot Daniel," quoted in Ward, *Miracles and the Medieval Mind*, 8).

91. Franz, 2:166: Primo sacerdos, qui missam celebraverit pro expellenda vastatione segetum et fructuum, accipiat stolam cum capa, et scolaris precedat cum cruce, et alii clerici processionaliter accedant, et in loco competenti seu ad benedictiones dedicato versus orientem dicat sacerdos sequentem orationem.

92. The Christian orientation of the churches toward the east and Jerusalem served as an indication of how, through Christ, the earthly Jerusalem had been replaced by the heavenly Jerusalem, with the turn east representing a turning toward the new heaven and the new earth,

This use of what I will term "directional prayer" is a common means by which to delineate sacred space, and it bears symbolic significance beyond its superficial simplicity, as I shall discuss below. The alliance of the blessing's power with the power of light and divinity is complemented in the final prayers of this benediction, when the celebrant asks God to "powerfully gird with an invincible wall the boundary of this village and of the whole kingdom, so that locusts and other noxious animals may not be able to approach freely, but destroy them in the power of your beloved son, Our Lord Jesus Christ."[93] This invocation explicitly states the often implicit notion that the blessing is a device by which to create a barrier against evil and pollution and thereby draw closer to God. The blessing is startling in its aim to protect not only the single community that its priest might speak for, but also to defend the entire realm of a kingdom from such evils of the natural world. Blessing appears here in the arsenal of the church as a potent weapon to guarantee prosperity and peace in its most fundamental economic activity, and (as important, I would argue) to ensure the continued good relationship between the divine and the human, as is demonstrated in the sixth and final prayer of this blessing, which concludes: "so that you might restore harvests to us which the locust, mildew and caterpillars completely devoured, in order that, with minds freed, we may be able to serve you and give thanks."[94] As anxiety can prevent a soul from focusing itself solely on service to God, the relief of such anxiety can, quid pro quo, benefit divinity as well as humanity. The negotiation here promises to maintain the proper balance of aid and gratitude between the divine and human worlds, a balance ensured by such a liturgy upon which the survival of the Christian cosmos and community de-

---

wherein justice dwelt and whence would come the *parousia*. Bouyer, *Rite and Man*, 170–71. The daily practice of prayer also supported this identification of the east with the divine, as Christians were exhorted to turn in this direction, where the holy land lay and whence Christ would return. See Richard C. Trexler, *The Christian at Prayer: An Illustrated Prayer Manual Attributed to Peter the Chanter* (Binghamton, N.Y.: Medieval and Renaissance Texts and Studies, 1987), 38. Another expression of this sentiment can be seen in the medieval Italian communal practice of burying the corpse in city cemeteries with its feet pointing east, "toward the rising sun, the direction from which Christ would come at the end of the world." Thompson, *Cities of God*, 409.

93. Franz, 2:167: muro inexpugnabili potenter precinge terminum huius ville et totius regni, ne locuste et alia noxia animalia amplius appropinquare possint, sed disperde ea in virtute dilecti filii tui, domini nostri Iesu Christi.

94. Ibid., 2:168: ut reddas nobis annos quos comedit locusta, brucus, rubigo et eruca, ut liberis tibi mentibus servire et gratias agere valeamus.

pends and which it continually reaffirms through its blessings and prayers.

The use of rubrics for motions and the use of physical objects in the creation of sacred space, seen in the preceding rite and the blessing of a cross presented in the introduction, are further developed in a final prayer of protection "Against the Worms Which Afflict Vegetables." In this blessing the celebrant is instructed:

> You ought to say this blessing of yours three times going around the garden before the rising of the sun, and sprinkle the vegetables with blessed water and say: Jesus. Basa Olea Basolea. I seek you, worms, and call on you, I adjure you and resist you, through the Father, Son and Holy Ghost, so that in this garden you may not spring up further, but may withdraw and die.[95]

The rubrics for this blessing suggest a conscious awareness of the importance of motion and time in the creation of sacred space.[96] The celebrant's circuit around the garden with holy water would seem to create a spiritual fortification, fancifully in the mode of a castle wall, against the powers of

95. Ibid.: Istam benediccionem debes dicere tribus vicibus circumeundo hortum ante solis ortum et asperge holera aqua benedicta et dic: Ysa. basa. olea. basolea. Quero vos et invoco vos, adiuro vos et contestor vos, vermes, per patrem et filium et spiritum sanctum, ut in his hortis ultra non crescatis, sed redeatis et moriamini. From the evidence of agricultural blessings alone, the belief in and fear of demonic pollution was widespread: demons and Satan and his tricks were specifically targeted in German, Swiss, and French rites of the tenth, eleventh, and fifteenth centuries; see the *RGP*'s "Blessing of Water for Crops against Vermin" and "Blessing of Water for Crops," the Old Spanish "Blessing of Seed," Prüm's "Blessing of a Cross," and Clm 22040's "Prayer in a Vineyard." While we might infer that fear of demons was a particularly northern perception, the evidence of domestic blessing and the reconciliation of churches and cemeteries undermines this interpretation. A fifteenth-century Spanish blessing of the bridal chamber (the Old Spanish "Ordo for Blessing the Bridal Chamber," examined in the next section of this chapter) focuses on driving out demonic powers, and the entire Roman *corpus* of ritual reconciliation from the tenth to the thirteenth century inveighs against the power of Satan and his evil spirits, who seek to pollute sacred places. This indicates that belief in demons was persistent and ubiquitous, although still subject to the influences of time and place.

96. Such ritual circuits of exorcism and purification manifest themselves first in the Christian consecration of churches, which themselves seem to have evolved from ritual practices designed to convert ancient pagan temples to Christian use. The Germanic peoples were especially conscious of the reality of a world alienated by demons that must be reconquered by and for the savior God through the aspersion of holy water mixed with salt, wine, and ashes, the so-called Gregorian water (Bouyer, *Rite and Man,* 187). For more discussion of this subject, see the discussion of the consecration and reconciliation of churches and cemeteries in the following section.

vermin to injure the delicate herbs and vegetables grown there. The repetition of the blessing enhances its efficacy, and perhaps adds the symbolic power of the number three and its associations with the Trinity to the ritual. The importance of performing this ritual before sunrise is less clear; possibly this is meant to prevent an encroachment of the worms before the day begins, thus catching the vermin unaware. Or perhaps this time was chosen as a "boundary time," a period between the end of night and the beginning of day, for such boundary times and places were often considered in popular folklore to be sites of magical potential, and thus the ritual would tap into this power to increase its chances of success.[97]

This short blessing is of great interest in understanding medieval people's conception of sacred space, in that it demonstrates how numinous locales, and their associated awe and power, could be invoked to create a new sacred space through a blessing. Witness the following prayer against the worms: "I adjure you through the name of the eternal God Adonay, the *tetragrammaton* and through the other names of the same one, through the Sun and the Moon and the other planets, through the stars and the sydera of heaven . . ."[98] This adjuration strikes the modern reader as unintelligible

---

97. One example of this idea can be found in the common practice of hanging criminals at crossroads, so that their spirits could not find their way in the waking world and harass their executioners. The importance of crossroads can be seen in later collections of ritual magic, such as the *Magica divina* of 1745, which requires the burial of a mirror at a crossroads in order that the mirror become magical. Some of these texts, originating with or inspired by medieval authors, place great emphasis on the magical qualities of such places: the *Key of Solomon*, for example, asserts that "the places best fitted for exercising and accomplishing Magical Arts and Operations are those which are concealed, removed and separated from the habitations of men. Wherefore desolate and uninhabited regions are most appropriate . . . but best of all are crossroads, and where four roads meet, during the depth and silence of the night" (Butler, *Ritual Magic*, 84). In Istria it was believed that *vucodlachi*, children born with a caul, would become spiritualists who went forth nocturnally (especially on Ember Days) to gather at crossroads and do battle with witches for the fertility of the coming season. See Klaniczay, *Uses of Supernatural Power*, 135.

98. Franz, 2:169: Adiuro vos per nomen eterni dei Adonay, tetragrammaton et per cetera nomina eiusdem, per solem et lunam et ceteras planetas, per stellas et sydera celi . . . The term *tetragrammaton* is composed of the four Hebrew letters used for the name of God, YHWH, or JHVH (as in Jehovah). It is commonly considered a mysterious symbol for the name of God (see *Oxford English Dictionary*, ed. J. A. Simpson and E. S. C. Weiner, 20 vols. [Oxford: Clarendon Press, 1989], 17:842). Kabbalists were the first to emphasize the mystery surrounding these letters, but they also often appear in Christian texts of ritual magic (Butler, *Ritual Magic*, 40, 63). The astronomical invocations in this adjuration closely resemble the invocation of

until one considers the awe with which heavenly bodies were regarded by the religious mentality of the high Middle Ages, which believed in the active power of heavenly bodies like the moon to influence the growth of both plants and animals.[99] The stars and planets were the creation of God, and reflected a more perfect form of reality (drawing on the works of Ptolemy and Aristotle), closer to God and his angels than the base world of terrestrial matter. Patristic authors and later Christian thinkers saw the world as governed by God's Providence, and the planets were thought to be instruments of that Providence, which God used to direct events according to his will. Planets' influence, however, extended only to material things; they were not granted influence over spiritual beings, namely, humanity's free will and soul.[100] That these bodies are invoked here against material creatures suggests that medieval Christians accepted this patristic notion, and the complementary notion that the power of the heavens, their very being, could be brought down to earth and employed for human uses, as long as they served to protect and preserve the Christian community and its resources from harm. Thus sacred space created by a blessing could be heavenly space, partaking in the same nature as the invisible world on which the Christian cosmology founded its belief system, and making both visible and invisible worlds more real and immediate for those who believed.

Heavenly bodies were not, however, the only source of sacred power to be accessed by the invocations of a blessing for sacred space; sacred time could also produce efficacious results in a blessing. The prayer discussed in the preceding paragraph continues: "Again I adjure you, worms . . . through the awesome Day of Judgment and through the incomparable delights of Heaven and through the intolerable punishments of Hell, so that you may

---

planetary thrones (archangels ruling over planets), angels of the Zodiac, and elements found in ritual magic texts such as the *Semiphoras et schemhamphoras salomonis regis* (Franz, 158). Such invocations also increasingly found their way into some secular rituals. For example, the oath taken by Rolando de Inglesci of Padua, the *podesta* of Vicenza, outlines God's rule over angelic choirs, the eight cosmic spheres, earth's four climactic zones (!), the creation of animals, and, finally, the creation of man, so as to ensure the oath's integrity and efficacy. See Thompson, *Cities of God*, 137.

99. Flint, *Rise of Magic*, 25. For example, Pseudo-Bede (among others) thought the movement of planets affected the atmosphere of earth, setting the winds in motion; see Pseudo-Bede, *De mundi celestis terrestrisque constitutione: A Treatise on the Universe and the Soul*, ed. Charles Burnett (London: Warburg Institute, University of London, 1985), 30.

100. Wildiers, *Theologian and His Universe*, 32. For further elaboration of this notion, see Boethius, *Consolation of Philosophy*, 134–42.

not grow further, but rather may you back away from these herbs and plants, and perish."[101] Again we see that the very nature of places imbued with the numinous, in both its divine and demonic forms, can fuel the power of blessings. Furthermore, the events of sacred history yet to come have a power to influence space in the natural world. They set it apart from the depredations of the forces of evil that will presumably be destroyed in the end times, making future elements of the cosmology meaningful and affecting daily life in the present.[102]

DWELLING PLACES AND PLACES OF WORK

While agricultural blessings such as those studied above formed a major portion of the corpus of blessings dealing with sacred space, these rituals by no mean exhaust medieval people's use of blessing to create holy places. Whereas agricultural blessings sought to hallow and sanctify the open and common places of the village community, blessings for homes and places of work offered the protection of the divine to the private and personal lives of medieval Christians, and stressed God's role as a defender and illuminator of the household. Greco-Roman culture gave to the medieval world its practice of delivering houses up to the protection of divinity, in ancient times the god Zeus or family deities. The Old Testament reveals that ancient Israel also knew of the consecration of a house, particularly of newly constructed homes.[103] In the New Testament Jesus' prescription "Peace be to this house" (Mt 10:12) suggests that the Christian house is to be put under God's protection, which scripture describes as the only true peace to be found in this world.[104] It seems reasonable, in agreement with Franz, to conclude that ancient Christians recommended their houses to God through prayer; Tertullian speaks of the sign of the cross being used too in the most serious incidents of daily life, which included the blessing, upon entry, of a fellow believer's home.[105] Still, liturgical and private formulas for the conse-

101. Franz, 2:169: Item adiuro vos, vermes ... per tremendum diem iudicii et per incomparabiles delicias celi et per intolerabiles penas inferni, ut ultra non crescatis, sed redeatis ab his herbis et hortis et pereatis.

102. This interpretation is paralleled by the scholarship of Mircea Eliade on preindustrial religious cultures, in which Eliade argues for the central role of myth in creating ritual and thereby making life meaningful; see *Sacred and Profane*, 99–100.

103. Franz, 1:604; Dt 20:5.

104. Franz, 1:604.

105. Tertullian, *De corona militis*, chap. 3, *PL* 2:80. The blessing takes the form here of

cration of houses are not found in the oldest sources of Christian liturgy, although masses were commonly said in homes in Christian antiquity.[106] The first Latin prayers for consecration of a house are found in the Gelasian sacramentary, and these deal with the protection of the house and the good fortune and prosperity of the inhabitants.[107] These were at first held universally, for both old and newly built houses, but later came to be used only for the inauguration of a new home.[108] While the Gregorian sacramentary proper lacks a house consecration, Benedict of Aniane's supplement has a blessing for a house, albeit a short one lacking a formal celebration of a Mass.[109] The formula for consecrating a house seems to have been fixed almost universally by the ninth century, with emphasis on God's role as defender and illuminator of the household, and later rituals studied by Franz vary only in the number and position of the prayers.

---

making the sign of the cross: "Lastly, we make the sign of the cross on our foreheads at every turn, at our going in and coming out of the house, while putting on our shoes, when we are taking a bath, before and after meals, when we light the lamps, when we go to bed or sit down, and in all the ordinary actions of daily life." The full translation of this chapter can be found in *Tertullian: Disciplinary, Moral and Ascetical Works*, ed. Rudolph Arbesmann, Emily Joseph Daly, and Edwin Quain (Washington, D.C.: The Catholic University of America Press, 1959), 236–37.

106. Franz 1:606. Augustine mentions the celebration of Mass in houses disturbed by demons in the *The City of God* (*De civitate dei* 22:8), and Ambrose was known to celebrate Mass in the houses of distinguished women. Augustine, *De civitate dei*, in *Corpus scriptorum ecclesiasticorum latinorum* 40, ed. Emanuel Hoffmann, (Vienna: F. Tempsky, 1899–1900), 602.

107. Franz, 1:606. These consist of book 3's *Orationes* 72: *Orationes intrantibus in domo sive benedictio*, which contains four prayers; 73, *Item orationes ad missas*, containing two collects, a secret, a prayer *Infra actionem*, and two post-Communion prayers; 74, *Orationes super venientes in domo*, spoken over visitors; and 75–76, a consecration of water for aspersion of a house. The prayers for visitors originate in the old monastic custom of receiving the visitor with prayer and accepting the prayers of the visitors.

108. Despite this shift in practice, old houses were commonly believed to hold the potential to manifest danger in the form of haunting by evil spirits, such as the Maison de l'ours et du lion on the Rou des Marmousets, which, in 1476, was "said to be hanted by a demon." See Michael Camille, "Signs of the City: Place, Power and Public Fantasy in Medieval Paris," in *Medieval Practices of Space*, ed. B. Hanawalt and Michal Kobialka (Minneapolis: University of Minnesota Press, 2000), 16.

109. Franz, 1:606–7. Franz was unable to determine the age of the use of consecrated water for blessing houses. The formula for *Benedictio aquae spargendae in domo* of the Gelasian sacramentary and the three connected prayers for the house and the inhabitants do not appear in later liturgical books, but the three prayers from the supplement for blessing water persisted into this century in the *Asperges* (ibid., 609).

Houses were traditionally blessed during Epiphany and the season of Easter, especially on Holy Saturday, a practice that derives from the old Roman custom in which the faithful sprinkled their houses, vineyards, fields, and fruits with baptismal water that had been blessed that day.[110] This tradition later evolved into an annual consecration, with the priest, not the laity, as the actor.[111] Five rituals have been selected as representative of the genre: a "Blessing of a House," from two of the manuscripts of Vogel and Elze's edition of the RGP;[112] another "Blessing of a House," from the same pontifical;[113] a "Blessing of the Wedding Bed," from the eleventh-century pontifical of the Benedictine house of Lyre in the diocese of Evreux;[114] an *Ordo* for Blessing the Bedroom or the Bridal Chamber," from the *Liber ordinum* of Silos;[115] and a "Blessing of a Furnace or Stone Forge," from a Carthusian *rituale*.[116]

The RGP's blessing, like the others in this pontifical, provides only prayers, not rubrics. The prayers reveal a deep concern that the power of the sacred be made to act as a defender of the home: "Hear us, Lord, holy Father, omnipotent eternal God, and deign to send your holy angel from heaven who may ward, cherish, protect, visit, and defend all dwelling in this house."[117] The importance of angels in protecting the house and its bed is a belief common to all regions during our period: German, French, English, and Spanish blessings from the tenth to the thirteenth century all desire the

110. Gy, "Benedictions," 178. German medieval *rituales* do not contain a house consecration at Easter or at Epiphany. For French praxis, see Hincmar of Rheims's *Capitula*, cited above. Only when the water consecration at Epiphany was introduced in Germany in the sixteenth century was a house blessing introduced, yet even then the ritual did not become general or universal (Franz, 1:610).

111. Franz, 1:609–10. The day of consecration became also a day for a parishwide fast.

112. *RGP* 2:354–55 (*ordo* 190). The MSS in question are the two German MSS B and G in Vogel's sigla and Vienna, Nationalbibliothek, *cod. lat.* 701, a pontifical written at the abbey of St. Alban, at Mainz, for the consecration of an oratory dedicated to St. Alban during the governance of Abbot Arnold (1070).

113. *RGP* 2:355 (*ordo* 191).

114. Franz, 2:181; see also Martène, *Antiquis Ecclesiae ritibus*, 2:129.

115. Franz, 2:180.

116. Ibid., 1:630. For the Carthusian *rituale* and this rite, see these MSS: Grenoble, Bibl. Municipale, MS 123, fol. 26; Grenoble, Bibl. Municipale, MS 606, fol. 164; and Marseille, Bibl. Municipale, MS 139 (seventeenth century). Three other rituals were also considered, as listed in the index.

117. *RGP* 2:354 (*ordo* 190.1): Exaudi nos, domine, sanctae pater, omnipotens aeterne Deus, et mittere dignare sanctum angelum tuum de caelis qui custodiat, foveat, protegat, visitet et defendat omnes habitantes in hoc habitaculo.

visitation and protection of angels.[118] This particular prayer is of great interest on two accounts: first, because it provides us with another example of the ways in which blessings served to define God's nature and call on the elements of that nature most appropriate to the current need for blessing; and second, because it conflates the house and its inhabitants. The prayer stresses the power of God and his nature as the origin of holiness and thus sacred power, a relationship appropriately cast in a familial light (the "holy father") that would resonate with the blessing of the family possessing the house.[119] Although the prayer calls for an angel, the emphasis on the role of protection and warding is characteristic of a constant view of divinity within this category of blessings, and indeed is a constant in the medieval understanding of the sacred: belief in the need for protection from the dangers of the outside world drives the RGP's blessings of homes, and as this theme appears in both Franco-Roman and English rituals from the tenth and fifteenth centuries, it seems to have been a constant in the conception of the medieval God who creates sacred space.[120] That the house itself is not marked out for special protection so much as the inhabitants therein reinforces the idea (seen in previous blessings) that the aim of the benediction is the protection of the human community, or in this case the families that make up the larger Christian congregation. The space itself seems to be of little importance in comparison with the human relationships that the space contains.

The RGP provides another "Blessing of a House" that develops these and other themes of interest. Belief in the power of the divine as a shield against spiritual suffering and aid to material prosperity is stated clearly:

> To you, God the Father omnipotent, we pray for this home and for the inhabitants of this house and we ask that you may deign to bless and sanctify and increase it by all good things. . . . Allot to them abundance from the dew of

118. The saints' usual position as intercessors seems to be usurped in domestic blessings by guardian angels; only the Carthusian blessing of a furnace makes use of a litany, whereas each of the six other rites of this genre invoke angels rather than saints. The significance of this anomaly is difficult to determine. Could it be that the perception of angels as numerous, even ubiquitous, made them more suitable guardians of ordinary people's homes, whereas saints' specific responsibilities as patrons and intercessors for local communities demanded all their time and attention?

119. Such an emphasis on God's nature also appears in the Salisbury missal's "Blessing of a Wedding Bed" (BAV Pal. lat. 501, fol. 263).

120. See the RGP's "Blessing of a Home" and "Blessing of a House," and the Salisbury missal's "Blessing of a Wedding Bed," discussed below.

heaven and the substance of life from the richness of the Earth, and may you guide the desire of their prayer to the reward of your mercy.[121]

The beauty of this prayer reveals not only the deep desire on the part of medieval men and women to use sacred power to enrich their lives, but also their clear understanding of the intimate link between that sacred power and the natural world in which they live. Appealing aptly to the paternal element of the Trinity, whose conceived nature echoes that of the head of the medieval household, this blessing ties their place of rest and communion to the benefits of nature in a way that eloquently demonstrates a desire to embrace the good things of the created world, not flee them from fear of pollution. That the desire for material prosperity and longevity present in domestic blessings seems universal to the genre, occurring in German, French, and English rituals from the tenth to the fifteenth century, only strengthens this conclusion.[122]

Protection is also sought in an alternative prayer included within this blessing. The celebrant addresses divinity thus in an alternative to the first blessing: "Eternal and omnipotent Lord, praying with one accord we ask on behalf of this home and all those dwelling in it, that the Lord might deign to assign to them the angel of peace, the angel of light, the angel of defense, and might keep them safe and protected."[123] God's role as defender, in the form of a variety of angels who (according to patristic theology) were ordained "companions of the faithful," is stressed to solidify the presence of the divine within the home and to qualify God as the bringer of light and thus the banisher of shadows, a motif present in the first blessing we examined, where God is asked to "enlighten this house by the bright eyes of your godliness."[124] As we have seen in other blessings, this invocation of di-

121. *RGP* 2:355 (*ordo* 191.1): Te, Deum patrem omnipotentem, oramus pro hac domo et pro domus huius habitatoribus ac petimus, ut eam benedicere et sanctificare et bonis omnibus amplificare digneris.... Tribue eis de rore caeli habundantiam et de pinguedine terrae vitae substantiam et desideria voti eorum ad effectum tuae miserationis perducas.

122. See the *RGP*'s "Blessing of a House," the eleventh-century Evreux "Blessing of a Wedding Bed," the Carthusian "Blessing of a Furnace or Stone Forge," the *PWD*'s "Blessing of a New House," and the Salisbury missal's "Blessing of a Wedding Bed."

123. *RGP* 2:355 (*ordo* 191.2): Aeternum atque omnipotentem dominum unanimiter orantes petimus pro hac domo atque omnibus habitantibus in ea, ut eis dominus angelum pacis, angelum lucis, angelum defensionis assignare dignetur, tutosque eos defensosque prestet.

124. Ibid., 2:354 (*ordo* 190.2): et hanc domum serenis oculis tuae pietatis illustra. This reference may draw upon knowledge of the pseudo-Dionysian understanding of light that

vine protection is accompanied by a conscious association of the current ritual with accepted elements of sacred history; in this case, the celebrant associates himself and his ritual with the founders of Israel: "Indeed may you deign to bless and to sanctify our entrance, just as you deigned to bless the home of Abraham, Isaac and Jacob, and within the walls of this home of yours may the angel of your light dwell."[125] This blessing makes the medieval home into an image of the home of the biblical patriarchs, connecting the power of the divine with the living and the dead, the past and present of the human community, and enriching both with the light that protects. This particular allusion appears in three of our rituals.[126]

Benedictions drew connections between people, their God, and their environment, but they were also a way to mold the morality of the recipients. An "*Ordo* for Blessing the Bedroom or the Bridal Chamber" provides a cogent example of this: following the sprinkling of salt in the third hour of Sunday (as was customary in the place where this ritual originated), the priest intones a short verse and then this longer prayer: "God, by whose blessing all things stand firm, bestow a blessing on this habitation prepared for marriage: so that a meeting of evil spirits will in no way touch it, but honest and clean conjugal things might alone occupy it."[127] The desire to exclude

---

was being popularized in the first centuries of the high Middle Ages. For the belief in guardian angels, see Jean Daniélou, *The Angels and Their Mission According to the Fathers of the Church* (Westminster, Md.: Newman Press, 1957), 68, quoting St. Basil, *Contra Eunomium libri quinque* 3.1, *PG* 29:654–58. Divinity and light are linked in house blessings such as this, and once in the blessing of a forge, again in an alternate blessing of a house from the *RGP*, and in the *PWD*, which adapted the *RGP*'s ritual; see *RGP* (*ordo* 191), "Blessing of a House," the *PWD*'s "Blessing of a New House," and the Carthusian "Blessing of a Furnace or Stone Forge." This theme does not appear in rituals of reconciliation, possibly because such rituals were more concerned with spiritual issues of sin and evil than with the natural world and its elements, as seems evident from the emphasis placed on original sin and the purity of the celebrant as the sine qua non for a successful reconciliation. For further discussion, see the following section.

125. *RGP* 2:355 (*ordo* 191.1): Introitum vero nostrum benedicere et sanctificare digneris sicut benedicere dignatus es domum Abrahae, Ysaac et Iacob et infra parietes domus istius angelus tuae lucis inhabitet.

126. The rituals are the *RGP*'s "Blessing of a House," the *PWD*'s "Blessing of a New House," and the eleventh-century Evereux "Blessing of a Wedding Bed." This common allusion appears in both the tenth and thirteenth centuries, so it is reasonable to assume that it was a *topos* for this genre. Comparison of these blessings does not reveal a clear trend, either increasing or decreasing, in the overall use of allusions.

127. Franz, 2:180: Deus, cuius benedictione plena consistunt, que in te nominis invocatione benedictionem percipiunt, benedictio huic habitaculo solius honestatis nuptui

the unclean, including immoral impulses on the part of the newlyweds, brings their private morality into accord with the accepted standards of sexual behavior espoused by the church, creating unity and order out of chaos. This goal is furthered in the second prayer of the blessing:

> May omnipotent God expend the abundance of his blessing on this matrimonial home and may he bless those coming together in it with perpetual sanctification. Amen. May all incursion of evil spirits flee from this place and may a sought-after angelic visitation come here. Amen. Thus, God granting, a celebration of marriage may be held here so that the honesty of the union may not be defiled. Amen. And thus may this work and discourse be useful for those entering the nuptial celebration . . . so that they might not be borne wantonly to the shipwreck of pleasure.[128]

Imbued with the power of the numinous, the central space of the medieval family is protected from pollution both of evil spirits and of carnal delights, ensuring the moral conduct of the affairs within and excluding the unclean from the human family, by means of sacred power that was conceived as a protection against both general and individual evils.[129]

---

preparato: ut in nullo illud malorum occursus contingat, sed honestas et mundita coniugalis sola possideat atque.

128. Ibid., 2:183: Omnipotens dominus huic receptaculo nuptiali copiam benedictionis sue inpendat et convenientes in eo sanctificatione perpetua benedicat. Amen. Omnis incursio malignorum spirituum ab hoc loco diffugiat et visitatio angelica hic obtata proveniat. Amen. Ita hic donante deo connubii celebritas habeatur, ut honestas coniugum non turpetur. Amen. Sicque hic intrantibus ad nuptialem celebritatem et opus et sermo sit utilis ... ut lascive non perferantur naufragium voluptatis. This prayer's emphasis on avoidance of pleasure in the marital bed reflects the belief in forms of pollution other than the demonic, in this case that of natural causes and the human will, mentioned by Gregory the Great in his letter to Augustine of Canterbury; see the Venerable Bede, *Historia ecclesiastica gentis anglorum*, ed. B. Colgrave and R. Mynors (Oxford: Clarendon Press, 1969), 1.27–28. It was also present in the concern for purity in rituals for the "churching" of women; see Joanne M. Pierce, "'Green Women' and Blood Pollution: Some Medieval Rituals for the Church of Women after Childbirth," *Studia Liturgica* 29 (1999): 191–215, esp. 196. This study is also an excellent example of the validity of a thematic study of liturgical rites employing anthropological theory, in this case that of Mary Douglas on pollution and taboo. A similar study demonstrating the importance of the customs and local needs of the Christian community in shaping liturgies of blessing is Daniel van Sylke, "The Churching of Women: Its Introduction and Spread," *Ephemerides Liturgicae* 115 (2001): 208–38.

129. This kind of concern with protection from general enemies and destructive entities, seen in agricultural blessings, is even more prominent in blessings of houses, where it appears in German, French, and English blessings from the tenth to the fifteenth century: the *RGP*'s

Other blessings of wedding chambers, however, reveal an equal concern with improving the material and spiritual lives of the recipients of the benediction. In the eleventh-century French "Blessing of the Wedding Bed," the couple is instructed to go at night to the wedding bed, where they are followed by a priest who draws close and blesses the bed and the couple: "Bless, Lord, this wedding bed of yours and all those dwelling in it, so that they may stand together in your peace and abide in your will and live in your love and grow old and be multiplied in the length of days."[130] This blessing is of interest as an example of how blessings were thought to exercise a power over the spirituality and morality of those blessed, expressing not only the ethos and appropriateness of the Christian life to this world, but also how the mysterious power of the sacred was thought capable of extending and enriching one's life in this world, even over an extended span of time. This blessing expresses the need to exclude pollution and danger from human dwelling places that we have seen in other blessings: "Then let him make a blessing over them, saying: 'May God bless your bodies and souls and give a blessing upon you, just as he blessed Abraham, Isaac and Jacob. Amen. May the hand of the Lord be above you and may he send his holy angel, who may guard you all the days of your life.'"[131] Here the power of the divine is explicitly invoked for both the body and soul, and is made potent by the recollection of the biblical blessings of the patriarchs. The protection of the sacred is made comprehensible in the image of a protecting hand and is augmented by the conjuring of a spiritual being to maintain the blessing spoken by the human agent of the divine. In this way the blessing enhances all aspects of human life within the blessed space and renders it safe from the disturbances of chaos and evil that afflict the unprotected space of the profane world.

In addition to houses, workplaces were often accorded distinct blessings

---

"Blessing of a House" and "Blessing of a Home," the Benedictine pontifical of Lyre's "Blessing of a Wedding Bed," the *PWD's* "Blessing of a New House," and the Sarum missal's "Blessing of a Wedding Bed" (see the index).

130. Franz, 2:181: Nocte vero cum ad lectum pervenerint, ac cedat presbyter et benedicat thalamum dicens: Benedic, domine, thalamum istum et omnes habitantes in eo, ut in tua pace consistant et in tua voluntate permaneant et in amore tuo vivant et senescant et multiplicentur in longitudinem dierum.

131. Ibid.: Deinde faciat super eos benedictionem dicens: Benedicat deus corpora et animas vestras et det super vos benedictionem, sicut benedixit Abraham, Isaac et Iacob. Amen. Manus domini sit super vos mittatque angelum suum sanctum, qui custodiat vos omnibus diebus vitae vestrae.

suited to their function. Numerous blessings spoken in the various chambers of the monastery entered into the pages of the Roman pontifical tradition, but other more secular places of work could also receive a blessing.[132] Such places include the forges of a blacksmith and furnace of the lime maker, places often associated with divine and mysterious forces in the cultures that preceded the Christian conversion of Europe.[133] The first reported blessing of a chalk oven occurs in the Greek church at Epiphany and employs water blessed by the sign of the cross.[134] Such a ritual is not found in the older Latin liturgical books; the first appearance of this type of blessing occurs in the first printing of the *manuale* of Lausanne (1451).[135] Another such ritual is the "Blessing of a Furnace or Stone Forge," drawn from a Carthusian *rituale*, in which we see the same use of holy water and the walking of a circuit we have observed in earlier blessings, but this time combined with the singing of the seven "penitential psalms" familiar to medieval believers, accompanied by the use of a litany to help solidify the boundaries of sacred space created by the blessed water.[136] The pronunciation of holy words and names would seem to be an efficacious way for medieval people to create sacred space, distributing power by symbolic and performative utterance through the association of the space with the speaking of the sacred words. While the sounds of the words themselves may have been conceived to hold a power to conjure the *numen's* protection, their content and meaning probably played an

132. For examples of such blessings, which were common within monastic houses, see *RGP* 2:357–59 (*ordos* 197–204).

133. The worship of Hephestus or Vulcan springs to mind, and the text of the Celtic lorica Patrick's Breastplate, which beseeches protection "against the spells cast by women, smiths and druids." Davies, *Celtic Spirituality*, 119.

134. Franz, 1:81. The Greek ritual employs references to the three youths cast into the fiery oven (Dn 3:21); the blessing invoked on the house of Laban through Jacob and on Potiphar through Joseph; the archangels Michael and Gabriel; and the saints Cyprian and Nikolaus. This ritual also employs aspersion of holy water.

135. Ibid., 1:630.

136. Ibid., 1:632: Primo fiat aqua benedicta et aspergatur furnellus per circuitum. Deinde cantantur septem psalmi poenitentiales cum letania ambulando per circuitum summitatis eius. The "penitential psalms" are Pss 7, 33, 39, 52, 103, 131, and 144. This ritual also appears in Martène, *Antiquis Ecclesiae ritibus*, 2:302, from the Codex Maioris Cartusiae (Grenoble, Bibl. Municipale, MS 123, fol. 26; Grenoble, Bibl. Municipale, MS 606, fol. 164; and Marseille, Bibl. Municipale, MS 139 [seventeenth century]). This is the only blessing of a home or workplace for which psalms were listed specifically, and as this rite is monastic in origin this probably reflects the different tastes of monastic copyists.

important role, as is clear from the readings from the four Gospels that follow.[137] The first reading is from Luke 1:26–38, recounting the dispatching of the angel Gabriel and the annunciation to Mary of the divine blessing about to be bestowed upon her.[138] While this story can be taken simply as a reminder of the holiness of Christ's birth and mission, it may have had a deeper relevance to the blessing of so prosaic an object as a furnace. When Mary asks Gabriel how she could conceive while still a virgin, Gabriel replies, "The Holy Spirit will come upon you, and the power of the Most High will overshadow you; therefore the child to be born will be holy."[139] The movement of the Holy Spirit in the creation of holiness seems apt here, in a ritual that beseeches the power of the divine to overshadow and embrace the workplace and make it holy. Thus in imitation of God's past acts with living souls this present power flows, through the performance of the sacred words, into inanimate objects. The next reading is drawn from Matthew 2:1–12 and continues the story of Christ's birth, with the journey of the wise men and the trickery of Herod, which interestingly enough focuses on the marking out of the stable of Bethlehem as a holy place, denoted by the star guiding the magi.[140] Such a passage reminds celebrant and audience of the divine's capacity to sanctify the most base and common of locales. In light of this, the blessing of a chalk oven is made sensible and readily credible.

This retelling of the sacred history of the church continues with a reading from the Gospel of Mark (16:14–20), a passage in which Jesus chastises the disciples for their lack of faith and their stubborn refusal to accept the stories of Jesus' resurrection as true. "And he said to them, 'Go into all the world and proclaim the good news to the whole creation. The one who believes and is baptized will be saved; but the one who does not believe will be condemned.'" This passage seems particularly appropriate for use in a ritual blessing, in which the good news of God's power to protect and succor humankind is acknowledged and affirmed by the recitation of the blessing, and the mention of baptism's saving grace fits neatly with the baptism through aspersion of the furnace, so that a grace purposed to the salvation of humans becomes a power to save a place from demonic malice. The blessing thus becomes a reenactment of the historical spread of grace. The power of the blessing to accomplish this seems enhanced by the final Gospel read-

137. Franz, 1:632: Quibus finitis dicuntur quatuor evangelia, videlicet.
138. Ibid.   139. Ibid.; see also Lk 1:34–35.
140. Franz, 1:632; Mt 2:9–11.

ing, from John 1:1–14, the "word became flesh" introit to the last canonical Gospel.

> All things came into being through him, and without him not one thing came into being. What has come into being in him was life, and the life was the light of all people. The light shines in the darkness and the darkness did not overcome it. There was a man sent from God, whose name was John. He came as a witness to testify to the light, so that all might believe through him. He himself was not the light, but he came to testify to the light. . . . He [Christ] was in the world, and the world came into being through him; yet the world did not know him. . . . But to all who received him, who believed in his name, he gave power to become children of God, who were born, not of blood or of the will of the flesh or of the will of man, but of God.[141]

Whereas the previous Gospel readings followed a more or less narrative course, this last reading provides us with not a historical but with a theological perspective on Christ and the divine, one with great relevance to the ritual of blessing. This reading stresses the ultimate being that is God, as much a distinct entity as the state of being itself. In this reading the celebrant declares the primacy of this being, the divine, over all other forces as the source of the real and the meaningful, using the metaphors of life and light (the latter most fitting for a blessing of fire) with which medieval people so often characterized and comprehended the mysterious power of the sacred. The supremacy of Christ as the ultimate manifestation of this reality is asserted by this reading, which neatly caps the previous historical accounts of Christ's life by implying the intense connection between all present reality and the life of the historical Messiah, thereby justifying the constant reiteration of that scriptural life throughout the blessings. The mention of John also seems significant, for what is the celebrant in this ritual but a herald, a witness to the power of divinity to effect a real change in the quality and the nature of a place? Through the reiteration of scripture, the celebrant symbolically fills the role of the great prophet of the new covenant, demarcating himself as a servant of true being and a channel for the power that Christ promises the faithful, the power of life against death, of light against darkness, and of sanctity against profanity in the places blessed to receive that power through ritual.

The reading of the Gospels is followed in this benediction by a selection

141. Jn 1:3–13.

from the Psalms, which serves once more to connect this profane place of the present life to the paradigmatic holy places of scripture. The psalm chosen is Psalm 86, which begins: "Lord, you were favorable to your land; you restored the fortunes of Jacob. You forgave the iniquity of your people; you pardoned all their sin. . . . Restore us again, O God of our salvation, and put away your indignation toward us."[142] By reiterating the favor that God bestowed upon the chosen people of Israel and the land on which their livelihood depended, the celebrant of this ritual implores divinity to act once again in a merciful manner, to re-create the blessing of scripture through his mediation for the benefit of the medieval soul charged with the operation of this furnace. If it was indeed sung in its entirety, this psalm offers in later passages the reassurance, so common to the blessings, that the proper relationship with the divine will ensure material prosperity for the Christian community: "Surely his salvation is at hand for those who fear him, that his glory may dwell in our land. . . . Faithfulness will spring up from the ground, and righteousness will look down from the sky. The Lord will give what is good, and our land will yield its increase."[143] Connected to the aspirations of the ancient psalmist, the celebrant re-creates the relationship of the human community with the divine through this ritual, negotiating with God for an abundance of physical prosperity in exchange for spiritual reverence, awe, and thanksgiving.

This blessing of the furnace continues with a selection of short prayers that emphasize the connection of this common place to the nature of the divine. Following a short and unremarkable invocation of blessing, the priest is directed to approach

> to the mouth of the furnace and let him bless the fire. . . . "Holy Lord, Father omnipotent, unfailing light and founder of all light, hear us your servants and bless this light, which was sanctified by you and blessed. And just as you illuminated Moses, thus may you deign to illuminate our hearts and our senses, so that we may merit to arrive at eternal life."[144]

142. Franz, 1:632: Postea dicitur psalmus "Benedixisti, domine, terram tuam."
143. Ibid.; Ps 86:9, 11.
144. Franz, 1:632: Deinde veniat sacerdos ad os furnelli et benedicat ignem. . . . Domine sancte, pater omnipotens, lumen indeficiens et conditor omnium luminum, exaudi nos famulos tuos et benedic hoc lumen, quod a te sanctificatum est atque benedictum. Et sicut tu illuminasti Moysen, ita illuminare digneris corda nostra, et sensus nostros, ut ad vitam aeternam pervenire mereamur.

In this prayer the light of the furnace's fire is tied explicitly in origin to the divine, the source of all light and energy, declaring God's nature to be intimately associated with all the benefits that light and fire bring to the medieval blacksmith and his community.[145] But this disquisition on the origin of fire is not the only message in this prayer; while the author of the ritual asserts God's power to aid the community's physical needs by his control of light, the author of the blessing also conjures the paradigm of Moses and the burning bush to make this ritual an opportunity for salvation. Morality and the material world are closely bound up by the ritual's use of this scriptural model, making the work of the furnace a reminder of God's marvelous power, both as it has been exercised in the past and as it will be exercised in the future of this now sanctified place for the betterment of the Christian community. It also represents another reenactment of the scene on Mount Sinai, making the wonders of the Old Testament vivid and immediate in the simple act of lighting the fire.

The fire having been blessed, the ritual blessing of a furnace concludes with the lighting of the furnace, accompanied by the singing of the hymn *Veni, creator*.[146] This last rubric suggests, I think, a metaphorical transition of the fire of the Holy Spirit to this place, a culmination of all the words and acts that have come before. The hymn seems a final invocation of the divine, a calling down of the power of the *numen* to the place of the furnace, an invocation that is empowered by the acknowledgement of God's role as the creator of all fire and light. Illuminated by divine flame, the forge is consecrated for the use of the human community, which has been duly reminded of the importance of the divine in its daily life, the contours of that relationship, and the community's obligation as created beings to worship the Creator.

PLACES OF BURIAL AND WORSHIP: CONSECRATIONS

The experience of the divine is often expressed in a spatial context, be it an internal locus within the soul or the hallowed structure of a hall of wor-

---

145. God's role as an illuminator, although it appears in only this one source for spatial blessings, is a significant complement to the notion of God as defender in other types of blessings, for it evokes a very traditional idea of divinity as the good light that opposes the evil darkness. This theme is paralleled in the reconciliation rituals for violated churches and cemeteries discussed below, where God is expressly defined as the essence of mercy and goodness. For a list of these rites, see the index.

146. Franz, 1:632.

ship. The sanctification of space brought about by contact with the spiritual need not, however, be merely a temporary phenomenon that fades with the passage of time. Instead, a spatial locale may be permanently connected with the divine by means of a ritual process, a process (as we have observed in the blessing of fields and other areas) that saturates the space concerned with the metaphysical presence of the divine. One such ritual of sanctification is the medieval rite for the blessing and consecration of a cemetery.[147] The rituals of blessing cemeteries and reconciling both churches and burial grounds found in the Franco-Roman liturgical tradition are, I would argue, a means of placing the cemetery at the nexus of three distinct planes of reality: heaven, the created world, and hell. This blessing closed off the site and its inhabitants from the profane world by the power of voice, gesture, and the use of sacred objects, thereby creating a community of the dead set apart from the mundane world. But before the full contours of the ritual's meaning can be explored, it is necessary to grasp the fundamental role of the dead and burial places as sacred ground within medieval culture and *mentalité*.

The Middle Ages ushered in a perception of the role of the dead and buried within Mediterranean and European society fundamentally different from that of classical antiquity. The pagan world had considered care of the newly dead to be merely part and parcel of one's human obligations, and the buried and decaying dead were sources of corruption and pollution to be excluded from the public world and the confines of settlements.[148] To the faithful Christian, however, death was the door to salvation, and the bodies of the dead represented the souls that had passed through this door.[149]

147. The bulk of this section's discussion of blessings of cemeteries first appeared as "*Consecratio cymiterii:* The Ritual Blessings of Cemeteries in the Central Middle Ages," *Comitatus* 35 (2004): 22–44.

148. Brown, *Cult of the Saints,* 24; Philippe Ariés, *The Hour of Our Death,* trans. H. Weaver (New York: Knopf, 1981), 29–31. For a general introduction to late antique and early Christian burial practices, see Brown, *Cult of the Saints,* 1–49. For a treatment of the evolution of the cult of the dead and its influence on Roman and Gallican liturgies, see Giles Constable, "The Commemoration of the Dead in the Early Middle Ages," in *Early Medieval Rome and the Christian West: Essays in Honor of Donald A. Bullough,* ed. Julia M. H. Smith (Boston: Brill, 2000), 169–95.

149. Paxton, *Christianizing Death,* 25. For an introduction to the issues of death and the dead in later medieval society, especially in Italy and the south, see Sharon T. Strocchia, "In Hallowed Ground: The Social Meaning of Burial Revenues at St. Maria del Carmine, 1350–1380," *Michigan Academician* 14, no. 4 (1982): 445–52; Strocchia, "Death Rites and the Ritual Family in Renaissance Florence," in *Life and Death in Fifteenth-Century Florence,* ed.

With the advent of the cult of the saints and the Christian establishment under Constantine, the ancient revulsion toward the buried dead began to be replaced by an explicit conception of the sanctity of the dead's bodies and presence.[150] In some ways this was a natural and unsurprising development that served Christianity well in its conversion efforts of later centuries, for while the classical world looked with revulsion on decaying corpses, in sub-antique and barbarian cultures the place of burial was often thought to be a locus of magic, as it barely contained the power of the dead, who could exude enormous supernatural powers.[151] By the sixth century, towns and cities had been invaded by cemeteries, as the living sought a closer physical com-

Marcel Tetel (Durham: Duke University Press, 1989), 120–45; Peter Burke, "Death in the Renaissance," *Dies illa: Death in the Middle Ages*, ed. Jane H. Taylor (Liverpool: Cairns, 1984), 59–66; A. R. Brown, "Death and the Human Body in the Later Middle Ages: The Legislation of Boniface VIII on the Division of the Corpse," *Viator* 12 (1981): 59–82; and Samuel K. Cohn Jr., "The Place of the Dead in Flanders and Tuscany: Towards a Comparative History of the Black Death," in *The Place of the Dead: Death and Remembrance in Late Medieval and Early Modern Europe*, ed. Bruce Gordon and Peter Marshall (New York: Cambridge University Press, 2000), 17–43.

150. Ariés, *Hour of Our Death*, 40; Paxton, *Christianizing Death*, 25. Augustine himself, in the *Civitate dei*, stresses the point that the bodies of the dead should not be despised; they are the temples of the Holy Spirit and part of human nature; see Roger Reynolds, "Death and Burial," *DMA* 4:118. Ariés provides an occasionally problematic yet extensive discussion of the development of cemeteries as a socioreligious institution and geographic feature (*Hour of Our Death*, 29–94); a more recent study is Michel Lauwers, "Le cimetière dans le Moyen Âge latin: Lieu sacré, saint et religeux," *Annales: Histoire, Sciences Sociales* 54, no. 5 (1999): 1047–72. For the placement of cemeteries in the central and later medieval periods, see Julia Barrow, "Urban Cemetery Location in the High Middle Ages," in *Death in Towns: Urban Responses to the Dying and the Dead, 100–1600*, ed. Steven Bassett (London: Leicester University Press, 1992), 94–95; and Norbert Fischer, "Topographie des Todes: Zur sozialhistorichen Bedeutung der Friedhofsverlegungen zwischen Mittelalter und Neuzeit," in *Aussenseiter zwischen Mittelalter und Neuzeit: Festschrift für Hans-Jürgen Goertz zum 60*, ed. Norbert Fischer and Marion Kobelt-Groch (New York: Brill, 1997), 81–97. For a brief discussion of the importance of cemeteries to rural communities, see Robert Fossier, *Peasant Life in the Medieval West*, trans. Juliet Vale (Oxford: Basil Blackwell, 1988), 53.

151. Flint, *Rise of Magic*, 213. In Norse cultures, burial mounds were considered to be of such power that if one sat or slept on one throughout the night one could gain supernatural aid or inspiration from the ancestors. A Christianized version of such stories may be seen in Bede's tale of the Christian poet Caedmon, who received the gift of prophecy from an angel who visited him at night as he lamented his inability to compose songs; see Davidson, *Myths and Symbols in Pagan Europe*, 130. Particularly ancient barrows could be feared and avoided for their alleged infestation with supernatural forces; see Sarah Semple, "A Fear of the Past: The Place of the Pre-Historic Burial Mound in the Ideology of Middle and Later Anglo-Saxon England," *World Archaeology* 30, no. 1 (1998): 109–26.

munion with the holy dead.[152] Burial *ad sanctos,* approximate to the body of the saint or martyr, was considered efficacious in assuring the departed salvation on the last day, and church authorities from St. Augustine to St. Julian affirmed the value of the saint's physical presence in fulfilling the prayers of those faithful who invoked God at the grave of the fallen saint.[153]

This belief in the bodies of the faithful dead as a conduit to God undoubtedly played a role in fueling the lay conviction that burial in consecrated ground, ground that had been imbued with sacred power, was a prerequisite to salvation.[154] By the twelfth century this conviction was enshrined in the canonical principle that all the baptized dead can and should be buried in sacred ground. If misfortune struck and a good Christian died and could not be buried in a cemetery, a priest would bless the isolated grave and erect a cross, to show that a Christian was there and make demons tremble.[155] The space of the cemetery itself, when occupied by Christian bodies, possessed a sacrality that inspired liturgical commentators such as Honorius of Au-

152. Ariès, *Hour of Our Death,* 29.

153. Ibid., 33, 42, citing St. Julian (*PL* 96, col. 474, Ariès translation): "The proximity of the memoriae of the martyrs is so advantageous to the deceased that if one commends to their patronage someone who had been buried in their vicinity, the effect of the prayer is increased."

154. Ibid., 31. The principle is reaffirmed in Durandus's commentary; see William Durandus, *The Symbolism of Churches and Church Ornaments: A Translation of the First Book of the "Rationales divinorum officiorum,"* ed. John Mason Neale and Benjamin Webb (London: T. W. Green, 1906), 81. Exceptions could and were made to this rule, however; the suicide, the excommunicate, the infant unbaptized, and (according to Durandus) even those found dead in doubtful circumstances could be denied burial in consecrated cemeteries (for a physical study of the exclusion of unbaptized and stillborn infants, see Seamus Donnelly, Colm Donnelly, and Eileen Murphy, "The Forgotten Dead: The *Cillíní* and Disused Burial Grounds of Ballintoy, County Antrim," *Ulster Journal of Archaeology* 3, no. 58 [1999]: 109–13). An example of such exclusion can be found in the account of the violation of the Hohenstaufen emperor Manfred's burial cairn (a tale reported by Dante in *Purgatorio* 3:125–35), which evoked the full strength of medieval horror at the thought of unconsecrated burial. For an example of the intentional exclusion of non-Christians from consecrated burial grounds, see Dominique Iogna-Prat, "La terre sainte disputée," *Médiévales* 41 (2001): 83–112.

155. Thompson, *Cities of God,* 409. The communal governments of Italian cities were especially concerned with the need to protect burial grounds from spiritual and physical pollution. Many enacted laws banning littering in the cemetery, requiring that maintenance funds be raised through taxation, and laying down special rules to govern the burial of women who died in childbirth and their unborn children. The rites for these unfortunates would be conducted outside the church building, as in the case of those who died by violence, lest the blood shed by either contaminate the holy precincts of the church.

tun and William Durandus to declare that the burial ground was not merely earth but the *dormitorium mortui et gremius ecclesiae,* the dormitory of the dead and the bosom of the church.[156] As a place "appropriated to prayers," the cemetery was a "sweet station, for there the bones of the departed rest sweetly, and expect the advent of their Savior."[157] As a holy place, the cemetery enjoyed the privilege of *ius asyli,* acting as a sanctuary for the persecuted and a supposed haven from earthly concerns.[158] Separated from the outside world by the presence of the dead and the rite of consecration, the space of the cemetery was a sacred land within the profane landscape. In this separated space the rite of consecration, in my view, created a *hierophany,* a manifestation of the sacred, divine power of the *numen* that unites and embraces not only the ontological worlds of divinity and the material realm, but also the realm of the dead, the underworld where the souls of the faithful departed lie sleeping in community until the end of the world. But before delving into an analysis of this process, a chronological history of the origin and development of these rites will place them clearly within the context of medieval liturgical trends and sources.

The rite for the blessing of a cemetery is reported to have existed as early

156. Honorius of Autun, *Gemma animae,* chap. 147. The notion of death as sleep for those awaiting resurrection had long been known in medieval thought; see Reynolds, "Death and Burial," 118. The conception of a cemetery as a place of dwelling is also a common motif, as is evident in the discussion of the cemetery as an abode by Messer Betto, a character from the *Decameron*'s ninth story of the sixth day; see Giovanni Boccaccio, *The Decameron,* trans. G. H. McWilliam (London: Penguin, 1972), 505.

157. Durandus, *Symbolism of Churches,* 71, 77–78. Durandus offers an intriguingly Scholastic schema, drawn apparently (as Lauwers argues) from late Roman law, for defining places dedicated to prayer: those that are holy (places with immunity or privilege), those that are sacred (where the feast of the Eucharist is celebrated), and religious places ("where the entire body of a man or at least the head is buried"). See ibid., 78, and Lauwers, "Cimetière dans le Moyen Âge." Cemeteries would appear to be places of dual sanctity, enjoying the status of being both holy and religious.

158. The canonical decrees and prohibitions regarding cemeteries, their violation, and their reconciliation are extensive. Aside from sanctuary, cemeteries were to be free from worldly business transactions, trials of civil or criminal cases, and socializing by the laity (see Canon 25, II General Council of Lyon [1274], in H. J. Schroeder, ed., *Disciplinary Decrees of the General Councils: Text, Translation and Commentary* [St. Louis: B. Herder, 1937], 354–55; Gratian, *Decretum* C. 2 q. 1 c. 23, *de immunitate ecclesiarum;* and Durandus, *Symbolism of Churches,* 77). Despite the canonical prohibitions, it is clear that medieval cemeteries were a focal point for the community, where everything from juridical affairs to dancing and feasting were enthusiastically carried out (see Ariés, *Hour of Our Death,* 52–53).

as the fifth century. Gregory of Tours, in his *De gloria confessorum,* is the first to mention a formalized rite for the blessing of a burial ground, yet the casualness of his remark suggests that such a rite was not new.[159] Despite the early date of Gregory's reference, the first extant manuscript containing this rite is the eighth-century *Liber pontificalis* of Egbert, archbishop of York (732 to 736).[160] This northern manuscript provides the earliest form of three essential prayers of consecration that compose the heart of the ritual in the Franco-Roman tradition of the high Middle Ages: *Deus qui es totius conditor* (hereafter designated A for ease of reference), *Domine sancte pater omnipotens trina maiestas* (B), and *Domine deus pater aeterne gloriae* (C). As well as these fundamental prayers, the ritual also provides significant rubrics for the celebrants.[161] The blessing begins with a bishop, accompanied by clerics, circling the bounds of the cemetery sprinkling holy water, all the while chanting the psalm *Miserere mei deus.*[162] The antiphon *Asperges me* ("Sprinkle me, Lord, with hyssop and I shall be cleansed, [resp.] you shall be washed by me, and I shall be made whiter than snow") is then sung, emphasizing the cleans-

159. Cornelius M. Power, *The Blessing of Cemeteries* (Washington, D.C.: The Catholic University of America Press, 1943), 4. For the reference in Gregory, see *MGH SRM* 1:104.

160. Power, *Blessing of Cemeteries,* 21. This manuscript has most recently been edited by H. M. J. Banting, ed., *Two Anglo-Saxon Pontificals: The Egbert and Sidney Sussex Pontificals* (London: Boydell Press, 1989), 57–59. The attribution of this pontifical to Egbert seems only partially correct; portions of the MS may be a product of the late ninth century (see Banting, *Two Anglo-Saxon Pontificals,* ix–xii).

161. As in all versions of these rituals, the celebrants are the only persons referred to in the text of the blessing. This fact, combined with the apparent silence of contemporary sources on the rites or their performance, makes exact conclusions regarding the audience for this rite impossible. It seems reasonable to assume, however, that since these rituals were often associated with the rites for consecrating churches (a very public ritual), there may have been a lay audience for this rite. Their reactions to the rite, however, will remain a mystery until relevant sources (if they exist) can be found and studied.

162. Banting, *Two Anglo-Saxon Pontificals,* 57: *Primitus cum aqua benedicta episcopus cum clericis suis circumdare debeat omne cimiterium cum psalmo.* For the origin of this form of aspersion, see above concerning the aspersion of fields. Blessings of cemeteries and reconciliations of churches and cemeteries are the only kind of spatial blessing that makes common use of specified psalmody. Only four of seventeen agricultural blessings studied here list psalms, and those that do are all oriented to blessing particular objects in that space: holy water, a cross, or the seed to be planted in the fields; see the Old Spanish "Blessing of Seed," the *RGP*'s "Blessing of Water for Crops against Vermin," Prüm's "Blessing of a Cross," and Lausanne's "Exorcism of Water." This suggests that the presence of holy water and the cross, two elements drawn from traditional church liturgical practice, may have encouraged authors to list traditional psalms as well.

ing process that the ritual imparts both to the earth and to the inhabitants of the cemetery.[163] This is followed by the speaking of the prayers mentioned above, the bishop and the clerics positioned in turn within three of the four cardinal corners of the cemetery, with a final prayer, *Omnipotens dominus qui es custos animarum* (D), offered in the northern corner of the cemetery.[164] A concluding oratio, *Adesto quesumus domine deus officio nostre servitutis* (E), is offered in the middle of the cemetery to complete the ritual.[165]

A later liturgical monument, the RGP of the tenth century, provides a similar ritual entitled *Consecratio Cymiterii*, which includes a near verbatim copy of the A, B, and C prayers of the Egbert pontifical.[166] Despite this similarity, there are differences between the two pontificals. Whereas Egbert includes directional and spatial instructions for the celebrants, accompanied by the sprinkling of holy water, the RGP merely provides the three basic prayers and the use of holy water.[167] The RGP rite also includes a new rubric for the singing of seven penitential psalms and the lighting of four candles around the bounds of the cemetery.[168]

The content of the three prayers common to the Anglo-Frankish and the Romano-Germanic rites focuses on creating a sanctified, purified resting place for the faithful dead. The celebrant calls on divinity "to bless and also purge this cemetery or burial ground," and "to allot perpetual purity for

163. Banting, *Two Anglo-Saxon Pontificals* 57; *CAO* 59.

164. Banting, *Two Anglo-Saxon Pontificals*, 59.

165. Ibid.

166. *RGP* 1:192–93 (*ordo* 54). The pivotal MS Vogel used in his edition of this ritual was Montecassino, Archivio della Badia, 451, fols. 49r–49v. This MS was copied in Beneventan script c. 1050 from a Rhenish MS interpolated at Rome in 999, the date of the emperor Otto's visit to Rome, as part and parcel of the *Renovatio imperii* (see Vogel, *Medieval Liturgy*, 230, 234, 237). Supporting MSS consulted include Rome, Bibl. Alessandrina 173, fols. 41r–41v; Rome, Bibl. Vallicelliana D.5, fols. 43v–47r; Vienna, Nationalbibliothek, *cod. lat.* 701, fols. 62r–63r; and Vendôme, Bibl. Mun., *cod.* 14, fols 43r–v.

167. *RGP* 1:192–93.

168. Ibid., 1:192, lines 4–5: Primitus canantur VII psalmi paenitentiae et in circuitu illuminentur IIII candelae. In addition to the differences in rubrics, there are subtle differences in the phrasing of the prayers that distinguish the northern tradition of this ritual from the southern. Where the Egbert ritual provides the B prayer with the conditional clause "ut hoc cymiterium in honore nominis tui compositum benedicere et sanctificare concedas," the *RGP* version of prayer B offers "ut hoc cymiterium in honore nominis tui compositum benedicere et sanctificare *digneris*" (emphasis added). The C prayer also varies between the two rites' incipits for this prayer: Egbert offers "Domine deus pastor aeterne gloriae," while the *RGP* offers "Domine deus *pater* eterne gloriae"; see Banting, *Two Anglo-Saxon Pontificals*, 58; *RGP* 1:192, line 22.

the human bodies of this place."[169] This act of purification takes aim at both physical and spiritual corruption: "we beseech you so that you might deign to bless, guard and cleanse this cemetery of your saints from all filthiness and the stain of unclean spirits."[170] The powers of evil are specifically warded off from the sacred ground by the blessing's power, as the celebrant begs protection "from all incursions of malevolent spirits."[171] The souls thus shielded are quite specifically those who partook of divinity's power within their lifetime, the faithful dead: the cemetery is said to be the preserve "of whosoever shall have received the sacrament of baptism and shall have persevered in the Catholic faith until the end of life."[172] Thus we observers of this ritual may perceive the manner in which ceremony, as defined by Grimes, can serve to protect the members of a community, to define it in opposition to others who have not chosen to embrace the community's ethos, and to provide the power of the sacred as a weapon to force compliance on the recalcitrant out of fear of the eternal damnation and vulnerability that is the lot of those buried in unconsecrated ground.

The prayers contextualize the cemetery and its inhabitants within sacred history. The inhabitants of the cemetery "await the trumpet of the first archangel," invoking the words of Paul from 1 Corinthians 15:52.[173] The rite provides its blessing ultimately so that the dead may participate in this prophecy, so that, "as the angelic trumpets sound, the material of the body and the soul united, they may lay hold of the everlasting reward of celestial joys."[174] Thus the power of the sacred is employed not only to bring to mind sacred history but to ensure that it is enacted in the lives of the community. The ritual also transforms the earth of the cemetery into a parallel of scripture, by associating it with "the land of Abraham the blessed patriarch, your familiar, [which], purchased from the sons of Hebron for use as a grave, you [God]

169. *RGP* 1:192–93 (A, C): ut hoc cymiterium sive poliandrium . . . sanctificare, purgare atque benedicere digneris . . . atque corporibus humanis huic loco advenientibus sinceritatem perpetuam tribuere.

170. Ibid., 1:193 (C): te flagitamus, ut hoc sanctorum tuorum cymiterium ab omni spurcitiae et inquinamento spirituum inmundorum custodire, mundare, benedicere digneris.

171. Ibid., 1:192 (B): ab omni incursione malorum spirituum.

172. Ibid.: et quicumque baptismi sacramentum perceperint, et in fide catholica usque ad vitae terminum perseverantes fuerint . . .

173. Ibid., lines 14–15 (A). The scriptural passage reads: "For the trumpet will sound, and the dead will be raised imperishable, and we will be changed." .

174. Ibid., 1:193 (C): angelicis tubis concrepantibus, materia corporis et animae unita, praemia caelestium gaudiorum sempiterna percipiant.

blessed."[175] This allusion to Genesis 23 establishes the ground of the medieval cemetery within the paradigmatic history of scripture, making the sacred time of medieval Christianity live again within the confines of this cemetery, and thus lending an aura of holiness to the site through association with Old Testament figures.

The content of these prayers was further disseminated in the territories affected by Roman liturgical practice by the agency of the next major liturgical collection, the Roman pontifical of the twelfth century.[176] This revision of the RGP provides two rituals for the sanctification of a burial ground: a short *Benedictio cimiterii* and a much longer episcopal *Benedictio cimiterii*.[177] The first ritual is merely a copy of the RGP's rubrics and three prayers, including the use of holy water, the lighting of candles, and the singing of the seven penitential psalms.[178] The presence of these psalms and objects, and the absence of any directional prayers such as are found in the Egbert pontifical, clearly indicate that this ritual is inspired by the RGP.

The longer episcopal rite of consecration is far more detailed. This ritual contains the fundamental A, B, and C prayers, and it also contains the prayer *Omnipotens Deus, qui es custos animarum,* the D prayer absent from the RGP.[179] It includes the use of directional rubrics and prayers as seen in Egbert, but on a far more complex level than in the northern ritual.[180] Of all the available rituals, this long benediction provides the most opportunities for meaningful discussion of content.

This ritual begins with the bishop taking up a position in the cemetery,

175. Ibid., 1:192 (B): qui Abrahae beati patriarchae famuli tui terram, a filiis Ebreon comparatam causa sepulturae, benedixisti. Abraham and the other patriarchs could often be portrayed as receivers of the faithful dead: in the *Liber ordinum* of Silos, one of the short prayers for a "Blessing for Consecrating a New Tomb" asks, "Receive, most pious God, the soul of your servant, N., into the bosom of the patriarch Abraham, and join him with all the saints and your elect" (*CB* no. 2015, 2:822).

176. For a discussion of the origin and significance of this pontifical, see Vogel, *Medieval Liturgy,* 249–51.

177. The short ritual of Andrieu's edition was drawn from a single MS: London, British Library, Add. 17005, fols. 130v–131r. The longer ritual was drawn from Lyon, Bib. Mun., 570, fols. 336–337r, an early modern copy of the renowned pontifical of Apamea, from the Latin patriarchate of Antioch, a pontifical originally copied from a Roman model at the end of the twelfth century (see Vogel, *Medieval Liturgy,* 250–51). The original version of the pontifical has since been found, and is now cataloged as London, British Library, Add. 57528.

178. *RP12th* 285 (*ordo* 52a.1).

179. Ibid., 287 (*ordo* 52b.10), lines 23–28.

180. Ibid., 286–88; Banting, *Two Anglo-Saxon Pontificals,* 57.

turning himself to face east and offering a short prayer. This *oratio* is unique in the tradition of the ritual up to its date of composition, although its statement of purpose is not: "We pray you shall deign to bless the place of this earth about to be dedicated to you so that it may be a cemetery, that is, quiet and sleep for the bodies of Christians to be buried therein."[181] A cemetery is thus defined by the qualities it bestows upon its inhabitants, and by connecting the space of the cemetery with the divine, the celebrant bestows upon the gathered dead a communal experience of the holy: "may the souls of the faithful, whose bodies to be buried here will be resurrected spirits at some time, merit to have a share and companionship with all the saints in eternal beatitude."[182] United thus under the shelter of the benediction's power, the souls may confidently await the final resurrection of the dead.

Next the bishop makes a circuit around the whole of the cemetery with his clerics, singing and sprinkling holy water. This physical act delineates the territory to be sanctified, enclosing it with the power of the blessed water and the voices of the celebrants chanting words of prayer and scripture.[183] The notion of purification is once again invoked, this time by the antiphon, as a central element in the creation of the cemetery's hierophany: "Sprinkle me, Lord, with hyssop and I shall be cleansed, [resp.] you shall be washed by me, and I shall be made whiter than snow."[184] As the cemetery is sprinkled with holy water, the celebrant invokes the cleansing power of anointing to add to the efficacy of the ritual. Then follows the psalm verse: "Be merciful to me, O God, be merciful to me, for in you my soul takes refuge; in the shadow

---

181. *RP12th* 286 (*ordo* 52b.2), lines 20–24: Oremus benedicere digneris . . . huius terrae locellum tibi domino Deo dedicandum, ut sit cimiterium, hoc est quies et dormitio corporum christianorum inibi sepeliendorum. The image of the grave as a place of rest and solace is a common one, and it is often described as a seat of refreshment, as in a brief prayer "In a Cemetery," in the *RGP* 2:356 (*ordo* 195).

182. *RP12th* 286 (*ordo* 52b.2), lines 25–27: animae fidelium, quorum hic corpora sepelienda sunt resurrectura quandoque spiritualia, in aeterna beatitudine partem et societatem cum sanctis omnibus habere mereantur. This association of the dead person with the concrete community of the servants of God can also be seen in liturgical texts for funeral rituals, which similarly link the dead and the cemetery with the elect beyond time (see McLaughlin, *Consorting with Saints*, 36).

183. A similar ritual use of circuits and sprinkling is to be found in the pontifical of Sens (MS Paris, Bibl. nat. lat. 934, fols. 38r–40v), a late twelfth-century manuscript; see Martène, *Antiquis Ecclesiae ritibus*, 2:295.

184. Ibid. Compare Banting, *Two Anglo-Saxon Pontificals*, 57; *CAO* 59: Asperges me, Domine, hyssopo et mundabor, lavabis me et super nivem dealbabor.

of your wings I will take refuge, until the destroying storms pass by."[185] By this invocation the cemetery is reinforced as a place of refuge, where a more immediate participation in the divine and its power is possible for the human soul.

After the circuit of the cemetery, the celebrants return to the bishop's point of origin, and turn to face east. In Christian cosmography, east is the direction associated with Christ himself, the sun of the universe; it is the auspicious quarter where light is born, and it represents infancy, purity, and paradise.[186] It is toward this direction, intimately associated with God, that the first *Pater noster* of the ritual is offered, and where the celebrant makes a personal address to God to hear the prayer favorably.[187] The prayer that is then offered up is the A *oratio*, which emphasizes the quality of purgation associated with the ritual and the need for purity on the part of the celebrant: "God, who is the creator of the whole world and the redeemer of the human race ... we earnestly beseech you with humble entreating voice and pure heart that you shall deign to bless and purge this cemetery."[188] The offering of this prayer, a personal address to God as both creator and savior, associates the prayer with the east's symbolic quality of purity and implicitly calls upon that purity to create the hierophany within the bounds of the cemetery.

The celebrants next cross to the opposite part of the cemetery, singing an antiphon and psalm. The former, *Placebo domino*, affirms the celebrant's desire to produce a ritual, and thereby a site, pleasing to God.[189] The psalm verse gives glory to God, ensuring a favorable response from the sacred world: "Not to us, Lord, not to us, but to your name give glory, for the sake of your steadfast love and your faithfulness."[190] Here the enduring nature of

185. *RP12th* 286 (ordo 52b.3); Ps 57:2.
186. Gertrude Jobes, *Dictionary of Mythology, Folklore and Symbols* (New York: Scarecrow Press, 1962), 486; Hans Sedlmayr, *Die Entstehung der Kathedrale* (Zurich: Atlantis Verlag, 1956), 119. Indeed, with the altar at the east and the baptistery at the west ends of churches, the procession of newly baptized Christians from the baptistery to the altar was seen in medieval times as a symbolic passage from the world of darkness to the world of light (Bouyer, *Rite and Man*, 184).
187. *RP12th* 286 (ordo 52b.3), lines 32–33: Domine exaudi orationem.
188. Ibid., 287 (ordo 52b.4): Deus qui es totius orbis conditor et humani generis redemptor ... te supplici voce ac puro corde exposcimus purgare atque benedicere digneris.
189. Ibid. (ordo 52b.5, line 4); *CAO* no. 403: Placebo Domino in regione vivorum.
190. *RP12th*; Ps 115:1.

God's guardianship is emphasized, undoubtedly in an effort to ensure that the blessing that invokes this wardship will endure until the last day, and to serve as a reminder to God to act in a consistent manner toward the human community. The sanctified space thus created will serve as a lasting focus of divine grace within the salvation history of the church, a spatial focus where a soul may arrive at a closer relationship with the divine force that drives history in the Christian cosmology.

The celebrants' motions now carry them to the outer limit of the cemetery, at which point they turn back to face west. This movement serves to re-emphasize the establishment of boundaries begun in the initial circuit of the celebrants; the length of the cemetery having been traversed, the celebrants turned their backs to the outside profane world and direct the power of their prayers toward the heart of the sacred space they are creating. The symbolism of direction again seems to play a significant role in the content of these prayers. The west in Christian thought is associated with darkness and death; it is the realm of sleep and sunsets, the land of darkness, of grief and death, the realm of the eternal mansions of the dead who await the resurrection of the Last Judgment.[191] It is toward this ominous and forbidding land that the first sequence of the *Kyries* is offered, in this context clearly beseeching mercy in the face of death and the shadows of the grave.[192] A second *Pater noster* is offered, probably with a similar intention of winning protection from the powers of darkness.[193] Following these prayers comes prayer B, the content of which seems entirely appropriate in its emphasis on the power of God: "Holy God, father omnipotent, triune majesty and one deity . . . author

191. Jobes, *Dictionary of Mythology*, 1674; Eliade, *Sacred and Profane*, 61; Sedlmayr, *Entsichung der Kathedrale*, 119. This symbolism is also reflected in the architecture of some churches. In the church of San Giovanni, in Florence, the west wall is "blind," without a door, to symbolize it as "the direction of darkness and the setting of the sun"; see Thompson, *Cities of God*, 31. And in the early liturgies of baptism, some rites had candidates for baptism "turned toward the West, the realm of the setting sun and death, the ritual seat of the prince of the world, 'who has the power of death' and rejected him [Satan] and his pomps directly . . . then they turned towards the East and professed their belief in God the Father and his Son, their redeemer, and in the Holy Spirit" (Kelly, *Devil at Baptism*, 11, 25). Ambrose of Milan, in his *De mysteriis*, also describes candidates for baptism facing west, "which is the symbolic realm of darkness, and as speaking as if he stood face to face with the Devil" (Kelly, *Devil at Baptism*, 99, quoting Ambrose of Milan, *De mysteriis*, ed. Otto Faller, Corpus Scriptorum Ecclesiasticorum Latinorum [Turnhout: Brepols, 1957], 2.5).

192. *RP12th* 287 (*ordo* 52b.5), line 5.

193. Ibid.

of justice, granter of grace, giver of good things, font of sanctity . . . grant favorably that you shall deign to bless and sanctify this cemetery constituted in honor of your name."[194] The might of divinity is stressed, and stressed significantly in the face of its opposite, the power of darkness and mortality. By voicing this prayer, the celebrants call down this power into the earth, to imbue the space of the cemetery with the holy aura of paradise as a counter to the power of darkness embodied in the physical graves and decaying bodies of the dead. This effort at balancing the presence of life and death within the cemetery is furthered by the use of the story of Abraham and the purchase of the grave site from Hebron, which can be read as contextualizing the physical reality of the grave with the sacred history of scripture, giving burial in this particular sacred ground a transcendent meaning by associating it with the numinous history of the founder of the covenant people.[195]

The motion of the celebrants continues with a procession to the "other part" of the cemetery, all the while singing an antiphon and psalm verse. While this "other part" of the cemetery is vague in the text, the fact that the celebrants then turn themselves toward the south suggests that the movement was to the north end of the cemetery, where a turn toward the south would parallel the closing off of the site as seen above.[196] The antiphon sung during the procession serves to reinforce the calling down of God into the space of the site: "Open the gates of justice for me, [resp.] Having entered them, I confess to the Lord; this gate of the Lord, the just shall enter into it."[197] By this antiphon, a metaphoric portal to divinity and its realm is called into being within the bounds of the burial ground, further strengthening the connection between the realms of divinity and humanity. The psalm verse that follows seems to be an attempt to validate the intention of the antiphon: "Praise the Lord with the lyre; make melody to him with the harp of ten strings, Sing to him a new song." (Ps 33:2).[198] By venerating and celebrating the power of God, the celebrant seems to encourage that power to affirm its residence within the bounds of the cemetery, enticing the divine to

194. Ibid. (*ordo* 52b.6), lines 8–9: Domine sancte, pater omnipotens, trina maiestas et una dietas . . . iustitiae auctor, veniae largitor, bonorum dator, sanctitatis origo . . . praesta propitius, ut hoc cimiterium in honore nominis tui compositum benedicere et sanctificare digneris.

195. Ibid.

196. Ibid. (*ordo* 52b.7), lines 10–12.

197. Ibid., line 10; *CAO* no. 53: Aperite mihi portas iustitiae, ingressus in eas confitebor Domino; haec porta Domini, iusti intrabunt in eam.

198. *RP12th* 287 (*ordo* 52b.7), line 11; Ps 33:2.

act in a predictably beneficent manner in exchange for the praise of the human community.[199] The psalm also stresses the joy and praise that shall be obtained by those making the passage into this new realm, reinforcing the cemetery as a place of peace and blessed repose.

Now turned toward the south, the celebrants render up another *Kyrie* and *Pater noster*, followed by a brief prayer. This prayer serves further to connect the space of the cemetery with the underworld: "From the gate of the grave, raise up, Lord, the souls of all the faithful dead."[200] Offered toward the south, associated with infernal regions but also with spiritual light and the saints, this prayer directs itself toward the infernal world.[201] As the antiphon *Aperite mihi portas* opened a gate to paradise, this prayer seeks to open the gate of the underworld or afterlife to the nexus of the cemetery. Following this prayer, the formulaic prayer C is offered up.[202] In this prayer, directed toward the region of spiritual light, divinity is cast as light embodied: "Lord God, father of eternal glory, light and honor of wisdom . . . we beseech you that you might deign to bless, guard and cleanse this cemetery of your saints from all dirt and the filth of unclean spirits."[203] The cemetery thus becomes the preserve and ward of the light toward which the celebrants turn themselves, both physically and spiritually. Through this prayer's description of the cemetery, the burial site becomes associated with the saints, so that mere occupancy of the cemetery seems to entitle one to membership in the company of the saints, a notion that both laity and clergy (steeped in the notion of burial *ad sanctos*) might find comforting.

With the next crossing of the cemetery and its accompanying songs, the emphasis on creating a dwelling place for divinity on earth again resurfaces. The antiphon "This is my rest in the world without end, [resp.] this I shall inhabit because I have chosen it" is sung, re-creating the space of the cemetery

---

199. The notion of such a contract between God and the faithful is also strongly represented in the Roman tradition of episcopal reconciliations of violated churches and cemeteries, where it no doubt received attention because of the need to reestablish the human-divine partnership that allowed prayers to be heard and departed souls to rest in peace.

200. *RP12th* 287 (*ordo* 52b.7), lines 13–14: A porta inferi, Erue domine, animas omnium fidelium defunctorum.

201. Jobes, *Dictionary of Mythology*, 1478.

202. *RP12th* 287 (*ordo* 52b.8), line 15.

203. Ibid.: Domine Deus pater aeternae gloriae, lux et honor sapientiae . . . te flagitamus ut hoc sanctorum tuorum cymiterium ab omni spurcitia et inquinamento spiritum immundorum custodire, mundare, benedicereque digneris.

as a dwelling place for both immortal souls and divinity.[204] A verse further defines the cemetery as the home of divine power: "O Lord, remember in David's favor all the hardships he endured; how he swore to the Lord and vowed to the mighty one of Jacob, 'I will not enter my house or get into my bed; I will not give sleep to my eyes or slumber to my eyelids, until I find a place for the Lord, a dwelling place for the mighty one of Jacob'" (Ps 132:1).[205] The creation of a sanctified space is reaffirmed by this canticle, as the celebrants' voices and motions shape the space of the cemetery into a residence for the divine within the profane world, a residence associated with the same holiness that had dwelt in the ancient temple of the Israelites.

Following the procession and the singing of these verses, the celebrants turn themselves to the north and offer up a *Kyrie* and a *Pater noster*, accompanied by a short prayer.[206] The north in the medieval *mentalité* was considered the inauspicious quarter, the mansion of frost, the realm of Satan, of faithlessness and spiritual darkness.[207] In the face of this evil, the celebrants use this short prayer to call again for the mercy of God to descend upon the space of the cemetery: "May you [God] not surrender the souls trusting in you to the beasts and nor shall you forget the souls of your poor in the end."[208] The sanctity of the space and of divinity is thus invoked to serve as both a physical and a spiritual shield for the community of the dead interred within the cemetery. This brief *oratio* is followed by prayer D, found first in the Egbert pontifical, which emphasizes the protective power of the divine: "Omnipotent God, who is the curate of souls and the guardian of the health of those believing the faith, provide favorably for the performance of our ser-

204. Ibid., *ordo* 52b.9, line 18; *CAO* 245: Haec requies mea in saeculum saeculi; hic habitabo quoniam elegieam.

205. *RP12th* 287 (*ordo* 52b.9), line 18; Ps 132:1. This psalm is thought to have been composed in the era immediately following the rebuilding of the Israelite temple, and its content is a general encouragement to belief in Jehovah's promise that David's house would enjoy dominion; as such, it may also have proved evocative to medieval people who sought comfort in the reassurance of God's salvific power in his residence, the cemetery. Kirkpatrick, *Book of Psalms*, 762.

206. *RP12th* 287 (*ordo* 52b.9), lines 19–22.

207. Jobes, *Dictionary of Mythology*, 1181. During this period the deacon's facing north while reading the Gospel during the Mass was interpreted as a challenge hurled at the powers of darkness, although in antiquity the west was regarded as the abode of dark powers (Bouyer, *Rite and Man*, 176).

208. *RP12th* 287 (*ordo* 52b.9), lines 20–21: Ne tradas bestiis animas confitentes tibi et animas pauperum tuorum ne obliviscaris in finem.

vice, so that this cemetery may be consecrated and sanctified and blessed at our entrance."[209] The efficacy of the ritual's benediction is here intriguingly tied to the performance of the celebrants, yet the power of sanctuary and holiness is still left to the agency of divinity and its presence as established by the ritual. This is yet another example of the cooperation, the negotiation, between the divine and the human at the heart of medieval blessings.

When the circuit of the cardinal directions within the cemetery has been completed by the celebrants, the bishop moves to the middle of the cemetery while intoning the response, "Free me, Lord, from eternal death," reinforcing the salvific power both of divinity and, implicitly, burial in the cemetery's consecrated ground.[210] Once in the cemetery's center, its symbolic heart, the bishop offers up a *Kyrie* and a *Pater noster,* facing east, in an apparent effort to center the cemetery itself in the divine associations of that direction.[211] The process of centering the site through appeal to the direction that was intimately associated with Christ, which can be seen as an attempt to center the cemetery within the person and power of Christ himself, is reinforced by the bishop's next offering up a prayer to the east that precedes the speaking of prayer E, the final prayer to be found within the Roman tradition.[212] The former of these two formulaic prayers both reinforces the personal nature of the earlier appeal and contextualizes the ritual within scriptural history:

> Be present, we beseech, Lord God, in our office visiting this place and in the ministry of our fragility and, just as you blessed the earth of the graves through the hand of the first fathers, namely, Abraham, Isaac and Jacob; and afterwards for the remedy of our salvation surrendered, scourged and at last crucified, with Joseph [of Arimathea] preparing it divinely, you sanctified the sepulcher through yourself, thus shall you deign to bless and to consecrate this cemetery.[213]

---

209. Ibid. (*ordo* 52b.10), lines 23–26: Omnipotens Deus, qui es custos animarum et tutela salutis fides credentium, respice propitius ad nostrae servitutis officium, ut ad introitum benedicatur, consecretur et sanctificetur hoc cimiterium.

210. Ibid. (*ordo* 52b.11), lines 29–30.

211. Ibid., lines 31–32.

212. Ibid. (*ordo* 52b.12), lines 34–37; 288, lines 1–5.

213. Ibid., lines 34–37; 288, lines 1–2: Adesto, quaesumus, domine Deus, officio nostro hunc locum visitanti et nostrae fragilitatis ministerio et, sicut benedixisti per manus patrum priorum, scilicet Abrahae, Yssac et Iacob, terram sepulturae et postmodum nostrae salutis remedio traditus, flagellatus tandemque crucifixus, per te ipsum, Ioseph divinitus praeparante, terrenum sanctificasti sepulcrum ita hoc cimiterium benedicere, consecrare.

This prayer, with its reiteration of the sufferings of Jesus for the sake of humanity, directly addresses itself to the crucified Christ and places the blessing of the cemetery in the tradition of the blessing God who provided for the earthly graves of the patriarchs, reinforcing the sacredness of the burial ground through association.

This ritual for the blessing of a cemetery concludes with the bishop returning to the church attached to the cemetery, once again reinforcing the power and the presence of divinity within the cemetery: "God, you who are the author of gifts about to be blessed, pour forth your blessing above this house of prayer, so that by all invoking your name here may be felt the aid of your defense."[214] This concluding prayer firmly opens the site to the divine within the church and, by association, within the precincts of the cemetery consecrated by the voice, gestures, and objects employed in the ritual benediction.

Another important ritual for the blessing of cemeteries is to be found within the last major Roman effort at pontifical creation in the medieval era, the pontifical of the Roman Curia. The creation of the pontificate of Innocent III, this ritual emerged in an era when a ritual of consecration had been firmly established as a canonical requirement, and draws its essential content from the RGP through the intermediary of the Apamea MS of the RP12th (c. 1200), yet it contains only a short prayer for the blessing of a cemetery.[215] Appended to a blessing for a church, this short prayer draws upon images developed in the formulaic prayers of earlier rituals: the cemetery is "sweet repose and the rest of the dead," consecrated by God who is "the sanctifier of all places and the reformer into better."[216] There are no ru-

214. Ibid., 288 (*ordo* 52b.13), lines 7–9: Deus qui sacrandorum tibi auctor es munerum, effunde super hanc orationis domum benedictionem tuam, ut ab omnibus hic invocantibus nomen tuum defensionis tuae auxilium sentiatur.

215. Power, *Blessing of Cemeteries*, 23–24. For a full discussion of this manuscript, see Vogel, *Medieval Liturgy*, 252; PRC 440–41.

216. PRC 440, lines 14–15, 11–12: Dulcis requies et pausatio mortuorum . . . locorum omnium sanctificator et reformator in melius. This emphasis on God as the sanctifier may be a response to heretical attacks on the value of consecrated ground, but in light of the formulaic nature of this text and the brevity of heretical statements regarding consecrated ground, such a conclusion can only be conjecture. For a discussion of twelfth- and thirteenth-century heretical opinions on consecrated ground, see Walter Wakefield and Austin Evans, eds., *Heresies of the High Middle Ages* (New York: Columbia University Press, 1991), 102–3, 117, 120, 172, 235, 348–49. This supposition is indirectly supported by the later commentary of Durandus; see the following discussion of this author's ritual for the reconciliation of churches and cemeteries.

brics, no use of song or objects, which suggests that the compiler of the pontifical regarded the consecration of a cemetery either as of little significance or as being largely covered by the preceding consecration of the church proper; it could also indicate that the book contained only the prayers said by the bishop, or a selection of items from *ordines* well known to all, or that the rubrics and chants were contained more fully in a different book.[217] Following the creation of this prayer, the Roman tradition of rituals for the blessing of cemeteries ceased to develop independently and ultimately gave way, in the fourteenth century, to the southern French liturgical forms contained within the pontifical of William Durandus, the last major source for this ritual we will examine.

The ritual for the blessing of a cemetery in the pontifical of Durandus displays a considerable augmentation of the symbolic elements of the blessings of the Roman tradition, as well as the addition of new elements and prayers. Durandus begins his blessing with a short commentary on the necessity for including such a blessing in his work: "Although very many assert a blessing of a cemetery to be unnecessary, saying a circuit around the church and the cemetery with sprinklings suffices for this, which they do when the church is dedicated, nevertheless it is not without cause to do the following blessing. Furthermore, very many cemeteries are separated from churches, and not all churches are consecrated."[218] This comment is quite revealing, not only in showing how blessings, while almost universally accepted as efficacious, could be a point of controversy among theologians, liturgists, and canonists, but also in demonstrating the manner in which blessings could be seen as cumulative and working in tandem.

The separate blessing of a cemetery justified, the ritual is begun with the placement of several crosses throughout the cemetery. These crosses are ordered to be placed a day before the actual performance of the ritual.[219] The

217. *PRC* 440–41 (*ordo* 24). It is also possible that this ritual was thought to be of little use in the long-Christianized district of the Holy See, where cemeteries were well established and little need was felt for new ones.

218. *PWD* 504 (*ordo* 2.5.1): Quamquam plerique asserant cimiterii benedictionem necessariam non esse, dicentes ad hoc sufficere circuitus extra ecclesiam et cimiterii aspersiones, que fiunt quando ecclesia dedicatur, non tamen supervacuum est sequentem benedictionem fieri. Sed et plerumque cimiteria sunt ab ecclesiis separata, nec omnes ecclesie consecrantur.

219. Ibid., 504–5 (*ordo* 2.5.2): Die namque precedenti fiunt in cimiterio benedicendo quinque lignee cruces. This rubric is also found in an earlier manuscript, which provides a simplified ritual in comparison with Durandus's work. The manuscript in question is the

reason for this early placement is ambiguous; perhaps it simplified and shortened the complex proceedings of the following day, or perhaps this early planting of the crosses was thought to "root" these potent symbols within the territory of the cemetery, so that their power might pervade the burial ground before the human celebrant began his invocation of the divine. In any case, the crosses are placed in a very specific pattern: "five crosses of wood at the height of a man are placed in the cemetery to be blessed, one in the middle [of the cemetery] which is made higher [than the other crosses], and another to the rising of the sun (east), a third to the setting (west), the fourth to the north, the fifth to the south."[220] The placement of these crosses stakes out the territory of the cemetery in a manner similar to the blessings that came before it, but this pattern adds a new element of symbolism to the meaning of the crosses. By employing five crosses in this order, Durandus creates not merely a space demarcated by the physical presence of crosses but a space that is itself re-created in the form of a cross, with a center and four points outlining a territory that now resonates with the power of the cross through sympathetic association.[221]

The blessing begins early the following morning, with the bishop dressed in the symbolic vestments of his role. With an amice, alb, stole, a white cope, simple miter, and pastoral staff, but without a maniple (a strip of silk sometimes worn by the ministers at Mass), the celebrant precedes the actual ritual with a discussion for the benefit of the laity present for the blessing: "And before everything he makes a short sermon for the people concerning the sanctity and freedom of the cemetery and similar things."[222]

---

pontifical of Archbishop Christian Moguntin, of the twelfth century; see Martène, *Antiquis Ecclesiae ritibus*, 1:295, and Martimort, *Church at Prayer*, no. 826. This blessing is of interest for this early appearance of a symbolic larger cross, and for the prayer *Sit nomen domini benedictum* (May the name of the Lord be a blessing), indicating the power held to reside within the name of God.

220. *PWD* 505 (*ordo* 2.5.2): fiunt in cimiterio benedicendo quinque lignee cruces, alte ad hominis staturam, una in medio que fit altior, alia ad ortum solis, tertia ad occasum, quarta ad septentrionem sive ad aquilonem, quinta ad austrum sive meridiem.

221. This is a perfect example of sacred space as a cosmological image and archetype, as elaborated in the work of Eliade and Bouyer, and of how sacred space uses the symbols of religious culture to order the chaos of profane space. For a discussion of this process, see the introduction to this chapter and Eliade, *Sacred and Profane*, 20–65.

222. *PWD* 505 (*ordo* 2.5.3): Et ante omnia facit populo brevem collationem de sanctitate et libertate cimiterii et similibus.

This instruction is remarkable for its concern with the understanding of the laity, who receive little if any mention in such rubrics, aside from their actions as recipients.[223] That the special qualities of the space of the cemetery should receive mention suggests that such qualities might be unknown to the laity, or (more probably) that they were ignored by customary practice in Durandus's time. Such a commentary may have been thought necessary following the heresies of the twelfth and thirteenth centuries and their condemnations of the theology of holy ground.[224] We can only speculate as to whether the blessing itself came under the rubric of "similar things" discussed by the bishop, but it seems reasonable to conclude that the blessing as a bestower of holiness and sanctity was mentioned before the crowd witnessed the ritual in action, to put them into the proper state of mind so necessary to a successful blessing.

The ritual proper begins immediately after the bishop's sermon to the gathered laity, with a symbolic gesture to drive away the powers of evil and pollution from the bounds of the cemetery. Fifteen candles are lit, three in front of each of the five crosses planted the day before.[225] These burning flames were probably meant to dispel the forces of darkness from the precincts of the burial ground, as in previous blessings, with the number three undoubtedly symbolizing the Holy Trinity. The objects of this ritual, then, all place the cemetery within the paradigms of the Christian faith, strengthening the power of the sacred by associating the site with the images, symbols, and numbers that medieval believers believed bore power within themselves.

The time at which this ritual is begun may also be significant; if *mane* is to be understood as "dawn" and not simply "morning," then this time may

223. For example, see the couples blessed in the blessing of nuptial beds (above), and the actions of pilgrims receiving blessings before departure for their holy destinations (see chapter 3).

224. Heretics especially disapproved of incense, song, and the ringing of church bells to sanctify spaces and persons; see Klaniczay, *Uses of Supernatural Power*, 37–38. See also Barbara H. Rosenwein, "Feudal War and Monastic Peace: Cluniac Liturgy as Ritual Aggression," *Viator* 2 (1971): 129–57.

225. *PWD* 505 (*ordo* 2.5.3): Postea illuminantur quindecim candele, tres videlicet ante quamlibet crucem, super aliquod lignum. It is possible, too, that this use of light is related to the long-standing Christian custom, which may have been a continuation of a Roman custom of using torches and candles at burial; see Martimort, *Church at Prayer*, 159. There are also many uses of light in scripture that could have inspired this usage: Ex 27:20, Lv 24:2–4, 1 Sm 3:3, Ex 25:31–40, Rv 4:5, Rv 1:12–13, and Acts 20:8.

have been chosen for its symbolic significance. Dawn signals the end not only of night but of the sway of the powers of darkness and evil. The bishop is instructed to speak the prayer *Omnipotens sempiterne Deus, qui es custos animarum et corporum,* drawn from the RP12th, facing the middle cross, the physical center of the cemetery and the heart of the symbolic cross that marks the cemetery as belonging to Christ.[226] The bishop then places a faldstool before the central cross "in the direction of the rising sun," and a cantor begins a litany, with a response from the attendant choir.[227]

> Then the bishop rising from his seat, holding the pastoral staff in the left hand, makes thrice the sign of the cross above the cemetery, saying first: "So that you might deign to purge and bless this cemetery. [We beseech] you." Secondly, he says: "May you deign to purge, to bless and to sanctify. [We beseech] you." Thirdly he says: "May you purge, bless, sanctify and consecrate. [We beseech] you."[228]

The litany is sung toward the quarter of light and Christ, greeting the rising sun with a conjuration designed to infuse the burial ground with the light that is Christ, the essence of medieval people's conception of the power of the divine. The sign of the cross and its repetition follow in the same manner as the physical crosses and candles, seeking to associate the cemetery with the forms, meaning, and being of the Christian faith. Also notable is the manner in which each phrase of the litany with its gesture seems to build in power and intensity, so that the purgation and blessing provided by the first phrase is augmented by the sanctification of the second, and the consecration of the final phrase caps this invocation with a further layer of divine protection for the cemetery.

Much of the remainder of this ritual is derived from the earlier Roman tradition of cemetery blessings. The bishop performs the aspersion of the points and precincts of the cemetery, accompanied by psalms and antiphons, as we saw in the Roman ritual and employing the RP12th prayers.[229] One interesting feature of this ritual is that, following the first circuit of the

226. *PWD* 505 (*ordo* 2.5.4); see RP12th (*ordo* 52b.10).

227. *PWD* 505 (*ordo* 2.5.4).

228. Ibid., (ordo 2.5.5): tunc pontifex surgens ab accubitu, baculum pastoralem in sinistra tenens, producit ter signum crucis super cimiterium, dicens primo: Ut hoc cimiterium purgare et benedicere digneris. Te. Secundo dicit: purgare, benedicere et sanctificare digneris. Te. Tertio dicit: purgare, benedicere, sanctificare et consecrare digneriis. Te.

229. Ibid., 506–7 (*ordo* 2.5.9–10); see also RP12th (*ordo* 52a.2–4).

cemetery, the bishop steps before the eastern cross and censes it before placing upon it the three burning candles lit at the beginning of the blessing,
one on the summit and one on each arm of the cross.[230] This is followed
by another circuit around the other crosses, with each treated in the same
manner as the eastern cross.[231] The meaning of this union of the crosses and
candles is ambiguous, but it probably represents the positive union of the
light of divinity with the suffering of the cross, perhaps as a metaphor for the
resurrection. Or it may have been performed to enhance the power of both
symbols to manifest the protective power of the divine summoned by the
blessing. There is mention in certain sources of the power of physical contact with the cross: for example, in Anglo-Saxon charms for healing we find
the assertion that lichen growing on a cross gains nearly miraculous virtues
by the contact, echoing how items touched by saints could exercise power by
that association.[232] In any case, the resurrection is invoked most explicitly by
the seventeenth prayer of the blessing, an original creation of this ritual said
before the northern cross:

> Lord Jesus Christ . . . we ask [you] to deign to consecrate this earth to the use
> of burial from out of the blessing of your buried body, and grant those buried
> together with you in baptism, about to be buried here in the flesh in the hope
> of your resurrection, to rest in the mercy of your redemption.[233]

230. *PWD* 506 (*ordo* 2.5.9): Deinde thurificat crucem et figit in summitate eius unam ex
tribus candelis accensam et alias duas in duobus brachiis crucis.

231. Ibid., 507–8 (*ordo* 2.5.14–16).

232. Jolly, *Popular Religion*, 161. In a similar fashion, herbs placed under an altar by the rubrics of charms could gain protection and blessing for those who used them. Also, in the *Vita
sancti Cuthberti*, the author records how a priest took soil from the ground where water used to
wash St. Cuthbert's body had been thrown, and used the soil to cure a demoniac boy. A similar
example can be found in the *Dialogi de miraculis sancti Benedicti* of Abbot Desiderius of Monte
Cassino, who recorded a story of how the monk Antony, injured in an accident, took dust from
St. Benedict's tomb and applied it to his injured limb and was immediately healed (*Dialogi de
miraculis sancti Benedicti*, 1116–17, and *Vita sancti Cuthberti anonymi, Two Lives of St. Cuthbert* 13, 130,
quoted in Ward, *Miracles and the Medieval Mind*, 45, 57). A perhaps more traditional story of
healing by association comes from thirteenth-century Italy, where in 1240 Donna Orvetana
lay her crippled son, Belbruno, on top of the sarcophagus of St. Ambrogio of Massa, and the
boy was cured (Thompson, *Cities of God*, citing the *Processus Ambrosii Massari* 73, p. 601).

233. *PWD* 508 (*ordo* 2.5.17): Domine Iesu Christe . . . hanc terram, quesumus ad usum
sepulture de benedictione tui sepulti corporis consecrare dignare et in baptismate tibi con-
sepultos in natura carnis hic consepeliendos sub spe tue resurrectionis in tue redemptionis
misericordia requiescere concede.

Here baptism is linked to burial, a striking image of death as rebirth, and the very corpse of Jesus is invoked, not as a source of pollution, as the ancient world would have conceived of it, but as a source of power for redemption and resurrection, a veritable source of blessing *manna* that could be summoned with action, object, and voice by the medieval priesthood.

The use of candles as a source of light and symbol of goodness is made explicit in the last prayer of note within this blessing. Following the prayer discussed above and another round of censing and sprinkling of holy water, the celebrant is directed to speak "with a medium voice" this preface prayer:

> He who is eternal day, light unfailing, clarity everlasting, who thus commanded his followers to walk in the light so that they might be able to evade the darkness of eternal night and to happily arrive to the homeland of light, who through assumed humanity wept for Lazarus, through the power of divinity restored [him] to life . . . through whom we humbly entreating pray you, Lord, so that whoever is buried in this cemetery, absolved from the bonds of sins and returned into eternal felicity and numbered among the assemblage of saints, may through you, who are eternal life, discover kindness and mercy in the last day when the horns of the angels shall have made a great noise, so that, exalting with all the saints, they may praise the author of life.[234]

This prayer offers us an excellent example of the medieval equation of light with the power of goodness and the divine, and provides powerful support for the interpretation of the use of candles as more than mere adornments. As a glimpse into "the homeland of light," the candles mounted on the cross, the ultimate symbol of humanity's triumph over death and darkness, served as a potent reminder not only to the participants of the ritual but also to the divine and demonic worlds themselves, that this space was now protected and separated from the rest of mundane space. The allusion to the resurrection of Lazarus emphasizes this point, reviving that ancient miracle for medieval participants in this blessing. It also declares the validity of their hope

---

234. Ibid., 509 (*ordo* 2.5.21): Qui est dies eternus, lux indeficiens, claritas sempiterna, qui sic sequaces suos in lucem precepit ambulare, ut noctis eterne valeant caliginem evadere et ad lucis patriam feliciter pervenire qui per humanitatem assumptam Lazarum flevit, per divinitatis potentiam vite reddidit . . . per quem te, domine, suppliciter deprecamur, quatenus qui in hoc sepelientur poliandro, in novissimo die, cum tube perstrepuerint angelorum, a peccatorum nexibus absoluti et eterne felicitati redditi et sanctorum cetibus annumerati, te, qui es vita eterna, benignum et misericordem inveniant, ut et auctorem vite exultantes cum omnibus sanctis collaudent.

of resurrection and God's obligation of consistent benevolence toward the faithful human community.

PLACES OF BURIAL AND WORSHIP: RECONCILIATIONS

The creation of sacred space by means of a blessing was often cast as an act that would suffice until the last day, or for as long as the recipients lived, as we see in the blessings for cemeteries and homes, respectively. But some circumstances could breach the extraordinary quality of sacred space: the spilling of blood through violence, the performance of carnal acts, and other acts that violated Christian morality.[235] When a shameful act was perpetrated within a sacred place, matters could not be left to rest as they were; the crime required a ritual act of cleansing by a bishop or priest to remove the pollution from the holy site and to banish the evil from the Christian collective, so that the site could once again serve as a meeting place of the divine and the human.

The act of ritual cleansing was designated a reconciliation, whether it dealt with a church or cemetery, a term that underscores the crucial importance of good relations between the different worlds that was essential if the blessings of the medieval church were to function properly.[236] A reconcilia-

235. For an introduction to the subject of the violation of churches and cemeteries, see Cornelius M. Power, "Cemeteries, Canon Law of," *NCE* 3:386–87; John T. Gulezynski, *The Desecration and Violation of Churches,* Catholic University of America CLS 159 (Washington, D.C.: The Catholic University of America Press, 1942); and A. C. Rush, *Death and Burial in Christian Antiquity,* Catholic University of America Studies in Christian Antiquity 1 (Washington, D.C.: The Catholic University of America Press, 1941). Under modern canon law, a violation of a cemetery results in a "temporary curtailment" of some effects of the blessing, which can be undone through the reconciliation (Power, "Cemeteries," 386). The violation of cemeteries or churches was always a serious offense, but nowhere more so than in the tightly knit communal society of the northern Italian cities of the central Middle Ages. There, violence was the most dramatic way one could rupture the fabric of communal society, and the offense required not only a reconciliation but a solemn public penance by the perpetrators (see Thompson, *Cities of God,* 302).

236. The subject of the consecration of churches, unlike many other forms of blessing, has received tremendous attention from talented scholars; nevertheless, such blessings have been excluded from this study (for reasons discussed in the introduction), and so a thorough look at this scholarship is not necessary at this point. For a brief introduction to this topic, see Daniel J. Sheerin, "Dedication of Churches," *DMA* 4:130–31; R. K. Seasoltz, "Churches, Dedication of," *NCE* 3:862–64; R. W. L. Muncey, *History of the Consecration of Churches and Churchyards* (Cambridge: W. Heffer and Sons, 1930); J. D. Crichton, *The Dedication of a Church* (Dublin: Dublin University Press, 1980); and Daniel J. Sheerin, "The Consecration of Churches

tion set matters right between the two parties, and because reconciliations were held to be vital in cases where the original blessing had been violated, they can reveal much about how and why medieval people understood blessings of space to work.

Reconciliations are lengthy rituals with many components, much like the dedication of churches, one of the most solemn and elaborate forms of ritual practiced in medieval culture. For the purposes of this study, I have chosen four reconciliations as the most representative and widespread forms of this ritual: a "Reconciliation of a Violated Church," contained in the RGP;[237] a blessing "In Reconciliation of the Altar, or a Sacred Place, or a Cemetery," from a twelfth-century manuscript originating either at Avranche or at Mont St. Michel;[238] a "Reconciliation of a Violated Church or Cemetery," found in the PRC;[239] and a ritual "Concerning the Reconciliation of a Church and Cemetery," from the PWD.[240] No significant supporting rites exist outside this small corpus of standard reconciliations, so all analysis will flow from these four blessings.

The earliest blessing of a violated church during our period is found in the RGP. So great was the seriousness of this blessing that, as often was the case in the consecration of churches, the reconciliation of a church involved the relics of the local saint's cult: "First the relics are to be lifted up and let the bishop come before this very church with the clergy and the people and say this prayer."[241] The elevation of the relics, the focal point of all the power of

---

Down to the Ninth Century," in *Further Essays in Early Roman Liturgy*, ed. Geoffrey G. Willis (London: S.P.C.K., 1968), 133–73.

237. *RGP* 1:182–85 (*ordo* 50). This ritual is found in nine of the manuscripts used in the modern edition of the *RGP*, which suggests that the importance attributed to this ritual was great enough to make it a standard element of most pontificals. The manuscripts are Rome, Biblioteca Alessandrina, *cod.* 173; Bamberg, Staatliche Bibliothek, *cod. lit.* 53; Montecassino, Archivo della Badia, *cod.* 451; Rome, Biblioteca Vallicelliana, *cod.* D. 5; Eichstätt, Bistumsarchiv, pontifical of Gondekar II; Pistoia, Archivo capitolare del Duomo, *cod.* 141; Lucca, Biblioteca capitolare, *cod.* 607; Vienna, Nationalbibliothek, *cod. lat.* 701; and Vendome, Bibliothèque municipale, *cod.* 14.

238. Martène, *Antiquis Ecclesiae ritibus*, 2:286–87. The full title is *In reconciliatione Altaris, vel sacri loci, seu cimiterii ubi sanguis fuerit effusus, aut homicidium factum aut aliqua spurcitia publice perpetrata*.

239. *PRC* 443–45 (*ordo* 26).

240. *PWD* 510–17 (*ordo* 2.6).

241. *RGP* 1:182 (*ordo* 50.1): Primum efferantur reliquie et veniat episcopus ante ipsam ecclesiam cum clero et populo et dicat hanc orationem.

the saints to protect their church, would serve both to honor the patrons and to involve them personally in the ritual so as to guarantee a propitious result. In fact, saints played a major role in the performance of such rituals.[242] The exclusion of relics from later rituals of reconciliation is not explained by contemporary authors, but it seems likely that these foci of holy power were excluded because of the changing nature of the sacraments in the high medieval church. Megan McLaughlin and Martha Newman have shown convincingly how a centralized clerical hierarchy whose position was based on the clerical monopoly of the sacraments, and the importance of these sacraments as the primary means of contact with the divine, overshadowed monastic prayer, saints' shrines, royal decisions, and relics as sources of sacred power from the twelfth century on.[243] The absence of relics from later reconciliations may be due to this decline in the relative importance of relics as sources of numinous power. Despite the absence of relics in later rituals, saints continued to be a powerful force in reconciling violated space with divinity. The predominance of saints in these reconciliations may be explainable, insofar as sacred ground in churches and cemeteries was the natural resting place of saints, and therefore their proximity made them appear to be the best intercessors to accomplish the blessing's goals.

In this concern with producing an acceptable ritual we are on familiar ground, but the prayer that is immediately spoken adds an interesting dimension to the performance of this blessing, in which the spiritual supremacy of the priesthood is asserted at the same time that it is invoked to justify the ritual:

> Let us pray. Omnipotent and merciful God, who conferred such great grace
> on your priests in comparison with others, so that whatever is done justly and
> perfectly in your name by them may be believed to be done by you, we ask your
> immense clemency that you may visit what we are about to visit in this way,
> and whatever may be blessed you may bless, and at the entrance of our hu-

242. Within the corpus of spatial blessings, saints most often appear when the blessing deals with holy ground, i.e., churches and their cemeteries. All of the five reconciliations studied make use of at least one litany, and early reconciliations (the *RGP* and the twelfth-century Mont-St. Michel's rites) also call for the use of relics, conduits of divine power. The two rituals cited are the *RGP*'s "Reconciliation of a Violated Church" and the Mont-St-Michel's "In Reconciliation of the Altar, or a Sacred Place, or a Cemetery."

243. McLaughlin, *Consorting with Saints*, 282–465; Martha G. Newman, *The Boundaries of Charity: Cistercian Culture and Ecclesiastical Reform, 1098–1180* (Stanford: Stanford University Press, 1996), 236.

mility may the ingress of angels of peace be the flight of demons through the merits of your saints.[244]

There are many levels of meaning in this complex prayer. On the surface there is a simple invocation to drive out the powers of the demonic, which, through the act of pollution, have violated the sanctity of the church, and to replace the demonic with divine peace through angelic intervention. Belief in the appropriateness of such a request finds support throughout innumerable medieval devotional texts, such as the Blickling Homily's exposition on St. Paul's *Qui ad ministrum summis:* "'Angels are spirits for ministering from God sent here into the world' for those who with spirit and with strength earn for God the eternal homeland, so that they are a help to those who must always fight against the corrupt spirits."[245] This battle with "corrupt spirits" could find no better field than a reconciliation, where the power of God was ministered through his agents to fight evil and corruption.

The second level of this prayer, the recapitulation of the special quality of the priesthood to administer God's grace through the sacraments, reminds all present of the divine sanction for this special status and reminds God that this ritual is undertaken by those who acknowledge themselves as his servants and accept the demand for moral probity that this special status entails.[246] The entire discussion of the priesthood in this prayer is predicated on the notion that the performance of a blessing is a partnership between the human and the divine, where the human agents carry out the physical actions required (motion, voice, and gesture), while God "follows up" these motions with the bestowal of power that will guarantee the success of the benediction.[247] This "cooperative approach" interpretation would have been well received, for as early as the church fathers there was the explicit notion of a partnership between the priesthood and the spiritual agents of God: an-

244. *RGP* 1:182: Oremus. Omnipotens et misericors Deus, qui sacerdotibus tuis prae ceteris tantam gratiam contulisti, ut quicquid in tuo nomine digne perfecteque ab eis agitur, a te fieri credatur, quaesumus immensam clementiam tuam, ut quod modo visitaturi sumus visites, et quicquid benedicturi benedicas, sitque ad nostrae humilitatis introitum, sanctorum tuorum meritis, fuga demonum, angeli pacis ingressus.

245. Boenig, "Blickling Homily," in *Anglo-Saxon Spirituality,* 77.

246. A similar phrase appears in the *RGP*'s *ordo* 214b.21, a "Blessing of Water against Vermin in the Crops."

247. This parallels the notion of "opus operatum" and "opus operantis" introduced by eleventh- and twelfth-century theologians writing on the sacraments. See Vorgrimler, *Sacramental Theology,* 52–53.

gels. Origen declares, "one might say, following Scripture, that there are two bishops in each church, one visible, the other invisible, and both are busied with the same task," that task being caring for and protecting the Christian community.[248]

The prayers following this initial *oratio* emphasize the need for the purity of those performing the ritual blessing. The second prayer implores God, "take away from us, Lord, we beseech, all our iniquities so that we may merit to approach with pure spirits to the place being purified by your name."[249] As we have seen before, the very name of God serves as a potent symbol, blessing the space in which it is spoken. This prayer asserts the need for spiritual cleanliness on the part of the celebrants of the ritual, demonstrating the close connection between interior issues of morality and the efficacy of blessings. Only a pure celebrant could hope to compel the power of the sacred for the just purpose of reclaiming a site for divine use; any other would merely contribute to the pollution already contaminating the sacred ground and lead either to no change or to negative results.

The ritual continues with an entrance into the church, accompanied by the singing of a litany.[250] The celebrant then speaks a prayer, while the people, at the order of the deacon, kneel in reverence.[251] This prayer highlights an important metaphor used in medieval benedictions, the image of God as a manifestation of sacred power:

> God, who by the passion of your son our Lord Jesus Christ has dissolved the inherited death of the ancient sin to which every following generation had succeeded, grant favorably that similar to your deed we may bear the image of heavenly grace by means of the sanctification of that same Christ our Lord, just as we have borne the image of an earthly parent by necessity of nature.[252]

This prayer suggests that the celebrant is imploring God to act in accordance with Christ's demonstrably merciful nature, as we in a sense act in accor-

248. Daniélou, *Angels and Their Mission*, 58 (quoting Origen's *Homily on Luke*, 13).

249. *RGP* 1:182 (*ordo* 50.2): Alia. Aufer a nobis, domine, quaesumus, omnes iniquitates nostras, ut ad loca tuo nomini purificanda puris mereamur mentibus accedere.

250. Ibid. (*ordo* 50.3).

251. Ibid., 1:183 (*ordo* 50.4).

252. Ibid.: Oremus. Deus qui peccati veteris hereditariam mortem, in qua posteritatis genus omne successerat, Christi filii tui domini nostri passione solvisti, dona propitius, ut conformes eiusdem facti, sicut imaginem terreni parentis naturae necessitate portavimus, ita imaginem caelestis gratiae sanctificatione portemus eiusdem Christi domini nostri.

dance with the human nature provided by our earthly parents. The blessing imparts to the participants the quality necessary to transmit the power of grace by means of the affinity between the human and divine worlds that was born from the Incarnation. The blessing, then, acts a conduit between these two realms, enabling power and worship to be exchanged in order to produce sacred space and its salutary qualities.

This reconciliation of a church then proceeds with a scattering of blessed water mingled with salt, wine, and ashes. This mixture, the so-called Gregorian water, was first used for sprinkling in the dedication of a church, with the salt and ashes added in the eighth century, the salt representing contrition and penitence and the ashes, mortality, mourning, and penance.[253] This procedure is followed by a prayer that invokes the Incarnation itself as an act of purification:

> We humbly implore, most beloved brothers, God, the pardoner of sins, God the cleanser of filth, God who by the splendor of his advent purified the physical world of original sin, so that the steadfast defender may assist us against the deceptions of the raging devil, in order that if something in this place is found defiled and corrupted with common infections by his poisonous shrewdness it may be made purged by the mercy of heaven . . . since our author restores lapses, makes firm the feeble and purges the corrupt.[254]

In this prayer of cleansing, the celebrant emphasizes the purgative powers of the divine to shape the power of God into an appropriate form and to reaffirm God's ability to heal the wounded space of the violated church.[255] The coming of Jesus into the world of humans is conjured in this blessing, drawing an analogy between the purgation of the human race and the purgation

253. E. J. Johnson, "Ashes, Liturgical Use of," *NCE* 1:948–49. It is possible that this use of ashes in aspersion is drawn from a practice mentioned in Nm 19:9, on the use of the ashes of a sacrificed heifer in the water used for cleansing and ritual purification of the Israelites.

254. *RGP* 1:183 (*ordo* 50.6): Deum indultorem criminum, Deus sordium mundatorem, Deum qui concretum peccatis originalibus mundum adventus sui nitore purificavit, fratres karissimi, suppliciter deprecemur, ut contra diaboli furentis insidias fortis nobis propugnator assistat, ut si quid eius virosa calliditate cotidianis infectationibus maculatum in isto loco invenitur atque corruptum, efficiatur caelesti miseratione purgatum . . . ita auctoris nostri est lapsa restituere, nutantia stabilire et corrupta purgare.

255. The Roman tradition in reconciliations of God as a cleanser and pardoner, although it is a common enough in Christianity, nevertheless addresses the specific purpose of the ritual and the need of the petitioning community: the removal of pollution, evil, and sin from the communal territory of the church.

of the place of its worship, as it draws power by re-creating the fact of the Incarnation for the assembled participants. And as in other blessings, the cleansing of space by the divine is considered to have the power to restore the proper moral state to those using and relying on the church, as well (by implication) as to those spirits that persist in resisting the resanctification of the house of God. This use of scripture is also typical of rites of reconciliation. All five reconciliations considered here make use of scripture, and these use stories from both the Old and the New Testament.[256]

With this recollection of the power of the divine to be manifest in and cleanse the human world, the formal consecration begins:

> God, whose goodness had no beginning and so will have no end, who, full with natural and divine good, chose rather to restore in us what was lost than to strike down what was about to perish, and if what negligence pollutes, or wrath commits, or drunkenness goads, or lust perverts, you would sustain by patient mercy, so that you might purify this place through grace.[257]

In this opening prayer we see the offering of praise for God with the reminder to God to live up to the obligations that humanity ascribes to the numinous. Despite all the possible means of pollution this prayer recounts, the blessing implicitly asserts that the power of grace transcends the human power to sin, realizing the Christian perspective on the conflict of good and evil in a comprehensible form. God's mercy is emphasized, since God has the power to punish but chooses instead to forgive. The reconciliation aims at a lasting infusion of this power into the fabric of the church:

> May all spiritual evils be absent and eliminated in the future. May the ill will of the ancient serpent be extinguished and the troop of the Devil driven out along with his deceptions. May it remove the worse stain which it carries, and about to be cut off at some time with everlasting prayers may it gather the worse seed of its works to be destroyed.[258]

---

256. There are two shared allusions: the role of the Incarnation in erasing original sin is mentioned in German, Roman, and French rituals, and the fall of the rebellious angels is present in the two French rituals studied (see the index). Both of these seem natural and appropriate, considering that the object of these rituals was the restoration of grace lost through sin.

257. *RGP* 1:183–84 (*ordo* 50.7): Deus cuius bonitas, ut non habuit principium, ita nec terminum habebit, qui, divina naturalique pietate plenus, elegis in nobis magis restitutere perdita quam percutere peritura, et si quid aut neglegentia polluit, aut ira committit, aut stimulat ebrietas, aut libido subvertit, clementi patientia sustines, ut hoc ante per gratiam purifices. . . .

258. Ibid.: Absint in posterum omnes nequitiae spirituales et eliminentur. Extinguatur

The stain of human sin is here intimately equated with the power of the demonic, which gains entry to divine places through human misconduct; it is therefore fitting that the human performance of a ritual blessing may undo what man has wrought, once again casting into relief the necessity of cooperation between the human world and the divine in maintaining the mutual points of contact, the sacred spaces of churches and cemeteries. This prayer reveals something of the medieval conception of blessing's lasting power when it states, "May the stain of the former contagion harm nothing here in the future, may there be nothing which remains polluted by the fraud of the enemy, when indeed it is seen to have been purged by the infusion of your spirit."[259] The Christian community's witnessing of the power of the sacred to cleanse this place here interestingly lends potency to the blessing, involving both celebrants and audience in the working of the ritual and the lasting purity it brings to the violated.

This long consecratory prayer concludes with a hopeful conjuration of the return of holiness to this violated site.

> May the pure simplicity of your church rise again, and may the candor of innocence until now stained rise again to glory when it shall have received grace so that the gathering crowd of your faithful people, when it has poured forth prayers of petition, may understand itself to have obtained the intercession of prayers.[260]

This call for a return to innocence for the violated church reveals both a desire to cleanse the site of pollution, thereby reestablishing its sanctity, and the importance attributed to the prayers of the celebrants. The infusion of the prayers of blessing and the grace they transmit revives the salvific power of the sacred place, and that power is directed specifically to confirming the faithful hopes of the Christians who gather to worship in the holy place. Thus comforted, they will render up the praises that are the human world's offering, bartered for the protection of the divine world. The ritual then con-

---

antiqui serpentis invidia et cum fraudibus suis diaboli turma propellatur. Efferat secum maculam quam ingessit et perennibus quandoque suppliciis deputandus operum suorum semina secum colligat peritura.

259. Ibid: Nihil hic in posterum noceat praeteriti culpa contagii, nihil sit quod remaneat inimici fraude pollutum, quando quidem per spiritus tui infusionem constat esse purgatum.

260. Ibid.: Resurgat aecclesiae tuae pura simplicitas, et candor innocentiae hactenus maculatus, dum receperit gratiam, resurgat ad gloriam, ut populorum istic fidelium turba conveniens, dum petitionis ingerit vota, votorum se sentiat obtinuisse suffragia.

cludes with the singing of the antiphon, *Exsurgat deus et dissipentur inimici eius* (Let God rise up, let his enemies be scattered, let those who hate him flee before him), which is taken from the text of Psalm 68, the theme of which is the march of God to victory and the triumph of Israel over all its enemies.[261] This psalm has always been a favorite of those who felt their cause was God's cause, in our period most notably crusaders and the radical Italian preacher Savonarola, and as such fits well with this blessing, which seeks the triumph of purity and the holy over the corrupt and profane.[262] The victory of God over his enemies in this psalm becomes the model for the present reconciliation, locating this particular church in the history of divine successes that benefited both the worship and the worshippers of God.

Following this antiphon, another kneeling prayer entreats the blessing's

261. Antiphons make appearances in each genre of spatial blessing, but only in reconciliations are they plentiful. There is no clear chronological pattern of evolution for the citation of antiphons in such blessings: antiphons for field blessings appear only in tenth- and eleventh-century German rituals, while we find them in domestic blessings only in the thirteenth-century *PWD*, and they are present in all the studied rituals for reconciliations; see the *RGP's* "Blessing of Water for Crops against Vermin," Prüm's "Blessing of a Cross," and the *PWD's* "Blessing of a New House." The most common antiphon, *Asperges me, domine*, is often used in connection with the Psalm *Miserere mei, deus*, which emphasizes purification as symbolized by the dew falling from heaven and reenacted in aspersion with holy water; for examples, see all the reconciliations studied here, the *RGP's* "Blessing of Water for Crops against Vermin," and the *PWD's* "Blessing of a New House." One clear regional characteristic, however, can be discerned: French sources specify more use of antiphons than do their Roman counterparts. The twelfth-century pontifical of Mont St-Michel expands the *RGP's* and *RP12th's* corpus of reconciliation antiphons from three (*Asperges me domine, Exurgat deus et dissipentur*, and *Confirma hoc*) to four by dropping *Confirma hoc* and adding the antiphons *Pax huic domui* and *Domine ad te dirigatur* (from "In Reconciliation of an Altar, or Sacred Place, or Cemetery"). The *PWD* does not list these new antiphons but retains *Confirma hoc* and adds *Introibo ad altare* (see Avranche/ Mont St.-Michel's "Reconciliation of a Violated Church"). While the citation of antiphons, and thus the specificity of spatial blessings, did not increase steadily, the regional variants do show that northern authors at least opted to cite more liturgical songs in their benedictions than southerners did. That all these antiphons share the common themes of beseeching God's intervention, cleansing, and in-dwelling suggests that the variation in antiphons was largely a matter of the author's taste.

262. Kirkpatrick, *Book of Psalms*, 375 (Ps 2). This psalm was most probably composed in the last decade of the Babylonian exile and derives from the blessing of Moses (Dt 33). Roman reconciliation rituals consistently use Psalm 57, *Miserere mei, deus*, and Psalm 68, *Exurgat deus, et dissipentur*, invoking mercy and calling for God's intercession, and this list was expanded by Durandus's pontifical, which added more verses of Psalm 68 and Psalm 34, *Benedicam dominum*, and Psalm 43, *Iudica me, deus*. As the *PWD* went on to become the standard pontifical text of the later Middle Ages, the specific mention of psalms probably became more common.

power to remain potent: "God . . . hearken to us, we entreat, and grant that in future times the inviolable consecration of this place may endure, and may the entirety of the holy church which prays merit the benefits of your gift."[263] With this prayer the relics are carried back into the church, accompanied by the antiphon *Confirma hoc:* "Make firm this, God, what you have done in us through your holy temple which is in Jerusalem, hallelujah hallelujah."[264] The antiphon seeks to assuage the concern of the celebrants that this reconciliation will endure, and ties this place of worship to the temple in Jerusalem, the spatial and spiritual heart of the Christian faith. The assurance that the Christian community will honor its pact with God is offered by the singing of the verse *Narrabo nomen tuam* and a Gloria.[265] A final short blessing of the altar is spoken by the celebrant, and the reconciliation is completed.

The RP12th's reconciliation of a violated church duplicates the RGP's rite, with some small differences in the rubrics (notably the absence of relics), and the addition of three verses: "Let those who fear the Lord praise Him, let all the seed of Jacob magnify Him"; "Let every seed of Israel fear Him, since He neither spurns nor despises the prayers of the poor"; and "Let Him not turn his face from me, and when I call to Him let Him hear me."[266] There is also a ritual in the PRC of the thirteenth century. The *Reconciliatio ecclesie violate et cimeterii secundum quosdam*[267] duplicates its predecessors. The rubrics first call for the bishop to equip himself in much greater detail than in previous rites: with a pastoral staff, ornate amice, stole, cope, and simple mitre, without a maniple.[268] The opening prayer is identical to the RP12th's, although the rubrics call for the bishop to approach to the head of the altar and seat himself on a faldstool until the end of the Mass. Once this is finished, the third prayer from the RGP is spoken, and an aspersion of the church with commingled water and salt is begun, as in the RP12th, but with the specification that he begin at the altar, turn to the right part of

263. *RGP* 1:184 (*ordo* 50.9): Deus . . . exaudi nos, quaesumus, et concede, ut in posterum inviolabilis huius loci permaneat consecratio, et beneficia tui muneris universitas sanctae ecclesiae quae supplicat mereatur.

264. *CAO* 1873: Confirma hoc, Deus, quod operatus es in nobis a templo sancto tuo quod est in Jerusalem, alleluia alleluia. This antiphon was also used on the fourth Sunday of Pentecost.

265. *RGP* 1:185 (*ordo* 50.10).

266. *RP12th* 195–97, esp. 197 (*ordo* 18, esp. 18.8).

267. *PRC* 443–45 (*ordo* 26).

268. Ibid. (*ordo* 26.1).

the church, then to the left part, until he returns to the place where he began to sing the antiphon *Asperges me*. Then the whole of the psalm *Miserere mei* is said, without a Gloria, and the antiphon is repeated.[269] The psalm *Exurgat Deus et dissipentur* is said in its entirety, without a Gloria, and the antiphon is repeated again. The verses of the RP12th are sung next, with a repetition of the antiphon *Confirma hoc*. The remaining prayers are mixed with these elements to conclude the ritual.[270]

The pontifical of William Durandus contains a lengthy reconciliation designed to deal with the violation of a church and cemetery, and both the complexity of the ritual and the effort Durandus devotes to justifying his ritual reveal the importance of this form of blessing to high medieval religion. The ritual is prefaced by a discussion in which he describes the disagreement over whether the blessing and thus pollution of a church and cemetery are intimately linked. Some commentators say that

> since the consecration and the immunity of both are one and the same, when either has been polluted or violated, whether it is thought to be cursed, profaned, violated or polluted, because unity does not take division; the form of the reconciliation ought thus to be one and the same . . . and the same ought to be said concerning an unconsecrated church, since one and the same immunity is held for it and the cemetery adjoining it.[271]

Despite this claim, Durandus points out, there are differences between local customs in handling such blessing rites:

> In most places, the use is interpreted so that, the church having been violated or polluted, the adjoining cemetery of that church is understood to be violated, according to the aforesaid; but not vice versa, since the church and the consecration of it is more worthy and primary. However, in some places when a church has been violated or polluted, the cemetery is scarcely thought to have been violated or polluted.[272]

269. Ibid. (*ordo* 26.1–4).
270. Ibid. (*ordo* 26.5–9).
271. *PWD* 511 (*ordo* 2.6.1): Unde, cum una et eadem utriusque sit consecratio et emunitas, altero eorum violato vel polluto, utrumque execratum, prophanatum, violatum vel pollutum esse censetur, quia unitas divisionem non capit; ideoque una et eadem esse debet forma reconcilliationis utriusque . . . Idemque dicendum est in ecclesia non consecrata, cum eius et cimiterii ei coherentis una et eadem emunitas habeatur.
272. Ibid.: In plerisque locis usus interpretatur ut, ecclesia violata vel polluta, cimiterium illi coherens violatum vel pollutum esse, iuxta premissa, intelligatur; sed non e converso, cum

This discussion of ritual reconciliation is important in its highlighting of the power that differences in region and custom could exercise over the understanding of blessings and their necessity.

Durandus's rite of reconciliation is an adaptation and expansion of the Roman pontificals' traditional rite. Much of this blessing is similar to the blessing of a cemetery provided by Durandus, with the bishop taking up a central position facing east on a faldstool placed over a small carpet, perhaps as a symbolic shield placed between the celebrant and the polluted earth.[273] A rubric provides for the placement of two vases of water, one in the southern quarter of the cemetery and the other in the southern part of the church, in the presbytery, to be used in combination with the wine, salt, and ashes we saw first in the reconciliation from the RGP.[274] The bishop is to be vested formally in an ornate mantle, surplice, stole, cope, and white miter without a maniple.[275] He then blesses the water, and there follows the antiphon *Asperges me* with the antiphonal psalm *Miserere mei, deus,* as the bishop makes an exterior circuit and sprinkles the water, with special attention to the contaminated spot.[276] The *Omnipotens et misericors deus qui sacerdotibus* prayer from the PRC is then said, followed by the short prayer *Aufer a nobis, domine* from the PRC, beseeching God to purify the participants of sin "so that we might merit to come with pure minds to the place about to be purified by your holy name."[277] This prayer seeks a sympathetic resonance between the participants and the goal of the ritual, a resonance enhanced by a passionate original prayer addressed to the divine in human guise:

---

ecclesia et eius consecratio dignior sit et principalis. Alicubi vero, ecclesia violata vel polluta, cimiterium violatum vel pollutum minime reputatur.

273. Ibid. (*ordo* 2.6.3): Paratis namque que ad hoc necessaria sunt, videlicet parato faldistorio super tapetum in medio cimiterii. This reinforces the texts of prayers that express concern over the purity of the agents or celebrants of blessings, albeit here in a physical rather than a spiritual sense.

274. Ibid. paratis etiam duobus vasis cum aqua, uno ibi et alio infra ecclesiam in presbiterio, provisio etiam quod ecclesia possit libere.

275. Ibid. Elements of this and the following portions of Durandus's rite are drawn from the *PRC*'s adaptation of the *RP12th* and the *RGP*.

276. Ibid. (*ordo* 2.6.4): aspergit cum ipsa aqua in circuitu deforis ecclesiam et totum cimiterium et specialiter loca contaminata, quando cimiterium est principaliter violatum seu pollutum.

277. Ibid. (*ordo* 2.6.5–6): ut ad loca tuo sancto nomini purificanda puris mereamur mentibus accedere. For the first prayer, see *PRC ordo* 26.1.

Holy Lord, who wished the potter's field to be bought with your blood price as
a burial place for pilgrims, we piously entreat, recall most clemently this your
ministry. You are truly our potter, Lord, you the field of our repose; you are
and you gave and you received the price of this field, from the ransom and in
the price of your life's blood you gave to us to be at rest; you, therefore, Lord,
who are the most merciful forgiver of our offenses, the most expectant judge,
one who shows the most abundant compassion in your judgments, hiding the
judgment of your just severity, after the kindness of your merciful redemption,
be present as the one who listens graciously to a prayer.[278]

Durandus emphasizes the two most relevant qualities of the divine in this
situation, judgment and mercy: judgment, in that this ritual occurs because
of an offense condemnable in both the eyes of humanity and God, and mercy, in that it is the forgiving God who can restore the benefits of this sacred place to a community that might justifiably be seen to have forfeited
the communal right to the cemetery and church owing to the individual sin
of one member of the congregation. The image of the Christian as a vessel
shaped by a divine potter serves to acknowledge the dependence of the human world on the divine, affirming the agreement negotiated in the initial
blessing of this violated place, as it reminds the participants in the ritual of
their proper place in the cosmos.

The image of the medieval Christian as a wanderer and traveler is further elaborated in the succeeding passages of this prayer. The cemetery is
described as

the mausoleum of your pilgrims desiring the dwelling place of the heavenly fa-
therland, do not diminish but glorify, purify, reconcile and revive both the bodies of the buried and of those who should be buried through the power and
the compassion of the resurrection to the glory of incorruptibility.[279]

278. *PWD* 512–13 (*ordo* 2.6.7): Domine pie, qui agrum figuli pretio sanguinis tui in sep-
ulturam peregrinorum comparari voluisti, quesumus, dignanter remiscere clementissimi huius ministerii tui. Tu es enim, domine, figulus noster; tu quietis nostre ager; tu agri huius es
pretium et dedisti etiam et suscepisti; tu de pretio et in pretio tui vivifici sanguinis nos requiescere donasti; tu ergo, domine, qui es offensionis nostre clementissimus indultor, expectan-
tissimus iudicator, iudicii tui superabundantissimus miserator, iudicium tue iuste severitatis,
abscondens, post miserationem tue pie redemptionis, adesto exauditor.

279. Ibid.: mausoleum peregrinorum tuorum celestis patrie incolatum expectantium, pu-
rifica et reconcilia, et hic tumulatorum et tumulandorum corpora de potentia et pietate resurrectionis ad gloriam incorruptionis non dampnans sed glorificans resuscita.

Infused with the power of the divine, with grace and majesty, the purified cemetery can once again fulfill its purpose as a static hierophany, a gateway for the righteous dead seeking the reward promised them by their faith.

The ritual then continues with short prayers, the bishop making the sign of the cross above the church and the cemetery, accompanied by a litany, the prayer *Deus qui peccata veteris hereditarium mortem,* from the PRC's ritual, and then blessing the water in the presbytry.[280] The verse *Ut obsequium servitutis nostre* is sung, and a tripartite prayer with the sign of the cross is made upon the church and altar, "So that you might deign to purge and reconcile this altar and cemetery and church," and reiterated, "So that you might deign to purge, reconcile, and sanctify this church and altar and cemetery."[281] The holy water is then sprinkled inside the church as the bishop and choir intone the antiphon *Exsurgat deus et dissipentur* and the entire psalm *In ecclesiis benedicite domine deo* (Bless God in the congregations, even the Lord, from the fountain of Israel), without a Gloria, is sung, followed by a repetition of the antiphon.[282] Again, this antiphon employs the promise of future victories of the divine as a means to assure such triumphs in this particular reconciliation. The psalm from which this verse is drawn deals with the march of God to victory, tracing the history of Israel and looking forward to the triumph of God over all the nations of the earth. In this context history and prophecy serve to reinforce the validity of the reconciliation, placing it within the framework of the sacred history of the world's redemption.[283] All parts of the church are covered in this aspersion, as in the Roman pontifical tradition, the walls receiving two aspersions (perhaps owing to their importance as barriers to the evils of the profane world outside), while the floor receives a single and final aspersion.[284]

The celebrants next turn their attention to the altar, speaking the prayers of the PRC, *Deum indultorum criminum, Deum sordium mundatorum,* and *Cuius immensa bonitas ut non habuit principium,* and then ascending to the altar accompanied by the antiphon *Introibo ad altare:* "I will go to the altar of God, to

280. Ibid., 513–14 (*ordos* 2.6.8–10).

281. Ibid., 513 (*ordo* 2.6.8): Ut hanc ecclesiam et altare hoc ac cimiterium purgare ac reconciliare digneris. . . . Ut hanc ecclesiam et altare hoc ac cimiterium purgare, reconciliare ac sanctificare digneris.

282. Ibid., 514 (*ordo* 2.6.11).

283. Kirkpatrick, *Book of Psalms,* 375 (Ps 68:27).

284. *PWD* 514 (*ordo* 2.6.12–13).

God my exceeding joy; and I will praise you with the harp, O God, my God," drawn from Psalm 43:4, presumably affirming the commitment to reopen the church and its altar for use through the proper offering of praise to divinity. The entire psalm *Iudica me deus,* without a Gloria, is then sung: "Judge me, O God, and plead my cause against an ungodly nation: O deliver me from the deceitful and unjust man."[285] This psalm recounts the distress of one who was unhappily and uncustomarily barred from worship in the sanctuary of the temple in Jerusalem, echoing the circumstances and emotions of a medieval congregation barred from using a defiled church.[286] More prayers and antiphons from the earlier ritual follow: *Deus qui in omni loco dominiationis tue* and *Deus, qui ecclesiam tuam de mundi finibus congreatiam* from the PRC, with modifications emphasizing the desire for the infusion of grace and mercy.[287] A Mass is then offered, for use at the bishop's discretion.[288] This Mass is of interest to our study for its collect, which expresses a clear desire to keep the channels of communication between the holy and human realms open: "God, who said 'My house shall be called a house of prayer,' may you deign to sanctify and cleanse this house contaminated with the filth of unbelievers, so that you may hearken to mercifully and kindly receive the prayers and offerings of all entreating you in this place."[289] This prayer suggests that the disorder of pollution has blocked the possibility of a benevolent reception of prayers by the divine, a possibility that must be reasserted through the blessing's invocation. With the path for prayer cleansed, the nexus of the divine and the human, the sacred and the profane, that is the church and cemetery may again perform its natural function, acting as a conduit between God and his faithful servants.

The remainder of the Mass contains an interesting selection of scriptural readings and verses that amplify the ideas developed in the earlier blessing. The epistle for this Mass is taken from the book of Revelation, 21:9–27, the vision of the New Jerusalem.[290] By selecting this scriptural passage the

---

285. Ibid., 515 (*ordo* 2.6.14–15); Ps 43:1. The two prayers are from *PRC* 2.6.3–4.

286. Kirkpatrick, *Book of Psalms,* 226.

287. *PWD* 515–16 (*ordo* 2.6.16–18). The prayers are from *PRC ordo* 2.6.7, 9.

288. *PWD* 515–16, (*ordo* 2.6.16–19).

289. Ibid., 516 (*ordo* 2.6.20): Deus, qui dixisti: "Domus mea domus orationis vocabitur," domum istam infidelium spurcitiis contaminatam mundare et significare digneris, ut omnium preces et voca hoc in loco ad te clamantium clementer exaudias et benigne suscipias.

290. Ibid. (*ordo* 2.6.21).

author draws an implicit connection between the glory of the New Jerusalem and the newly purified space of the church, the jewels and adornments of the New Jerusalem adding luster by association to the restored church, an imagined realization of the future glories of the Christian cosmos.[291] The last section of the reading lends the spiritual purity and strength of the New Jerusalem to the space of the church:

> And the city has no need of sun or moon to shine on it, for the glory of God is its light, and its lamp is the Lamb. The nations will walk by its light, and the kings of the earth will bring their glory into it. Its gates will never be shut by day—and there will be no night there. People will bring into it the glory and the honor of the nations. But nothing unclean will enter into it, nor anyone who practices abomination or falsehood, but only those who are written in the Lamb's book of life.[292]

The glory of the new city finds its reflection in the space of the reconciled church, where the peoples and rulers of the Christian community will walk and worship, a place where the darkness of night, either spiritual or worldly, will never descend. The concern for keeping the communication between God and humans open is expressed in the gates "that will never be shut by day," maintaining a constant communion between God and his people as the church maintains the connection between its congregation and the divine through its worship. Finally, this reading uses scripture, the word of God spoken through a prophet, to act as a further guard against pollution, so that neither physical pollution nor the moral failings of humanity might corrupt the space of the church again. Buttressed by the holy prophecy of scripture and the blessing that imparts its power into the fabric of the church, the power of sacred words ensures that this place of worship can once again serve as point of contact between the divine and the human, for the benefit of both parties.

The Gospel reading of this Mass is also of interest, in that it presents an image of the divine incarnate, Christ, both traveling like the celebrants and acting to save the lost. The reading is from Luke 19:1 and recounts the story of Jesus' journey through Jericho and his calling on the tax collector Zacchaeus, ending with Jesus blessing Zacchaeus, saying, "Today salvation has come to this house, because he [Zacchaeus] too is a son of Abraham. For the Son of

291. Ibid.
292. Ibid.; Rv 21:23–27.

Man came to seek out and save the lost."[293] Like the house of the tax collector, the defiled church has been entered to effect its salvation, with the celebrants mimicking the actions of Christ in the Gospel through their ritual entry.

Two last prayers in the Mass reveal the power of the blessing of space to change the internal landscape as well as the external. In the secret of the Mass, the celebrant speaks softly, "We ask, Lord, may this gift both purify this place from all uncleanness, and always and everywhere deliver to you our acceptable requests."[294] While this prayer seeks to maintain the connection of prayer we have noted above, it also implies that this blessing's power may extend outward throughout the physical world to bring the power of the divine into contact with all places. The post-Communion prayer enlarges this power to affect the material world to include the spiritual landscape of the individual believer, offering entreating prayers to God, "so that this temple and this cemetery, cleansed of the stains of the unbelieving, may remain sanctified by your blessing, and our hearts may be devoted always to you and alienated from all the filth of vices."[295] This invocation brings the blessing full circle, offering a final entreaty for the cleansing of profaned space as it offers up a sincere desire for the human congregation to receive this blessing, so that the proper relationship between the divine and the people may continue uninterrupted. The precincts of the violated church have, through the blessing, become a model for the human heart stained by sin, both places to be healed by the power of the blessing.

The reconciliation of a cemetery alone, without the reconciliation of a church, is provided for in the PWD as a shortened version of the blessing studied above.[296] While this blessing yields nothing significantly new, there is another blessing that does, a twelfth-century French blessing "In Reconciliation of the Altar, or a Sacred Place, or a Cemetery." This ritual begins with the bishop and a cleric coming before the people and church and singing the antiphon *Deus in sancto via supra* (God upon the holy way), suggesting that the author conceives of this ritual as a means to reestablish this site as an ave-

293. *PWD* 516 (*ordo* 2.6.23); Lk 19:9.
294. *PWD* 516 (*ordo* 2.6.25): Hec hostia, quesumus, domine, et locum istum ab omnibus immunditiis expurget et supplicationes nostras semper et ubique tibi redat acceptas.
295. Ibid., 517 (*ordo* 2.6.27): ut templum hoc et cimiterium, infidelium inquinamentis emundatum, tua benedictione maneat sanctificatum et pectora nostra ab omni sorde vitiorum alienata tibique devota semper existant.
296. Ibid., 517–18 (*ordo* 2.7).

nue to "the holy way" of the divine. Prayers drawn from the Roman pontifical tradition then follow, and the entrance of the bishop into the church is
appropriately accompanied by the singing of the antiphon *Pax huic domui*, establishing a cordial relationship between this holy place and the celebrant.[297]
Then comes the mingling of ashes, salt, water, and wine we have noted before,
accompanied by a blessing of the mixture that asks that through the power,
grace, and blessing of God the place might be made to endure "perpetually consecrated to invoking the name of the Lord," again reminding us of the
power attributed to the spoken name of God.[298] Many of the ceremonial acts
and prayers that follow are drawn directly from the Roman pontifical tradition, although one striking allusion is made comparing the restoration of a
sacred place by a blessing to the resurrection: "We ask, Lord, may the stain
of the former contagion harm nothing here, may there be nothing which remains polluted by the fraud of the enemy. Indeed, may the pure simplicity of
this place and the unstained whiteness of pristine innocence rise again, and
when it has received grace may it be returned to glory."[299] In language evocative of other prayers studied above, this blessing partakes of the same power
that returned Jesus from the land of the dead, and through this association it
is not only a reminder of sacred history but a re-creation of the act of resurrection itself in the present world to confirm the faith of the congregation, to
preserve inviolate the place consecrated with the power of the divine, and to
keep sacred history alive within the life of the community.

This prayer is followed by a censing of the bounds of the site, with the
singing of the antiphon *Domine ad te dirigatur* (May it be arranged for you by
the Lord), invoking the power of the *numen* to come and cleanse the tainted
site.[300] A lengthy prayer then is spoken, which again evokes the cosmological history of the Christian world to contextualize the present blessing:

> God, who dwelling in holy things formed by the guiding of supernal piety the
> pure earth of the world, which, stained also by the addition of the first violator
> cast out from the heavenly seats, you dwelt near, having pitied the primitives
> of the paradise you created, may you deign to cleanse and wipe away all conta-

297. Martène, *Antiquis Ecclesiae ritibus*, 2:286.
298. Ibid.: ac perpetualiter ad invocandum nomen domini consecratum permaneat.
299. Ibid.: Nihil hic, quesumus Domine, postmodum noceat praeteriti culpa contagii, nihil sit quod maneat inimici fraude pollutum. Resurgat vero huius loci pura simplicitas et candor innocentiae pristinae immaculatus, et dum recipit gratiam revertatur ad gloriam.
300. Ibid.

gion of transgression by means of the holy pouring forth of blood and also of your own self of old.[301]

This invocation of the first sin, the disobedience of Satan and the rebellious angels, demonstrates the power of the divine will for purification in action and serves as a paradigm for the purification of the polluted church, realizing Christian mythology and connecting the mundane blessing to the awesome power of mythic history. It reminds the congregation of the presence of the divine within any pure part of the creation, allowing the Christian community license to enjoy the fruits of the physical world while hearkening after the benefits of the spiritual life.

It is the community itself, indeed, that this blessing seeks to protect by maintaining the connection to the divine within this sacred place:

> even now may you bless with your heavenly blessing the place stained by the fault of the same transgression, so that those who under fear and love of your name shall have assembled in this oratory for seeking the pardon of their sins, or shall have been buried in this cemetery, may rejoice to seek the pardon of all sins in perpetuity.[302]

Again we see the concern for the maintenance of the proper status of the holy place, as a channel for the power of salvation that can be granted by the divine in exchange for the moral probity of the believers, whose participation and acceptance of the power of the blessing enables them to continue to fulfill their obligations to God in the hope of eternal reward. This blessing concludes with the return of the relics to the church and the singing of the verse *Sanctum est verum lumen,* and several concluding prayers found in the Franco-Roman liturgical tradition.[303]

A final word about reconciliation blessings and their use of scripture is in order here. The increase in scriptural passages in twelfth- and thirteenth-century rituals suggests that these solemn blessings had a tendency to be-

301. Ibid.: Deus qui in sanctis habitans supernae moderamine pietatis terram mundus mundam formasti, quam etiam primi praevaricatoris de supernis ejecti sedibis suggestione maculatam priscis misertus paradisi quos creasti accolis pii effusione cruoris ac proprii antiquae ab omni praevaricationis contagio mundare et abstergere dignatus es.

302. Ibid., 2:287: quamvis iam eiusdem naevo praevaricationis maculatam tua caelisti benedictione benedicas, ut qui sub timore et amore tui nominis ad hoc oratorium pro impetranda suorum venia peccatorum convenerint, vel in hoc cimitierio sepulti fuerint, se in perpetuum omnium veniam peccatorum impetrare gaudeant.

303. Ibid.

come more elaborate over time. This particular change most probably is the result of an increasing desire to make the faithful aware of some of the fundamental scriptural events, patristic theology, and canon law that the clergy wished them to accept as articles of faith (for example, original sin and the Incarnation's mitigation of it, the coming of the New Jerusalem, and the authority of priests as ministers of sacraments).[304] This desire would have been felt as an especially urgent need in the face of heretical movements arising in the twelfth and thirteenth centuries, notably the Cathars of southern France and northern Italy, which attacked core orthodox belief in the Incarnation, the resurrection of the body, the authority of priests, and the validity of the sacraments.[305] That a concern for the power of priests and the validity of sacraments first appears in a twelfth-century ritual, the origin point of both the new sacramental theology and the new heresies of the high Middle Ages, and that it is reiterated in a Roman and southern French pontifical of the thirteenth century, strongly suggests that this change in reconciliation blessings was a direct response to the theological and devotional ferment of twelfth- and thirteenth-century Christianity. Quotation of scripture in blessings, then, was not mere decoration or recollection but an active force used to affirm doctrine and reinforce the faith.

This chapter has also described some of the central elements of the blessings' piety: belief in the adaptability of the sacred; anxiety about God's consistent benevolence; participation of the divine at all levels of community life, external and internal; the ritual "reminding" of divinity and the natural world of its obligations to the Christian community; blessings' role as injectors of meaning into a seemingly chaotic natural world; the use of scripture to connect the present world to the numinous sacred history of Christianity; the use of object, word, and gesture to create sacred space; the positive view of the natural world and humanity's connection to it; and the power of blessings to keep alive the memory of God's role in the creation of the living world. With these elements in mind, we may now turn to an examination of rituals that focused on blessing the lay individuals and communities who made use of sacred power to heal, exalt, and protect themselves.

304. The authority of priests is stressed particularly in *RP12th ordo* 18.1; PRC *ordo* 26.1; and *PWD ordo* 2.6.5.

305. Wakefield and Evans, *Heresies of the High Middle Ages*, 26–40, 189–242; "Cathari (or Cathars)," E. A. Livingstone, ed., *Oxford Dictionary of the Christian Church*, 3d ed. (Oxford: Oxford University Press, 1997), 301.

Chapter 3

SACRED PERSONS   *Blessing the Laity*

SACRED PEOPLE: A BRIEF SURVEY

The civilization of the Latin West during the Middle Ages understood sacred qualities and power to pass to individuals primarily through ritualized formulas of ordination and consecration. These rituals were performed by individuals placed high within the hierarchy of the church, who imparted the grace and sacrality they themselves had acquired through apostolic and priestly succession dating back to the beginning times of the church.[1] The earliest rituals of ordination and consecration of persons were kept in separate *libelli*, the first collection of which is the *Sacramentarium veronense,* or Leonine sacramentary. Ordination prayers for the clergy are found within this and later sacramentaries, often with instructional rubrics, as well as in the thirty-forth, thirty-fifth, and thirty-sixth *Ordines romani* of Andrieu's edition.[2]

---

1. The Middle Ages saw little difference between ordination and consecration, and when an individual sought to enter the clergy he was thought to enter simultaneously into both orders and a specific order, the definitions of which were the subject of constant debate. In general, holy orders were considered to be a special status conferred on a member of the clergy, while the specific order entered into was an individual grade or status within the clergy. For a survey of the liturgical rituals employed, see Roger Reynolds, "Ordination, Clerical," *DMA* 9:263–69.

2. These rituals were later included in the newly devised pontificals for the use of bishops, who performed these rites on certain days deemed, since the early years of the church, most appropriate for ordination. Such ceremonies were held in the chief basilicas of a city or town, preferably at the bishop's cathedral, where ordinands were examined by the bishop and accepted or rejected (at least in the *RGP*) at the will of the congregation (ibid., 263–64). Bad behavior could disqualify a candidate from office, and even (within monastic communities) exclude the offender from receiving any blessings. See *Rule of St. Benedict,* chap. 25.

At the heart of these Latin rituals were the prayers and the benedictions spoken by the bishop. Blessings were spoken over both the ordinands and their instruments of office, which acted both as symbols of their new status and obligations and as a focus for the power and authority with which they were entrusted.[3] While these elements are characteristic of the consecration of clergy and have been much studied, similar ritual elements manifest themselves in blessings of the laity that have received less attention.[4] During the high Middle Ages, the church made a concerted effort to extend participation in holy activities and vocations to a laity growing dissatisfied with their secondary role in the worship of the church. In particular, rituals were developed to distinguish the occupation of pilgrim, crusader, and knight from mundane professions, rituals that marked the persons and created sacred insignia for their profession in much the same way that older ordination rituals conferred sacred status on the clergy.[5] It is these rituals, partaking in the character of ecclesiastical ordinations but set apart from the institutional hierarchy of the church, that interest me for what they can reveal about the popular medieval understanding of the blessing and its uses. Together with blessings for individuals fallen prey to illness and travail, these rituals are the subject of this chapter.

PILGRIMS, TRAVELERS, AND WAYFARERS

The words of blessing spoken over expectant pilgrims in the votive masses and rites of the late medieval liturgy served a dual transformational purpose. As an act that essentially restored God's creation to its former goodness, blessings hallowed the person of the pilgrim, beseeching inter-

3. Reynolds, "Ordination, Clerical," 266. The *traditio instrumentorum,* a solemn handing over of the instruments, was an important part of these rites, as were the gestures of the participants.

4. Baptism, marriage, and death rituals fit this category, but their association with the formal sacraments makes them unsuitable for this study. I focus instead on three types of blessings: for pilgrims, for knights, and for health. Portions of the first section of this chapter have appeared in Derek A. Rivard, "*Pro iter agentibus:* The Ritual Blessings of Pilgrims and Their Insignia in a Pontifical of Southern Italy," *Journal of Medieval History* 27 (2001): 365–98.

5. This may be seen in the rise not only of these rituals but also of lay penitential groups, a common feature of twelfth- and thirteenth-century cities, especially Italian communes. Such penitential groups are of interest here because some adopted a simple blessing, much less complex than the blessing of a monk's habit, for their own simple "habit" worn during their public and private life in the commune. See Thompson, *Cities of God,* 84, 102.

cession from divine powers and instilling in the pilgrim's mind remembrance of the duty to fulfill the dictum of St. Jerome to become an itinerant monk on the road to spiritual reformation. These rites also bestowed upon the pilgrimage unique items, "marking insignia," the possession of which separated the pilgrim from mundane society: by carrying the staff and scrip of the pious wayfarer, the pilgrim was protected and designated as a member of a special order of Christians bound for immediate contact with the sacred. Blessings were thus used to transform ordinary moments of sensible life into contact with the divine, to turn common items into things holy. Understanding their content—for example, the prayers and psalms of pilgrimage rites—can therefore enable modern scholars to understand what medieval piety sought from God, what it expected to experience in its search for this communion, and how it placed its own experiences within the framework of the sacred stories that structured its history. The traveling gear was invested with the power of the sacred through liturgical rituals that associated these items with the deeds of scripture and thus summoned the protection of God for the pilgrim, a helpless traveler in strange lands. By means of the liturgical rite, which formally separated the pilgrim from the local community, the church could retain spiritual control over the unique camaraderie and bonding that existed beyond the borders of the parish: its genesis and dissolution were channeled through the church's language of piety, and thus expressed in an approved fashion the feelings of freedom and community whose free expression might otherwise have threatened the medieval social order.

Medievalists have paid little attention to the category of pilgrimage blessings. I have therefore sought new understandings of this liturgy within the context of anthropological research on the common culture of the religious wanderer.[6] Anthropologists have described pilgrimage as a phenomenon with its own culture, one that crosses religious boundaries to produce

---

6. The work of Victor Turner remains seminal in the historical anthropology of pilgrimage; see especially Victor Turner and Edith Turner, "Pilgrimage as Social Process," in their *Image and Pilgrimage in Christian Culture: Anthropological Perspectives* (New York: Columbia University Press, 1978), 94–120; Victor Turner, "The Center Out There: Pilgrim's Goal," *History of Religions* 12, no. 3 (1973): 32–54; and Victor Turner, *The Ritual Process: Structure and Anti-Structure* (Chicago: Aldine, 1969). For crucial concepts of historical anthropology, see also Arnold van Gennep, *The Rites of Passage*, trans. Monika B. Vizedom and Gabrielle L. Caffee (Chicago: University of Chicago Press, 1960).

a common set of practices focused around two conceptual frameworks: liminality and the state of *communitas*.[7] Such frameworks rest upon a bipolar definition of pilgrimage: "daily, relatively sedentary life in a village, town, city, and fields is lived at one pole; the rare bout of nomadism that is pilgrimage over many roads and hills constitutes the other pole."[8] Medieval Christian theology contributes a sacred-profane dichotomy to this bipolarity. The sacred and profane worlds were considered essentially incompatible; passage between them required an intermediate stage, a liminal state, in which social and religious boundaries were formally crossed. These are what Van Gennep's pioneering work has termed "rites of passage" and what I perceive as the fundamental nature of the rites for blessing pilgrims.[9] In the case of pilgrimage, the pilgrims become involved in the process by segregating themselves from their community through participation in rituals of blessing, journeying to a shrine, returning, and being welcomed back into their home. While thus segregated from their community, the pilgrims partake of a unique form of society of equals, which Victor Turner has termed "social anti-structure," or *communitas*.[10] *Communitas* is a form of social bonding that combines qualities of lowliness, sacredness, homogeneity, and comradeship; it arises spontaneously in all types of groups separated from traditional society; and as the camaraderie it creates often dissolves the governing norms of society instilled in its participants, it is often seen as both holy and threatening to traditional society.[11]

Pilgrims take part in *communitas* when they receive the blessed items of the "order" of pilgrims, coming together with others of similar intent who would otherwise never have united: peasant and baron, bishop and vicar, artisan and aristocrat all carried the staff and scrip, walked the roads, and met in shrines from Compostela to Canterbury, Jerusalem to Rome. William Melczer has noted the perceived existence of a "community of pilgrims" in the documentation of the Compostela pilgrimage, a trait of *communitas* that consistently reappears in the warm companionship described in the travel diaries of

7. For a case study of the latter phenomenon, see John M. Theilman, "Communitas among Fifteenth-Century Pilgrims," *Reflexions Historiques* 311 (1984): 253–70.

8. Turner and Turner, "Pilgrimage as Social Process," 171.

9. Van Gennep, *Rites of Passage*, 1.

10. Turner and Turner, "Pilgrimage as Social Process," 169–70.

11. Theilman, "Communitas among Fifteenth-Century Pilgrims," 255. For a fuller discussion of Turner's work and theory, see the Introduction.

medieval pilgrims.[12] Although medievalists have noted some difficulties with employing this anthropological model to explain the historical past, it seems clear that the liminality-*communitas* paradigm still has great utility in understanding the benedictional rites contained in the rituals examined here.[13] The rites served as a solemn ritual of initiation and separation from mundane society, propelling the pilgrim by the power of invocation and scriptural association into a special order of pious wayfarers, singled out by their distinctive dress and accoutrements. In this liminal state, the pilgrims progressed toward their spiritual goal, armed with the sanctified symbols provided them by the priest of their community, side by side in a pilgrim band, with a cross-section of the rigidly stratified medieval social hierarchy.

12. William Melczer, *The Pilgrim's Guide to Santiago de Compostela* (New York: Italica Press, 1993), 35–38.

13. As Theilman has pointed out, while transition (or marginality) is clearly evident in pilgrimages, separation and reintegration can be difficult to observe. The possibility of multiple pilgrimages also calls into question van Gennep's insistence on rites of passage as a once-in-a-lifetime experience, and contemporary texts clearly that indicate medieval pilgrims, unlike their modern counterparts, did not submerge their social identity ("Communitas among Fifteenth-Century Pilgrims," 254, 264). Such criticisms have some validity, but they ignore the importance of the liturgical rites for the blessings of pilgrimage. Later medieval pilgrims began their journey with a solemn, ritualized, and public ceremony, traits that are fundamental to van Gennep's conception of the rites of passage. Separation is thus achieved through the device of a liturgical rite, but what of reintegration? Medieval ecclesiastics also developed a formula for the community's reception of returning pilgrims, and it clearly is of the same fundamental nature as the benedictional rites for departing pilgrims. The criticism of medieval pilgrims' retention of social rank does seem to conflict with a strict interpretation of *communitas*, but in this case it is worthwhile to remember the Turners' disclaimer: "While the pilgrimage system does not eliminate structural divisions; it attenuates them, removes their sting" ("Pilgrimage as Social Process," 205). Although pilgrims may strive for pure *communitas*, they are ultimately bound by social mores: even camaraderie has its limits when pilgrims must travel through lands accustomed to traditional forms of social heirarchy (171). The criticism of the repetitive nature of medieval pilgrimage has the most validity; it warns against too readily adopting the theory of other disciplines to explain the complexity of the past. But again, the warning of the Turners must be heeded: "*Communitas* itself in time becomes structure-bound and comes to be regarded as a symbol or remote possibility rather than as a concrete realization of universal relatedness" (206). Can the repetitive nature of pilgrimage have derived from the church's liturgical efforts to structure pilgrim *communitas* in order to channel and control the piety of the teeming masses of pious travelers flooding the roads of the later Middle Ages? Possibly, but without a contemporary commentary on the topic of pilgrim benedictions, we may never gain an adequate understanding of the church liturgy's impact on the *communitas* of medieval pilgrims.

Pilgrimage, travel as an expression of piety, traces its early origins in the Christian West back to the time of the imperial Roman era.[14] As scriptural notions filtered into the *mentalité* of the early church, the empire's repression of Christians heightened the conception of pilgrimage as a crucial element of Christian life.[15] As outsiders and outcasts, early Christians enacted devotional journeys to the sites of Christ's life in Palestine in the second and third centuries, despite the official hostility of imperial authorities. Such journeys sought to mirror the *via crucis* by reenacting the events of Christ's life through meditation and prayer upon the holy soil of Palestine. By the close of the third century, this form of pilgrimage to Jerusalem and other holy locales was an established Christian practice.[16]

With Constantine's official sanction of Christianity, pilgrimage was transformed throughout the Roman world. Jerusalem and Rome had many shrines honoring the graves of martyrs and apostles, sites that were ideal for the veneration of these saints because they held their earthly remains. Contact with such remains, whose sacred character was held to consecrate the immediate environment in which they lay, became the "brightest hope" of late antique Christians for an immediate end to physical, mental, or spiritual suffering.[17] The pursuit of these contacts with the sacred dominated expressions of pilgrims' piety throughout the patristic and medieval eras, playing a crucial role in the development of the later medieval cult of the saints.

---

14. For a full introduction to the origins of pilgrimage, see Jonathan Sumption, *Pilgrimage: An Image of Medieval Religion* (London: Faber and Faber, 1975), 11–21, 89–97. Christian pilgrimage joined Hellenic ideas of exile, expressed in classical works of mythology such as Homer's *Odyssey* and the legends of Orpheus, to Hebraic ideas of the "holy traveler" or pilgrim. See Julia B. Holloway, "The Pilgrim in the Poem: Dante, Langland, and Chaucer," in *Allegoresis: The Craft of Allegory in the Middle Ages*, ed. J. S. Russell (New York: Garland Publishing, 1988), 1. Scripture is replete with images of pilgrimage: in Exodus, the wandering of the Israelites in the desert; in the book of Tobit, the journeys of Tobit; in the Gospels, the tale of Jesus at the Inn of Emmaus. Indeed, the entire life of Christ would come to be seen in the medieval era as a recapitulation of the pilgrimage of Israel, as a sign of Jesus' role as the suffering servant. See C. K. Zacher, *Curiosity and Pilgrimage: The Literature of Discovery in Fourteenth-Century England* (Baltimore: Johns Hopkins University Press, 1976), 45.

15. Sumption, *Pilgrimage*, 11–21. The empire's view of non-Roman citizens as *peregrini*, rootless outsiders, was gladly adopted by the early church, which took onto its persecuted shoulders the mantle of the outcast and the despised traveler who shunned the ways of a wicked world.

16. Richard Barber, *Pilgrimages* (Woodbridge, UK: Boydell Press, 1991), 14.

17. Melczer, *Pilgrim's Guide to Santiago de Compostela*, 1–2.

The expansion of pilgrimage in Christian life provoked numerous responses from the fathers of the church, responses that colored medieval notions of this institution. Augustine of Hippo's works convey the importance of pilgrimage in medieval thought: images of travel and of "losing the way" dominate the *Confessions;* the archetype of humanity as the prodigal, the Christian as a member of a pilgrimage community, and the concept of human beings driven to pilgrimage by an inner need for truth dominate the *Civitas Dei.*[18] For prescriptive practice, however, Jerome had the greatest impact on medieval pilgrimage. To Jerome, the pilgrim was no mere vulgar tourist but a monk whose manner of life was far more important than the journey through it.[19] Through Jerome's influence, pilgrimage was incorporated into the church's tradition of spiritual reformation as a means of a renunciation of the world and its values, making pilgrimage a truly spiritual venture. The emphasis on the moral reformation of those who set out on a pilgrimage characterized ecclesiastical thought on the subject until the Reformation, and indeed led to the full development in the high Middle Ages of the penitential pilgrimage, a journey imposed upon lay persons by their confessors as a means of atoning for past sins.[20] Although many pilgrims surely set out with such pious motives, seeking through physical hardship to achieve a sort of second baptism, there must have been a great multitude who took to the roads for more mundane reasons: curiosity, dissatisfaction, hunger for adventure, or criminal motives.[21]

18. Paul G. Kuntz, "Augustine: From Homo Erro to Homo Viator," in *Itinerarium: The Idea of Journey,* ed. L. Bowman (Salzburg: Institut für Anglisitik und Amerikanistik, Universität Salzburg, 1983), 30–41. Concepts of *via, viator,* and *peregrini* were crucial to medieval life and thought. See Gerhart B. Ladner, "Homo Viator: Medieval Ideas of Alienation and Order," *Speculum* 17 (1967): 233.

19. Sumption, *Pilgrimage,* 95.

20. Ibid., 98–113. For the influence of the idea of pilgrimage as moral reform in preaching, see ibid., 125. Recent scholarship has suggested that the idea of pilgrimage as a penitential punishment may have developed as a result of sophisticated thought about the uses of space in punishment in early monastic movements, and have speculated that the spatial distance traversed during the pilgrimage was fitted to the level of rehabilitation desired. See Valerie J. Flint, "Space and Discipline in Early Medieval Europe," in Hanawalt and Kobialka, *Medieval Practices of Space,* 150, 161.

21. Sumption, *Pilgrimage,* 114. For a discussion of alternative motives to pilgrimage, see Zacher, *Curiosity and Pilgrimage;* Giles Constable, "Opposition to Pilgrimage in the Middle Ages," *Studia Gratiana* 19 (1976): 125–46; and John M. Theilman, "Medieval Pilgrims and the Origins of Tourism," *Journal of Popular Culture* 20, no. 4 (1986): 93–102.

But there is no doubt that an important motivation for pilgrimage in the medieval era was the hope for a miracle by venerating the relics of a particular saint. Physical movement toward the holy place of a saint's relics, the site of a theophany, was thought to be a movement toward heaven, at once a quest beyond oneself and a transformation within oneself.[22] By means of such a journey and the devoted supplications offered up at the saint's shrine, medieval Christians sought by the intercession of the holy dead to achieve supernatural relief from worldly woes. An arduous journey and veneration of the saint's relics were undertaken in order to establish a patron-client relationship between the saint and the supplicant, by means of which pilgrims would receive the grace of the saint and be healed of their afflictions.[23]

While such devotion to the powers of saints had existed throughout the entire medieval period, its importance exploded in the eleventh through thirteenth centuries, a period characterized as the "golden age of pilgrimage."[24] With the opening of the overland route to Jerusalem in the late tenth century, and the decline of the Ummayad caliphate of Cordoba, the roads to the great shrines of Christianity were once again safe to travel. As Jonathan Sumption has argued, millenarian concerns and monastic renewal (especially the movement of Cluniac reform) in the eleventh century emphasized to the laity the need for remission of sins, and the laity responded enthusiastically to the call to attend upon shrines; a new devotion to the humanity of the crucified Christ in the twelfth century inspired medieval Christians to walk once again the earth where the physical Christ had trod.[25] According to Sumption, pilgrims wished "to tear down the barrier of remoteness that separated a man of the twelfth century from the events of the first . . . they wished to enter the mind and body of the crucified Christ, and take on Christ's sufferings in their persons."[26] While this interpretation is but one among many drawn by scholars of pilgrimage, it is nevertheless the most

22. Leonard J. Bowman, "Itinerarium: The Shape of the Metaphor," in Bowman, *Itinerarium*, 6.

23. For a full discussion of this patron-client relationship, see Thomas Head, "I Vow Myself to Be Your Servant: An Eleventh-Century Pilgrim, His Chronicler and His Saint," *Historical Reflections* 11, no. 3 (1984): 215–30. Alternatively, in the later Middle Ages, a miracle often preceded a pilgrimage, making the journey an offering of thanks rather than a supplication (for discussion of this phenomenon, see Sumption, *Pilgrimage*, 257–288).

24. Sumption, *Pilgrimage*, 115.

25. Ibid., 118–35. For a discussion of the importance of Cluny to the growth of pilgrimage, see J. Houser, "Pilgrimage," *DMA* 9:654–61.

26. Sumption, *Pilgrimage*, 94.

plausible. A difficult journey to the holy land, or to a nearer holy locale of a more personal saint, could provide ample opportunity for the pilgrim to experience the earthly suffering, despair, redemption, and triumph associated with the Crucifixion in a survivable undertaking that would leave pilgrims closer to the divine when their normal life resumed.

The enthusiasm for pilgrimage was also encouraged by the initial successes of the military Crusades first called by Urban II in 1095. While the conquest and dispersal of Islamic power around the holy sites of Palestine opened the region for safe journey by Christians, the development of indulgences spurred on by Urban II in the late eleventh century inspired both militant and pacific pilgrims to take up the cross and earn salvation through travel to the holy land.[27] In addition to this, the immense popularity of the Crusades and the concomitant social difficulties caused by absent pilgrims prompted extensive legal proscriptions to protect pilgrims' property and establish for them a unique status and garb.

Accompanying the socio-legal developments was the evolution of sophisticated liturgical rites for the blessing of the pilgrims and their marking insignia. Although a Mass for the blessing of pilgrims and travelers was composed as early as the eighth century, a particular rite for the blessing of a pilgrim's traveling garb, a *baculus* (staff) and *pera* (wallet), does not appear until the eleventh century.[28] The blessing conferred on the departing crusaders in 1099 seems to have spurred on the sophistication of pilgrim benedictions.[29] Such novel rites formed a part of the Church's eleventh- and twelfth-century efforts to stimulate lay piety by assigning special status to a layperson who performed certain spiritual functions: the dubbing of a knight is the most familiar of the new ceremonies, and the presentation of the pilgrim's staff bears many resemblances to the presentation of a knight's martial gear. Thus the specialized "marking insignia" of the pilgrim announced to the world

27. Houser, "Pilgrimage," 657.

28. See Franz, 2:271–87. Staves themselves, if associated with holy people, could themselves be bearers of power, as can be seen in the Welsh poem "Padarn's Staff": "May his staff, bright and much loved, offer protection, / Its holy power reaching three parts of the world, / No other relic is like Cyrwen [the staff], / A wonderful gift was Padarn's staff" (Davies, *Celtic Spirituality*, 267).

29. Sumption, *Pilgrimage*, 172. For a description of the development of the rite for taking the cross of crusade, see John A. Brundage, "Cruce signari: The Rite for Taking the Sign of the Cross in England," *Traditio* 22 (1966): 289–310. Brundage edited several Anglo-Norman pontificals in this article, and I have used his transcriptions in the discussion of parallel texts that follows this section.

that he was on a journey not only through this world but also out of it, away from the mundane into the spiritual.[30]

In the case of pilgrimage blessings, which provide a rich source for the study of blessings both in terms of their sheer numbers and in their diverse and copious use of scriptural references, we will confine ourselves to examining a series of short prayers composed for the blessing of travelers and pilgrims in the centuries before and after the high medieval explosion of pilgrimage and its attendant blessings.[31]

Since the early Middle Ages, the Latin church had met the needs of the traveler with votive masses, particularly masses *ad proficiscendum in itinere.* The Gelasian sacramentary has such a ritual, and Benedict of Aniane's supplement to the Gregorian sacramentary also has a Mass *Pro iter agentibus* and *Pro navigantibus.*[32] Prayers outside of the Mass that were common for travelers vary in both form and content from the former, but all such prayers were built upon the foundations of the prayers of the Gelasian and Gregorian sacramentaries.[33] The earliest blessing of interest for our purposes is a

30. Barber, *Pilgrimages,* 154. Lay efforts at ensuring a felicitous end to a journey can be seen in the French poem "La paternostre saint Julien," a prayer spoken by pilgrims and travelers in hopes of receiving hospitality on the journey. See Paul Meyer, "De l'alliteration en roman de France," *Romania* 2 (1882): 577, quoted in Camille, "Signs of the City," 8.

31. For a treatment of longer rituals and prayers for pilgrims, their equipment, and their journey, see Rivard, *"Pro iter agentibus."*

32. Franz, 2:262–63. The Gelasian's prayers are in book 3, 24–25, consisting of a ritual with three collects, a secret, two prayers *infra actionem,* and two post-Communion services. They also contain two oratios *pro iter agentibus* characteristic of this genre of blessing. Some of these prayers reappear in the Bobbio missal. Benedict of Aniane's ritual borrowed all of its prayers up to the post-Communion from the Gelasian.

33. Ibid. Travel blessings performed privately differed greatly from solemn liturgical blessings, although they still maintained a connection to the liturgical forms. One example Franz gives of such blessings are the *itineraria* prayers of priests and monks, in which the cult of the three magi figured heavily from the twelfth century onward in German blessings, especially since the translation of their relics to Cologne by Archbishop Rainald of Dassel in 1164 (ibid., 2:266–67); for an example of their presence, see the twelfth-century prayerbook of Elisabeth of Schönau. This cult was first confessed by St. Caesarius of Arles (d. 542), and the three kings' names occur (with great variation in spelling) in liturgical texts from the eighth century onward, finally reaching a stable form in the names Kaspar, Melchior, and Balthasar. Their efficacy as patrons of travelers was attested to by Johannes of Hildesheim's *Historia trium regum* (c. 1370), which reported that after their death God granted many miracles in their name for travelers (2:267). German vernacular travel blessings sought protection agains itemized dangers facing the traveler and eventually developed from simple forms into extremely lengthy "Tobias blessings," which both ennumerated more dangers and added more biblical

"Blessing for Those Making a Journey," found in the tenth-century benedictional of Archbishop Robert of Jumièges.[34] This early blessing manifests an element universal among the blessings of travelers, the invocation of the angels as protectors and defenders. The second clause of this ritual reads: "Perpetually may you merit to have as a companion the college of angels . . . fortified by the consolation of which may you pass unharmed in coming and going along the ways of narrow paths."[35] We have already noted how since patristic times the angels were considered to be the special agents of protection for individuals and communities. St. Basil especially promoted the belief in a guardian angel who protects us in the voyage of this life: "We pray to God who is well disposed toward men in order that he might give us a companion to protect us."[36] Angels were considered the "chosen activators" of God's will and thus played the most prominent role of all created beings in God's dealings with the supernatural forces of the world.[37] Their protection was actively sought by those encountering the perils of foreign lands and

allusions. Some of these German blessings include incidents from the life of Christ and elements of Christianity that were found in Latin and German blessings against sickness but were not present in the Latin travel blessings (2:269). The German formulas later expanded to include prayers against enemies and the weapons of enemies, and for the success and potency of the traveler's weapons. These occasionally call for worship or masses but more often include superstititious customs (such as the use of "letters of safe conduct" written by Irish saints, Pope Leo III to Charlemagne, and others), which were ineffectually condemned by strict moral theologians. The most popular saints in these texts were St. Gertrud of Nivelles (a particular patron of ships at sea) and St. Julian Hospitator, as well as others better known from Latin blessings (2:270–71).

34. *CB* no. 1543. The manuscript is Rouen, Bibl. Munic. 369 (Y 37); see also H. A. Wilson, ed., *The Benedictional of Archbishop Robert,* Henry Bradshaw Society 24 (London: Henry Bradshaw Society, 1903). Franz also notes that the *praefatio* of the missal of Jumièges is the first to specifically catalogue the dangers faced by the traveler (Franz, 2:262–63).

35. *CB* no. 1543b: Angelorum iugiter collegium habere mereamini comitem . . . quorum solatio muniti, eundo et redeundo semitarum vestigia transeatis illaesi.

36. St. Basil, *Epistles,* 1:11, quoted in Daniélou, *Angels and Their Mission,* 74.

37. Flint, *Rise of Magic,* 167. See also St. Augustine's writings and Rabanus's *Commentaria in Exodum* 1:13 (*PL* 108:33) and *De magicis artibus* (*PL* 110:1099). The early tradition of guardian angels posited that each soul had an angel and a demon within it, as exemplified by the Gregory of Nyssa: "After our nature had fallen in sin, we were not abandoned in our fall by God, but an angel, one of the beings who have an incorporeal nature, was set up to aid the life of each of us. The destroyer of our nature, in his turn, did just the same by sending us an evil, pernicious angel to the detriment of human nature. It now depends upon man . . . to make the one triumph over the other." Gregory of Nyssa, *De vita Moysis, PG* 44:337D–340A, quoted in Daniélou, *Angels and Their Mission,* 81.

strange peoples. While such invocations could remain general, they were often directed to a particularly appropriate agent of divine will, the Archangel
Raphael: "May Raphael, the great protector and guide of Tobias, be with you,
so that you might avoid diabolical and human craftiness, and might merit to
have as companion Christ of the way, the truth and the life."[38] Raphael, who
accompanied the Old Testament traveler Tobias, is called upon to reenact
his role as the shield of the traveler, lending the certainty and power of this
historical paradigm to the present supplicant.

The invocation of divine power and the sacred past is continued in this
blessing's structuring of the traveler's experience through scriptural allusion.
The third clause begins: "As you would test the path of this age together, so
may you both shun the charms of Egypt, and also through the road of justice
arrive at the imperishable reward of happiness."[39] The paradigm of Egypt, a
land familiar to medieval Christians as heathen country and the historical
land of the Israelites' imprisonment, where their faith was tempted by the
hardship of slavery and the opulence of the pharaoh's realm, is of particular
interest in this prayer. It casts the voyage being blessed as a kind of moral
journey, injecting what may have been a simple journey to a saint's shrine, or
even a business trip, with the significance of the scriptural struggle of faith
in the covenant with hardship and alien religions. Everyday voyages become
through this blessing a reenactment of that ancient struggle, a part of the
ongoing sacred history of Christianity.

Scripture is again found to be a potent source for the empowerment of
the words of a benediction in a "Blessing for Those Making a Journey" found
in the sacramentary of St. Thierry of Rheims, from the end of the tenth century.[40] The second clause of this blessing beseeches, "May he bring to you the
Archangel Raphael as guide, and may he, made appeased, remove from you

38. *CB* no. 1543d: Adsit vobis Raphael magnus Tobiae custos et praevius, ut humanam
et diabolicam devitetis calliditatem, et Christum viae, veritatis et vitae mereamini habere comitem. This prayer also appears in the Canterbury benedictional from the second quarter of
the eleventh century: London, British Library, Harl. MS 2892; for an edited version, see R. W.
Wooley, *The Canterbury Benedictional* (*Brit. Mus., Harley ms. 2892*), Henry Bradshaw Society 51
(London: Henry Bradshaw Society, 1917; reprint, 1995), 178.

39. *CB* no. 1543c: Quatenus instantis aevi tramitem sic communiter compensetis, ut et
illecebras Aegypti devitetis, atque per viam iustitiae ad immarcescibile felicitatis praemium
perveniatis.

40. Ibid., no. 383. The MS in question is MS Rheims, Bibl. Munic. 214 (F. 418); see also
Deshusses, *Sacramentaire grégorien*.

every lack of ease and contrariness."[41] Once more the archangel is invoked as a guide whose credibility was established by holy scripture. God himself is also invoked, in the first clause: "May the most blessed guardian adhere inseparably to you, and may he mercifully direct your journey by means of his favor."[42] The absence of the formal name of God in this prayer is another example of the manner in which blessings sought to contextualize God in accordance with the goal of the blessing: in this case, God assumes the mantle of protector and guardian we have seen so often in other blessings.

The final notable short blessing of travelers reveals another important component of this type of blessing, the power of blessing to address all eventualities. In "Another [Blessing for a Journey]," from the Gelasian sacramentary of Angoulême, the first clause seems a variant of the notion of sacred power's adaptability we saw in previous blessings: "May the God of things bringing us salvation make a prosperous journey for us, and may he lead us on straight roads through the steep places of mountains, the hollows of valleys, the plains of fields, the shallows of rivers, the secrets of forests."[43] This prayer adapts the power of the sacred to meet every exigency on the road, providing protection in all locales, extending God's power throughout the created world.

The themes seen in these rituals are elaborated and enhanced with new paradigms in the pilgrimage blessings of the pontifical of William Durandus. In the PWD's "Blessing of Staves and Wallets of Pilgrims," the quality of divinity as that which reforms and cleanses human sin is emphasized throughout the opening addresses to God: "Lord Jesus Christ, redeemer of the world, you who . . . through the mouth of your blessed apostle Paul instructed us not to cling to this existing city, but always to seek after the future city. . . . Omnipotent eternal God, reformer and author of the human race . . ."[44] These invocations emphasize the penitential nature of pilgrim-

41. *CB* b: Ducem vobis archangelum Raphaelem adhibeat, et omnem a vobis incommoditatem contrarietatemque propitiatus amoveat.

42. Ibid., a: Benigissimus custos vobis inseparabiliter inhaereat, et iter vestrum beneplacito suo misericorditer dirigat.

43. Ibid., no. 1881a: Prosperum iter faciet nobis Deus salutarium nostrorum, perducatque in vias directas, ardua montium, convexa valium, plana camporum, vada fluminum, secreta silvarum.

44. *PWD* 543–44 (*ordo* 2.31.1): Domine Iesu Christe, redemptor mundi, qui . . . per os beati apostoli tui Pauli innotuisti non habere nos hic manentem civitatem, sed futuram debere hic semper inquirere. . . . Omnipotens sempiterne Deus, humani generis reformator et auctor.

age as a journey to reform the internal person, marking out divinity's special role in this process as well as using scripture to tie this particular journey to the larger journey of the Christian who seeks to live in this world but belong to the next. This image is developed further with an allusion to the flowering staff of Aaron:

> bless these supporting staves, so that carrying them as the sign of pilgrimage and support for their bodies they may be empowered to lay hold of the plenitude of heavenly grace and protection of your blessing and, just as you blessed the staff of Aaron to defend against the faithlessness of the rebelling Jews . . .[45]

With this recasting of the blessing of the pilgrim's staff as a reenactment of God's miracles against the faithless, the blessing of the medieval pilgrim's aid and defense becomes another way to remedy the spiritual failings of the pilgrim, making pilgrimage a continuing journey of moral reformation.

The concern for right intention, crucial to the success of pilgrimage as reformation, is reaffirmed in the final prayer of this blessing:

> God of infinite mercy and immense majesty, whom neither the space of places nor the interval of times separates from those whom you watch, be with your present servants believing in you in all places and, through every road which they are about to take, deign to be leader and companion to them . . . so that whatever they seek with just desire will happen quickly under the power of your right hand.[46]

Once again the power of the divine in all places is asserted, but most particularly for those with a "just desire" to worship or seek benison from God. The blessing thus reassures the expectant pilgrim that those with good intentions can expect divine guidance and protection on their spiritual journey.

One final ritual of blessing in Durandus's pontifical is of interest, a ritual intended not simply for pilgrims but for those undertaking any journey. The *"Ordo* for Those About to Journey" seems to have been intended for high

---

45. Ibid.: hos sustentationis baculos benedicere, quatenus portantes eos in peregrinationis signum et suorum corporum sustentationem, celestis gratie plenitudinem in eis et munimen valeant tue benedictionis percipere, et, quemadmodum virgam Aaron ad rebellium Iudeorum perfidiam repellandam benedixisti . . .

46. Ibid., 545 (*ordo* 2.31.5): Deus infinite misericordie et maiestatis immense, quem nec spatia locorum nec intervalla temporum ab hiis quos tueris abiungunt, adesto presentibus famulis tuis in te ubique fidentibus et, per omnem quam ituri sunt viam, dux eis et comes esse digneris . . . ut, sub ope dextere tue quicquid iusto expetierint desiderio, celeri consequantur effectu.

clergy intending some trip, for the opening rubric refers to "a bishop about to make a journey," who is (interestingly enough) to begin the antiphon *In viam pacem* as a verse after mounting his horse, performing the *ordo* while *in processu*, as it were.[47] This is followed by a psalm *Benedictus dominus deus Israel*, which praises Jehovah as the giver of victory and offers a prayer for intercession on the psalmist's behalf against the faithless:

> Blessed be the Lord, my rock, who trains my hands for war, and my fingers for battle; my rock and my fortress, my stronghold and my deliverer, my shield, in whom I take refuge. . . . Rescue me from the cruel sword, and deliver me from the hands of aliens, whose mouths speak lies, and whose right hands are false.[48]

This invocation against the treachery of foreigners is aptly suited to the subject of the blessing, and speaks to the fears and desires of those who received the blessing in the hope of a safe journey. The use of metaphors evoking strength, rootedness, and stability ("stronghold" and "fortress") suggests that these images of security were most comforting to those about to enter into the uncertainty of a long trip. The antiphon *In viam pacem*, imploring an uneventful voyage, is then repeated: "Direct us, omnipotent and merciful Lord, in the way of peace and prosperity, and may the angel Raphael accompany us on the road, so that we may return to our own with peace and joy."[49] While the intent of the antiphon is familiar, it is intriguing to note how even with a common voyage the journey merges metaphorically (in the language of the antiphon) with the "way of peace and prosperity," so that the prayer requests a good trip at the same time that it asks God for a prosperous life in language reminiscent of pilgrimage.

This ritual blessing makes vivid use of scriptural history to contextualize the everyday journey and impregnate it with meaning. In the ritual's first prayer, which follows several short psalm verses imploring the protection of God, the celebrant says:

47. Ibid., 619 (*ordo* 3.10.1): Prelatus incipiens iter agere hunc ordinem dicit. Postquam enim equum ascenderit, inchoat ant. In viam pacis.

48. Ibid., 620 (*ordo* 3.10.2); Kirkpatrick, *Book of Psalms*, 807–8 (Ps 144:1–2, 11). This psalm probably originated as a patchwork from other psalms and dates from a later period, despite its Davidic attribution.

49. *PWD* 620 (*ordo* 3.10.2): In viam pacis et prosperitatis dirigat nos omnipotens et misericors dominus et angelus Raphael comitetur nobiscum in via, ut cum pace et gaudio revertamur ad propria.

Lord, you who made the sons of Israel to walk through the middle of the sea on a dry track, and who with a star as guide laid bare for the three magi the journey to you, grant us, we ask, a prosperous journey and tranquil weather, so that, with your holy angel as companion, we may be able to arrive at that place which we seek and at last at the harbor of eternal salvation.[50]

A similar invocation is to be found in a twelfth-century *rituale* from Lambach: "God, who conducted the three blessed wisemen Caspar, Balthazar, and Melchior star-led from the East without peril to the crib of your coeternal Son, teaching the faith of the Holy Trinity through their mystic gifts so that they might revere you with mystic gifts."[51] The mythic events of ancient Israel are brought forth by the former blessing to remind both the travelers and God of the great deeds worked for the righteous, to comfort the travelers and prod the Creator to act in a consistent manner toward the present band of wayfarers. The reference to the gifts carried by the magi, and their equation with the mystical wisdom that could accept the notion of a triune God, confirm the belief in the Trinity, presenting a worldview well adapted to the world as it is.[52] By such allusions the medieval journey enters a kind of timeless realm, approaching and actualizing the sacred history that kept the Christian community close to its God and in touch with reality. This is further exemplified in another prayer from the PWD: "God, you who guarded your child Abraham, led out unharmed from Ur of the Chaldeans through all the roads of his wandering, we ask that you might deign to guard us, your servants."[53] A connection is created with this use of scripture, making the struggles of the patriarch a paradigm for the struggles of clergy on the road,

50. Ibid. (*ordo* 3.10.3): Deus, qui filios Israel per maris medium sicco vestigio ire fecisti, quique tribus Magis iter ad te stella duce pandisti, tribue nobis, quesumus, iter prosperum tempusque tranquillum, ut, angelo tuo sancto comite, ad eum quo pergimus locum ac demum ad eterne salutis portum pervenire feliciter valeamus.

51. Franz, 2:267: Deus, qui beatos tres magos orientales Caspar, Walthesar, Melichor ad coeterni filii tui cunabula, ut te misticis revererentur muneribus, stella duce ab oriente sive periculo conduxisti, misticis ipsorum muneribus fidem sancte trinitatis insinuans (Codex Lambacensis 73, an illuminated manuscript described in Franz, *Rituale Floriani*, 25–28).

52. Clifford Geertz has argued that this demonstration is at the heart of religious symbolism and ritual. See Geertz, "Religion as a Cultural System," and Geertz, *The Interpretation of Cultures* (New York: Basic Books, 1973).

53. *PWD* 620 (*ordo* 3.10.4): Deus, qui Abraham puerum tuum de Ur Chaldeorum eductum per omnes sue peregrinationis vias illesum custodisti, quesumus, ut nos famulos tuos custodire digneris.

blending the ancient world of scripture with the medieval world into a seamless union. This connection is very similar to that described in Eliade's study of ritual and myth. Although some might argue that medieval Christians' belief in divine scripture as revelation would elevate it above most myths' credibility, at a fundamental level scripture and myth can be equated: both recount unquestionable "histories" of creation for their believers, explaining how the world came to be and the role of humans in it. The salvation history of the Old Testament presented the medieval Christian with just such a history, and the ritual of blessing that invoked it rooted that history as a real fact in the consciousness of the faithful.

While divinity and its mythic acts are conjured up by these prayers, there is also further evidence in this blessing for the argument that, to medieval Christians, the power of the divine was supremely adaptable to human use. The prayer discussed above continues: "Be for us, Lord, support during preparation, solace on the road and a shady place in hot days, a covering in rain and cold, a conveyance in weariness, protection in adversity, a staff in a slippery place, a port in shipwreck, so that, led by you, we may arrive prosperously and at last may return unharmed to our own."[54] God in this prayer becomes leader and all helpful things to these travelers, adapting the divine to the present circumstances in such detail that it only serves to highlight the medieval belief in a world permeated by the power of the holy, a world where any object or living thing could become a vessel for the sacred power that guarded those human beings willing to venerate the divine.

While blessings for pilgrims helped place them and their struggles within the sacred history of biblical times, they also helped to contextualize the individual spiritual experience of pilgrimage within the larger metaphors of service to the risen Savior. In an *"Ordo* for the Imposing of the Pouches of Pilgrims," psalmody is used to provide guidance and deliverance to the pilgrim:

> To you, O Lord, I lift up my soul. O my God, in you I trust; do not let me be put to shame; do not let my enemies exult over me. Do not let those who wait for you be put to shame; let them be ashamed who are wantonly treacherous.

54. Ibid.: Esto nobis, domine, in procinctu suffragium, in via solatium et in estu umbraculum, in pluvia et frigore tegumentum, in lassitudine vehiculum, in adversitate presidium, in lubrico baculus, in naufragio portus, ut, te duce, quo tendimus prospere perveniamus et demum incolumes ad propria redeamus.

> Make me to know your ways, O Lord; teach me your paths. Lead me in your truth.[55]

The protection this psalm seeks is well suited to the needs of pilgrims, who faced constant danger from bandits, thieves, and others who would betray the pious traveler for profit. This psalm seeks to avoid that "shame"—indeed, it seeks to turn the tables on the treacherous—but it also draws a metaphorical connection between the life of the devout believer and the way of the pilgrim: the celebrants seek guidance in "your [God's] paths" and to be led to truth, much as a pilgrim sought the path to his sacred destination, so that the steps of that one become not only a progress toward a sacred destination but a journey toward greater devotion to God.

The second psalm presented is Psalm 91, *Qui habitat,* which describes the security of the godly person under Jehovah's protection amid the perils of life.

> You who live in the shelter of the Most High, who abide in the shadow of the Almighty, will say to the Lord, "My refuge and my fortress; my God, in whom I trust." . . . You will not fear the terror of the night, or the arrow that flies by day, or the pestilence that stalks in the darkness, or the destruction that wastes at noonday. . . . Because you have made the Lord your refuge, the Most High your dwelling place, no evil shall befall you, no scourge come near your tent. Those who love me, I will deliver; I will protect those who know my name.[56]

Divinity is itself cast as sacred space in this psalm, both as a fortress and as a dwelling place, and those who acknowledge God's power in their lives ("I will protect those who know my name") and trust in it will receive spiritual protection from the earthly perils involved in a pilgrimage, another example of how the reciprocal relationship between the human and the divine manifests itself in the blessings. The psalm also demonstrates how this relationship was predicated on the moral probity of its human element, as only the just enjoy God's largesse: "When they call to me, I will answer them; I will be with them in trouble, I will rescue them and honor them. With long life I will satisfy them, and show them my salvation."[57] This psalm, then, presents

---

55. Franz, 2:278–80. The rite is drawn from the Rituale Wratislaviense (pp. 107–18) of 1496 (second edition printed in 1510), preserved in the state library of Breslau; Ps 25:1–5. For a discussion of this psalm's contents, see Kirkpatrick, *Book of Psalms,* 131.

56. Kirkpatrick, *Book of Psalms,* 553–54 (Ps 91:1–2, 5–6, 9–10, 14).

57. Ps 91:15–16.

God as a powerful ally to the righteous pilgrim, one who never strays from the side of those who never falter in their faith.

The third and final psalm of this ritual is Psalm 119, the "great psalm of the law." The psalm acknowledges the blessing of revelation and expresses the psalmist's fervent wish to make God's law the governing principle of his conduct: "Happy are those whose way is blameless, who walk in the way of the Lord. Happy are those who keep his decrees, who seek him with their whole heart, who also do no wrong, but walk in his ways."[58] Again, the obedience to divine will is cast in metaphors of travel and motion that connect the inner moral transformation of pilgrimage with the physical movement of the pilgrims from their starting point to their destination. Inward sincerity is also stressed in this psalm, for only those who seek God "with their whole heart" will arrive at the promised end of the body and soul. The author of this rite singles out the importance of a beneficial relationship between human and divinity as expressed in the psalm: "Deal bountifully with your servant, so that I may live and observe your word."[59] This statement goes to the heart of the contractual relationship that governs the operation of the benedictions: God is implored to give blessings in exchange for the reverence and worship that is embodied in the faithful's living out of the Christian ethic. But despite the confidence with which this psalm is spoken, there lingers in the mentality of the rite an uncertainty regarding the benevolence of divinity. The optimistic psalms are followed by the antiphon *Ne reminiscaris:* "Do not, Lord, remember my sin or that of my parents, neither take vengeance on account of my sins."[60] While such invocations are commonplace in Christian prayer, evincing the necessity of forgiveness and contrition in the salvation of the human soul, they also serve as evidence of the fundamental ambiguity at the heart of the blessings' understanding of the divine as an unpredictable force that can bring both prosperity and suffering, however well deserved.

Despite this doubt, the primary sentiment expressed in this rite is the desire to follow God's will. Service to the person of Jesus as the risen Savior follows these psalms and antiphon, when the descent from heaven of the Holy Spirit in Christ is invoked, and the saving action of Christ is presented

58. Kirkpatrick, *Book of Psalms,* 700–703 (Ps 119:1–3).
59. Ps 119:17. This passage is specifically included in Franz's edition of the rite.
60. *CAO* no. 3861: Ne reminiscaris, Domine, delicta mea vel parentum meorum, neque vindictam sumas de peccatis meis.

through the parable of the lost lamb: "you [Christ] desired to seek out the sheep lost through diabolical seduction and carry it back on your shoulders to the flock of the heavenly homeland."[61] The image is suitable to the subject of the blessing, as the journey of the pilgrim can be seen, especially in its penitential aspect, as a guided trek back to the bosom of God for the sinful Christian soul. The "heavenly homeland" in this context could stand for both the worldly destination (a shrine) and also for the reformed moral state that was the spiritual goal of many pilgrims. By this imagery, the pilgrim's journey becomes a metaphor for the return of the soul to God, a microcosm of the central experience of the Christian believer.

The stress placed on the relationship of the pilgrim to the person of Christ in the *ordo* for imposing the small pouches of pilgrims is further strengthened by the equation of the accoutrements of the pilgrim with the spiritual burdens of the faithful Christian: "In the name of the holy and indivisible trinity, may the yoke of Christ be mild and light for you, so that you might merit with the guardianship of his protection accompanying you in all places to be sustained mercifully to the harbor of healing remission and to thoroughly and happily enjoy the glory of eternal blessing."[62] As we have seen in other pilgrimage rituals, this *ordo*'s equation of the wallet and staff with the "yoke" of obedience to the message of Christ firmly roots the pilgrimage experience within the greater experience of the Christian life, a life of service to the higher power of the sacred. With this connection established by the words of the blessing, the pilgrimage is now more than an effort to seek healing or forgiveness for sins: it is a path to further embody the sacred words of scripture and to participate, in this life, in the being and meaning contained in the Gospels.

Blessings for pilgrims and crusaders to the holy land found in sources other than the central manuscripts of the Roman pontifical tradition present many similarities to the Roman sources in both form and content. In particular, we find an approach to God that emphasizes not only his mercy but his unconquerable power. In a "Blessing Made for Affixing the Sign of

61. Franz, 2:279: ovemque deperditam dyabolica seductione voluisti querere atque propriis humeris ad celestis patrie gregem reportare.

62. Ibid., 2:280 (Ordo ad imponendas capsellas peregrinis): In nomine sancte et individue trinitatis sit tibi hoc iugum Christi mansuetum et leve, ut sue protectionis custodia te ubique comitante ad portum salutifere remissionis misericorditer merearis attolli atque eterne benedictionis gloria feliciter perfrui.

the Cross, " from the benedictional of Meissen (1512), the celebrant follows the stitching of the red cross onto the crusader's surplice with the prayer: "Unconquerable Lord, we ask, guard by your power the one whom you have granted to be fortified by the sign of the most holy cross against your and your holy church's obstinate enemies."[63] The granting of this invincible power could comfort the crusader facing probable death in the service of Christ, while it also reinforced the expectation of the Christian community that God was indeed suited to their needs. Psalm 34, *Benedicam dominum in omni tempore,* follows this prayer, and quite aptly fits into the prayer's theme of unconquerable divine protection:

> I will bless the Lord at all times, his praise shall continually be in my mouth. My soul makes its boast in the Lord; let the humble hear and be glad. O magnify the Lord with me, and let us exalt his name forever. I sought the Lord, and he answered me, and delivered me from all my fears. Look to him and be radiant, so that your faces shall never be ashamed.[64]

God here is portrayed as the ultimate deliverer, one who can erase the fears of those taking the Cross and make their hearts firm, removing all their doubt and strengthening their faith and courage. Such a message would have been of great comfort to a prospective crusader, and its inclusion is further support for the view that the blessings responded to the deep-seated needs and fears of the medieval laity. But even this psalm contains the repeated warning that the benefits of the blessed flow first and foremost from the purity of their own relation to the divine:

> Many are the afflictions of the righteous, but the Lord rescues them from them all. He keeps all their bones; not one of them will be broken. Evil brings death to the wicked, and those who hate the righteous will be condemned. The Lord redeems the life of his servants; none of those who take refuge in him will be condemned.[65]

This psalm stresses that righteousness, or moral probity, is the foundation of humanity's positive relationship with God and the source of all the benefits that flow from that relationship.

---

63. Ibid., 2:306: Insuperabili, quesumus, domine, tua virtute custodi, quem signo sanctissime crucis contra tuos et ecclesie tue sancte pertinaces adversarios muniri tribuisti.
64. Kirkpatrick, *Book of Psalms,* 169–70 (Ps 34:1–5).
65. Ps 34:19–22.

But despite this confidence in God's beneficent nature, there always remained the sense that for such rituals of blessing to be efficacious, they must be performed with the proper attitude: "Omnipotent and merciful God, the consolation of the suffering, strength of the laboring, may the prayers of the Christian people reach you, so that they may rejoice that your mercy, which they seek in the spirit of humility against the opponents of your blessed cross, was present for them in their gravely imminent needs."[66] The concern for the maintenance of an open channel to the sacred realm is clear in the desires for prayers to be heard, and it is significant that mercy is sought "in the spirit of humility," the proper manner so important to a successful blessing.

The blessing of crusader-pilgrims also manifests an important element of the typical medieval blessing, the desire for restoration of baptismal grace. To a "Prayer for Those Crossing over [the Sea] against the Turks," from a manuscript dated sometime after the crusading bull of Pope Nicholas V (30 September 1453), there is appended a "form of absolution," which reads:

> May our Lord Jesus Christ absolve you, and I by the authority of the same and of the most holy Lord Pope N. . . . By the same authority I bestow the most full remission of all sins on you and with the baptismal [state] of innocence having been restored, I recommend your soul to the holy angels, so that if proceeding against the Turks death may befall you, they may without delay and without almost any taste of purgatory soon return it [your soul] to the heavenly kingdom.[67]

The slain crusader's direct ascent to heaven presented here is an idea familiar to scholars of holy war, but the restoration of "innocence" is less so. This

66. Franz, 2:306: Omnipotens et misericors deus, mestorum consolatio, laborantium fortitudo, perveniant ad te preces populi Christiani, ut in necessitatibus sibi graviter imminentibus misericordiam tuam, quam in spiritu humilitatis contra adversarios benedicte crucis tue humiliter exquirunt, sibi gaudeant adfuisse.

67. Ibid., 2:304–6: Dominus noster Iesus Christus te absolvat et ego auctoritate eiusdem ac sanctissimi domni N. pape. . . . Eadem auctoritate tibi plenissimam omnium peccatorum remissionem impendo ac innocencie baptismali te restituto sanctisque angelis animam tuam recommendo, ut, si contra Turcos pergendo mori te contingat, eam sine mora et sine purgatorii pene degustacione mox ad regna celestia te referant. The blessing is drawn from Codex Kremifanensis, Benediktinerstift Kremsmünster 225, fols. 347r–347v. The text of this blessing contains many familiar elements: the allusion to the rod of Aaron flowering against the rebellious, the invocation of the angel Raphael of Tobias as a guardian, and the call of Christ to take up the Cross and follow him (to which is appended the phrase "against the Turks," perhaps not a happy marriage of concepts to the modern mind, but quite acceptable to the medieval).

restoration would have been considered by medieval men and women to be a tremendous gift, erasing the sins of the adult Christian and squaring the account between the individual soul and God.[68] Its inclusion in this ritual no doubt reflects a need for such rebirth expressed since the early Middle Ages, in the *Asperges* of the Mass if nowhere else. The blessing thus becomes analogous to a sacrament in this later ritual, shoring up the power of the established sacrament of baptism with the power of the spoken word. Such words of blessings were not restricted to warriors formally dedicated to holy war, however; ordinary knights, too, could find themselves the beneficiaries of liturgical blessings in the central and later Middle Ages, and it is to these rituals that we now turn.

KNIGHTS AND WAR

The blessing, or dubbing, of knights is one form of medieval ritual that has moved beyond the circle of scholars of this period to affect the imagination of the general public, as an image of gallantry and the ideals of the knight, understood romantically. Indeed, the religious interpretation of knighthood's purpose has been so powerful in the scholarship of the dubbing ritual that one early historian of knighthood considered it an eighth sacrament, and this view was until recently accepted without question by numerous scholars.[69] Despite its influence on the popular imagination of the Middle Ages, the historian looking to construct a clear picture of the actual historical practice of dubbing is faced with a glaring lack of reliable sources describing actual knightings.[70] While there is some reason to see this ritual as imbued with re-

68. This absolution and its reliance on the power of the pope parallels the earliest definitions of absolution to be found in the *RGP*, which Mary C. Mansfield discusses in her study of public penance in thirteenth-century France; see Mansfield, *Humiliation of Sinners*, 197–98.

69. The scholar in question is Leon Gautier, author of *La chevalerie* (Paris: Senard and Derangeon, 1884), 250, 286ff. This sacramental understanding of the dubbing ceremony also appears in the work of Georges Duby, who in his study of chivalry and society mentions briefly that the church converted the ceremony of dubbing into a "real sacrament" sometime during the eleventh or twelfth century (Georges Duby, *The Chivalrous Society* [London: Edward Arnold, 1979], 180). C. Warren Hollister, in his summary of knighthood in the medieval period, calls dubbing a "sacrament of knighthood" (Hollister, "Knights and Knight Service," *DMA* 7:277).

70. For a brief survey of the study of dubbing and the limitation of the sources, see Jeffrey D. Hass, "The Development of the Medieval Dubbing Ceremony," *Michigan Academician* 28 (1996): 123–33.

ligious significance for Christian knights, this view obscures significant secular elements of a ceremony that is probably rooted in the traditions of early medieval Germanic war bands.[71]

Before the development of the idea and ideals of chivalry, the delivery of arms was the most common form of secular dubbing found in written accounts of the creation of knighthoods. This ceremony was conducted at the time of the warrior's coming of age and his inclusion into the war band of a military and political leader, a source of glory and worth to the young warrior.[72] In this period records exist only for the highest stratum of warriors: in ninth-century England young Athelstan is recorded as having received his arms from his grandfather, King Alfred; and in Carolingian Europe we have a record of Charlemagne bestowing arms on his son, Louis.[73] While this ritual was a purely secular affair, Maurice Keen has argued that the secular ritual of delivery was paralleled by the development of the ecclesiastical blessing of a warrior's sword. Keen contends that this ecclesiastical ritual seems to have been the source of all the later liturgies of making knights, which we will examine in this section.[74] These two distinct strands of development in the historical evolution of dubbing to knighthood, Keen argues, existed side by side until the creation of the Roman pontifical and the pontifical of Durandus, whose liturgies fused secular and religious traditions, endowing the ceremony of dubbing with Christian, secular, and social significance.[75] Before addressing the validity of this theory, however, we must examine in detail the ritual's components and their evolution.

As we have seen in the previous discussion, blessings of objects of daily use were a common element in the early pontificals and sacramentaries of

71. Ibid., 123–25; Maurice Keen, "The Ceremony of Dubbing to Knighthood," in his *Chivalry* (New Haven: Yale University Press, 1984), 73.

72. Keen, "Ceremony of Dubbing to Knighthood," 66–69.

73. For these events, see William of Malmesbury, *De gestis regnum anglorum*, book 5, *Historiae novellae* 3, ed. William Stubbs (London: Eyre and Spottiswoode, 1887), 145; and "Anonymonius de gesta francorum" quoted in Hass, "Medieval Dubbing Ceremony," 124.

74. Keen, "Ceremony of Dubbing to Knighthood," 71. While numerous scholars of chivalry and the evolution of knighthood mention dubbing, few study it in any detail. Maurice Keen offers one of the most substantive treatments to date and is correspondingly predominant in my discussion of this ritual. See also Hass, "Medieval Dubbing Ceremony," 131.

75. Jean Flori reached a similar conclusion regarding the origins of dubbing in "Les origines de l'adoubement chevaleresque: Étude des remises d'armes et du vocabulaire qui les exprime," *Traditio* 35 (1979): 209–72. See also Keen, "Ceremony of Dubbing to Knighthood," 73.

the medieval church, and the sword was no exception.⁷⁶ This particular ritual blessing was the product of the age of the barbarian invasions, and the ritual stresses the defense of God's church from heathens who threaten it. The warrior-heroes who led this struggle were compared in these texts to the heroes of the Old Testament, and the church provided rituals for all who sought its blessing.⁷⁷ In Germany the blessing of a sword was first accompanied in the twelfth century by the blessing of a spear and shield, a practice that became customary in France by the thirteenth century.⁷⁸ Blessing a sword has an interesting connection to another form of blessing, the earliest coronation rituals, for the latter contain a blessing of a sword, and both have an injunction to defend the widow and the orphan, as well as prayers for victory.⁷⁹ As we shall see, the first blessing of a sword in the RGP seems to be intended for use more by some great man than by an ordinary knight, which reminds us that knighthood, even in the eleventh and twelfth centuries, when lesser men commonly began to receive arms, never entirely divested itself of its secular connections with lordship and magisterial functions.⁸⁰

76. Keen, "Ceremony of Dubbing to Knighthood," 73.

77. Ibid. For examples the previously cited rite, see *RGP ordo* 244, the Leofric missal's *Oratio super militantes* (in F. E. Warren, ed., *The Leofric Missal* [Oxford: Clarendon Press, 1883], 230), and the other rituals examined below.

78. Franz, 2:291–92. Weapons other than the spear and sword were not blessed by liturgical rituals, the only exception being the small arrows consecrated on the day of St. Sebastian and carried by the laity as a defense against plague (ibid., 2:299). The preferred date in Germany for weapon blessings and dubbing was the feast day of St. Gregory. In Italy the Feast of St. Francis was preferred, and the young knights were often decked in wreaths reminiscent of the laurels of imperial Rome (ibid., 2:292–93). Franz also mentions the existence of popular Latin and German blessings that sought to empower the recipients' weapons while rendering the weapons of their enemies impotent. These rituals often included superstitious or kabbalistic signs or made use of charms or magical letters. See Bede, *Historia ecclesiastica gentis anglorum,* ed. B. Colgrave and R. Mynors (Oxford: Clarendon Press, 1969), 401–5; Franz, 2:299–300.

79. Keen, "Ceremony of Dubbing to Knighthood," 72. The early texts invoke God's blessing on the king, while the later sources invoke that blessing for knighthood at large. For a brief introduction to the copious literature of coronation rituals, see Cornelius A. Bouman, *Sacring and Crowning: The Development of the Latin Ritual for the Anointing of Kings and the Coronation of an Emperor before the Eleventh Century* (Groningen: J. B. Wolters, 1957); Jean Pierre Bayard, *Le sacre des rois* (Paris, 1964); Elizabeth A. R. Brown, *"Franks, Burgundians and Aquitanians" and the Royal Coronation Ceremony in France* (Philadelphia: American Philosophical Society, 1992); and Henry G. Richardson, "The Coronation in Medieval England," *Traditio* 16 (1960): 111–202.

80. Keen, "Ceremony of Dubbing to Knighthood," 72–73.

For this period, then, Keen's thesis is plausible and fits the existing evidence.

With the dawning of the high medieval period, however, more detailed sources for the dubbing ritual become available. The first full account of a dubbing appears in 1128, with John of Marmoutier's description of the knighting of Geoffrey of Anjou.[81] This ritual appears to have been not only a military rite of passage but also a significant social event. Geoffrey received a horse, shield, helmet, and chain mail suit as his military equipment. These were accompanied by a ritual bath, the wearing of fantastic clothing at the ceremony, and a week-long celebration and tournament held in his honor. Keen views this era, particularly the time of Pope Urban II's call to knights to take up the sword in the defense of Christendom overseas some thirty years earlier, as a time of major transformation in the tradition of dubbing. Church liturgies for the making of a knight could now, according to Keen, symbolize the primacy of the knight's obligation to the ecclesiastical order and authority that called the crusade; and in accordance with the Gregorian reformers' efforts to build a papal monarchy as the head of Latin Christendom, the church vigorously sought to make dubbing a liturgical ritual with priests, not warlords, as the central actors. Again, Keen's thesis is consistent with the known goals of the papacy and with the increase in ecclesiastical rituals related to knighthood and the Crusades.

Despite the creation of new and more elaborate rituals for the dubbing of knights, Keen argues that the ecclesiastical aims were not fully realized and that the church never achieved a monopoly over the making of knights; indeed, he notes that almost all recorded incidents of an ecclesiastic performing the central office in dubbing involve princely bishops who were also great secular lords.[82] Even in the thirteenth century, when the practice

81. John of Marmoutier, "Historia Gaufredi ducis normannorum et comitis Andegavorum," in *Chroniques des comtes d'Anjou et des seigneurs d'Amboise*, ed. Louis Halphen and Rene Poupardin (Paris: A. Picard, 1913), 178–80, quoted in Hass, "Medieval Dubbing Ceremony," 124. Previous accounts of dubbing do exist, such as those by Orderic Vitalis, but they limit themselves to a simple mention of someone being knighted by the girding on of a sword. See Orderic Vitalis, *Ecclesiastical History*, ed. Marjorie Chibnall (Oxford: Clarendon Press, 1999), 6:191.

82. Keen, "Ceremony of Dubbing to Knighthood," 74–75. Well-known dubbings include Henry IV taking his sword from Archbishop Eberhard of Trier on 29 March 1065 (Franz, 2:292ff.); King Geisa II of Hungary being dubbed by the church before the battle of Leitha (1146) (Franz, 2:293ff.); Orderic Vitalis's description of Henry I of England being girded by Bishop Lanfranc (Franz, 2:294ff.); and the dubbing of Simon de Montfort's son Amalrich by the bishops of Orleans and Auxerre in 1213 (Franz, 2:296ff.).

of making knights inside a church was most common, there are just as many incidents of men being knighted outside a church, with ecclesiastics playing no part in the ceremony. The reasons for this are somewhat ambiguous, but Keen argues that it is likely that the secular service of knighthood was an ideal too deeply rooted in Germanic culture, one of the building blocks of medieval civilization, for any other obligation to challenge its priority.[83]

Despite the failure of the reformers' agenda to make the ceremony religious, Keen does acknowledge that since dubbing was often done in a church it impressed on the minds of all present that knighthood was a Christian calling, imposing a modicum of Christian morality and ethics upon a fundamentally violent occupation.[84] This is supported by another major source in the history of dubbing, the late thirteenth-century *Book of the Ordre of Chyvalry* by Raymon Lull, a Catalan, which described a detailed ceremony for dubbing that reflected the three major influences in his life: chivalry, military ideals, and religion.[85] According to Lull, the ceremony was to occur

> on the day of a great church feast so that it would be well attended. The squire, after he was tested and found worthy of honor, was to bathe, go to confession, spend the night in the church in prayer and fasting, and in the morning attend Mass. The dubbing was to occur after the homily, in which the prelate was to expound upon the Ten Commandments, the twelve articles of the faith, and the seven sacraments. The squire was to kneel before the knight who was to dub him with his eyes and arms directed upward. The knight then girded the squire with a sword, kissed him, and slapped him. After the ceremony the new knight was to ride throughout the town and show himself to the people. A great feast was to be thrown, and knights were to exchange gifts.[86]

This elaborate ritual and social event, with its explicit religious overtones, may not have been the standard course for every dubbing, but it certainly reflects a strong consciousness of the role of the church in the creation of new knights. The ceremony of Durandus's pontifical, composed at roughly the same time, is a much shorter ritual, as we shall see, and bears little resemblance to Lull's or previous accounts, but its placement of the cleric as

---

83. Keen, "Ceremony of Dubbing to Knighthood," 74–76.

84. Ibid.

85. Hass, "Medieval Dubbing Ceremony," 127–28; Ramon Lull, *The Book of the Ordre of Chyvalry,* trans. William Caxton, ed. Albert T. P. Byles (Oxford: Oxford University Press, 1926).

86. Lull, *Book of Chyvalry,* 66–75, quoted in Hass, "Medieval Dubbing Ceremony," 128.

the one to confer knighthood significantly alters the "balance of power" between the secular and the sacred; the status of knight was now dependent upon the clergy, not upon the knights themselves. This displacement of a knight as the agent of knighthood, seen as early as the eleventh century in the pontificals of Besançon and Rheims, is typical of the ecclesiastical rituals that Keen dismisses as infrequent and as overshadowed by the secular tradition of dubbing.[87]

In the final analysis, Keen's emphasis on the secular concerns in dubbing does have merit. Certainly many knights received the insignia of their class independent of clergy, many on the battlefield, where no one but their secular lord was present to bestow it. I would argue, however, that dismissing the ecclesiastical blessing of knights gives insufficient weight to the religious concerns that played themselves out in the minds of liturgical authors, celebrants, and would-be knights. The numerous themes of Christian piety that appear in the rites suggest that they are being aimed at recipients already conscious of these issues, which would especially be the case for anyone seeking to become a *miles Christi*. These blessings of knights reveal important elements of the Christian perspective on the military class, and the connection of that class to the piety of its age.

To illuminate these issues, I have chosen eight rituals as representative of the genre: a "Blessing of a Newly Girded Sword," from the RGP;[88] a "Blessing of the Standards of War," from the RGP;[89] a "Prayer for an Army," from the RGP;[90] a "Blessing of a City against the Gentiles," also from the RGP;[91] a "Blessing of a Sword," from the twelfth-century pontifical of Besançon";[92] an "*Ordo* for Arming the Defenders of the Church or Another Knight";[93] a ritual "Concerning the Blessing of Armor," from the PWD;[94] and a ritual "Concerning the Blessing of New Knights," from the same pontifical.[95]

The "Blessing of a Newly Girded Sword," from the RGP, presents the

---

87. Ibid., 129–30.

88. *RGP* 2:379 (*ordo* 244).

89. Ibid., 2:378 (*ordo* 243).

90. Ibid., 2:380 (*ordo* 245).

91. Ibid., 2:378 (*ordo* 242).

92. Franz, 2:294; the ritual is also found in Martène, *Antiquis Ecclesiae ritibus,* 2:239.

93. Franz, 2:295–97. This ritual is drawn from Melchior Hittorp's *De divinis catholicae ecclesiae officiis ac mysteris* (Paris, 1610), which indicates neither time nor origin but is most probably from the thirteenth century or later.

94. *PWD* 549 (*ordo* 2.38).

95. Ibid., 447–50 (*ordo* 1.28); this rite also appears in Franz, 2:294–95.

sword as both the instrument of Christian righteousness and an insignia of the knightly class to be invested with power, as seen in this first prayer:

> Hearken to our prayers we entreat, Lord, and may you deign by the right hand of your majesty to bless this sword, with which this your servant N. desires to be girded about, in so far as it can be the defense and protection of churches, widows, orphans and of all those serving God, against the ferocity of the pagans, and may it be dread, terror and fear for others laying snares.[96]

By this blessing the sword is converted to a dual purpose: to terrify the wicked (and note the interesting anthropomorphizing of the sword into a human emotion) and uphold the weak. The emphasis on the obligation of the knight or lord to defend the helpless through the blessed sword represents not only these two purposes but also the effort described by André Vauchez to involve the laity more deeply in the life of the church, in this case by creating a consecrated position for the military elite of the feudal era.[97] This emphasis appears in three rites analyzed here and one other supporting rite, and seems to have been a major element of the church's efforts to control the creation and intention of knights. By converting a tool of violence into a blessed object, the author of this rite distinguishes the knight from other orders of society and orients his class to a closer adherence to the terms of the relationship between the human community and the divine: worship, veneration, and obedience to the mandates of scripture. Thus the promise of good behavior that we have seen in other rites underlies the efficacy of this ritual; it anticipates the wider tradition of ritual blessings of insignia that were extended to the less exalted category of pilgrims, perhaps in imitation of the knightly class's new ritualized prestige.

The blessing of a sword demonstrates another theme common to martial blessings: the affirmation of a divinely sanctioned social order. A "Blessing of a Sword," from the twelfth-century pontifical of Besançon, has a second prayer that begins:

---

96. *RGP* 2:379 (*ordo* 244.1): Exaudi, quesumus, domine, preces nostras, et hunc ensem, quo hic famulus tuus N. se circumcingi desiderat, maiestatis tue dextra benedicere dignare, quatenus defensio atque protectio possit esse aeclesiarum, viduarum, orphanorum omniumque Deo servientium contra sevitiam paganorum, aliisque insidiantibus sit pavor, terror et formido.

97. André Vauchez, *La spiritualité du Moyen Âge occidental: VIIIe–XIIe siècles* (Paris: Presses Universitaires de France, 1975), 75–137, esp. 105–37.

God, who constituted three orders of men in the whole world after the fall of Adam, by means of which your faithful people may remain quiet, secure and free from all the violence of evil, be present by our supplications and make use of this sword, which we bless by the invocation of your name . . . so that he may both repress the enemies of the church of God laying snares and powerfully defend himself by means of your protection from all the fraud of the enemy.[98]

The idea of three orders of medieval society is a familiar one, but it was not vigorously promoted until the feudal age of the eleventh and twelfth centuries (the latter being the date of composition of this ritual), and this ritual blessing seems to serve as a public confirmation of the validity of this social model by providing it with divine origins.[99] This prayer also provides an example of the power believed to reside within the ritual invocation of God's name, a protection that (following a theme found in the blessings of pilgrims and others) extended beyond simple physical protection to offer a spiritual shield against inner temptation and deception.

This blessing of a sword also benefited from associative power created by placing its existence within the context of sacred history. The victories of the heroes of ancient Israel empowered the weapon of the medieval knight:

God, guardian and protector of those hoping in you . . . grant to this your servant, who with a sincere heart endeavors to gird upon himself a sword for the

98. Franz, 2:294: Deus, qui trinos gradus hominum post lapsum Adae in toto orbe constituisti, quo plebs tua fidelis immunis ab omni impetu nequitie secura et quieta permaneret: adesto supplicationibus nostris et hunc ensem, quem invocatione tui nominis benedicimus, ita famulus tuus . . . utatur, quatenus et hostes ecclesiae dei insidiantes reprimat et se ipsum ab omni fraude inimici tua protectione potenter defendat. The invocation of the name of God, while rare in blessings for illness and healing (being present only in two Swiss and German supporting rituals from the tenth and fifteenth centuries), is plentiful in blessings of knights and blessings for war (see St. Gall's "Blessing upon Infirm Eyes" and the *RGP*'s "Blessing of Cross Water"). German, French, and English martial rituals all manifest this type of invocation, and while it does appear twice in rituals from the tenth and twelfth centuries, it is most common in blessings of the thirteenth century or later (see the *RGP*'s "Blessing of a New Sword," Besançon's "Blessing of a Sword," the *Ordo* for Arming the Defenders of the Church," the *PWD*'s "Blessing of New Knights," and Magdeburg's "Another Blessing in Time of War"). Why this is the case is unclear, although it may reflect a belief that the name of God was equivalent in sacred power to other essential elements of the divine, notably the wounds of Christ and tears of Christ venerated in the Passion-oriented faith of the later Middle Ages. This interpretation is supported by the Israelite tradition of cursing discussed in the previous chapter.

99. For an introduction to this idea, see Georges Duby, *The Three Orders: Feudal Society Imagined,* trans. Arthur Goldhammer (Chicago: University of Chicago Press, 1980).

first time . . . and just as you granted victory by the power of your strength to David and Judith against the enemies of your people, thus fortified by your aid against the fury of his enemies may he [the recipient] be everywhere a victor, and may he contribute to the safety of the holy church.[100]

The triumph of biblical heroes becomes a model for the sought-after gift of victory that the blessing implores from divinity, seeking to re-create the past in the present and reminding God of his obligations to protect the human world. Such contextualization is common among the rituals of this genre of blessings, appearing in six blessings in all.[101] Only two of these manuscripts, however, share a common biblical allusion: reference to the military victories won by King David. Although no clear chronological patterns of development can be found in these rites, when one examines their disparate allusions one is struck by the complete absence of references to the New Testament; all of the biblical references are to the Old Testament, and these are heavily weighted to the warlike aspect of Jehovah and the martial tools and triumphs he brought to Israel.[102] This emphasis is important evidence for interpreting these rituals as being responsive, in their content, to the needs, desires, and hopes of the laity who received them. While the Son might give comfort to the victims of war, it was the Father in his terrible glory that knights and soldiers undoubtedly wanted at their side to guarantee them victory. This blessing also demonstrates the importance of intention to the blessing's efficacy, declaring the "sincere heart" that drives the request of the supplicant and is vital to the success of any performative act, such as a blessing. Finally, the prayer of this ritual emphasizes the obligation of the

100. Franz, 2:294: Deus custos et in te sperantium protector . . . concede huic famulo tuo, qui sincero corde gladio se primum nititur praecingere . . . et sicut David et Iudith contra gentis tuae hostes fortitudinis tuae potentia victoriam tribuisti, ita tuo auxilio munitus contra hostium suorum saevitiam victor ubique existat et ad sanctae ecclesiae tutelam proficiat. Rituals seeking to strengthen the military defenses of the Christian community emphasize God's role as protector. We see this in French rites from the twelfth and thirteenth centuries, the major period of these rituals' development. See the pontifical of Besançon's "Blessing of a Sword" and the "*Ordo* for Arming the Church's Defenders or Another Knight."

101. These rites are found in French, German, Spanish, and English manuscripts ranging from the tenth to the thirteenth century (see the *RGP*'s "Blessing of a City," the *PWD*'s "Blessing of Armor," the Besançon pontifical's "Blessing of a Sword" and "*Ordo* for Arming the Defenders of the Church or a Knight," the Canterbury benedictional's "Blessing in Time of War, or against the Danes," and the Longlonde's "Blessing for Peace in a Time of War").

102. See the index, and the previous note, for the different manuscripts and references.

militant recipient to put this tool of violence to the use of peace, protecting the church and its clients and thereby ensuring the continued existence of the ties binding the human and divine worlds.

Along with the blessing of swords, medieval warriors and kings also sought blessings for the other accoutrements of war. In a "Blessing of the Standards of War," from the RGP, we first notice the equation of God with power and success on the battlefield:

> Omnipotent eternal God, who are the blessing of all and the strength of the triumphant, look favorably on the prayers of our humility, and sanctify with a heavenly blessing this standard, which has been prepared for military use, so that it may be mighty and covered on all sides by your rampart against adversaries and rebel nations, and may it be terrible to the enemies of the Christian people and also a solid foundation and the sure confidence of victory to those believing in you.[103]

The divine in the opening lines of the prayer is the source of military victory, but this prayer also provides an example of how blessings linked the power they bestowed with the interior condition of the recipient, offering courage and constancy to humble believers.[104] The insignia of war, invested with the *numen*'s power, thus not only defends the faith but promotes its growth within the hearts of believers.

While this prayer serves to increase the confidence of those going off to war, it nevertheless contains hints of the underlying anxiety about the

103. *RGP* 378 (*ordo* 243): Omnipotens sempiterne Deus, qui es cunctorum benedictio et triumphantium fortitudo, respice propicius ad preces humilitatis nostrae, et hoc vexillum, quod bellico usui preparatum est, caelesti benedictione sanctifica, ut contra adversarias et rebelles nationes sit validum tuoque munimine circumseptum, sitque inimicis christiani populi terribile atque in te confidentibus solidamentum et victoriae certa fiducia. The association of God with strength and invincibility is made in the prayers of the *RGP*'s "Blessing of Standards," the *PWD*'s "Blessing of Armor," and the Canterbury benedictional's "Blessing in a Time of War, or against the Danes," all examined below (see the index for the presence of this association in the manuscripts studied). God as strength also appears in the St. Gall "Adjuration against Fevers," an indication of the versatility of sacred power to both heal and harm.

104. Standards were, of course, used all across medieval Europe's battlefields, but they served more purposes than mere identification on the battlefield. For example, the banners and banner wagons for the communes of Italy became important symbols of civic identity, eventually becoming the center of their own cults. They embodied the history, pride, and independence of the city; to lose one in battle was deeply shameful, while taking an enemy's cart brought glory to the victor and allowed the victorious city to offer the prize as a votive offering to God and the city's patron saint. See Thompson, *Cities of God*, 125–27.

constancy of God that we have seen in other ritual blessings. This is evident in the concluding lines of the blessing: "For you are God who destroys war, and provides the help of a heavenly defense to those hoping in you."[105] God's nature is here reaffirmed in the eyes of the lay recipients of the blessing through a commonplace in Christian texts, the use of military language to describe an avowedly peace-loving God. The use of the phrase *Tu es enim Deus,* however, does highlight the muted uncertainty buried in the language of the blessings that God will not live up to his perceived nature and may fail to end the suffering of such conflicts unless he is reminded by the blessing.

Among the insignia of war, armor received blessings that reflect the church's efforts to convert the unfortunate practice of war into a device for spreading the faith. Durandus's ritual "Concerning the Blessing of Armor" emphasizes the need to put arms to a spiritual purpose: "Let the seal and the blessing of omnipotent God the Father, Son and Holy Spirit be upon these arms, and upon the one wearing them, through which let him be garbed for the guarding of justice asking you that you may protect and defend him, Lord God."[106] The blessing imparts the power of the divine for an appropriate Christian use of these arms, in this case guarding justice. This is further elaborated in the second prayer of this blessing, which frames this use within the paradigm of the sacred past:

> Omnipotent God, in whose hand complete victory firmly stands, and who also granted David marvelous powers for overthrowing the rebel Goliath, we beseech your clemency by humble prayer that you might deign to bless these arms with beneficent piety and grant your servant N., desiring to carry the same, that for the protection and defense of holy mother church, of orphans and widows, against the attack of visible and invisible enemies, he may use these freely and victoriously.[107]

105. *RGP* 378: Tu es enim Deus, qui conteris bella et caelestis presidii sperantibus in te prestas auxilium.

106. *PWD* 549 (*ordo* 2.38.1): Signaculum et benedictio Dei omnipotentis, patris, et filii et spiritus sancti sit super hec arma, et super induentem ea, quibus ad tuendam iustitiam induatur domine Deus, ut illum protegas et defendas.

107. Ibid. (*ordo* 2.28.2): Deus omnipotens, in cuius manu victoria plena consistit, quique etiam David ad expugnandum rebellem Goliam vires mirabiles tribuisti, clementiam tuam humili prece deposcimus, ut hec arma almifica pietate benedicere dignare et concede famulo tuo N. eadem gestare cupienti, ut ad munimen ac defensionem sancte matris ecclesie, pupillorum et viduarum, contra visibilium et invisibilium hostium impugnationem, ipsis libere et victoriose utatur.

This use of arms "freely and victoriously" highlights the status and qualities of this class, with its aura of power, freedom, and command.[108] The power to triumph on the battlefield is another form God's potency may take, but its use is conditioned by the obligation to employ said power to promote the close connection of the divine and human worlds, through the protection of the church and those especially favored by God.

This ritual blessing of armor highlights the manner in which such rituals could define and distinguish the Christian people in opposition to other cultures. Following a sprinkling of holy water on the arms, the priest recites a final prayer to their recipients: "Accept the standard sanctified by a heavenly blessing, and may it be terrible to the enemies of the Christian people. May the Lord give you grace so that for his name and honor, safe and secure, you may powerfully pierce the enemies' ranks with it."[109] Through this blessing these arms become a potent tool in the struggle to ensure the survival of the Christian world, and it is interesting to note how the author represents God's power as a double-edged sword, providing balm and protection to the faithful and death and destruction to those outside the bounds of the accepted community.[110]

While the blessing of objects of war served the medieval church in many ways, the most versatile agents to serve such purposes were the knights themselves. The ritual "Concerning the Blessing of New Knights," from the pontifical of Durandus, reveals how the devout contextualized the secular profession of knighthood within the religious cosmology of the medieval world.[111] First the sword of the knight is blessed, using the first and third prayers from the RGP's blessing of a sword (which instruct the knight in his obligation to protect the weak and innocent, and implore victory for him and his weapon), and then the psalm *Domine exaudi* is sung.[112] This psalm is

108. This phrase appears in no other blessing, although a similar notion does appear in a blessing for impotence, which requests that the couple being blessed be able "freely" to create children.

109. *PWD* 550 (*ordo* 2.28.6): Accipe vexillum celesti benedictione sanctificatum, sitque inimicis populi Christiani terribile. Det tibi dominus gratiam, ut ad ipsius nomen et honorem cum illo hostium cuneos potenter penetres incolumis et securus.

110. This fits well with Grimes's notion of how ceremony can both create community and set that community in opposition against the outside and foreign.

111. *PWD* 447–50 (*ordo* 28).

112. Ibid., 447–48 (*ordo* 28.1–2); Ps 143. This is one of the "penitential psalms" used on Ash Wednesday. This ritual is also presented in Martène, *Antiquis Ecclesiae ritibus*, 2:239ff. The *RGP*'s ritual is *ordo* 244. Only the later ritual texts of the thirteenth century for

a recognition by God's servant that his sufferings are a merited punishment for sin yet also a plea for a merciful hearing:

> Hear my prayer, O Lord; give ear to my supplications in your faithfulness; answer me in your righteousness. . . . For my enemy pursues me; he has crushed my life to the ground; he has left me dwelling in the dark, like those long dead . . . I remember the days of old; I meditate on all your doings. The works of your hands I ponder. I stretch out my hands to you; my soul thirsts for you like parched land.[113]

This psalm focuses on the psalmist's concern for direction, instruction, deliverance, and the destruction of his enemies, all of which naturally would be of great concern to a soldier for whom violent death was an occupational hazard. But this psalm also encourages the knight meditate on the divine, a reflection perhaps unfamiliar to the rough life of his class. The call to reflect upon the sacred past of scripture seems aimed at creating a more pious warrior, one who through ritual and devotion can attain a closer connection between himself and God.

Following these blessings and psalmody, there is an elaborate rubric in which the bishop gives the knight his sword and girds it on him, the knight brandishes his sword three times, and the bishop applies "the mark of a soldier" upon the recipient. The bishop then kisses the knight and says to him: "Be a knight peaceful, steadfast, faithful and devoted to God." The *ordo* continues: "And then he gives the knight a light blow on the cheek, saying: 'You will have awakened from the sleep of evil and stay awake in the faith of Christ and worthy renown.'"[114] This is another example of the manner in which martial blessings sought to make the profession of a warrior into a spiritual experience and place the secular order of knighthood at the service of the reformed church of the high Middle Ages. The image of awakening from sleep suggests that this is a rite of passage from a secular state to a holy

---

blessing knights include psalmody (see the "*Ordo* for Arming Defenders of the Church or Another Knight," and this blessing from the *PWD*).

113. Ps 143:1, 3, 5–6.

114. *PWD* 449 (*ordo* 28.7–11): Post haec pontifex ensem nudum sumit de altari et ponit illum in dextera manu illius dicens: Accipe gladium in nomine etc. Deinde ense in vagina reposito cingit illi ensem cum vagina et cingendo dicit: Accingere gladio super femur *etc*. Ense igitur acto miles novus illum de vagina educit et evaginatum ter in manu vibrat. Et eo super brachio terso mox in vaginam reponit. Quo facto insigniens illum charactere militari dat illi osculum pacis dicens: Esto miles pacificus, strenuus, fidelis et deo devotus. Et mox dat sibi alapam leviter dicens: Exciteris a somno malitiae et vigila in fide Christi et fama laudabili.

state, represented by sleep and wakefulness, respectively, and the vigil intimately associates this state with the religious ideals of the monastic orders. Despite the overtly religious character of this prayer, this text addresses the central secular concern of the knightly class: the desire for glory and renown. But earthly glory seems here transformed into a higher form by the blessing's "*worthy* renown" (emphasis added), the entry into which parallels the metaphor of awakening from a profane into a sacred state. The profession of knighthood thus realigned toward service to God, the medieval blessing of knights is one more example of how such rituals sought to bring the divine and the human worlds into closer alignment, for the benefit of both parties.

The themes we perceive in this blessing of knights and the previous blessings of arms and armor are evident in a much more elaborate ritual: the "*Ordo* for Arming the Church's Defenders or Another Knight." The ritual begins with the blessing of a sword found in the RGP, and then adds a blessing for a lance:

> Lord God omnipotent, light and life of the fabric of the world, who through the hand of Tubalcain instituted smithing for the use of men: look favorably upon the prayer of our office for blessing this lance, for military use, you who permitted the side of your Son, our Lord Jesus Christ, hanging on the cross for our salvation, to be pierced by a soldier with a lance, and through the name of that same one, your Son, may you deign to bless and consecrate it thus, so that you may give to him who shall bear it the prosperous sign of your defense, just as you gave it to Gideon, Saul, and King David, so that always supported by your aid he may rejoice and be glad in you in his prosperities.[115]

This complex invocation draws upon many sacred paradigms from biblical history to frame the blessing and reception of this lance by the medieval warrior. Tubalcain, credited in Genesis as the first human armorer, connects the knight to the sacred history of war.[116] The allusion to the wounding of Christ in the side by the Roman centurion, a story that gained prominence

---

115. Franz, 2:295–96: Domine deus omnipotens, lux et vita fabricae mundi, qui per manus Tubalcain ad usus hominum fabrilia opera instituisti: respice propitius nostri deprecationem officii ad benedicendam hanc lanceam militaris instrumenti, qui a milite latus filii tui, domini nostri Iesu Christi pro nostra salute in cruce pendentis permisisti lancea perforari, et per nomen eiusdem filii tui eam sic consecrare et benedicere digneris, ut is, qui eam tulerit, des ei prosperum signum tuae defensionis, sicut dedisti Gedeoni, Sauli, David quoque regi, ut tuis semper fultus auxiliis congaudeat et laetetur in te in omnibus prosperitatibus suis.
116. Gn 4:22.

following the supposedly miraculous discovery of the Holy Lance by the first crusaders, directly connects the life of the knight or king bearing his less august lance with the sufferings of Christ, lending new life to the power and mystery of that moment as it imbues this insignia of knighthood with the power of the numinous.[117] Such investments occur in six of the eight blessings examined here. That God allowed Christ to be wounded in this manner somehow brought a dignity and power to the lance, an aura that could bolster the confidence of anyone entering a battle in its blessed presence. The reference to biblical kings suggests that this rite may have been designed for the use of a monarch, or at least a leader, and associates the struggles of the current recipient with the struggles and divine power that led to victory in the mythic past.

The third prayer of this ritual blessing extends this association. In this invocation, the leadership of kings is joined with angelic power to guard the knight:

> Lord Jesus, Savior of all and redeemer of souls, incline the ears of your love to the prayers of our humility and through the intervention of the blessed Michael, your archangel, and all the heavenly powers, hold forth the aid of your right hand for this man, and just as you blessed Abraham triumphing against the five kings, and king David conducting triumphal battles in praise of your name...[118]

The conjuration of the archangel Michael, a warrior angel and the patron of many medieval knights, associates the knight or king with the triumphs of this angelic being over the hosts of Satan, an association that brings mythic

---

117. For a discussion of this relic and its discovery, see John H. Hill, "Crusades and Crusader States: To 1192," *DMA* 4:35; Marshall W. Baldwin, ed., *The First Hundred Years,* vol. 1 of *A History of the Crusades,* ed. Kenneth Setton (Madison: University of Wisconsin Press, 1969), 321, 323, 356; Wolfgang Giese, "Die 'lancea Domini' von Antiochia," in *Fälschungen im Mittelalter: Internationaler Kongress der Monumenta Germaniae Historica, München, 16–19 September 1986,* ed. Wolfram Setz (Hanover: Hahnsche Buchhandlung, 1988), 5:485–504; and Randall Rogers, "Peter Bartholomew and the Role of 'the Poor' in the First Crusade," in *Warriors and Churchmen in the High Middle Ages: Essays Presented to Karl Leyser,* ed. Timothy Reuter (London: Hambledon Press, 1992), 109–22.

118. Franz, 2:296: Inclina, domine Iesu, salvator omnium ac redemptor animarum, aures tuae pietatis ad preces nostrae humilitatis et per interventum beati Michaelis, archangeli tui, omniumque coelestium virtutum praesta huic viro auxilium dexterae tuae, et sicut benedixisti Abraham adversum quinque reges triumphantem atque David regem in tue nominis laude triumphales congressus exercentem...

history to life in medieval times. Abraham's and David's victories lend their aura of power and the numinous intervention of God to the efficacy of the blessing and the potency of the knight. This efficacy is complemented by the further invocation, in the eleventh prayer of this ritual, of Christian saints associated with war and conflict: "Lord God, who destroys war and who is the helper and protector of all those hoping in you: hearken kindly to our invocation and through the merits of your martyred saints and knights Mauritius, Sebastian and George, extend victory for this man over his enemies."[119] These saints were often called upon during our period as the special benefactors of soldiers.[120] Such patrons were undoubtedly considered the best intermediaries for channeling the power of the divine into battlefield success owing to their association with the practice of war. Martial blessings include invocations of such warrior saints, but only when the ritual in question is aimed at defending the Christian community or church from external threats.[121] This is significant, in that it calls to mind the feudal relationship of lords as patrons and protectors of their vassals, a relationship that schol-

119. Ibid., 2:297: Domine deus, qui conteris bella et adiutor et protector es omnium in te sperantium: respice propitius invocationem nostram et per merita sanctorum martyrum tuorum et militum Mauritii, Sebastiani, Georgii praesta huic viro victoriam de hostibus suis.

120. Farmer, *Oxford Dictionary of the Saints,* 429, 197–98. Legend has it that St. Sebastian, a Roman martyr who died under the persecutions of Diocletian (c. 300), was a captain of the praetorian guards who comforted the confessors Mark and Marcellian in prison, for which Diocletian had him shot to death with arrows. Sebastian thus came to be the patron saint of archers and soldiers and was one of "the fourteen holy helpers," a group of saints with a collective cult in the Rhineland from the fourteenth century onward. St. George, a martyr (d. c. 303) and eventually the patron saint of England, was also believed to have been a soldier, and George held a position of honor by the time of the Angevin king Richard I as the patron saint of knights, archers, armorers, and common soldiers. The identification of St. Mauritius is more problematic, but the reference is most probably to St. Maurice, a popular soldier-saint who was martyred around 287. The saint was thought to have been Egyptian and the principal officer of the Theban Legion under the command of the emperor Maximian in a campaign against rebellious Gauls. The legend claims that Maurice refused the emperor's order that all legions should offer sacrifice to the gods for military success, and when his legion supported him, Maurice and every last member of the legion were said to have willingly accepted martyrdom at the hands of the emperor and his army. Maurice was a very popular saint in the West, known principally as a patron of soldiers. Although Maurice was martyred at this time, there is no substantive evidence about the willing martyrdom of the entire legion, and the numbers of those thought slain are obviously grossly exaggerated. See ibid., 331–32; *AS* (September 7, 1757): 308–403, 895–926.

121. See the "*Ordo* for Arming the Defense of the Church," and the *RGP*'s "Blessing of a City."

ars such as Thomas Head have discerned in hagiographic sources.[122] Saints in these blessings act as feudal lords, protecting their clients from their enemies.

That God could be conceived of as supporting both peace and war may seem strange to modern minds, but we must remember that medieval people would have seen no conflict in this union of opposites. Since St. Augustine's discussion of just war, the Christian world had accepted that war carried out in defense of the church and the Christian people was an acceptable use of violence by the devout.[123] The call for crusade first issued by Urban II at Clermont was a natural extension of this concept. Hence the blessing's curious invocation of the God "who destroys war" as the sponsor of the medieval soldier fits well with the use of blessings we have seen before, namely, as a tool for preserving the Christian community in the face of the hostile forces of the natural and human world. This desire is also expressed in two other blessings examined here, from the Gellone sacramentary and the pontifical of Roda.[124] One wonders if an end to war was something all knights would have welcomed; this text seems closer to the ideals of the clerical author than to the militant recipients of the blessing, but despite this conflict

---

122. Head, "I Vow Myself to Be Your Servant," 215–30. It was also commonly believe that honoring the mutual responsibilities established between patron saints and their people could prevent supernaturally bad weather and natural disaster. See Ward, *Miracles and the Medieval Mind*, 36.

123. For a discussion of this issue, see Frederick H. Russel, *The Just War in the Middle Ages* (New York: Cambridge University Press, 1975); Carl Erdmann, *The Origin of the Idea of Crusade*, trans. Marshall W. Baldwin and Walter Goffart (Princeton: Princeton University Press, 1977); E. O. Blake, "The Formation of the 'Crusade Idea,'" *Journal of Ecclesiastical History* 21 (1970): 11–31; Herbert E. J. Cowdrey, "Canon Law and the First Crusade," in *The Horns of Hattin: Proceedings of the Second Conference of the Society for the Study of the Crusades and the Latin East, Jerusalem and Haifa, 2–6 July 1987*, ed. Benjamin Z. Kedar (Jerusalem: Variorum, 1992), 41–48; Cowdrey, "The Genesis of the Crusades: The Springs of Western Ideas of Holy War," in Murphy, *Holy War*, 9–32; John A. Brundage, "Holy War and the Medieval Lawyers," in Murphy, *Holy War*, 99–140; and John R. E. Bliese, "The Just War as Concept and Motive in the Central Middle Ages," *Medievalia et Humanistica*, new ser., 17 (1991): 1–26. Augustine's position in brief was that a just war is one that avenges injuries, including injuries done to God. God can authorize war in such cases, and the church had the authority to command such imperial persecutions of sinners and heretics. This idea was adopted by the eleventh-century church and used to define holy war in defense of God as the duty of every knight.

124. The blessing in the pontifical of Roda also appears in the pontifical of Odon of Montaigu, bishop of Elne, 1423 (Paris, Bibl. Nat. lat. 967), whose episcopal blessings are drawn from the pontifical of Durandus.

of interest the prayer is a good example of how the sacred could be adapted to meet the needs of medieval culture.[125] The contrast between these two images of God, and the multitudinous other roles blessings attributed to the divine, highlights the inclusive conception of the sacred held by medieval Christians as a power that embraced any virtue needed by those who ritually implored it.[126]

As the recipient of this blessing was empowered and defended by God, so too are the insignia of his class imbued with the power of the divine. After having said numerous prayers, the bishop girds the knight with his sword and says, "Accept this sword given to you with the blessing of God, in whom you may be able through the power of the Holy Spirit to resist and drive out all your enemies and any adversaries of the holy church of God."[127] Here the power of the *numen*, in the form of the Holy Spirit, is directly conjured for success in the knight's personal battles, but more important in the defense of the interests of the church and the Christian community that it represents. Through this insignia and instrument of the knightly class, the self-interest of both the warrior and the divine world is served, bringing both closer together and ensuring their continued cooperation. The blessings that impart the numinous to the sword, shield, spurs, and other equipment of knights act on the same principle as blessings of the staves and wallets of pilgrims: they imbue the visible and tangible elements of a special social status with divine power.[128]

125. A similarly contradictory juxtaposition appears in the casting of God as a granter of victory in Durandus's blessing of a sword and in a supporting eleventh-century English blessing in times of war, and on the other hand as a destroyer of war, a concept also present in the *RGP* (in the "Blessing of Standards") and in later French rituals, including the "Blessing of Armor" from the thirteenth-century *PWD*.

126. Further evidence for this view may be found in how God was portrayed as a savior and as light itself in the thirteenth-century *ordo* for arming the defenders of the church, as a refuge and solace for the suffering in the *RGP*'s prayer for a besieged city, and as a commander in the twelfth-century pontifical of Besançon's blessing of a sword.

127. Franz, 2:296: Accipe hunc gladium cum dei benedictione tibi collatum, in quo per virtutem spiritus sancti resistere et eicere valeas omnes inimicos tuos et cunctos sanctae dei ecclesiae adversarios adiuvante domino nostro Iesu Christo.

128. The principal ritual actions of blessings for knights are made in the bishop's bestowal of arms and armor on the new knight. While the early blessings of the *RGP* include only prayers, the *PWD* offers a rite for the blessing of armor that includes aspersion with holy water. Durandus's ritual for blessing a knight adds to the earlier rituals by calling for the recipient to brandish his sword, the celebrant to deliver a kiss of peace to the knight, and local nobles to affix the spurs of the new knight to his person.

This theme seems principally a trait of German rituals: four of the six blessings in which it appears are from the tenth-century RGP, which probably set the norm for later rituals, since this theme also appears in the thirteenth-century PWD and a later source.[129] While it is possible that both these blessings and the blessings of pilgrims and crusaders invest insignia merely because of their subject matter (i.e., they are blessings of a particular class of person), it seems more likely that this is an example of the process of incorporating the laity into the sacramental life of the church described by Vauchez and Swanson.[130] Comparative analysis of this theme may reveal a closer connection between these two groups of rites, but that kind of analysis is beyond the scope of this study.

Following this prayer several antiphons and psalms are sung. The first is the antiphon *Speciosus* [*forma prae filiis hominum*] and the answering verse *Accingere* [*gladio tuo super femur tuum potentissime*], both drawn from Psalm 44:3–4 ("For they got not the land in possession by their own sword, neither did their own arm save them: But thy right hand, and thine arm, and the light of thy countenance, because thou hadst a favor unto them").[131] These sacred words reinforce the idea that the knight derives his power from God and God alone, thereby making appropriate moral behavior even more critical to the success of a new knight. This is followed by a *Gloria* and the antiphon *Specie tua* ("Your appearance and your beauty stretch forth, advance and favorably reign").[132] This antiphon invokes God's glory and might as it encourages the knight to go forward and fulfill the duties of his class. A selection

129. See the *RGP*'s "Blessing of a Sword," "Blessing of Standards," "Prayer for an Army," and "Blessing of a City," the "*Ordo* for Arming Defenders of the Church or Another Knight," and the *PWD*'s "Blessing of Armor."

130. André Vauchez, *Spirituality of the Medieval West, 700–1100*, trans. Colette Friedlander (Kalamazoo: Cistercian Publications, 1993), 75–145; Swanson, *Religion and Devotion in Europe*, 21–25, 102–35.

131. Antiphons, like psalms, are infrequently included in blessings of persons. In martial blessings such as this one, the antiphon *Speciosus* is the only specific antiphon mentioned, appearing first in the *RGP*'s blessing of a new sword and subsequently in this rite. Antiphonal song is somewhat more frequently ordered in blessings for health and healing, as versicles appear in several rituals, but no entire antiphon is prescribed by any of this subcategory of blessings (the *RGP*'s "For the Health of One of the Living" includes psalmody but no specific antiphon; the *PWD*'s "Blessing of a Fetus" also contains psalmody).

132. *CAO* 4987: Specie tua et pulchritudine tua, intende prospere procede et regna. This antiphon was also used during the Feast of St. Agnetis, the Purification and Annunciation of St. Mary, the Feast of St. Agatha, the Assumption and Nativity of Mary, the Feast of St. Cecilia, the Common of a Virgin, and the Feast of St. Mary Magdalene.

from the Psalter follows: "In your majesty ride on victoriously for the cause of truth and to defend the right; let your right hand teach you dread deeds. Your arrows are sharp in the hearts of the king's enemies; the peoples fall under you. Your throne, O God, endures forever and ever. Your royal scepter is a scepter of equity."[133] This passage, drawn from a nuptial ode celebrating the marriage of a king to a king's daughter, encourages the pursuit of the godly form of knighthood so desired by the high medieval church, as it affirms the ultimate triumph and justice of God.[134] Its militant imagery accords well with the subject of the rite and implicitly connects the present knight's conduct and attributes with the sacred paradigm presented in scripture.

While this blessing seeks to impart the power of the sacred to serve the interests of the larger institution of the church, it also places surprising emphasis on a kind of worldly happiness we might not initially associate with a liturgical rite composed by a medieval cleric. The ninth prayer of the ritual consists of a blessing for the knight's shield:

> Lord God, Savior of the world, without whom the salvation of man is in vain, hearken to the prayer of our humility and infuse the gift of your blessing upon this shield, a covering of the human body . . . may he [the knight] have you as a shield and defense against the enemies of soul and body, so that fortified on both sides and protected he may bless the name of your glory in all his works.[135]

In this prayer we see a concern for *both* the soul and the body, another instance of how medieval blessings played to the needs, desires, and anxieties of the laity even though composed by clerical and monastic authors who ostensibly subordinated material life to life in the next world. If nothing else, this reflects the fact that the common human experience of ill health, shared by all members of the Christian community, was a powerful influence on

133. Ps 45:5–6.

134. Kirkpatrick, *Book of Psalms*, 242. The "king" of the psalm has been understood since ancient times to mean the Messiah, but Kirkpatrick argues that this interpretation is untenable. The king must be one of the house of David, either Jehoram or Solomon, probably the latter. Despite this, the messianic significance of the psalm is almost universally recognized (ibid., 243–45).

135. Franz, 2:296–97: Domine deus, salvator mundi, sine quo vana salus est hominis, intende deprecationem nostrae humilitatis et super hoc scutum, humani corporis tegumentum, infunde benedictionis tuae donum . . . scutum et tutelam te habeat contra inimicos animae et corporis, ut in utroque vallatus et protectus benedicat nomen gloriae tuae in omnibus suis operibus.

the composition of the blessing. This concern may also be seen in the final prayer of this ritual: "Preserve your servant, we ask, Lord, and return him secure from all adversities, so that he might rejoice in the present life and in the future."[136] The typical concern for the future life in the next world is present in this prayer, but it is again joined to a desire for joy and fulfillment in this life. Thus a rite of blessing could address both facets of medieval existence, using the power of the holy to promote the kind of life in which the individual can be free to fulfill his obligations to God in happiness and thereby maintain the balance that ensures the survival of the larger community as well.

From the preceding analysis it is clear that rituals for creating knights underwent significant change and growth during the period of our study. This was most probably the result of a combination of factors: an ecclesiastical desire to assert the church's spiritual and temporal authority over the increasingly powerful knightly class of feudal Europe; the influence of clerical and monastic efforts to promote the idea of crusade and to make war in the service of the church into both a holy occupation and an aid to personal salvation; and the desire of the laity, particularly the powerful and wealthy, to experience holiness and the religious life in their own station. As numerous forces undoubtedly influenced the elaboration of dubbing rituals, it is also likely that the meaning of such rituals varied depending on perspective. For the recipient knight, such a ritual would probably not be the first blessing he received, but it would be unique in that it marked his coming of age and elevation to a new social order, represented in the insignia blessed during the ritual, as it bestowed upon him the special blessing of God for the Christian warrior. For the celebrant, the blessing was an opportunity not simply to create a new knight but to create a defender of the church by holding up a model of the ideal Christian warrior, a model promoted vigorously by both the secular and regular clergy, and to encourage the knight's obedience to the

136. Ibid., 2:297: Conserva, quaesumus, domine, famulum tuum illum et ab omnibus adversitatibus redde securum, ut in praesenti vita gaudeat et in futura. A similar concern is also expressed in the Roman liturgy for the ritual care of the sick, as preserved in the Vatican Gelasian sacramentary of the sixth century, as examined by Frederick Paxton. Prayers in the Mass for the sick, which are probably slightly older than the Gelasian, seek to restore sick brothers and sisters to the community of worshippers, and they show that the early Roman church did not dwell on the connection between physical disease and sin so emphasized by some scholars; see Paxton, *Christianizing Death*, 30–32. Prayers in the Bobbio missal's mass for the sick have the same concern for the physical health and restoration of the life of the recipient (32).

authority by which the church preached holy war and blessed its crusaders and defenders.

As God could protect the individual and his accoutrements on the battlefield, so too could the larger gathering of an army be blessed through ritual. Since antiquity the church had accompanied Christian armies to battle, with many early medieval liturgical collections containing votive masses and prayers in time of war or for the blessing of armies and their royal commanders.[137] The RGP's "Prayer for an Army" at once casts the army's actions within the framework of biblical history and expresses a concern for the quality of life in this world:

> Grant, Lord, the aid of your mercy for our army, and under clear skies maintain for them the aid sought in setting out and, just as you granted the protection of security for Israel hastening out of Egypt, thus direct an angel, a source of light, for your people going forth into battle, who may defend them by day and by night from all adversity. May the accomplishing of the journeying be without labor for them, in all places the planned-for result, a way without dread, a way of life without monotony, moderate weakness without fear, strength without terror, and an abundance of things and a correct will for giving battle, and when, with your angel as leader, the conqueror will have stood forth, he would not allocate triumph to his own forces but would reflect thanks to the true victor, Christ, your Son, who by the humiliation of his passion on the cross triumphed over death and the prince of death.[138]

137. Franz, 2:300. The Gelasian sacramentary has a Mass *Tempore belli* (an ancient Roman ritual from the German invasions of late antiquity), and the Catholic Visigothic kings of Spain often sought the blessing of the church of Toledo before setting out to battle (see the rich ceremony of the *Liber ordinum* of Silos, Mon. Liturg. 5:149–53). In times of war and before battles, each side in medieval conflicts tried to use church blessings to gain divine assistance and protection. For a pertinent study, see Claude Gaier, "Le rôle militaire des reliques et de l'étendard de Saint Lambert dans la principauté de Liège," *Le Moyen Âge* 72 (1966): 235–50.

138. *RGP* 2:380 (*ordo* 245): Praebe, domine, misericordiae tuae opem exercitui nostro, et sub aeris clariate presta eis optatum proficiscendi auxilium, et, sicut Israheli properanti ex Egypto securitatis prebuisti munimen, ita populo tuo in prelium pergenti lucis auctorem dirige angelum, qui eos die noctuque ab omni adversitate defendat. Sit eis itinerandi sine labore profectus, ubique providus eventus, meatus sine formidine, conversatio sine fastidio, moderate fragilitas sine metu, fortitudo sine terrore, copia rerum et proeliandi recta voluntas, et, cum, tuo angelo duce, victor extiterit, non suis tribuat viribus, sed ipsi victori Christo filio tuo gratias referat de triumpho, qui humilitate suae passionis de morte mortisque principe in cruce triumphavit.

The exodus of the Israelites is an appropriate metaphor for the excursion of an army, going forth in both confidence and anxiety toward an uncertain future, with only the promise of success to sustain them. Yet the adoption of this paradigm from sacred history demonstrates the manner in which the meaning of scripture could be adapted to fit the needs of the ritual blessing, glossing over the difference between an exodus of unarmed, impoverished former slaves and a well-armed force advancing on an enemy in order to lend the aura of power and triumph of the former to the latter and thus a kind of reversal of sense that exalts both parties. With the invocation of the angelic guardian, we note an intense concern (not unlike that demonstrated in the blessings of pilgrims for the road) that God's power be employed to improve the life of the soldiers in *this* world, easing their burdens on the campaign trail as it strengthened their inner resolve, extracting every harmful thing while preserving the beneficial: "a way *without* dread . . . weakness *without* fear, strength *without* terror" (emphasis added). The invocation of an angel of defense is typical of knights and war: they appear as agents of defense in three rituals and one supporting rite examined here.[139]

Finally, this blessing provides another example of how the incidents of Christ's life could serve as the ultimate paradigm for a blessing, empowering the soldiers of the army with the triumph of Christ by bringing that ancient victory to life and making it real. The insistence that this victory be attributed to God and Christ's sacrifice, not to an individual's strength, also reveals the tension we have noted previously between religious ideals and knightly character, as well as the contractual relationship of God and knight. This relationship, expanded to include the Christian people as well as the knight himself, appears explicitly in four rituals for knightly and war blessings, drawn from French and German sources of the ninth, eleventh, and thirteenth centuries, which suggests that it was an important element of this kind of blessing.[140]

139. See the *RGP*'s "Prayer for an Army" and "Blessing of a City," the "*Ordo*" for Arming the Defenders of the Church," and the Canterbury benedictional's "Blessing in Time of War, or against the Danes." As in house blessings and the blessings of pilgrims, angels are invoked in these German and English rituals of the tenth to the thirteenth century to shield and protect the recipients of the blessings. This association of angels with defense is further strengthened by the fact that all the invocations appear in rituals specifically designed to defend groups: an army, a city, the church at large, and in a blessing against the depredations of Danish raiders. But, as we shall see below, angels gave way to other powers in cases of extreme physical need.

140. See the Gellone sacramentary's "Blessing in Time of War," the *RGP*'s "Prayer for an Army" and "Blessing of a City," and the *PWD*'s "Blessing of Armor."

The arsenal of martial blessings could even be expended to protect entire urban communities in danger of attack from forces outside the bounds of the Christian community. The subject of holy combat on this scale is too immense to warrant a thorough treatment here, but it is worth considering how such rites as the RGP's "Blessing of a City against the Gentiles" fit into this tradition. Augustine Thompson has skillfully shown how, in the Italian communes of the central Middle Ages, wars between cities and their enemies were often accompanied by rhetoric of divine favor and holy war that implied strongly that God and his saints, especially the patron saint of the city, led the commune in battle.[141] This relationship parallels the kind of contractual relationship seen in many blessings. As Thompson puts it, "Cities and their patrons had a reciprocal relationship. The saints in heaven protected their cities, by intercession with God; the cities on earth celebrated their patrons with acts of devotion and homage."[142] In some cases, faith in the divine clearly played a significant role in battles, at least in the minds of its participants: when the city of Gubbio underwent a siege in the twelfth century, Bishop Ubaldo gave a special episcopal blessing to the whole city, leading ultimately to victory, a vast slaughter of the enemy, and "much rejoicing."[143]

While much of the RGP's "Blessing of a City against the Gentiles" is a formulaic invocation for protection, it does demonstrate the familiar adaptability of God's power:

> God, refuge of the sorrowful, consoler of the afflicted, we humbly entreat your clemency that, applying the aid of your defense to those afflicted by the op-

141. Thompson, *Cities of God*, 108–9. Angels could also serve as patrons, such as Michael at the battle for Vicenza in 1264, but Mary held the highest and most special place as patron and protector of the peace. As the thirteenth century progressed, invocations of holy protectors by the communes multiplied almost to the point of obsession, as happened in Florence in 1325, when the city fathers invoked God, the Virgin, St. Michael, John the Baptist, Peter, Paul, Philip, James, Barnabas, Reparata, Cenobius, Miriatius, and (for good measure) "all the saints of God" (ibid., 114). A similar pattern can be observed in the blessings of the sick and in ordeals, discussed later in this chapter and in the following one.

142. Ibid., 119–20. One must note that such relationships between saints and their devotees is a common feature of medieval piety, and not one limited to either the act of war or the instrument of blessings. For an example of this, see Head, "I Vow Myself to Be Your Servant."

143. Thompson, *Cities of God*, 158–59, citing Giordano of Città di Castello, *Vita Beati Ubaldi Eugubini Episcopi*, 14.6–15, p. 101. Belief in the power of such protectors may also be seen in art, as in Verona's Romanesque church of St. Zeno, where the sculpture of the bishop saint holds his pastoral staff and blesses the communal militia, commemorating the independence of the city from imperial rule and establishment of the commune in the 1130s (ibid., 115–16).

pression of the peoples, you might deign to save and deliver us. Give, we entreat, strength to the weary, assistance to the laboring, solace to the sorrowful, help to those beset.[144]

The sacred here becomes an all-purpose remedy for the ills of a besieged community. This blessing is explicit in its conjuration of the power of the holy into the very walls of the town:

encircle this city by the defense of your power, and defend all remaining in it by the help of your immense godliness; on its walls and gates place a watch of angels, the aid of salvation, the fortifications of all your saints, so that we who are justly cast down for our sins, trusting in your mercy alone, may be assisted.[145]

The power of the divine becomes another layer of protection through this ritual, imbuing the very fabric of the city's defense with its potency, and conscripting all manner of heavenly beings, angels and saints, to maintain that protection. God here takes on a tangible quality, working in perfect accord with the natural elements of the town to ensure the survival of the faithful human community.

ILLNESS, HEALING, RECOVERY, AND CHILDBIRTH

Of all the uses to which the sacred power of blessings was put, one of the most frequent was healing and the easing of pain. The problem of disease and medicine in the early Middle Ages was one that occupied the theologians and legislators of the church to a great degree. As Valerie Flint has demonstrated, this problem was a major concern in the early medieval church's conflict with practitioners of magic, who offered an alternative method of healing that (aside from being attributed to dubious, even demonic, origins) was distasteful to churchmen for the competition it offered the church as a source of solace.[146] The church's desire to control the dispensation of healing was a

144. *RGP* 2:378 (*ordo* 242): Mestorum refugium, Deus, tribulatorum consolator, clementiam tuam suppliciter exoramus, ut afflictis oppressione gentium auxilium tuae defensionis impendens eripere nos et salvare digneris. Tribue, quesumus, fortitudinem fessis, laborantibus opem, solatium tristibus, adiutorium tribulatis.

145. Ibid.: Circumda civitatem hanc virtutis tuae presidio, et omnes in ea manentes immensae pietatis defende iuvamine; pone in muris et in portis eius angelorum custodiam, salutis auxilia, munitionem omnium sanctorum tuorum, ut, qui pro peccatis nostris iuste affligimur, de sola tua misericordia, confidentes, miserationis tuae munere adiuvemur.

146. Flint, *Rise of Magic*, 240–41. Flint has also explored hagiographic evidence to illuminate the complex relationship between early medieval medical practitioners, or *medici*, and

natural outgrowth of its core value of ministering to the sick, and of the belief that disease was the result of the action of evil angels, or demons, who could inflict pestilence and other maladies to torment or punish human beings.[147] Dependent on this belief was the complementary conviction some held that illness was the direct result of sin, which, along with witchcraft and possession by the Devil, has typically been identified in histories of medieval medicine as the range of medieval explanations for the origins of disease. This view, however, ignores the evidence of numerous historical, hagiographical, and liturgical sources that show that sin was offered as an explanation for illness only in a very limited set of circumstances.[148] Belief in a connection between the demonic and illness, however, was universal, and it is to this belief, as well as to the fear of natural illnesses, that blessings ministered.

Prayers of exorcism and charms for health were extraordinarily impor-

---

saints and their cults, and has found that while hagiographical authors often cast the *medicus* as a foil to the powers of their saintly patron, the *medicus* could and often did hold a place of respect in the eyes of the Christian community, and could be an ally in assisting the guardians of shrines in their constant competition with enchanters and their magical, demonic wonders. See Valerie J. Flint, "The Early Medieval 'Medicus,' the Saint—and the Enchanter," *Social History of Medicine* 2, no. 2 (1989): 127–45. For the conflicting notions of saint's healing *potentia* and paganism's "do-it-yourself" healing in late Roman Gaul, see Brown, *Cult of the Saints*, 113–20.

147. This power was somewhat ambiguous, as some claimed that it could inflict disease only by the will of God or his good angels, while others associated it with the inherent nature of demons or saw illness as the result of human sin. See Flint, *Rise of Magic*, 163; Darrel W. Amundsen, *Medicine, Society and Faith in the Ancient and Medieval Worlds* (Baltimore: Johns Hopkins University Press, 1996), 187–88. The diagnosis of the origins of disease seems to have played a major role in determining the prescription for healing. While the church and *magi* relied on exorcism, ritual, prayer, and incantations to heal the sick, formally trained *medici* eschewed these devices and relied almost exclusively on naturalistic remedies such as herbal ointments and mixtures. See Nancy G. Siraisi, *Medieval and Early Renaissance Medicine: An Introduction to Knowledge and Practice* (Chicago: University of Chicago Press, 1990), 149.

148. See Jerome Kroll and Bernard Bachrach, "Sin and the Etiology of Disease in Pre-Crusade Europe," *Journal of the History of Medicine and Allied Sciences* 41 (1986): 395–414. Kroll and Bachrach convincingly demonstrate through traditional and quantitative analysis of chronicles and hagiographical sources that God's involvement in inflicting disease as a punishment for sin occurs only when medieval authors had a fundamental grievance against the sick; in the absence of such animosity, sin is not cited as a cause (395–96 and 409–11). This being said, it is clear from similar sources that the laity recognized and feared illness brought on by sin. Benedicta Ward has studied numerous miracle stories that reflect this attitude. Two in particular are revealing: in one, a boy refuses to accompany his parents on a pilgrimage to Canterbury to seek forgiveness for their sins and is struck down by a grave illness that quickly persuades him to make the pilgrimage; in the other, from the *Miraculi S. Anselmi*, a story of three knights on pilgrimage to Santiago de Compostela, when one of the knights becomes ill,

tant in the church's efforts to deal with disease; and central to the exercise of these remedies was the action of angels, especially Michael, Raphael, and Gabriel.[149] These Christian supernatural practices for curing often came perilously close to the magical praxis so virulently condemned by the church, particularly in cures involving relics, Christian writings used as talismans imbued with healing power, and cures that employed incantations, invoking names from scripture to heal.[150] Some of the best examples of such charms and prayers can be found in Anglo-Saxon sources, many of which mingle prayers and incoherent mistranslations of Latin scripture to protect and heal those suffering from a variety of diseases, such as the "elf-shot" charms of tenth- and eleventh-century Anglo-Saxon England.[151]

While enchantments and incantations of dubious origin were condemned by reformers of the early Middle Ages, there were acceptable forms of healing that differed from such magical praxis principally in their origins: liturgical prayers, rituals of blessing, and masses for the healing of illness.[152] The divine, so readily adaptable to the needs of individuals and communities, was one of the most potent remedies for the multitudinous afflictions suffered by people living in an age that lacked effective medicine. In particular, blessings were used to combat several specific maladies and circumstances that reveal further dimensions of their nature and use within medieval culture: blessings against general plagues affecting humans and livestock, against various fevers and ailments in individuals, blessings against the maladies of human eyes, the sterility of women, and those suffering impotence

---

the other two are convinced that his illness is caused by a secret sin of which he must repent in order to be healed. Ward, *Miracles and the Medieval Mind*, 96, 114.

149. Flint, *Rise of Magic*, 153, 164; see also E. A. Lowe, ed., *The Bobbio Missal*, Henry Bradshaw Society 58 (London: Boydell Press, 1920; reprint, 1991), 153.

150. Flint, *Rise of Magic*, 303. Flint argues that the reverence given to such objects made them very adaptable to this purpose.

151. Ibid., 315; Jolly, *Popular Religion*, 96–169. Cures that invoked the power of healing herbs through charms were a special target for Anglo-Saxon reformers such as Aelfric, who despised the recourse to such bogus forms of healing. Instead, he commanded that "none shall enchant a herb with magic, but, with God's word shall bless it and so eat it." See Jolly, *Popular Religion*, 309; see also *The Passion of St. Bartholomew the Apostle*, ed. B. Thorpe, in *The Homilies of the Anglo-Saxon Church* (London: Aelfric Society, 1884–86), 475, 477.

152. For an excellent study of the church's struggle to use liturgy as the predominant form of medicine in the early Middle Ages, see Frederick Paxton, "Liturgy and Healing in an Early Medieval Saint's Cult: The Mass *in honore sancti Sigismundi* for the Cure of Fevers," *Traditio* 49 (1994): 23–44; Paxton, *Christianizing Death*.

or infertility, and for both the woman and the fetus during and following pregnancy. Owing to the multitudinous purposes of these rituals, I have enlarged the sample of rites studied for this category of blessings to twelve: a "Blessing against Fevers," from a ninth-century manuscript;[153] an "Adjuration against Fevers," from a tenth-century St. Gall manuscript;[154] "Prayers Begun against Chills," from a tenth- or eleventh-century Burgundian manuscript;[155] a "Blessing in a Time of Pestilence," from the mid-eleventh-century Canterbury benedictional;[156] a "Prayer for a Mass for Female Sterility," from the RGP;[157] "Other [Prayers] for the Sterility of Women," also from the RGP;[158] a "Blessing after Birth," from an eleventh- or twelfth-century manuscript of Salzburg;[159] a "Blessing against Pestilence," from the later thirteenth-century benedictional of John Longlonde, bishop of Lincoln;[160] a ritual "Concerning the Blessing of a Fetus in the Womb of the Mother," from the PWD;[161] an "Adjuration against Cataracts," from a Germanic manuscript dating to the first half of the fourteenth century;[162] a "Blessing of Eyes," from a fifteenth-century Germanic manuscript;[163] and a "Prayer for the Impeded in Matrimony on Account of a Demon or Evil Doers," drawn from a Dominican missal of 1519.[164] As these themes cross over divisions into subcategories (for example, eye blessings versus pregnancy blessings), the differentiation between types of healing blessings is of secondary importance and occurs therefore at a secondary level. Numerous other benedictions corroborate the themes and issues analyzed here, and these data have been indexed at the end of this work.

153. Franz, 2:480–81; the ritual is drawn from Clm 14179, fol. 55.

154. Ibid., 2:481; the ritual is drawn from CSG *cod.* 550, p. 55.

155. Ibid., 2:482–84; the ritual is drawn from BAV Pal. lat. 235, fols. 44–45. The presence of Saint Simphorianus, a martyr of Autun (c. 180, venerated especially in Autun and Trevoux), and Saint Sigismund, king of Burgundy (d. 524), strongly suggests that its origin is Burgundian; see the analysis below, and Pierre Salmon, *Les manuscrits liturgiques latins de la Bibliothèque Vaticane*, 5 vols. (Vatican City: Biblioteca Apostolica Vaticana, 1968–72), 5:71 (no. 315).

156. *CB* no. 1239.   157. *RGP* 2:420–21 (*ordo* 257).

158. Ibid., 2:421 (*ordo* 258).

159. Franz, 2:210; the ritual is drawn from CVP lat. 2090, fol. 95v.

160. *CB* no. 1175.   161. *PWD* 678–80, appendix 3.

162. Franz, 2:494–95; from Clm 4350, fol. 81, written or copied in 1338. Franz states that this popular *ordo* contains older ecclesiastical prayers and adjurations but does not list these sources (2:491).

163. Ibid., 2:496–98, from Clm 7021, fol. 168vb.

164. Ibid., 2:184; in the Paris edition of the missal, edited by Wolfgang Hopylio, fol. 43.

The blessing rites for the prevention or elimination of pestilence are some of the earliest blessings of interest for our purposes. A group of rites from the eleventh century reveals in particular how blessings for health were aimed at converting a physical disease into an opportunity for spiritual growth. In the Canterbury benedictional's "Blessing in a Time of Pestilence," an *ordo* found also in the Lanalet and Sherborne pontificals and the benedictional of Archbishop Robert of Jumièges, the first clause reveals the intimate connection medieval people perceived between the nature of physical diseases and spiritual failings: "Deign, our Lord God, to bestow a heavenly blessing upon the people, to take away diseased pestilence and sicknesses, not only of the body, but also of the soul."[165] This connection of illness with the spirituality of the afflicted person is explicitly referred to in eight rituals examined by this author. Six of the rituals originate in Germany, two in England, and one in France, and occur in the ninth, tenth, eleventh, thirteenth, and fifteenth centuries, with clusters of three and two blessings occurring in the tenth and thirteenth centuries, respectively.[166] This theme thus appears to be a major element in the high medieval conception of sickness and the sacred, and in the connection of medieval people's lives to the numinous world.

The second clause of the blessing extends the connection by focusing on one of several causes of disease accepted by medieval believers, sin: "And may despair not depress those who are afflicted justly for sins and repent with deserving merits, but may God bring them to hope in heaven."[167] The affliction of disease, seen as the result of sin in this and the final part of the

165. *CB* no. 1239 a: Dignare, domine deus noster, caelestem super populum impertiri benedictionem, pestilentias morbidasque aegritudines auferre, non tantum corporis, sed et animae. For the other appearances of this *ordo*, see G. H. Doble, ed., *Pontifical Lanalatense: A Pontifical Formerly in Use at St. Germans, Cornwall,* Henry Bradshaw Society 74 (London: Harrison and Sons, 1937), 65c; and Paris, Bibl. Nat. lat. 943 (late tenth century, from the pontifical of St. Dunstan of Sherborne).

166. See the Canterbury benedictional's "Blessing in Time of Pestilence," the Longlonde benedictional's "Blessing against Pestilence," Clm 14179's "Blessing versus Fever," the *PWD*'s "Blessing of a Fetus," Clm 7021's "Blessing of Eyes," the *RGP*'s "Blessing for Health," the "Blessing for Cross Water," and a "Blessing against Bleeding." A similar connection is evident in blessings that posit a link between human health and an individual's morality. From the eleven rituals examined that contain this theme, it is clear that the theme is a particularly German one: it appears from the eighth to the thirteenth century but clusters mainly in the tenth (four blessings), eleventh, and twelfth (two blessings).

167. *CB* no. 1239 b: Et, qui iuste pro peccatis affliguntur meritisque condignis conteruntur, hos desperatio non deprimat, sed sperare superna perficiat.

blessing, where it is explained that "thus your [God's] paternity corrects and lashes its sons,"[168] is further made by the blessing into an opportunity for developing a closer relationship with the divine world, one founded on repentance and faith. This relationship fits well into the general medieval conception of illness evident in other sources treating the topic, notably in the pastoral handbook of Pope Gregory the Great, in which Gregory commands that "the sick are to be admonished to realize that they are sons of God by the very fact that the scourge of discipline [i.e., disease] chastises them."[169]

A similar notion may be perceived in a later text, namely, the thirteenth-century benedictional of John Longlonde, bishop of Lincoln. This text, a "Blessing against Pestilence," employs scripture, as we have seen in previous rituals. The blessings for health and recovery make the greatest use of scripture that we have encountered in blessings thus far. Fifteen rituals employ scriptural allusion and/or Christian legend to contextualize and empower their prayers.[170] Through such stories, allusions, and recitations of scriptural history, blessings of persons made these figures and moments live again in the lives of the persons receiving the sacred power mediated by the benedictions, connecting them with the meaningful and defining moments of their cosmos. This particular blessing uses an allusion to the Old Testament figure of King David to illustrate God's power to transform physical suffering

168. Ibid., c: Paternitas tua, Christe, sic filios corrigat et flagellet.

169. Gregory the Great, *Pastoral Care* 3.12, trans. Henry Davis (New York: Newman Press, 1950), 122.

170. See Clm 14179's "Blessing versus Fevers," the *RGP*'s "Mass for Female Sterility," BAV Pal. lat. 2090's "Blessing after Birth," the Longlonde benedictional's "Blessing against Pestilence," the *PWD*'s "Blessing of a Fetus in the Womb," Clm 7021's "Blessing of Eyes," the Dominican missal's "Prayers against Impeded Matrimony [impotence]," the *RGP*'s "Prayers for Sterility," St. Gall's "Prayers versus Chills," the Gellone sacramentary's "Blessing versus Mortality," Vienna 1888's "Blessing of Salt" and "Blessing of Eyes," Helmstädt 493's "Blessing of Salt," the St. Zeno "Blessing in Bed," and St. Gall's "Blessing on Infirm Eyes." The allusions are scattered so diffusely throughout the period of our study that no discernible overall pattern of development can be found in them. They draw nearly equally on the Old and New Testaments, with the inclusion of one Christian legend. But it is possible to find certain allusions common to specific subcategories of blessings for health. The most plentiful of these can be found in blessings for pregnancy, childbirth, and recovery: the miracle of Sarah's restored fertility, the role of Mary as the quintessential mother, and the story of Elizabeth, the wife of Zacharias, all appear in multiple rituals of this subcategory. Blessings for eye ailments and eye illness also share common themes, in this case the restoration of sight to the aged Tobias in the Old Testament (which appears in two blessings), and the illumination of the blind man at the pool of Siloh in the New Testament (appearing in three rituals).

into spiritual redemption: "And may he, who restrained the destroying angel for the sake of the humiliated David at the latter's prayers, change the sighs of his scourged people to the perpetual reward of himself in the glory and honor of his name."[171] Pestilence and disease afflict the medieval community as they did King David when he begged for mercy from the wrath of God, both afflicted for their sin and unworthiness to serve God. Both David and medieval people hoped for release from divine retribution through prayer, which serves as a model for the larger expectation of this blessing: that the prayers of the celebrant will liberate the people from the burden of ill health. Divinity is invoked as the power that has already proved its capacity to effect such a resolution, and God is reminded by this invocation to fulfill his obligation to protect the human community from plague. In exchange for this protection, the "sighs" of the people will be transformed into praise and glory for the name of God, the principal benefit for divinity in the contractual obligation understood to exist between humanity and divinity. Contractual statements like this are common in blessings for illness and healing, appearing in eight of the total blessings examined in this category.[172]

Rites invoking the divine power of protection against chills and fevers exhibit these and other themes. Popular belief attributed the existence of fever or chills to the presence of demons, which authors numbered anywhere between seven and seventy, each responsible for a unique type of fever.[173] The presence of the demonic in the healing blessings reflects this widespread belief in the power of demons to inflict illness, either through sheer malice or through the will of God, who tests and chastises the Christian community

171. *CB* no. 1175 c: Quique David humiliato ipsius precibus angelum compescuit exterminatorem, populi sui flagellati suspiria in fructum ipsius perpetuum, in sui nominis convertat gloriam et honorem. The biblical reference is to 1 Chr 21:15–17, 2 Sm 24:15–17.

172. See the Longlonde benedictional's "Blessing against Pestilence," the *RGP*'s "Mass for a Sterile Woman" and "Prayers for Feminine Sterility," Vienna 2090's "Blessing after Birth," the *PWD*'s "Blessing of a Fetus," and Clm 7021's "Blessing of Eyes." The theme is widespread geographically, being present in blessings from German, French, Austrian, and English sources. The majority of these, four of the six, appear in blessings for women, suggesting that the efficacy of such rites was thought to rely most heavily on the maintenance of the relationship between God and the mother and child, in order to ensure continuity of worship for the one and survival for the other two. The presence of contractual elements does not explain fully, though, the process of blessings for health, as many of the rites emphasize healing as a simple gift from God or see it as an exorcism of evil powers.

173. Franz, 2:467–68. An excellent example of such a fever may be seen in Frederick Paxton's discussion of the quartain fever and St. Sigismund (see above, note 152).

with illness, and demonstrates the influence these beliefs had on liturgical authors.[174] Remedies for such fevers were numerous, but the most popular included visits to holy wells, appeal to the saints, a small number of ecclesiastical blessings that invoked the pains and sufferings of Christ in an attempt to draw God's mercy down upon the sick, and the touch or immersion of a cross in water or wine, the holiness of which was believed to transfer to the liquid it touched.[175] The use of this "cross water" or "cross wine" spread from England to the continent in the seventh century, its spread no doubt assisted by the *Immersio crucis* (the consecration of water during Epiphany), which served as a model for the dispensation of such liquid as a sovereign remedy for fevers and other illnesses.[176] The customary practice of blessing

174. While mention of the demonic occurs in only one of the blessings for knights and war, namely, the twelfth-century pontifical of Besançon's blessing of a sword, it is relatively common in blessings for illness and recovery. In this category demons figure in four rites, of which three are for women (see the *RGP*'s "Blessing of Cross Water," Lambach's "Blessing after Birth," *PWD*'s "Blessing of a Fetus," and the Dominican Missal's "Blessing against Impeded Matrimony"). The rituals originate in France and Germany and span the entire period of our study, appearing in the tenth, twelfth, thirteenth, and sixteenth centuries. That these rituals are all northern supports Franz's assertion that Roman liturgical authors accorded demons a much smaller role in the etiology of disease (Franz, 2:212–13), and that they predominate in blessings for women suggests that these northern authors saw feminine biology as particularly susceptible to the powers of evil spirits, possibly owing to assumptions about woman's "weaker" nature inherited from antiquity and Christian scripture.

175. Franz, 2:467–69, 474. Ritual blessings could and did include both ritual prayer and the use of a cross. There are numerous prayers and votive masses for healing in the sacramentaries of the early Middle Ages: the Gelasian sacramentary has prayers against plague (3.38), sterility (3.43, 3.54), and sickness (3.69–71); and the Gregorian sacramentary has prayers for the health of the living (nos. 126, 127, 129), against plague (no. 167), feminine sterility (no. 202), sickness (no. 203), and fevers (no. 211); see Mohlberg, *Liber sacramentorum;* and Deshusses, *Sacramentaire grégorien.* An example of a holy well can be found in the description of the stream that issued forth north of the altar at the shrine of Monte Gargano: "There was a glass vessel next to this stream, hanging by a silver chain, that received this pleasant water. It was the custom there of that people when they had gone to the eucharist to go up to that glass vessel along a ladder and there receive and taste that heavenly liquid. It was then pleasant to taste and healthful to the innards. This is also a miracle, that many people with fever and various other diseases would immediately be healed through the taste of this liquid." Boenig, "Dedication of the Church of St. Michael," in *Anglo-Saxon Spirituality,* 76–77.

176. Franz, 2:467–69. By the ninth century a ritual prayer for the consecration of water by the submersion of a cross can be found (see BAV Pal. lat. 485), and from the eleventh century, rituals employing wine for the same purpose may also be found. In addition to the *Immersio crucis,* support for this practice could come (as Amalarius of Metz mentions) from the *Adoratio crucis* on Good Friday, when the Cross was carried outside the church for this purpose. Amalarius

water and wine varied greatly from region to region: in one diocese a person might drink it on three successive Fridays to effect a cure; in another area, one might drink the water once before dawn and once in the late evening; others might drink from only square or angular containers.[177]

The custom of immersion was popular not only with the laity but also within certain monastic communities, and the blessed liquid was undoubtedly distributed to the monastery's dependents and the needy as required.[178] Saints' relics provided a similar healing function.[179] Popular folklore and magical practice had their own cures for fevers, mingling blessings of water and salt with the blessing and consumption of bread, apples, and cheeses in an effort to heal the victim through sympathetic magic.[180] Monastic sources also provided their own, similar rites, such as are contained within the *Physica* of Hildegarde of Bingen.[181] Alongside ecclesiastical blessings, many for-

---

of Metz, *Amalarii episcopi opera liturgica omnia*, ed. Johanne M. Hanssens (Vatican City: Biblioteca Apostolica Vaticana, 1948), vol. 2, chap. 14, 99–107. Franz remarks that this practice is reminiscent of Bede's account of St. Oswald, who, in 635, begged victory for his army at the foot of a cross, since all crosses were thought to have sacred power. Bede tells how in another instance the saint had small rods cut from this cross, immersed these in water, then distributed the water among sick persons or animals to speed their recovery. Bede, *Ecclesiastical History*, 215.

177. Franz, 2:470–71. All of these special conditions attributed a special meaning or power to the water or wine.

178. Ibid., 2:473–74. Wine was consecrated for use against fever on the feast day of St. Gall, who was chosen for this honor because St. Gall had been prevented by fever from traveling to Italy with St. Columba, a delay that led St. Gall to found his own monastery. The Carmelites in the late Middle Ages also used water made sacred by the immersion of the relic of St. Albertus.

179. One example comes from Ralph of Tortaire, a monk of Fleury, who wrote of *saint vinage*, water in which relics had been dipped that was then given to the sick to drink and pour over their maimed parts; see *Histoire littéraire de la France* 7:102, 125, quoted in Ward, *Miracles and the Medieval Mind*, 49.

180. Franz, 2:469. The custom of immersion was even the subject of a bitter controversy in the late Middle Ages between the University of Vienna's theological masters and a local preacher who had condemned the practice. The debate ultimately led to Magister Johannes Geuss's commission to write and teach the clergy and people the orthodox interpretation of this ritual's use and meaning. For a complete discussion of this incident, see ibid., 2:471–73; the source is Johannes Geuss, *Sermo de potacione vini, cui immergitur lignum sanctae crucis, et de potacione sancti Iohannis* (in BAV Pal. lat. 442, fols. 359v–366r). The treatise concluded that the prayer and immersion of the cross do not unconditionally guarantee recovery; rather, the soul's condition is of primary importance in determining who will be healed. A suffering believer must beg for healing in eucharistic love and prayer and with confidence in Christ.

181. *PL* 197:1125–1352. Monastics, as allegedly holy people, often fulfilled a similar role

mulas, called benedictions or adjurations, were not sponsored but tolerated de facto by the church as remedies for fever.[182] We shall examine some of these below, but first it is worth remarking on the use and function of ritual action within blessings for healing and alleviation of fever. The blessings for illness, healing, and recovery include only a few instances of prescribed ritual actions, but some of those are significant and intriguing. Aspersion is relatively rare, appearing in only two rites: the thirteenth-century supplemental blessing of a fetus found in some copies of the pontifical of Durandus, and in the supporting blessing of a woman after birth found in the twelfth-century Lambach pontifical (although the use of holy water is implicit in the rites for blessing of salt for the eyes).[183] More interesting than aspersion, though, is the use of ritual imitation in blessings for eyes. The healing of the blind man at the pool of Siloh recounted in the Gospel of John is explicitly imitated in the rubrics of two fifteenth-century blessings, either in the use of the spittle to make mud to place a cross above the afflicted eyes or in the covering of the eyes with the mud.[184]

---

themselves, as in the story told by Hugh Farsit, canon of St. Jean des Vignes, who recounts how an ill girl was cured by the abbess Mathilda (see the *Libellus de miraculis Beatae Mariae, PL* 179:1779–80).

182. Franz, 2:474–75. These blessings and adjurations contain ecclesiastical phrases and terms corresponding to the popular view of the demonic origin of fevers. For example, they refer to the "seven sisters," demons who inflicted a variety of fevers and were abjured to cease their evil by these rituals. Such popular blessings also called on the Trinity, the Christian mysteries, and patron saints (especially the seven sleepers, St. Benedict, St. Vitus, St. Gallus, and St. Gumbertus) to effect their cures, but many also went beyond orthodox belief, threatening demons with angelic wrath and using the Gospel of John's preface as a magical incantation to ward off the demons. This practice itself, however, could claim some legitimacy from the common practice in rural areas all across Europe of chanting the opening verses of the Gospels while crossing fields, since these texts were "pregnant with sacred power, symbolically containing the whole of the following Gospel. Chanting the four Gospels toward the cardinal directions could [also] cleanse and protect a sacred building" (Thompson, *Cities of God,* 155–56). Old German fever blessings, however, clearly have their origin in Latin ecclesiastical blessings, and they use ecclesiastical adjuration formulas as well as saints' names from the Latin benedictions, stressing the torture of Christ on the Cross as a power to heal the sick (Franz, 2:476).

183. See Vienna 1888's "Blessing of Salt" and Helmstädt's "Blessing of Salt for the Eyes of Men."

184. See St. Gall's "Blessing upon Infirm Eyes" and Clm 7021's "Blessing of Eyes." The scripture is Jn 9:1–41. This ritual imitation is a good example of both Eliade's and Geertz's notion of ritual as reenacting sacred time, making contemporary events resonate with the deeds of divine and mythical figures, and connecting the participants to the stories that give their world meaning.

In addition to scriptural reenactments such as these, blessings also drew upon less authoritative sources, including Christian legend and folklore. In a "Blessing against Fevers," from the ninth-century manuscript Munich, Bayerische Staatsbibliothek, Clm 14179, one incident invoked from the sacred history of medieval Christianity was the legend of the seven sleepers:

> In the city of Ephesus on Mount Celius there rest seven sleepers: Maximinianus, Malchus, Martinianus, Constantinus, Dionysus, Johannes, and Serapion. In the name of the Father, Son, and Holy Spirit, through their merit and intercession may omnipotent God deign to save this servant N. from all infirmity of fever or chills.[185]

This allusion refers to a sixth-century legend in which seven early Christians of Ephesus were walled up in a cave, while hiding from the persecution of the emperor Decius, and left to die. God intervened by placing them in a deep sleep, and two hundred years later they awoke to marvel at their city, which was then a Christian stronghold. After seeing their city transformed, all dropped dead and were immediately venerated as saints.[186] This legend may have been adopted as a numerological counter to the power of the fevers known as the "seven sisters," or as a metaphor for awakening: as the sleepers awoke to joy in this life and entry into the new life of heaven, so too

---

185. Franz, 2:480–81 (V): In Ephasa civitate in monte Celio ibi requiescunt VII dormientes: Maximinianus, Malchus, Martinianus, Constantinus, Dionisius, Iohannes, Serapion. In nomine patris et filii et spiritus sancti. Per merita et intercessionem eorum omnipotens deus dignetur salvare istum famulum illum ab omni infirmitate febris vel frigoris. This story resembles other narratives inserted into healing blessings; see the discussion of eye blessings below. It is difficult to know why the seven sleepers were included only in these ninth- and tenth-century blessings, or what they meant to the participants in fever blessings beyond the general power of intercession. The legend of the seven sleepers is thought to have been created as a means of demonstrating the truth of bodily resurrection of the dead, particularly in connection with the Origenist controversies, appearing first in the East (known by Jacob of Sarug) and the West (known by St. Gregory of Tours) in the sixth century. Pilgrims visited the supposed shrine of the sleepers until the conquest of Asia Minor by the Turks; see "Seven Sleepers of Ephesus," Livingstone, *Oxford Dictionary of the Christian Church*, 1489–90.

186. Farmer, *Oxford Dictionary of the Saints*, 433. Some scholars have suggested that this legend represents a Christianization of the ancient story modernized in Washington Irving's *Rip van Winkle*. This tale bears similarity to other cultures' folklore, from the Celtic tales of benighted souls who spend an evening in fairyland and return to a human world that no longer remembers them, as well as to the Japanese tale of Urashima Taro; see Jobes, *Dictionary of Mythology*, 1628. Its inclusion in liturgical blessings suggests that it was both a familiar and a serious element of medieval legend and culture.

does the blessing seek to awaken the Christian "sleeping" in sin and sickness to health and new life. Such an awakening can be interpreted, I would argue, as a rite of passage, one that transforms the Christian not merely from a condition of illness to one of health, but also from sin to salvation, especially since illness and sin are often equated in other blessings. A similar connection between health and morality may be found in prayers against plague and for the health of women. The use of the story serves as another example of how such rites set a contemporary event within the framework of Christian history, tapping the sacred power of God exercised in the past to give new life in the present.

The "Blessing against Fevers" in Clm 14179 includes pleas for intercession to many other saints than the legendary sleepers of Ephesus. Their intercession is linked in the first prayer of the rite with the spiritual rejuvenation brought about by the blessing:

> And like resting infants, not knowing labor or sorrow or death, in this servant of God N. may that one feel neither in sleeping nor in waking the infirmity of fever or chills. In the name of the Father, Son and Holy Spirit. [Sts.] Eugenius, Stephen, Protasius, Sambatius, Dionysius, Chelisius, Quirianus, by aiding the servant of God N. from fever or chill.[187]

The allusion to the resting infant suggests a connection between the infant's condition of innocence and freedom from fever, implicitly joining sin and disease by equating their opposites: innocence and health. Saints are ubiq-

---

187. Franz, 2:480–81 (V): Et sicut illi more infantium quiescentium non sentientes laborem neque dolorem neque mortem, in isto famulo dei illo neque dormiendo neque vigilando sentiat infirmitatem febris vel frigoris. In nomine patris et filii et spiritus sancti. Eugenius, Stephanus, Protasius, Sambatius, Dionisius, Chelisius, Quirianus adiuvando famulo dei illi a febre vel frigore. As for the saintly intercessors of this rite, St. Dionysius may refer to St. Denys, bishop of Paris (d. c. 250), the "apostle" to France and later patron saint of that country, or to the companion of Paul, or pope (d. 272), or bishop of Corinth (second century), or bishop of Milan (d. c. 371); Chelisius, possibly for Celsus or Celsius, a first-century Milanese martyr; Quirianus, possibly for Quirinus, an early martyr. See Farmer, *Oxford Dictionary of the Saints*, 131; Caraffa and Morelli, *Bibliotheca sanctorum*, 632–62 (Dionysius), 1216 (Protasius), 1238–1334 (Quirinus), and 1376–95 (Stephen). Denys's cult may have gained popularity and impetus from the false identification of him in the ninth century with the influential fifth-century Neoplatonic, Pseudo-Dionysius the Areopagite. Others in the list are equally well known, or at least share names with famous saints: Eugenius, possibly either the bishop of Cartagena (d. 505), or pope (d. 657), or archbishop of Milan (eighth century); Stephen, the protomartyr, or pope (d. 260), or bishop of Lyon (d. c. 512), or bishop of Bourges (d. 845); and Protasius, bishop of Milan (d. 352).

uitous in each subcategory of healing blessings, appearing in early, high, and late medieval texts, but they are employed primarily as agents of adjuration and exorcism, much as they were in the adjurations of fields and gardens. Healing blessings occasionally invoke the corporate body of the sainted, but far more common is the inclusion of individual saints with other principalities and powers called upon to drive out illness.[188] The most popular intercessor was the Virgin Mary, who appears in four blessings.[189]

There is a discernible pattern in the appearance of saints in blessings for pilgrims, knights, and the sick. This pattern is visible when we consider one predominant desire that drives each of these types of blessings: protection and salvation from physical danger. Whereas angels dominate as intercessors in blessings of space, blessings of persons seek out the aid of the more tangible saints. Saints most frequently appear in blessings having to do with either preventing or partaking in some physical danger to the faithful Christian.[190] Having once lived as humans, the sainted dead and their relics may have been more accessible to the celebrants and laity than the angels, who were after all incorporeal, spiritual beings. Those who themselves had suf-

188. Individual saints are included in the following rituals: Clm 14179's "Blessing against Fever," BAV Pal. lat. 235's "Prayers against Chills," the *RGP*'s "Prayers for Female Sterility," the Dominican missal's "Prayer for Impeded Matrimony," Clm 4350's "Adjuration against Cataracts," and Clm 7021's "Blessing of Eyes."

189. Mary appears in the following rituals: Clm 14179's "Blessing against Fever," BAV Pal. lat. 235's "Prayers against Chills," the Dominican missal's "Prayer for Impeded Matrimony," and Clm 7021's "Blessing of Eyes."

190. The presence of saints as intercessors also clearly suggests that blessings responded to the piety of their audience and recipients. Numerous scholars, among them historians such as Vauchez and Duffy, have pointed out how the medieval laity valued saints as intercessors better able to bring solace than direct prayer to God, who, while beneficent, was also considered somewhat distant from human affairs. Vauchez, *Laity in the Middle Ages*, 3–26; Eamon Duffy, *The Stripping of the Altars: Traditional Religion in England, 1480–1600* (New Haven: Yale University Press, 1992), 161–83. Divine power could be mediated through saints in numerous ways: Fredrick Paxton has shown how liturgy functioned as a mediating agent for healing, bringing the power of the saints' intercession into the lives of those suffering from fever, and Richard Kieckhefer's work on the hagiography of late medieval society has shown how saints, by willingly embracing affliction in an age of unusual suffering, were so incomprehensible to the common person that they were judged to be the best intercessors with God. Paxton, "Liturgy and Healing," 23–44; Kieckhefer, *Unquiet Souls: 14th-Century Saints and Their Religious Milieu* (Chicago: University of Chicago Press, 1984), 89–121. Saints' greater presence in blessings against bodily suffering is reasonable in light of this scholarship: as humans who bore great suffering of the body, saints were the best patrons for healing the faithful suffering from similar afflictions.

fered illness, faced the dangers of a lengthy pilgrimage, and confronted the violence of the human world head on, knew best how much aid and succor the living required on a day-to-day basis. This is most notable in prayers to the Virgin Mary found in blessings for birth and recovery, in which her maternity is recalled in such a way as to connect it to the hoped-for fertility sought by impotent couples, and the easy childbirth and recovery sought by the pregnant.[191] On the other hand, it is conceivable that saints were seen as intercessors not because of their shared human experience but because they transcended nature and could lend their supernatural power to those suffering from the afflictions of the physical world.[192] While apparently contradictory, both of these interpretations have the same point of departure: the humanity of the saint. Whether it is embraced or transcended, the humanity of the saint is the foundation upon which belief in his or her intercessory power is built, and binds the living Christian community to the community of the sainted dead.

To return now to the rite that began this discussion, this blessing invokes the aid of the archangel Michael, St. John the Baptist, and a host of scriptural figures and icons (notably the Cross), a trait common to rites that were often presented as adjurations of the diseased person: of the twelve rituals studied here, five contain specific adjurations of illness by the celebrant, while two contain similar conjurations of disease.[193] Sickness, caused by demons, could be driven out by the numinous power of God, and his servants thus invoked this power through blessing and adjuration.

In the similar "Adjuration against Fevers" from the tenth-century St. Gall MS, recourse is again made to the intercession of departed saints to protect the living against illness. It also refers to God as the founder of world, thus invoking the idea that the created world itself is more than a product of God's power; it is an object through which God's power can work:

191. For examples of this, see the *RGP ordo* 262.2, the "Prayer for a Mass for a Sterile Woman," the second prayer of the 1519 Dominican missal's *Oratio pro impeditis in matrimonio a daemone vel maleficiis* (Franz, 2:184).

192. This possibility supports Kieckhefer's thesis that later medieval saints held the physical world and human society in contempt and sought to rise above them to a spiritual union with God; see Kieckhefer, *Unquiet Souls*, 1–15.

193. All of the studied rituals against fever and eye illness contain adjurations. The "Prayers Begun against Chills" of BAV Pal. lat. 235, and Clm 7021's "Blessing of Eyes," contain both adjurations and conjurations.

In the name of the Father, Son and Holy Spirit. I adjure you, chill, through the Father, Son and Holy Spirit, through the three testaments, through the four evangelists, through the twelve prophets, through the angels of heaven, through the hinges of the world, through which God made the world . . . so that further you might not harm that man of [St.] Leopold neither by labor nor fear. . . . Holy God, holy strength, holy immortal, who bears the sin of the world, take pity on this man of [St.] Leopold.[194]

The clients of St. Leopold are freed through the power of this ritual invocation of their relationship to the heavenly intercessor.[195] Such invocations of specific saints within the body of blessing texts is a distinctive feature of this category of blessing: five of the twelve rituals studied here contain such invocations, while in the entire body of rituals examined in this study only two others mention specific saints.[196] The prevalence of intercessory invocations such as this within the blessings of healing, and the paucity of such specificity in other rituals, suggests that the very human essence of this kind of physical suffering must have been seen as more suitable to this most personal aspect of the divine. This prayer also uses the created nature of the world to act as a focus for the holy power of the Creator, through its invoca-

194. Franz, 2:481: In nomine patris et filii et spiritus sancti. Adiuro te, frigor, per patrum et filium et spiritum sanctum, per tria testimonia, per IIII evangelistas, per XII prophetas, per angelos celi, per cardines mundi, per quem deus fecit mundum . . . ut amplius non noceatis isto homini Leotolti non labore nec tremore. . . . Sanctus deus, sanctus fortis, sanctus inmortalis, qui tollis peccata mundi, miserere isto homini Leotolti.

195. The identification of St. Leopold is problematic. There is no saint listed by this name in the *AS, Bibliotheca hagiographica latina antiquae et mediae aetatis,* or *Bibliotheca sanctorum* before the eleventh century (this being the military governor of Austria, b. 1073 in Melk, brother-in-law to the holy Roman emperor Henry V, after whose death Leopold refused to succeed to the throne and retreated to a monastic life; see Rev. Sabine Baring-Gould, *The Lives of the Saints: with an introduction and additional lives of English Martyrs, Cornish, Scottish and Welsh Saints, and a full index to the entire work,* 16 vols. [Edinburgh: John Grant, 1914], 14:340), but Franz identifies the MS source for this rite as originating in the tenth century. Either the blessing refers to some obscure local saint of St. Gall, or Franz's dating is faulty. In either case, the problem of Leopold's identity cannot be resolved without direct examination of the MS, which is not possible at this time.

196. These two rituals come from the blessings of knights and war and from rituals of ordeals. While specific saints are not mentioned in the majority of blessings, saints were not totally absent. They made their appearance most often in the form of litanies (which occur in seven rituals and whose content was at the discretion of the celebrant) and in adjurations, where they are addressed as a nameless body (as in five of the healing rituals, discussed above), in blessings of fields and crops (in two rituals discussed above), and in ordeals, which relied heavily on adjurations of the elements of the ordeals to ensure their efficacy (five of the ordeal rituals examined include such adjurations; see below).

tion of "the hinges of the world."[197] This conjuration demonstrates the medieval view of the holy as being absolutely pervasive in the essence of the world, within the personal and impersonal elements of creation, yet not activated or accessible without recourse to the ritualized human action that the blessings represent. This view finds support, if not in popular literature and culture, then in the texts of Plato and Aristotle known to the early and high Middle Ages. Platonic thought studied in the universities of the latter period posited that the world was more than inanimate matter: in his *Dialogues*, Plato asserted that "using the language of probability, we may say that the world became a living creature truly endowed with soul and intelligence by the Providence of God."[198] This view of the world as an intelligence was adapted by Aristotle, whose work shows that he believed that stars and planets should be considered animate beings to which one must attribute a certain intelligence.[199] It is possible that the notion of using matter that we moderns consider inanimate would have posed no problem to medieval liturgical authors familiar with classical thought, who already accepted as a given that the matter of earth and the heavens were to some extent driven by a divine intelligence that could be appealed to in times of need.

This belief in the power of the natural bodies of the world to work an influence on the shape of human life manifests itself through astrological references. In the blessing "Prayers Begun against Chills," from a tenth- or eleventh-century Burgundian manuscript, an adjuration of chills begins: "I adjure you, chills and fevers, whether daily or every second day or third day or every fourth day or every fifth day, that you not harm this servant of God in the day or night, waking or sleeping, by waxing or waning moon."[200] The

197. This phrase echoes Eliade's discussion of the sacred as a creating force for the "axis of the world." See Eliade, *Sacred and Profane*, 32–36.

198. Plato, *The Dialogues of Plato*, trans. B Jowett, (Oxford: Clarendon Press, 1964), 3:450, quoted in Wildiers, *Theologian and His Universe*, 20–21.

199. Wildiers, *Theologian and His Universe*, 24. Christian scholars and theologians later interpreted these "intelligences" as angels.

200. Franz, 2:482: coniuro vos, frigores et febres, sive cotidianas sive secundarias sive tercianas sive quartanas sive quiintanas, ut non noceatis huic famulo dei nec in die nec in nocte nec vigilanti nec dormienti, nec luna crescente neque descrescente. The ritual is found in BAV Pal. lat. 235, fols. 44–45. A preceding prayer invokes the assistance of the seven sleepers and St. Christopher, the early martyr; St. Stephen, one of several possible saints; St. Simphorianus, a martyr of Autun, c. 180, venerated especially in Autun and Trevoux; and St. Sigismund, king of Burgundy (d. 524), who was venerated especially in Cremona and Bohemia for the curing of quartain fevers. For Sigismund's cult, see Paxton, "Liturgy and Healing."

final pair in the list probably reflects a belief in astrological influence on human health, and indeed there is ample confirmation of such belief in other rituals, popular writings, and the proscriptions of preachers and would-be reformers of lay belief.[201] In the medieval view of the cosmos, the macrocosmic moon could exert an influence on the microcosm of the human body, as could more vast and general elements of the natural world: "I adjure you, chills and fevers, through the Father, Son and Holy Spirit . . . through the three testimonies and through the depths of heaven and through the hinge of the world and through all the creatures of God, so that you may presume nothing more upon this servant of God . . ."[202] Here every creation of God becomes a channel for divine power, an instrument put to the service of human beings, who stand atop, but not apart from, the natural order. As the created world serves the divine and the human in this way, so too does the human embodiment of the divine, namely, Christ and the incidents of his life: "I bind you together by oath, from whatever nation you are, through the Father, Son and Holy Spirit and through the nativity of Christ and through the baptism of Christ."[203] The mythic events of the Savior's life, through the juridical restrictive act of the adjuration, make the events become a source of power and salvation in the present world, reactualized for the believers who receive the benefit of their protection.

This prayer develops the picture of the medieval perception of God's nature. The final part of the blessing invokes sacred history to shape the power of the divine for its own purposes: "Lord God Omnipotent, who freed Jonah from the belly of the whale, the three boys from the chamber of fire, . . . Peter from the waves, Paul from prison, free this your servant from fevers and from chills, and from all evil."[204] God is portrayed in all these paradigms as

---

201. Flint, *Rise of Magic*, 92–102, 128–56, 303. For a complete history of astrology in the West, see S. J. Tester, *A History of Western Astrology*, chapter 5, "The Latin Middle Ages" (Bury St. Edmunds, UK: Boydell Press, 1987), 98–203. Astrology also plays a role in blessings against illnesses of the eye, as we shall see below.

202. Franz, 2:483: Adiuro vos, frigores et febres, per patrem . . . per tria testimonia et per abyssos celi et per cardinem mundi et per omnes creaturas dei, ut non presumatis istum famulum dei N. nihil amplius . . .

203. Ibid.: coniuro vos, de quacunque natione estis, per patrem et filium et spiritum sanctum et per navitatem Christi, per baptismum Christi.

204. Ibid., 2:484: Domine deus omnipotens, qui liberasti Ionam de ventre ceti, tres pueros de camino ignis, . . . Petrum de fluentibus, Paulum de carcere, libera hunc famulum tuum de febribus et de frigoribus, atque ab omni malo. I owe thanks to Dr. Frederick Paxton for

the bringer of freedom, a liberator who sets captives free from malevolent powers. The same quality of God's nature is invoked in prayers for the eyes, such as in the rite in the fourteenth-century Munich MS, Clm 4350, and in those for pregnancy.[205] Such a great power would be required to liberate a suffering person from the agony of grave illness, and the adaptable power of the divine is molded by appeal to these mythohistorical incidents. In order to prod God to take on his liberating and saving aspect, he is reminded in the appeal of how he has worked in the past.

Another important category of blessings for healing are those designed to remedy illnesses of the eyes. The science of ophthalmology, inherited from antiquity and elaborated by the Islamic world, remained largely stagnant in the medieval West.[206] The theory and explanation of diseases of the eye fit solidly into traditional medical thought for all illnesses, which ascribed to the body four "humors," liquids whose balance created health and whose imbalance brought illness. The task of the physician was to restore the patient's humors to their natural balance.[207] Medical treatments for the eye

---

drawing my attention to the citation of nearly identical incidents in the *Libera domine* prayer of the antemortem phase of the death ritual in the Gellone sacramentary. As he notes, the purpose of these selections from scripture is clear: "Each of the comparisons is to a person, to a moment in human history in which God intervened to save one of his faithful.... Their shared recitation created community, not only among the attendants at the death [or the participants of the ordeal] but between them and those who had gone before them in sacred history." Paxton, *Christianizing Death*, 118–19.

205. For further details, see the index.

206. Much of the science of the ancient world passed to the Arabs through their contact with (and conquest of) Byzantium. Arab ophthalmologists made great advances in the field of optics and returned to the Hippocratic principles of observing and codifying diseases, turning away from the mysticism that had worn away the science in Byzantium. Salerno was the preeminent center for the Hippocratic and Gallenic study of ophthalmology in the West, where many translations of Arabic texts were completed. Despite the contributions of a few notable scholars, Roger Bacon (1214–92) being the greatest, there were few original contributions to the field in the West. See George E. Arrington Jr., *A History of Ophthalmology* (New York: MD Publications, 1959), 62. For a good general survey of ophthalmology, see also Julius Hirschberg, *Geschichte der Augenheilkunde*, vols. 12–14 of the *Handbuch der gesamten Augenheilkunde*, ed. A. K. Graefe and Theodor Saemisch (Leipzig: Wilhelm Engelmann, 1899–1911).

207. Many different materials and activities were thought to cause eye illness; a short example of some of them is provided in the *Regimen sanitatis salernitatem*, a textbook at use in Salerno during the high medieval period: "Now you shall see what is hurtful for sight / Wine, Women, Bathes, by art to nature wrought, / Leeks, Onions, Garlic, Mustardseed, fire and light, / Smoke, bruises, dust, Pepper to powder brought, / Beans, Lentils, Strains, Wind Tears,

ranged from cautery (application of hot irons), phlebotomy (bloodletting), pharmacology (such as herbal wrappings or poultices made from egg yolks), to eye drops, blowing into the eyes, and surgery combined with prayer, as when a surgeon, having pierced the eye with a needle and drawn a cataract down to the bottom of the eye, proceeded to say four or five *Pater nosters* to ensure that the cataract remained in the well of the eye.[208] Salt was especially valued in treatment, as is recounted in the *vita* of St. Columba.[209] Access to trained specialists seems to have been extremely limited, even in the high and late Middle Ages, and so it is not surprising that the church should provide the more accessible remedy of liturgical blessings.[210] Alongside Latin ecclesiastical formulas, vernacular German prayers for the healing of eye illness are found as early as the eighth and ninth centuries.[211] The ecclesiasti-

---

and Phoebus bright, / And all sharp things our eye sight do molest: / yet watching hurts them more than all the rest." Quoted in Arrington, *History of Ophthalmology*, 59.

208. Franz, 2:485. For the treatment of cataract, see Beneventus Grassus, *The Wonderful Art of the Eye: A Critical Edition of the Middle English Translation of His "De probatissima art oculorum,"* ed. L. M. Eldredge (East Lansing: Michigan State University Press, 1996), 14, 19–20. Grassus remains a mysterious figure, probably Italian, a well-traveled peripatetic specialist in ophthalmology, probably from the late thirteenth century (ibid., 1–5).

209. Adomnano Abbate Hiensi, *Vita S. Columbae*, ed. A. O. Anderson and M. O. Anderson (Oxford: Clarendon Press, 1991), 2.7. One exception to the prescription of salt was provided by the abbess Hildegard of Bingen, who eschewed it altogether. Hildegard thought the eye consisted of fire and water, the fire holding the eye together and giving it endurance and the water providing the power to see; she believed it could be harmed by the application of salt. In her treatise on the causes and cures of illnesses, she asserted that an imbalance in the blood and water impaired vision. She also gives a fascinating discussion on the causes of cataract: "If the human brain somehow becomes too fat, the fat sends an injurious juice and sweat into the eyes. If this juice and sweat attack the eyes often, then they acquire a white skin. If this skin is not taken off while it is still fresh, it becomes so thick that later it cannot be removed because it is as thick as gallbladder. . . . The white skin also develops as a consequence of cold humours and bile." Hildegard of Bingen, *Holistic Healing*, trans. Manfred Pawlik, Patrick Madigan, and John Kulas, with Mary Palmquist (Collegeville, Minn.: Liturgical Press, 1994), 81–83.

210. Grassus, *Wonderful Art of the Eye*, 15.

211. Franz, 2:492. See also Walter de Gray Birch, *The Book of Nunnaminster, i.e., the British Museum MS Harley 2965* (Hampshire: Hampshire Record Society, 1889), 96. Franz provides a good discussion of several vernacular German eye blessings, many of them based on Latin models in their wording and rubrics. Franz notes, however, that they add distinctive elements, such as the invocation of St. Odilia (said to have been born blind and to have received sight at her baptism) in fourteenth-century texts, or the centurion Longinus (who legend claimed was born half-blind and received sight in his blind eye when he touched the organ with hands coated in the blood of Jesus). Franz, 2:488–89, 492.

cal prayers are for the most part short and simple in composition, consisting of one or two general blessing prayers or adjurations. While the blessing prayers address God, the adjurations address the actual illness, demanding that it withdraw from the afflicted one. These blessings may also include a blessing of salt or water to act as a healing agent. The more complex rituals, such as Munich Clm 7021's "Blessing of Eyes" and the St. Gall manuscript's "Blessing upon Infirm Eyes," incorporate all these elements and add rubrics commanding the celebrants to perform certain acts thought healing for eyes.[212]

While scripture played an important role in drawing down the power of the sacred for the supplicant, some eye blessings took this connection with scripture a step further. In the "Adjuration against Cataracts," the celebrant addresses God as he appears personally to repeat the actions of Christ:

> The Lord made mud from spittle, and anointed the eyes of the one born blind, who went and washed and saw and believed in God [cf. Jn 9:11]. Thus, Lord Jesus Christ, anoint these eyes with the medicine of your health, so that . . . seeing he might believe you are the true God and with praise he would bless you as the best physician.[213]

The description of God as a physician is evident in rites from French, German, and Austrian blessings from the tenth to the fourteenth centuries, and so must be accepted as a common understanding of the divine's nature.[214] In any event, if we can infer that a reenactment of the miracle described in John 9:11 is occurring here through the hands of the celebrant, this re-creation of miracle makes it all the more potent and real for the believer. The blessing also calls for the recipient to fulfill his obligation to "bless" or revere God with praises, the expected exchange for divine healing in the negotiation of

212. For a fuller discussion of these prayers and rubrics, see below.

213. Franz, 2:494–95 (*ordo* V): Lutum fecit dominus ex sputo et liniuit oculos ceci nati et abiit et lavit et vidit et credidit deo [paraphrasing Jn 9:11]. Sic, domine Iesu Christe, unge oculos istos medicamento tue salutis, ut ista . . . videns te verum deum credat et optimum medicum te laudando benedicat.

214. See Vienna 2090's "Blessing after Birth," Clm 4350's "Adjuration against Cataracts," the *PWD*'s "Blessing of a Fetus," and Vienna 1888's "Blessing of Salt." God was portrayed not only as a healer but as a liberator, freeing the body from physical suffering as he freed the soul from the taint of sin for which the illness was a punishment. This attribution appears in a fifteenth-century rite from Dubrovnik, as well as in the supplementary blessing of a fetus found in some French recensions of Durandus's pontifical. The Dubrovnik rite is found in Vatican City, BAV, Barb. lat. 412.

these rites. This re-creation of numinous action appears, or is referred to, in two other rites, as listed in the index. God is here the "best doctor," who as Creator stands above every other healer, a possible criticism of other sources of healing not approved by the church, such as the *magi* discussed by Flint.

This rite demonstrates several other general themes common to this type of blessing. The second adjuration is spoken thus: "Again I adjure you [cataracts] through the ethereal throne, through the sun and the moon and stars and all the sydera of heaven, through the nine choruses of angels."[215] Long lists of various beings and bodies are typical of the adjurations that appear in medieval blessings of all kinds, but here it is important to note the recurrence of a belief in the power of celestial objects to act as conduits for the power of the divine, reflecting perhaps both a popular belief in astrology and a more sophisticated idea of the diffusion of the holy throughout the created world.[216] There is also the distinct invocation of a personal intercessor: "Lawrence the deacon did good work, who through the sign of the cross illuminated blind men. . . . May St. Mark, St. Matthew, St. Luke and St. John the Evangelist heal these eyes, through the true God, through the living God."[217] The conjuration of St. Lawrence and reference to his past miracles is an explicit example of the manner in which such blessings seek to re-create the sacred past for the benefit of the worldly present. While few details of his miracles are known, St. Lawrence was renowned as "the Illuminator" for his teaching and miracles performed in the diocese of Spoleto after his election as bishop.[218] The association of the evangelists with eye ailments is less clear, but it is plausible that their reputation as "illuminators" who opened the spiritual eyes of souls to

215. Franz, 2:494–95: Iterum adiuro te per thronum ethereum, per solem et lunam et stellas et omnia sydera celorum, per novem choros angelorum.

216. This same belief may also be seen in the devotional Celtic "Litany of Creation": "I beseech you by the tenth order on the compact earth; I beseech praiseworthy Michael to help me against demons. Together with Michael, I beseech you by land and by sea unceasingly; I beseech you respectfully by every quality of God the Father . . . I beseech you by water and the cruel air; I beseech you by fire, I beseech you by earth . . . I beseech you by the Triad of wind, sun and moon" (in Davies, *Celtic Spirituality*, 298).

217. Franz, 2:494–95: Levita Laurentius bonum opus operatus est, qui per signum crucis cecos illuminavit. . . . Sanctus Marcus, sanctus Lucas, sanctus Matheus, sanctus Iohannes evangelista sanent et salvent oculos istos, per deum verum, per deum vivum.

218. Baring-Gould, *Lives of the Saints*, 2:49. St. Lawrence is said to have come to Italy from Syria with other illustrious clergy and confessors during Diocletian's reign. He was later elected bishop in Spoleto, where he preached and performed many miracles. Lawrence's feast day is 3 February.

the word of God could be seen as analogous to the opening of physical eyes to the light of day. They may also have been invoked simply for their prestige and status in the heavenly hierarchy of intercessors. In any case, both of these invocations ask God to act consistently with the deeds of these illuminators, and they seek the intercession of patrons associated with God's potency to power their healing ritual, making their miracles meaningful for the sufferer by re-creating them in the present.

Blessings of the eyes, indeed, healing blessings in general, contain many invocations of saints and other elements familiar in lay piety. The "Blessing of Eyes" in the fifteenth-century Munich MS asks: "Draw away, Lord, this cataract, just as you dragged away the spots from holy Job. . . . Ianuarius, Felicius, Philip, Salanus, Alexander, Vitalis, Martialis, the seven brothers, the sons of Felicity, may they come to our aid."[219] Neither Franz nor I have been able to determine the reason for the inclusion of these seven martyred brothers; it may be that they were confused with the seven sleepers who opened their eyes after a long sleep, but this is only conjecture.[220] These conjurations of intercession by spiritual agencies are complemented in this blessing by the aid believed to reside within central elements of the Christian salvation narrative: "Again I conjure you through the power of the Holy Cross, through the blood of the Lord, though his wounds. . . . St. Christopher, the dagger of holy Abraham or divine Aquilina, St. Saturnina, may you aid us."[221] Abraham's connection to eyes is unclear. St. Christopher was probably considered a patron of eyes because of a story common to the legends surrounding this mysterious saint, in which one of the arrows ordered shot at Christopher by his royal persecutor reversed its course and lodged in one of the king's eyes. Christopher is said to have then addressed the king:

> "I tell thee, King Dagon, that tomorrow I shall gain my crown [of martyrdom]; and the Christians will take my body, and will put it in the place where

219. Franz, 2:496 (*ordo* VIII): Abstrahe, domine, maculam istam, sicut abstraxisti maculam a sancto Iob in nomine patris etc. . . . Ianuarius, Felicius, Philippus, Salanus, Alexander, Vitalis, Martialis, septem fratres, filii Felicitatis, veniant in adiutorium nostrum.

220. The legend of the seven brothers declared them to be sons of the Roman martyr Felicity, who shared both captivity and execution with them for their refusal to apostatize and sacrifice to pagan gods. See Farmer, *Oxford Dictionary of the Saints*, 432–33.

221. Franz, 2:496: Item coniuro te per virtutem sancte crucis, per sanguinem dominis, per vulnera eius. . . . Sanctus Christoforus, sanctus Abraham siculum sive divina Inclina, sancta Saturnina, tu nos adiuva.

they pray. Then do thou make clay with my blood, and apply it to the blind eye, and it will recover sight." Then there fell a voice from heaven: "It shall be as thou hast prayed not only where thy body is, but also where it is not." After the saint's martyrdom, the king did as instructed and recovered sight in his maimed eye.[222]

This story, which clearly mimics the illuminations performed by Jesus in the Gospels, offers a double justification of itself: as saints mimic Christ, celebrants mimic saints in calling upon the power of divinity to heal eyes, acts that justify and empower their blessings. The inclusion of Aquilina with Christopher is reasonable, since Aquilina was considered to be one of the two women who, prior to the wounding of the king, had been sent by the ruler to tempt Christopher into apostasy. Instead of doing the king's will, the women fell prostrate before Christopher, were converted, and then were martyred by the furious king. Aquilina's loss of both eyes to the torturer provides another reason for her inclusion in this ritual.[223] The last saint invoked, St. Saturnina, has no clear connection to eyes or eye illness. A young virgin from Germany who died defending her chastity while in France, Saturnina and her story are

222. Baring-Gould, *Lives of the Saints*, 8:557. The saint's feast day was 25 July. Nothing of this saint's history is known except that he died in Asia Minor. Indeed, the church now has serious doubts as to the existence of Christopher and has relegated his feast day to particular calendars because of the legendary nature of the accounts of his life. Several legends of Christopher were known to medieval Christians. The most familiar and accepted states that Christopher was a Caananite giant who had first pledged to serve the Devil, but upon seeing that the Devil feared Christ and his Cross decided to serve Christ instead. A hermit instructs the giant in the faith and makes it Christopher's Christian duty to ferry travelers across a dangerous river on his back. The final and most difficult passenger is a boy whose weight seems that of the whole world. The boy, of course, is Christ, who declares that he bears the weight of the world and its sins and commands Christopher to plant his staff in the ground so that it will bear flowers and dates on the following day as proof of Christ's words. It does so, and subsequently Christopher preaches successfully in Lycia. He is then imprisoned under the persecution of an evil king (whose identity varies according to author, but most likely was Decius) for refusing to sacrifice to the pagan gods, is beaten, shot, and eventually beheaded (Farmer, *Oxford Dictionary of the Saints*, 98). The passage cited in the text is drawn from a far more bizarre form of the biography, in which Christopher is said to be a dog-headed man who is transformed into a human when he accepts Christ as his redeemer, and who withstands incredible torture at the hands of the wicked king Dagon in order to attest to the truth of Christianity (for the entire text, see Baring-Gould, *Lives of the Saints*, 8:553–56). For the original texts, see *AS* (July 6), 125–49; and *AB* 1 (1882): 121–48, and *AB* 10 (1891): 393–405.

223. Baring-Gould, *Lives of the Saints*, 8:556.

probably pure legend, but her status as a virgin martyr alone would seem reason enough to consider her a good intercessor for the faithful.[224]

The subsequent invocation of the blood and wounds of Christ reflects the cult of the physical manifestations of Christ's suffering that emerged as a dominant element in high and late medieval religion.[225] The Crusades in particular brought a new impetus to the devotion to the Passion, with St. Bernard of Clairvaux preaching and promoting a special devotion to the five wounds of Christ. This devotion to the sacred humanity of Christ, the events and experiences of his life, served for St. Bernard as a means of arousing an emotional response to the love of Christ for suffering humanity, a response that ideally allowed the believer to move beyond mere emotion to reach a mystical union with Christ.[226] While devotion to the five wounds did become a major theme of later medieval mystics' meditations, in the case of this ritual what seems more relevant is the connection between Christ's suffering and the suffering of the blind, a physical similarity that through this allusion sympathetically empowers the blessing to remove the physical affliction of the supplicant.

This lengthy blessing also includes the story of three female saints thought to be particularly efficacious in the restoration of vision: "St. Tecla, St. Clina, St. Nazarena sat above the sea very early in the morning. Tecla said: 'Let us go.' Clina said: 'Let us go.' Nazarena said: 'Let us seat ourselves and work the Lord's will on the blemishes of eyes and let us not neglect the will of the Lord in any hour, in day or in night.'"[227] This narrative invocation closely resembles the *historiolae*, or "microstories," described by Edina

224. For her life and *Passio,* see *Bibliotheca hagiographica latina antiquae et mediae aetatis* 2:1085;*AS* (May 5), 178–79nn8–9;*AS* (October 4), 218n30.

225. J. P. Bruni, "Wounds of Our Lord, Devotion to," *NCE* 13:1035–36; Swanson, *Religion and Devotion in Europe,* 142–43; Francis Oakley, *The Western Church in the Later Middle Ages* (Ithaca: Cornell University Press, 1979), 82–89. The wounds of Christ were considered to be redemptive, to testify to Christ's willingness to bear the maximum suffering out of love for sinners (see Jn 15:13), the visible tokens of the New Covenant sealed in his blood (Heb 9) that plead perpetually for humanity (Heb 9:11–12, Jn 14:2). See J. P. Schanz, "Wounds of Our Lord, Theological Significance," *NCE* 13:1036–37.

226. J. P. Bruni, "Sacred Humanity, Devotion to the," *NCE* 12:829.

227. Franz, 2:496: Sancta Tecla, sancta Clina, sancta Nazarena sederunt super mare valde mane. Tecla dixit: "eamus nos." Clina dixit: "eamus nos." Nazarena dixit: "sedeamus nos et faciamus voluntatem domini in maculis oculorum et non pretermittamus voluntatem domini in aliqua hora, in die, in nocte."

Bozóky in her study of narrative magical incantations.[228] In these formulas a sequence of mythical events is enumerated in which the recounting of episodes similar to the present circumstances assures that the present situation is assimilated into the mythic universe and is thereby resolved successfully.[229] The inclusion of this story within a liturgical blessing and its similarities to taboo magical praxis strongly suggest that popular beliefs in the power of incantations exercised an influence over both author and audience of this ritual, obscuring the sometimes fine line between ecclesiastical ritual and magical spell.

228. Edina Bozóky, "Mythic Mediation in Healing Incantations," in *Health, Disease and Healing in Medieval Culture*, ed. Sheila Campbell, Bert Hall, and David Klausner (New York: St. Martin's Press, 1992), 84–85. In a typical formula, the officiator (be he healer, sorcerer, or patient) assumes the role of mediator between the sick person and the malevolent forces that have caused the illness. In a narrative incantation, on the other hand, the magical power is at least partially transferred to the protagonist of the microstory, thus transposing the mediation from the "actual" to the mythic level. This fits the definition of "mythic incantation" in Marcel Mauss's study of magic, which explains these narratives in much the same way as we have examined the use of scriptural allusion in the blessings: "One assimilates the present situation to the situation described as a prototype, with this reasoning: if a god, hero, or saint had been able to do something, often something very difficult, in a certain circumstance, can he not do the same thing in the present situation, which is analogous?" (ibid., 88). See also Marcel Mauss, "Esquisse d'une théorie générale de la magie," in his *Sociologie et anthropologie* (Paris: Presses Universitaires de France, 1950), 49.

229. Bozóky, "Mythic Mediation," 89. Bozóky notes that a symbolic location often figures prominently in such *historiola*, and that the action (for example, Mount Sinai in Bozóky's study of the story of the three angels [86–87]) often occurs in "intermediate" places (before a gate or threshold or on a bridge) that recall the transition from illness to healing; other places suggest mediation between two elements: a mountain (where heaven and earth meet) or a seaside (where water and earth meet); see ibid., 90. Our story of the three sisters conforms to this model, as it takes place on the seashore, and so does the story of the seven sleepers of Ephesus, discussed above, who sleep within a mountain. This type of narrative in magical praxis can also be seen as another way in which medieval people sought to impose order on a chaotic cosmos: in Todorov's analysis of the discourse of magic, he notes that for such narratives, "the function of the comparison is not to make resemblances emerge, but rather to affirm the possibility of a relationship between events belonging to quite different categories, to permit putting the universe in order. It is thus that the perturbing act, unknown, finds itself integrated into a reassuring order." Tzvetan Todorov, "Le discours de la magie," *L'Homme* 18 (1973): 52, quoted in ibid., 89. In this view disease is not isolated but is part of a natural order that has been disturbed by the intrusion of supernatural forces. I would argue that the same perception of disease lies behind the blessing's appeal to the story of Tecla, and that the ritual is an effort to assure that the evil of eye disease is expunged through an acceptable mediator, the trio of saints.

As to the role of Tecla in such blessings, Franz notes that her name appears in Latin formulas for the blessing of eyes from the twelfth century onward, although her biography offers no special reason why she was considered a patron of the eyes.[230] She is often accompanied in blessings by Saints Nazarena and Clina, who with Tecla form a trio of sisters or virgins who sit at the seashore and work to heal afflicted eyes.[231] Scriptural allusions often accompany these popular legends of sanctity. In particular, incidents in which God restores vision appear in the fifteenth-century Munich rite, reminding God to act in a consistent manner toward suffering in the present day:

> Cure, Lord, the eyes of your servant N., just as you cured the eyes of Tobias and of the two blind men whom we commemorate in the Gospel. Purge and expel the motes and sands and membranes and pustules and all which harm the eyes, and make apparent your mercy in the whole world, God, and may your name be magnified.[232]

This biblical allusion not only enhances the blessing's potency, it also encourages God to remember the benefits that accrue to him if he acts in accordance with the relationship between the sacred and the human established by performance of the ritual. There is also the invocation of the archangel

230. Franz, 2:486–90. Franz believed that a possible justification may lie in the story in which Tecla saw a rock open miraculously to conceal her from pursuers bent upon rape (see R. A. Bonet and M. Bonet, eds., *Acta Apostolorum Apocrypha*, vol. 1 [Darmstadt: Wissenschaftliche Buchgesellschaft, 1959], 271). For an English translation of the *Acts of Paul and Thecla*, see J. K. Elliott, *The Apocryphal New Testament: A Collection of Apocryphal Christian Literature in an English Translation* (Oxford: Clarendon Press, 1993), 365–74. While Franz is correct in observing that no direct connection between Thecla and eyes is stated in her *vita*, it is possible that her great reputation as a healer of the sick qualified her as an intercessor against eye illness, and the fact that she was once guided by "a cloud of light" and commanded her would-be rapists to "wait . . . that you might *see* the glory of the Lord" (emphasis added) may have been seized upon by the author as justification enough for invoking her in the blessing (Elliott, *Apocryphal New Testament*, 372–74).

231. Franz, 2:489–90. Franz argues that the name Nazarena was formed from the original Nazarius (or Nazarenus), and Clina, from mutilating the name Aquilina, in order to produce a feminine triad of saints as patrons for these rituals (2:496). Nazarius was a martyr of Nero, who at his trial was said to have been bathed in a golden light that struck the emperor and his court blind. Aquilina was a female martyr who had her eyes gouged out by the hot awl of a hangman (see *AS* [13 June] 2:167nn).

232. Franz, 2:496: Sana, domine oculos famuli tui N., sicut sanasti oculos Tobye et duorum cecorum, quos in evangelio commemoramus. Purga et expelle festucas et harenas et membranas et pustulas et omne, quod nocet oculis, et appareat misericordia tua, deus, in toto orbe et magnificetur nomen tuum.

Raphael, the angel most intimately associated with healing (and, as we saw above, with pilgrims), owing largely to his role in aiding and healing Tobias.[233] And finally, this ritual blessing of the eyes includes a reenactment of Christ's healing of the blind man at the pool of Siloh.[234] Thus the events of Christianity's sacred history are resurrected in the present, making them real and forging an unbreakable link between the different ages of the church.

The last subcategory of healing blessings comprises those performed for women and the family, most especially women suffering from sterility, undergoing childbirth, or whose children's lives are endangered by some illness. The RGP's ordo 257 provides an early example in a "Prayer for a Mass for a Sterile Woman," a mass set adapted from the Gelasian sacramentary.[235] This Mass uses the convention of biblical allusion, but with particular reference to episodes in which God involved himself in the process of birth: "God, who permitted Sarah's barren womb to be fertilized by Abraham's seed, so that against hope offspring might be born again for him, look kindly upon the preceding prayers of your female servant for her sterility."[236] While this blessing refers to the prayers of the woman, it is interesting to note how the benefits all seem to be for the sake of Abraham, while Sarah appears almost incidental: the womb is made fecund for *his* semen, and although the dative *ei* of the quotation can be translated as either "him" or "her," the prior reference to Abraham suggests that the hope is his more than hers. This emphasis no doubt reflects the widespread belief in the passive role of women in procreation, and it demonstrates the deeply ingrained belief in patriarchal dominance typical of biblical culture, which played a major role in shaping medieval culture.[237] But we must also acknowledge that many blessings for

233. Ibid., 2:498.

234. Ibid., 2:497–98, in imitation of Jn 9:1–7. Medieval medical thought also recommended this practice; see Arnold of Villanova, *Medicina salernitana, id est conservandae bonae valetudinis pracepta cum luculenta et succincta Arnold Villanovani in singula capitula exegesi per Iohannem Curionem recognita et purgata* (Erfurt: Jacobus Stoer, 1591), 17; Franz, 2:492.

235. *RGP* 2:420 (*ordo* 257).

236. Ibid. (*ordo* 257.1): Deus, qui emortuam vulvam Sarae ita per Abrahae semen faecundari dignatus es, ut ei etiam contra spem suboles nasceretur, preces famulae tuae pro sua sterilitate precantis propitius respice. This allusion is also found in the *RGP*'s ordo 236, a "Blessing against Bleeding."

237. From the late twelfth century, Aristotelian physiology played an especially strong role in cementing this belief in Western consciousness. In his *De generatione animalum*, Aristotle reduced the role of women in procreation to the state of "prime matter" awaiting the "forming" or "moving" agency of a man's semen, from which Aristotle concluded that women were

health place their recipients in a passive role, wherein they receive the intercession of saints, angels, or God himself to heal them when they themselves cannot. In this case the passivity of the recipient seems amplified by her gender, particularly in the biblical allusions of the alternative collect for the Mass: "Omnipotent eternal God, who did not deny the maternal state to the holy, ever-virgin Mary, who bore our redeemer, grant kindly that by the prayers of the same mother of God your female servant may be worthy to be a mother."[238] Mary was both mother and virgin through God's grace, but she humbly accepted the honor and travail of her divine pregnancy much as Sarah did. Mary, the only woman of nearly equal dignity to the figures of the Trinity, in the piety of the high and late Middle Ages, acts as intercessor, healing a woman who cannot heal herself.

While this Mass and others like it were designed principally for the benefit of individuals and their families, such rituals were also thought to benefit the entire community. In the proper *Hanc igitur* of the canon of the Mass for a sterile woman, God is beseeched, "so that you might hearken to her prayers and, absolving her womb from the fetter of sterility, grant offspring in whom your name may be blessed, and our days as well."[239] The final words of this prayer stress how the power of the blessing of an individual could, through the connection of that individual with the sacred body of the church, help bless and support the life of the entire community. The reference to absolving the woman's womb from "the fetter of sterility" is another clue to popular attitudes toward sin and illness, for it was popularly believed that the affliction of sterility, which in the eyes of the church robbed women of their primary raison d'être, was punishment for some grievous sin or personal failing. A blessing, then, could be not only a means of protection

---

an inferior form of men: "A woman is, as it were, an infertile male; the female, in fact, is female on account of an inability of a sort, that is, it lacks the power to concoct semen out of the final state of nourishment . . . because of the coldness of its nature." For this and further passages on Aristotelian views of women, see Alcuin Blamires, with Karen Pratt and C. W. Marx, eds., *Women Defamed and Women Defended: An Anthology of Medieval Texts* (Oxford: Clarendon Press, 1992), 38–41; Thomas Kiernan, ed., "Female," in his *Aristotle Dictionary* (London: Peter Owen, 1962), 261–62.

238. *RGP* 2:420 (*ordo* 257.2): Omnipotens sempiterne deus, qui maternum affectum nec in ipsa sacra semper virgine Maria quae redemptorem nostrum genuit denegasti, concede propitius, ut eiusdem Dei genetricis precibus famula tua esse genetrix mereatur.

239. Ibid. (*ordo* 257.4): ut orationes eius exaudias et eius uterum vinculo sterilitatis absolvens prolem in qua nomen tuum benedicatur concedas, diesque nostros.

and healing but also a form of absolution from sins affecting the body. God's versatility once more rises to the occasion in this blessing, offering a multitude of benefits to those willing to enter into the web of obligations the ritual created.

A second blessing in the RGP serves to strengthen the impression of women as secondary participants in the process of blessing. A set of "Other [Prayers] for the Sterility of Women" reminds God and the audience of the conception of Anna in scripture: "Omnipotent eternal God who, after prayers were extended to you, turned the continuous plaint of Anna to joy when you made her fertile, kindly fulfill the desire of your servant that she be made fertile, and mercifully turn away from her the disgrace of infertility for the glory of your name."[240] While the prayers of Anna and the woman receiving the blessing are acknowledged by this author, the blessing is ultimately performed for the greater glory of God, that is, for the praise and worship demanded by the divine in the negotiated process of the blessing, not solely for the woman's own need. Moreover, granting this need does not serve the woman's personal desires so much as it removes the "disgrace of infertility" from her and her family, offering further evidence for the popular view of sterility as the result of some grave sin or failing on the woman's part, and a source of great concern (not to mention acute embarrassment) for the husband. Along with the invocation of Anna, the mother of Mary, the Mass also invokes the name of Elizabeth, the wife of Zechariah and the mother of John the Baptist, nudging God further to perform consistently and grant the same beneficence to this medieval woman.[241]

The final alternative prayer concludes with the celebrant praying: "God, who looking mercifully upon the anxiety of the sterile, may miraculously cause fertility in them even in their desperation, grant kindly that your servant by the prayers of your servant Gregory may merit to obtain the bearing of children which she is unable to do on her own."[242] In this prayer the suffering of the woman is at last addressed as an important reason for the

240. Ibid., 2:421 (*ordo* 258.3): Omnipotens sempiterne deus, qui continuum etiam post fusas ad te preces gemitum Annae dum eam fecundares in gaudium convertisti, desiderium famulae tuae, ut fecundetur, propitius perfice et ad laudem gloriae tuae ab ea obprobrium sterilitatis benignus averte.

241. For the reference to Elizabeth, see ibid. (*ordo* 248.4).

242. Ibid. (*ordo* 258.5): Deus, qui anxietatem sterilium pie respiciens in eis faecunditatem etiam in sua desperatione mirabiliter operaris, concede propitius, ut famula tua de percipienda sobole quod per se non valet servi tui Gregorii mereatur precibus obtinere.

blessing. While the proper desire of the supplicant is not laid out by this author, given the emphasis of the other prayers it seems reasonable to conclude that it would be deemed appropriate to desire children to please a husband, or to fulfill the biblical injunction to be fruitful and multiply and thereby please God.

The inability to conceive was not the only gestational difficulty treatable by blessing; following conception, a fetus itself could be blessed. In the pontifical of William Durandus, a rite "Concerning the Blessing of a Fetus in the Womb of the Mother" reveals the distinct image of God depicted in healing blessings, while also offering new interpretations of the sacred past.[243] Following the singing of several versicles and responses and a brief prayer emphasizing the truth and being of the Trinity, the ritual presents an alternative prayer:

> Lord God, creator of all, strong and terrible, just and merciful, who alone is good and godly, the only excellent king, the only just king, omnipotent and eternal, who liberates Israel from all evil, who chose certain fathers in the womb after conception and sanctified them by the gift of the Holy Spirit, namely, Jeremiah, John the Baptist and the glorious Virgin . . . accept the sacrifice of a contrite heart, we entreat, and the fervent desire of your afflicted servant humbly praying for the preservation of weak offspring, which you gave her to conceive, and guard your portion and sanctify it by the immense blessing of your grace and defend it from all deceit and injury of the fearful Enemy, and also from whatever cruel adversities and iniquities you please, so that he or she may come unharmed to the most joyful light of this present life, by means of your delivering hand, and let him or her serve you always and in all things, and may he or she finally merit to obtain everlasting life.[244]

243. *PWD* 678–80 (apppendix 3). This *ordo* is not found in the three books of the pontifical itself; according to Andrieu the ritual was added by a copyist, probably from Provence.

244. Ibid., 679 (appendix 3.3): V. Salvam fac ancillam tuam et prolem suam. R. Deus meus sperantem in te [possibly an adaptation of Ps 86:16 and 86:2]. V. Esto eis, domine, turris fortitudinis. R. A facie inimici [Ps 61:4]. V. Nihil proficiat inimicus eis. R. Et filius iniquitatus non apponat nocere eis [adapted from Ps 89:23]. *V. Mitte eis, domine, auxilium de sancto. R. Et de Syon tuere eos* [adapted from Ps 20:3] Domine deus, omnium creator, fortis et terribilis, iustus atque misericors, qui solus es bonus et pius, rex solus prestans, solus iustus, omnipotens et eternus, qui de omni malo liberas Israel, qui fecisti patres electos quoslibet et sanctificasti eos munere sancti spiritus, Iheremiam videlicet, Iohannem Baptistam ac virginem gloriosam in uter post conceptum . . . accipe sacrificium cordis contriti, quesumus, ac fervens desiderium famule tue anxie humiliter supplicantis pro conservatione prolis debilis, quam dedisti eam concipere, et custodi partem tuam atque sanctifica immensa benedictione tue gratie et

As well as Creator, God here is portrayed as a midwife equipped with skills particularly suited to the task at hand, namely, the care and delivery of the gestating and newborn.[245] This is remarkable, considering the masculine identity of God in scripture and other blessings, and given than midwifery was a field of expertise left in the hands of women alone.[246] That God could assimilate this role into his aspect demonstrates again the flexibility that was attributed to divine power by medieval believers. This prayer invokes figures out of the sacred history of the Christian cosmos that are associated with childbirth and the water of new life: Jeremiah, whom scripture declares was consecrated as a prophet while still in the womb; the Virgin Mary, whose association with childbirth is obvious; and John the Baptist, whose kicking in the womb when Mary visited John's mother was probably a factor in associating him with fetuses and the womb. It thus draws on the awe and power that surrounded those numinous personages to ensure a safe term and delivery for the woman receiving the blessing.[247] And finally we see that this prayer seeks not only the physical well-being of the child but also seeks to impart the child with God's power in order to convert the newborn into a model Christian and ensure his or her salvation. Thus material concerns are wedded to spiritual, benefiting all by granting health to the human child and worship and service to the deity.

---

defende ab omni dolo et iniuria diri hostis necnon a quibuslibet adversitatibus crudelibus et iniquis, ut ad lucem presentis vite iocundissimam, obstetricante manu tua, veniat incolumis tibique iugiter in omnibus deserviat et vitam consequi perpetuam finaliter mereatur.

245. God as creator is a common theme in these rites, appearing in Swiss, French, and German blessings of the tenth, twelfth, and thirteenth centuries; see St. Gall's "Adjuration against Fevers," the *PWD*'s "Blessing of a Fetus," and Lambach's "Blessing after Birth." God as a just king is a common theme within ordeal blessings, as will be discussed in the next chapter.

246. For a discussion of midwifery, see Jean Donnison, "The Office of Midwife," in her *Midwives and Medical Men: A History of Inter-Professional Rivalries and Women's Rights* (London: Heinemann, 1977), 1–20; Diane Bornstein, "Family, Western European," *DMA* 4:600; Thomas Rogers Forbes, *The Midwife and the Witch* (New Haven: Yale University Press, 1966); Lucille Pinto, "The Folk Practice of Obstetrics and Gynecology in the Middle Ages," *Bulletin of the History of Medicine* 47 (1973): 513–23; Helen Lemay, "Women and the Literature of Obstetrics and Gynecology," in *Medieval Women and the Sources of Medieval History*, ed. Joel T. Rosenthal (Athens: University of Georgia Press, 1990), 189–209; and Carol Leslie Neuman de Vegvar, "Images of Women in Anglo-Saxon Art, II: Midwifery in Harley 603," *Old English Newsletter* 25, no. 1 (1991): 54–56.

247. Jer 1:4–5: "Now the word of the Lord came to me saying, 'Before I formed you in the womb I knew you, and before you were born I consecrated you; I appointed you a prophet to the nations.'" Also Lk 1:35–45.

After this lengthy prayer, the rite continues with a sprinkling of the mother and the singing of the psalm *Deus misereatur nostri* (May God be merciful to us and bless us and make his face to shine upon us, that your way may be known upon earth, your saving power among all nations), followed by the singing of more verses: "*Versus:* Let us bless the Father and the Son with the Holy Spirit. *Responsum:* Let us praise and exalt him on high in the world. *Versus:* God commanded his angels concerning you. *Responsum:* So that they might guard you in all your ways."[248] With praise yielded up in the opening verses, angelic protection is then invoked by associating the pregnant mother with one divinely favored.[249] This protection would help the woman throughout her pregnancy, placing her directly in God's care.

The final prayer reveals a fascinating medieval perspective on the human body as more than simply a vehicle or even a microcosm, but as a significant object in its own right: "Visit, we entreat, Lord, this entire habitation of yours and drive far off all the deceits of the enemy from it and from your present servant, and let dwell in it your holy angels, who may guard her and her children in peace."[250] In language reminiscent of the RGP's two house blessings and Durandus's "Blessing of a House," this blessing describes the body of the woman as a habitation for divine power, a repository of angelic beings that can guard and preserve her through the agency of this ritual prayer.[251] This suggests belief in an intimate link between the spaces in

248. The first verse and response appears to be an adaptation of the canticle of the three youths (the story is mentioned in the apocryphal additions to Daniel inserted between Dn 3:23 and 3:24; for the text of the canticle, see the song of the three Jews, 1:23–68); the second set is from Ps 91:11 (also in Mt 4:6, Lk 4:10); *PWD* 680 (appendix 3.4): V. Benedicamus patrem et filium cum sancto spiritu. R. Laudemus et super exaltemus eum in secula. V. Angelis suis Deus mandavit de te. R. Ut custodiant te in omnibus viis tuis. There is little citation of psalms in blessings for health and healing, and the majority of these are clustered in the blessings of women before and after birth (see the BAV Pal. lat. 235's "Prayers versus Chills," Vienna 2090's "Blessing after Birth," the *PWD*'s "Blessing of a Fetus," and Lambach's "Blessing after Birth"). These psalms all focus on turning away God's righteous wrath, acknowledging God's law, and seeking God's mercy to end suffering.

249. The ultimate exemplar of one divinely favored is, of course, Christ.

250. *PWD* 680 (appendix 3.5): Visita, quesumus, domine, cunctam habitationem istam et omnes insidias inimici ab ea et presenti famula tua longe repelle, et angeli tui sancti habitent in ea, qui eam et eius prolem in pace custodiant.

251. For similar passages, see *PWD* 546 (*ordo* 33.2); *RGP* 2:354–55 (*ordo* 190.1, 3); *RGP* 2:355 (*ordo* 191.2). All of these prayers call for angels to visit and defend the homes in question, and there is a concrete parallel to the notion of the human body's connection to communal space in the *PWD* blessing, which lumps together the house and its human

which human beings live and their very bodies, binding the natural world outside and the personal, inner world of the individual into an harmonious whole that acknowledges no fundamental distinction of worth between the physical and spiritual parts of our lives.

While such blessings could protect the married and their offspring, this was not their only function. Such rituals could also ensure the proper functioning of the marriage, at least so far as this was understood by the church that sanctioned such unions, a functioning that could (in the minds of the laity) be maliciously attacked through the powers of magic.[252] A "Prayer for the Impeded in Matrimony on Account of a Demon or Evildoers," drawn from a Dominican missal of 1519, unlike earlier blessings examined above, emphasizes the blessing of both partners:

> Lord Jesus Christ, son of the living God, who miraculously made fecund the womb of the blessed virgin Mary so that through the Holy Spirit she might conceive, carry, deliver and nourish: we invoke you, God and man, through your mercy, that you may deign to give fertility to these your servants N. and N.[253]

The prayer highlights the joining of two married people as a partnership, at least in so far as conception is concerned. This point is supported by an appeal to the sainted dead in the first prayer of the rite: "may you deign, through the merit and the prayers of the most blessed Virgin Mary, your mother, and of all the male and female saints to bless those whom you have joined matrimonially."[254] The appeal to both male and female saints is significant,

---

inhabitants when it asks "that they [the house and inhabitants] might be filled storehouses of good things" (*PWD* 546, *ordo* 33.3: ut sint promptuaria eorum plena).

252. An example of such concern is evident in the Burchard of Worms *Decretum* (c. 1008 to 1012), book 19, chap. 5, which shows that ordinary peasants of the eleventh century and even earlier clearly feared being bewitched into impotence (see Cohn, *Europe's Inner Demons*, 211). Another example is provided in the autobiography of the monk Guibert of Nogent, who tells how his father was made impotent by *maleficium* and his mother was then approached by an incubus, which fortunately was driven off by the appearance of a "good spirit" (ibid., 32).

253. Franz, 2:184: Domine Iesu Christe, fili dei vivi, qui uterum beate Marie virginis mirabiliter fecundasti, ut de spiritu sancto conciperet, portaret, pareret ac nutriret: te deum ac hominem invocamus per clementiam tuam, ut his famulis tuis N. et N. fecunditatem donare digneris. It is an interesting commentary on the prevailing double standard that ruled medieval gender relations that in the penitential manuals of the time, a woman yielding to the advances of an incubus was said to imperil her eternal salvation, but for a man to be approached by a succubus was "less dangerous" (Cohn, *Europe's Inner Demons*, 33).

254. Franz, 2:184: tu per merita et preces beatissime virginis Marie, matris tue, et omnium sanctorum et sanctarum tuarum digneris hos, quos matrimonialiter coniunxisti, benedicere.

reinforcing the cooperation of the male and the female joined in marriage by creating a similar alliance between the gendered forces of divinity. This prayer is a good example of how rituals of blessing could connect the trials and travails of medieval Christians to the paradigmatic events of sacred scripture, in this case seen through the allusion to the conception of Mary. The rite presents other such allusions, which seem to provide a way to actualize what medieval Christians assumed to be truths of their cosmology:

> Lord Jesus Christ, son of God and the blessed Virgin, who in the terrestrial paradise instituted marriage in the duty and conservation and multiplication of human nature and miraculously honored marriage itself in your advent with the first of your miracles [at Canaan] . . . may you give fertility and grace, so that they may be able to freely use their marriage for begetting, conceiving, carrying, bearing and nourishing offspring pleasing to God and human beings.[255]

This long invocation reasserts the divine origins of marriage and associates this human institution with the honor and glory of the Messiah's advent, sanctifying earthly union with divine grace. The prayer also makes the mythic time of marriage's origin come alive in the lives of the couple in distress, re-creating it for a new generation and preserving its memory for the community, which relies on the assumed truth of such stories to regulate social and sexual relations.

Scripture is also brought to life in blessings dealing with the aftermath of delivery. The older sacramentaries of the Latin West do not contain a formal blessing for the mother in childbed following a birth.[256] By the twelfth century, however, such rituals had developed, so that a priest performed such a blessing in the home of the mother on the eighth day after birth.[257] In a

255. Ibid.: Domine Iesu Christe, dei et beate virginis filius, qui in paradiso terrestri matrimonium instituisti in officium et conservationem et multiplicationem humane nature et ipsum matrimonium mirabiliter honorasti in adventu tuo ex primordiis miraculorum tuorum . . . dare fecunditatem et gratiam, ut libere possint uti matrimonio suo ad generandum, concipiendum, portandum, pariendum et nutriendum proles gratas deo et hominibus.

256. Ibid., 2:209. The Gelasian sacramentary does contain a Mass *In natale genuinum* for the anniversary of a birth, but the prayer is for the child, not the woman (Mohlberg, *Liber sacramentorum, ordo* 53, 211). In the Greek East, St. Chrysostamus attacked numerous heathen and superstitious practices concerning the mother in childbed and the newborn that were designed to protect them from evil spirits. The West had similar practices, some born from the appeasement of ancient Roman gods (Franz, 2:213).

257. Franz, 2:210–12. The German liturgical manuscripts Franz studied first show blessings after birth in the eleventh and twelfth centuries, but even at this time they were not

"Blessing after Birth," from an eleventh- or twelfth-century manuscript of Salzburg, the singing of several psalms initiates the blessing: Psalm 41, *Beatus, qui intelligit* (Blessed are those who consider the poor, the Lord delivers them in the day of trouble); Psalm 67, *Deus misereatur* (May God be gracious to us and bless us and make his face to shine upon us, *selah*); and Psalm 128, *Beati omnes* (Blessed is everyone who fears the Lord, who walks in his ways). The first psalm is one in which illness and treachery threaten the psalmist, who nonetheless remains confident in his faith.[258] This would be a positive exhortation, reassuring the recipient that her struggle to give birth was in accord with her faith, and that God would not abandon her to postpartum illness. The second psalm is both a thanksgiving and a recollection of deliverance from danger, an apt description of a new mother recovering from her delivery.[259] The third psalm's theme is that prosperity and domestic happiness will be the lot of those who obey divine mandates, both an assurance to the recipient and a reminder to continue in her devotion to God.

Following the psalmody, the celebrant speaks this prayer over the new mother: "God, father of our Lord Jesus Christ, God of all mercy, who rules the living and the dead, who is the doctor of souls, favorably look upon this your servant . . . and visit her with your heavenly visitation, just as you deigned to visit the mother-in-law of Symeon, and Sarah your maidservant, through your only begotten Son."[260] This prayer provides numerous in-

---

universally practiced; their existence is specifically confirmed, for example, in the liturgy of the Christophorus, bishop of Trent (ibid., 2:209). Only the older prayers touch upon the relations of the mother and (unlike Greek prayers) make only an indirect allusion to the pollution of the new mother. Franz also notes that, while popular belief in the demonic's grave threat to the mother and child was strong, all but eight Latin formulas he studied were silent on this issue. Only the twelfth-century Lambach *rituale* (Lambach, Bibliothek des Benediktinerstift Clb. 73) requests aid for the mother and child against evil spirits (Franz, 2:212–13). This manuscript fortuitously provides an illumination for its *Benedictio mulieris post partum*, which shows a priest, with an accompanying servant carrying holy water, entering the recovery room of the mother. The priest holds a book in his left hand and blesses the bed with his right hand, with the mother lying half-prone in it. A cradle sits next to the bed and an attendant sits by the foot of the bed, presumably as a guardian (2:209–10).

258. Kirkpatrick, *Book of Psalms*, 215–16. This psalm is probably Davidic in origin, composed when the ill David saw growing disloyalty at court leading to the revolt of his son, Absalom.

259. Ibid., 372–73. While this psalm was probably composed for use after the gathering in of the harvest, it clearly has relevance to someone suffering from physical distress, such as a new mother.

260. Franz, 2:210: Deus, pater domini nostri Iesu Christi, deus tocius misericordie,

sights. First, it gives us another example of the theme of God as physician, one whose spiritual nature grants him dominion over both living and dead "patients," such as the ailing mother in this ritual. Second, it emphasizes the nature of God as a *father*, one intimately familiar with the needs and desires of parents and therefore well suited to assisting them in their time of need. Finally, by alluding to past instances in which God played a role in ensuring a smooth delivery and recovery, this prayer both makes these events live again the mind of the medieval family, and reminds God of his past beneficence and his obligation to continue this service for the faithful.

It is worth pointing out some commonalities between blessings for health and blessings for knights and pilgrims and their equipment. There is a common interest in healing and knightly blessings to associate with the spiritual world a physical or worldly state, the condition of being ill, and the state of being a knight. Blessings of knights as early as the tenth century show a desire to associate the occupation with the spiritual life of the Christian, but on the whole this concern appears principally in the thirteenth and fourteenth centuries, in three studied rituals from German and French sources.[261] This is slightly later than the period that, according to Vauchez and Keen, was the greatest flowering of knightly dubbing as a religious ritual, but that these rituals appear slightly later is reasonable considering the typically slow rate of innovation within the medieval liturgy.

Finally, as with blessings of places, all benedictions for persons reveal a conception of the sacred or divine that is fundamentally adaptable and versatile. God could both protect and attack, heal and harm, consecrate and exorcise. As a city's defenses could be strengthened by the invocation of divine power, so too could the body of the fever wracked; as a blessing of a knight incorporated him into the spiritual hierarchy of Christian society, a blessing could also cast out demons who prevented conception and harmed pregnant mothers seeking to perpetuate the community of the faithful. But divine aid was never guaranteed; it had to be constantly recalled through rituals that acknowledged the saving acts of God at the same time that they anxious-

---

qui dominaris vite et mortis, qui es medicus animarum, respice propicius super hanc famulam tuam N . . . et visita eam visitacione tua celesti, sicut per unigenitum tuum filium visitare dignatus es socrum Symeonis et Saram, ancillam tuam. The allusions are to Mt 8:14 and Gn 18:9–15.

261. See the *RGP*'s "Blessing of a New Sword," the "*Ordo* for Arming the Defenders of the Church," the *PWD*'s "Blessing of Armor," and the *PWD*'s "Blessing of New Knights."

ly reminded God of his obligations to the faithful. The numinous power of God touched individuals and communities through this ritual negotiation, assisting them, identifying them, placing them in the context of the sacred history recounted in scripture, and giving their lives meaning.

The blessings of knights and the sick further reveal a *mentalité* that looked at the world not simply as a source of corruption but also as a font of holy power to be drawn upon at need. In curing the sick, blessings called upon the elements and the very structure of the world, its "hinges," to cast out natural and diabolical torments.[262] Other rituals invoked the heavenly bodies and every created thing to act as channels of divine power, conjuring healing from the power of the *numen* that lingered in the world it had created. The natural and physical components of creation were valued for their power to effect both physical and spiritual change in persons, and this power was equally applied to the spirit and the body of the believer. This concern for both halves of our nature upsets any effort to depict the medieval perspective as purely Augustinian, or at least Neoplatonic, as a view of the material world as imperfect and imperfectible and the immaterial world of spirit as innately perfect. Blessings show us instead how medieval religion could both condemn and commend the world, acknowledging the presence of sin and evil in it while appealing to the goodness and sacred power imbued within the cosmos during its divine creation.

262. See St. Gall's "Adjuration against Fevers" and Dalmatia's "Prayers Begun against Chills" (BAV Pal. lat. 245).

Chapter 4

SACRED VESSELS, OBJECTS, AND EVENTS

SACRED THINGS: A BRIEF SURVEY

In the study of the blessings of places and persons, we have already noted how frequently medieval Christianity blessed objects and particular times, imbuing them with a power beyond their mere physical presence. But in all of these blessings, the objects or times being blessed were of secondary importance, because the rituals in question were designed primarily to bless and assist the persons and places and the instruments of their consecration. There is, however, a group of blessings that elevate objects or events to a primary position. Many of these rituals deal with items associated with particular moments in the church's liturgical calendar: the blessing of palm fronds on Palm Sunday and candles on the feast of Candlemass are two of the best-known examples of such rites.[1] Others focus on items that play an important role in the daily liturgy of Christian worship: blessings of altars, chalices, bells, and clerical vestments being but a few of these numerous rituals.[2]

While these blessings undoubtedly are worthy of analysis in their own right, they will not be discussed in this work because of their close association with, and physical proximity to, the formal liturgy and the physical structure of the churches in which they were employed. In keeping with the focus on extraliturgical blessings outside the formal sacramental system of the high and late medieval church, this chapter examines ritual blessings of

---

1. For an excellent study and commentary on these rituals, see Franz, 1:445–55, 470–507.

2. Examples of all these diverse kinds of blessings may be found within the printed critical editions of the Roman pontifical tradition that I have used extensively in this study; for a sample, see *PWD ordos* 2.3–4 and 2.7–22.

items and events that mattered greatly to the laity but did not have a place within the formal sacramental liturgy of the church: blessings of ships, their crews, and nets; blessings of wells, dishes, and vessels; and blessings of ordeals, trials, and judicial duels.

SHIPS, NETS, AND MARITIME EQUIPMENT

The sea has always been a place of great ambiguity and mystery for humankind. In the imaginations of cultures around the world the ocean represents both the fear of an awesome unknown and the challenge, adventure, creativity, and romance of exploring distant lands. A source of life and livelihood for mariners, it is also a realm of death, where the turning of a tide or a slight shift in the wind could portend the coming of violent storms and dangerous currents that could steal away the lives of unwary sailors and fishermen.[3] This danger so impressed itself upon the mind of mariners that the forces of marine nature have consistently been attributed a malicious personality in Europe since ancient times, the sea thought of as one manifestation of the waters of Chaos, the enemy of universal order that ever threatened to cover the earth and revoke the authority of the gods who formed the cosmos from its waters.[4] The Israelites called the ocean Tehom, the "face of the water" over which God moved in the creation story of Genesis, and early secular written sources of this culture attributed an evil and dangerous nature to the waves, with Hebrew epic poetry portraying a constant war between Yahweh and Yam (the sea) and its monsters. This view was supported by biblical texts, which affirmed the existence of sea monsters, the greatest of which was the monstrous Leviathan.[5] Apprehension of similar ma-

3. Michel Mollat du Jourdin, *Europe and the Sea* (Oxford: Blackwell, 1993), 192; Elisha Linder, "Human Apprehension of the Sea," in *The Sea and History*, ed. E. E. Rice (Phoenix Mill, UK: Sutton Publishing, 1996), 15.

4. Linder, "Human Apprehension of the Sea," 15, 19; Mollat du Jourdin, *Europe and the Sea*, 193. One common belief that reflects the death and evil that the sea could represent was that the cries of seagulls expressed the wailing of the souls of the dead who were lost at sea and thus deprived of a proper burial (Mollat du Jourdin, *Europe and the Sea*, 194).

5. Linder, "Human Apprehension of the Sea," 15, 19 (see Gn 1:2, Is 27:1, 51:9, Ps 75:13–14, Jb 7:12); see also C. H. Gordon, "Leviathan: Symbol of Evil," in *Biblical Motifs*, ed. A. Altman (Cambridge, Mass.: Harvard University Press, 1966), 1–10. In the later biblical prophetic texts, the struggles of Yahweh and the sea's monsters turns into the struggle of Israel against its enemies, a case of cosmogony changing into history (Linder, "Human Apprehension of the Sea," 19). In medieval culture, especially in Germanic countries, Leviathan was often equated

leficent forces led to the development of taboos, divinatory and propitiatory gestures, and ritual precautions that were carried out before the departure of mariners in pre-Christian times, many of which survived into the medieval era despite the best efforts of the church to eradicate them.[6] With all the dangers, imagined and real, that the sea posed for medieval mariners, it is unsurprising that they turned to the power of the divine to protect themselves. While little is known directly of shipboard life besides its hazards, we do know something about the rituals that launched ships on their perilous courses.[7] One of the principal forms this protection took was the invocation of a blessing for ships.

In the early medieval period the Greek church offered blessings during the construction and the launch of a new ship, but Latin formulas from this period are rare. The Latin formulas of the high and late Middle Ages, however, evolved into a form even richer than that of the Greek blessings.[8] Latin blessings for the launching of ships appear as early as the eighth century, often in a simple form mingling prayers with the aspersion of holy water. Five rituals present a representative sample of such maritime blessings: a "Blessing of a Ship," from the *Liber ordinum* of Silos;[9] a "Blessing When One Boards a Ship," from (among others) the sacramentary of Angoulême,

---

with the Midgard serpent, who held the earth in its coils and whose motions caused earthquakes; see Rudolf Simek, *Heaven and Earth in the Middle Ages: The Physical World before Columbus*, trans. Angela Hall (Woodbridge, UK: Boydell and Brewer, 1996), 102.

6. Mollat, *Europe and the Sea*, 193. As taboos, Mollat mentions the ban on pregnant women aboard a ship and the fear of loading or eating rabbit meat onboard; divinatory gestures such as the interpretation of the sea's movement and the prediction of winds on certain days of the year, as well as the power of dream premonitions; propitiatory gestures such as hiding coins in the step of the main mast; and such precautions as consulting an astrologer before setting out on a journey.

7. Norbert Ohler, *The Medieval Traveler*, trans. Caroline Hillier (Woodbridge, UK: Boydell, 1989), 37.

8. Franz, 1:626–27. The Greek blessing appeals to heavenly aid, making reference to Noah's ark and the voyage of Jesus and the apostles on the Sea of Galilee. Other rituals call upon the aid of St. Michael and St. Nikolaus, refer to the stilling of the storm on Lake Genesareth, and make use of Ps 121. All of these rituals seek protection from the sea, pirates, and inclement weather. The Latin rituals, as we shall see, add to these elements richer allusions to biblical history, and insert psalms and Gospel readings.

9. Franz, 1:628; the MS is Silos, Biblioteca del Monastero *cod.* 4; Mon. Liturg. 5:173. The manuscript dates to 1052; see Klaus Gamber, *Codices liturgici latini antiquiores*, 2d ed. (Freiberg: Universitätsverlag Schweiz, 1968), 66, no. 390, and the following pages for other copies of the Old Spanish, Visigothic, or Mozarabic *Liber ordinum*.

a version of the Gelasian sacramentary composed circa 800;[10] a "Blessing of Nets," from the *Liber ordinum* of Silos;[11] a "Blessing of Nets for Catching Fish," from the RGP;[12] and a "Blessing of a Ship or a Boat," from a Dalmatian manuscript of the fifteenth century.[13]

The Frankish "Blessing When One Boards a Ship" demonstrates well one of the common themes of such blessings, the union through ritual of the physical vessel with its moral counterpart in the world of the spirit: "May this your people, Lord, be guided by your aid and protected by the arm of your majesty; may the water of the raging sea not trouble them, nor may they be affrighted by the face of the tempest. . . . Build the ship of their salvation, so that their heart may be filled by the increase of health-giving faith."[14] As

10. *CB* no. 1393. This blessing appears in nine other sources used by Moeller: Cambridge, Fitzwilliam Museum, MS. J 27; the unedited Benedictional of Augsburg, fols. 81v–82r (no. 216); the Gellone sacramentary (Dumas, *Liber sacramentorum*, no. 2099); the Lanalet pontifical of Cornwall (Doble, *Pontifical lanalatense*, no. 110a); the eleventh-century Roda pontifical MS Lerida, Archivo de la Cathedral de Lérida, fols. 143–179 (J. Rius Serra, ed., "Benediciones episcopales en un manuscrito de Roda," *Hispana Sacra* 10 [1957]: 161–210, esp. no. 187); the late tenth-century sacramentary of St. Thierry of Rheims (*PL* 78:625, 2); the episcopal blessing collection of Warmond, bishop of Ivrea, c. 969–c. 1014 (F. dell'Oro, ed., "Le 'benedictiones episcopales' del codice Warmondiano," *Archiv für Liturgiewissenschaft* 12 [1970]: 148–254, no. 98); Paris, Bibl. Nat. lat. MS 961, of Paris, or pontifical of Louis Beaumont—La Forêt, bishop of Paris (c. 1473–92) (Victor Leroquais, *Les pontificaux manuscrits des bibliothèques publiques de France* [Paris: Macon, 1937], 2:69–76, esp. 75, no. 110); Paris, Bibl. Nat. lat. MS 967, a pontifical of William Durandus or the "Pontifical of Jêrome d'Ochon, Bishop of Elne," 1423 (Leroquais, *Pontificaux manuscrits* 2:89–91, esp. no. 115); and Paris, Bibl. Nat. lat. MS 13315, a twelfth-century pontifical of Trèves, adapted to the usage of Saint-Germain-des-Prés.

11. Franz, 1:624–25; see Férotin's edition of the *Liber ordinum* of Silos, Mon. Liturg. 5:174.

12. *RGP* 2:377 (*ordo* 241). The rite appears in manuscripts B, C, D, and G from Vogel's sigla.

13. Franz, 1:629. The ritual is drawn from Vatican City, BAV, Barb. lat. 412, fols. 41–41v. Salmon, *Manuscrits liturgiques latins*, 61 (no. 152), believes that the MS is probably Dalmatian, an opinion confirmed by the personal inspection of the MS by Dr. Richard F. Gyug, who kindly provided me with his observations to help confirm this attribution. He points out that the Dalmatian martyrs Lawrence, Peter, and Andrew are cited in a litany during the liturgy for the dead (fol. 97r); Blaise, the patron of Dubrovnik, is cited in a blessing of bread (in an addition on 3r), in the litany noted above (96v), and in a blessing against clouds (146v); and finally there is a prayer added in Slavic (3r–v). This strongly suggests that the MS originated in Dubrovnik.

14. *CB* no. 1393a–b: Hic populus tuus, Domine, tuo gubernetur auxilio et brachio tuae maiestatis protegatur, non eum pelagi furentis unda turbet, nec a tempestatis facie terreatur. . . . Navem eorum salutis construe, ut cor eorum fidei salutari augmento impleatur. It is likely that this rite was composed with clerics or monks in mind, but its content and presentation suggest that it could also be applied to the laity.

the blessing offers protection from the physical dangers of the sea, so too does the blessing of the earthly ship strengthen the "ship of salvation," the church, by augmenting the faith of those who make use of this blessed vessel: "May they be held by the anchor of the Catholic faith, so that they might traverse secure the waves of the fierce world."[15] The physical world and the daily life of sailors within it is united with the moral domain of the spiritual life of the church through the power of this ritual, and the blessing of the material vessel becomes another opportunity to strengthen the bonds between God and his chosen people. This connection of spirituality and morality to the natural, physical world is fundamental to blessings of both ships and nets, and it appears in rituals as early as the eighth century and as late as the eleventh century, in both Frankish and Spanish collections.[16]

The association of sailing vessels with the body of the church is a metaphor found in other blessings of ships as well. In the Old Spanish "Blessing of a Ship," from the Silos *Liber ordinum,* the words of Jesus are invoked to strengthen this comparison:

> Lord Jesus Christ, who ordered the ark of your church to be made in the likeness of a ship, so that with the flood overflowing they alone who were found in it [i.e., the ark] might be saved, and who also deigned to stretch forth your right hand from the ship for the sinking Peter: we ask your clemency, that you might turn the opposition of every wind far away from this ship.[17]

15. Ibid., c: Catholicae fidei anchora teneantur, ut undas saeculi saevientis securi pertranseant.

16. See the Frankish "Blessing on Boarding a Ship" and the Old Spanish "Blessing of Nets." This theme also appears in the tenth-century *RGP*'s blessing of a new well and is strongly present in two studied and three supporting ordeal blessings, which were composed in the ninth, tenth, and eleventh centuries; two are of German, two of French, and one of Swiss origin. (See Geneva's "Blessing of Iron," the Gondekar pontifical's "Blessing of Frigid Water," the Montpellier "Blessing of Water," the Parisian "*Ordo* for Water Judgments," and the Bamberg pontifical's "Blessing of a Small Jug.") This theme is accompanied by an emphasis on the mutual benefits reaped by divinity and humanity in blessings. This appears in four blessings of ships and nets from ninth- and tenth-century France and Spain. It highlights the businesslike relationship between God and humans so often expressed in blessings (see the Frankish "Blessing on Boarding a Ship," the Old Spanish "Blessing of a Ship" and "Blessing of Nets," and the *RGP*'s "Blessing of Nets").

17. Franz, 1:628: Domine Iesu Christe, qui in similitudinem navis ecclesie tue arcam fieri iussisti, ut inundante diluvio soli, qui in ea inventi sunt, salvarentur, quique etiam Petro mergenti dexteram de navi dignatus es porrigere: rogamus clementiam tuam, ut ab hac nave omnium ventorum adversitatem procul avertas.

The reference to the Old and New Testaments, and the familiarity of church-men with these naval metaphors, undoubtedly enhanced the potency and ef-ficacy of this ritual in the minds of its author and audience.[18] In its scriptur-al allusion the blessing presents a reasonable fear of nature and a desire to subdue it, and in a secondary sense it is an example of how a ceremony such as ritual blessing establishes identity for its participants through opposi-tion to the outside world: the ark marks out not only those who will survive the flood but those whose souls will be saved and carried home to God.[19] The reference to Christ's life-saving action for the drowning Peter, like so many other biblical allusions we have studied, could serve a double purpose: on the one hand, it provides a model of divinity's beneficent past behavior, with which the human celebrant can encourage the divine to act consistent-ly and protect these mortals in a similar fashion; on the other, it associates the perils of medieval sailors with the saving acts of sacred history, making the Gospel come alive for the recipients of the blessing and thus keeping the mythology of the Christian cosmos alive and real for the present generation of believers.

As we have seen with the reference to Noah's ark above, blessings of ships appealed to the Old Testament in their search for a way to successfully tap the power of the divine. The Dalmatian "Blessing of a Ship or a Boat" re-actualizes the saving acts of God involving water through invoking the pa-triarchs of ancient Israel:

> God, who led our fathers through the Red Sea and carried them singing
> the praise of your name through the overflowing waters: we humbly entreating

18. The use of scriptural allusion, a common element of other blessings, is also quite fre-quent in the three subcategories of blessings of vessels, objects, and events. Scripture was of-ten employed in blessings of ships and nets, appearing in five of the six studied rituals, and three of the four allusions made in these rituals are common to two or more rituals (see the Old Spanish "Blessing of a Ship" and "Blessing of Nets," the *RGP*'s "Blessing of Nets," the *PWD*'s "Blessing of a Ship," and the Dalmatian "Blessing of a Ship or Boat"). The first of these was a generic allusion to the blessing of God received by Abraham, Isaac, and Jacob, which is present in three rituals; the second, a more "on-topic" allusion to Noah surviving the deluge, is present in three blessings; and the walking of St. Peter on the water is invoked in two bless-ings. The last, a solitary allusion, is made by the Old Spanish "Blessing of Nets," which recalls the apostles casting their nets at Jesus' command. The Old and New Testaments each have two references.

19. This, I would argue, implies an "us-versus-them" relationship similar to the one dis-cussed by Grimes in his definition of ritual.

pray you, that you may kindly bless this ship or boat of your servants and with all the adversities bearing upon it having been repulsed . . .[20]

The parting of the Red Sea becomes an example of how God could grant freedom from the suffering and death the sea can so swiftly and savagely bring, moving aside this chaotic danger in order to make way for orderly divine will.[21]

As we have seen before, however, the most typical appeal to sacred history was to the distant antediluvian world God chose to punish for its sinfulness:

> Bless, Lord, the procession of our feet and the vessel of your servants, and bless the master of the ship and those sailing with him, just as you deigned to bless the ark of Noah wandering in the waves of the Deluge, and just as you blessed Abraham, Isaac and Jacob. Stretch forth your right hand for your servants, Lord, just as you stretched it forth for Peter walking upon the sea; give them, Lord, bodily health and your mercy and may you deign to lead them through to safe harbor.[22]

Unpredictable and often inexplicable, the actions of the sea could easily be seen as an instrument both of chaos and of God's wrath, and this unpleasant thought must have preyed upon the minds of sailors and nervous passengers, who have ever been concerned to guarantee a safe journey and

20. Franz, 1:629 (Barb. lat. 412, fols. 40r–41v): Deus, qui transduxisti patres nostros per mare rubrum et transvexisti eos per aquam nimiam laudam tui nominis decantantes: te supplices deprecamur, ut hanc navem vel naviculam famulorum tuorum propitius benedicas cunctisque in ea vehendis repulsis adversitatibus . . .

21. See the *PWD*'s "Blessing of a Ship," the *RGP*'s "Blessing of Frigid Water," and Saint Florian's "Judgment of Hot Iron." It is likely that the sign of the cross was also a ritual gesture common in blessings: it may have been taken for granted by medieval liturgical authors, or it may be indicated in blessings by the sign of the cross, which modern editors of blessings (with the notable exception of Andrieu) typically omit from their editions. For examples of Andrieu's inclusion of the sign of the cross, see *PWD ordo* 2.34, "Concerning the Blessing of a Ship." Ritual action in blessings of objects and events is largely confined to such aspersion, as in this blessing. It occurs in maritime blessings of the thirteenth and fifteenth centuries, ordeals of the eleventh and twelfth centuries, and not at all in blessings of wells and vessels (although the blessing of a neglected font mentions salt being added to the water in the font).

22. Franz, 1:629: Benedic, domine, ingressum pedum nostrorum et navigium famulorum tuorum et benedic nauclerum et cum eo navigantes, sicut benedicere dignatus es arcam Noe ambulantem in undis diluvii et sicut benedixisti Abraam, Yssac [*sic*] et Iacob. Porrige, domine, famulis tuis dexteram tuam, sicut porrexisti Petro ambulanti super mare; dona eis, domine, corporis sanitatem et misericordiam tuam et ad portum salutis eos perducere digneris illesos.

return home. The allusions to Noah's ark and the rescue of Peter could comfort them in the knowledge that God's mercy would set sail with them, and would act for them just as it had for much mightier servants from the living past of Christian history, especially considering the protection granted by aspersion of the ship with blessed water such as baptized Christ.[23] Such a combination of invocation and action as this blessing presents must have been powerful in its appeal, as we may see it appear again within the rite "For the Blessing of a Ship" from the thirteenth-century PWD:

> Deign to be favorable to our supplications, Lord, and with your right hand
> bless this very ship and all who are carried in it, just as you deigned to bless
> the ark of Noah wandering in the deluge, and Abraham, and Isaac and Jacob.
> Stretch forth your right hand for them, Lord, just as you stretched it forth
> for Peter walking upon the sea, and send your holy angel from heaven, who
> may liberate it and guard it always from all perils . . . and, with adversaries re-
> pulsed, may you always support your servants in it with an always calm port
> and voyage, and with all business completed and rightly conducted, again may
> you deign to recall them to their own with all joy.[24]

The prayer duplicates most of the previous prayer but adds an important new emphasis on the action of angels in the protection of sailors.[25] This is unsurprising, as we have seen angels fulfilling many similar roles in other blessings. The commercial emphasis (*negotiis*) and related definition of voyaging as out and back are other additions. It is also of interest for its explicit desire to invoke protection from "all perils," the chaotic nature and active malevolence of which drove the medieval laity to seek shelter in the ritual blessings offered

23. Ohler, *Medieval Traveler*, 45. The aspersion found here has a precedent in the story, related by Bede, of how monks had stilled the raging waves of the North Sea by sprinkling oil provided them by Bishop Aidan onto the waters; see Bede, *Ecclesiastical History*, 3.15, p. 134.

24. *PWD* 547 (*ordo* 2.34.1): Propitiare dignare, domine, supplicationibus nostris et benedic navem istam dextera sancta tua et omnes qui in ea vehentur, sicut dignatus es benedicere archam Noe ambulantem in diluvio et Abraham, Yssac [*sic*] et Iacob. Porrige eis, domine, dexteram tuam, sicut porrexisti beato Petro ambulanti supra mare, et mitte sanctum angelum tuum de celis, qui liberet et custodiet eam semper a periculis universis . . . et in ea famulos tuos, repulsis adversitatibus, portu semper cursuque tranquillo tuearis, transactisque riteque perfectis negotiis omnibus, iterato tempore, ad propria cum omni gaudio revocare digneris. Andrieu notes that this blessing is found in a shorter form in *RGP* 2:377 (*ordo* 244, *Oratio in nave*); this prayer also appears in Franz, 1:627–28 (in a *Benedictio navis* from Clm 100, fol. 127) and 2:285 (in the first part of an *Ordo benedictionis ad peregrinos navigare volentes ad terram sanctam*).

25. Saints are notably absent from the blessings of ships and nets, as well as from those of wells and vessels discussed in the next section.

by the church. Through voice, gesture, and action, such rites assuaged believers' fears in the same moment as they actualized the significant events of the
history upon which they based their understanding of the world.

While ships were an essential element of the sailor's life and thus in
need of divine protection, smaller tools of the fisherman's trade were also
thought to require divine assistance. The blessing of nets is a practice as ancient as that of ships, with the first significant rite appearing in the RGP. A
"Blessing of Nets for Catching Fish" invokes the power of God for the fishermen thus:

> we pray your goodness, that you might bless with your powerful right hand
> these nets woven for the capturing of fish, so that when the catch of fish in
> these nets shall have happened for the use of your servants, we may yield to
> you, Lord, the granter of good works, deserved thanks for the granted ben-
> efits.[26]

This blessing interweaves the power of the *numen* into the woven nets, but
it also expresses the contractual relationship so typical of blessings. In this
case, the human celebrant promises thanks and praise in exchange for an
ample catch of fish to feed the fishermen and their families, binding the
community of believers closer to God through a web of interdependence.

This relationship could provide more than simply material benefits to the
humans who invoked it through rituals of blessing. In the Old Spanish *Liber
ordinum*'s "Blessing of Nets," which duplicates the RGP's prayer for its second
invocation, we see the recipients of the blessing benefit on many levels:

> Omnipotent, eternal Father and Lord, you who are the indulger of highest pi-
> ety, the grantor of eternal grace. . . . Do not allow any art of adversaries to bind
> the net nor the most wicked words of incantations to entangle it; and you who
> granted your most blessed and holy apostles, by throwing a net into the sea,
> to pull out an abundance of fish from the waters of the sea. . . . Grant us, Lord,
> that by the use of this net we might be refreshed and made to rejoice through
> the gifts of your grace, just as both refreshed by temporal food we might al-
> ways express the due abundance of thanks to you in eternal reward.[27]

26. *RGP* 2:377 (*ordo* 241): oramus pietatem tuam, ut haec retia ad capiendos pisces in-
texta potenti benedicas dextera, quatinus, dum tuorum usibus famulorum piscium in eis cap-
tura provenerit, tibi domino bonorum operum largitori pro concessis beneficiis debitas gratias referamus.

27. Franz, 1:624–25: Omnipotens sempiterne pater et domine, qui es summe pietatis

This prayer's call for grace to accompany the full nets of the fishermen creates a parallel between the temporal and the spiritual that reflects the deep connection medieval people perceived between the world of the spirit and the material world. There is also a noticeable concern over the power of sorcery to adversely affect the daily catch, through "adversaries" whose incantations and ill will can bring disaster, a theme echoed in the pontifical of Durandus's "Blessing of a Ship."[28] This represents not only a general belief in the powers of the demonic and magical but also the common belief in evil magic as a threat to survival of the faithful.[29] And finally, reference to Christ's commands to the apostles to cast out their nets provides an eminently appropriate paradigm from sacred history to empower the fishermen's task, and to connect their daily life with the meaningful events of the Christian cosmos.[30]

WELLS, DISHES, AND DRINKING VESSELS

A crucial element of any society's life is access to clean sources of drinking water, and medieval societies were no exception. When human ingenuity and knowledge proved inadequate to the task of securing good water, medieval people turned to God, in this way following the ancient world's precedent of associating the beneficent powers of wells and springs with gods and spirits. Isidore of Seville's *Etymologiae* preserved the legend of numerous wells that both provided drinking water and produced miraculous effects on those who drank from them; many "holy wells" throughout the British Isles continue to attract the needy to this day.[31] In the Christian era, the powers of

---

indultor, eterne gratie contributor. . . . Non eum sinas adversantium arte aliqua inligare nec verbis incantantium pessimis irretiri. Quique beatissimis tuisque sanctis apostolis sagenam iactantibus in mare dedisti copiam piscium a marinis gurgitibus abstrahere. . . . Presta nobis, deus, ut huius retis exhibitione repleamur et gratie tue muneribus gratulemur, qualiter et cibo temporali refecti eterno in premio debitam tibi semper copiam gratiarum pandamus.

28. *PWD* 547 (*ordo* 34.1).

29. For example, see the numerous blessings against thunderstorms and lightning summoned by sorcery and incantations (Franz, 2:19–74).

30. A similar invocation of Christ's command to cast out nets can be found in a "Blessing of Nets or Fish Hooks," found in Franz's collection. The rite begins with the reading of Lk 5:1 and the prayer: "Lord Jesus Christ, who commanded your apostles so that they might loose nets into a catch of fish, and they filled up with a copious multitude of fish: bless, we ask, these nets with your abundant blessing" (Franz, 1:625).

31. Simek, *Heaven and Earth*, 108. Simek mentions several wells discussed by Isidore: two Greek wells, one that strengthened memory and one that caused forgetfulness (*Etymologiae*

the numinous were frequently called upon for the protection and purification of water, and numerous blessings for wells, dishes, and drinking vessels can be found in the liturgical texts of the high and later Middle Ages.[32] These rites, like those that used blessed water to sanctify houses and cemeteries, are particularly valuable for the insights they provide on medieval ideas of pollution and the nature of the divine as a source of purification for both the spiritual and the physical worlds.

The issue of pollution and the demonic is most frequently addressed in blessings of wells and vessels, many of which are explicitly designed to cleanse and purify the polluted vessels so that they may be used safely by Christians. In the process of this purification, grace is made the central agent of cleansing the pollution. All of the four rites examined are German and Spanish in origin, and all were composed in the tenth and eleventh centuries.[33] The prayers of these blessings of wells and vessels most frequently mention demonic or diabolic influence as a pollutant to be removed: it appears in all but the *ordo* for a neglected font or spring.[34] Why this *ordo* does not mention demons is not entirely clear, but if it is for a church font it may be because the font's placement within the walls of a consecrated church was

---

13.12.3–4); two Sicilian springs, one that made women pregnant and one that caused infertility (13.13.5); and others in Greece that increased one's libido (13.12.3–4). Healing springs and wells were also known throughout Europe and the British Isles. See Swanson, *Religion and Devotion in Europe*, 186; Arthur Gribben, *Holy Wells and Sacred Water Sources in Britain and Ireland: An Annotated Bibliography* (New York: Garland Publishing, 1992), esp. 15–20; Warwick Rodwell, *Archaeology of Religious Places: Churches and Cemeteries in Britain*, rev. ed. (Philadelphia: University of Pennsylvania Press, 1989), 154; Richard K. Morris, *The Church in British Archaeology*, CBA Research Report 47 (London: Council for British Archaeology, 1983), 19–48; and for a general survey of Ireland's wells and springs, see Nigel Pennick, *Celtic Sacred Landscapes* (York, UK: Thames and Hudson, 1996).

32. For a fuller discussion and collection of such blessings, see Franz, 1:610–23.

33. See the Old Spanish "Blessing of an Unclean Vessel," and the *RGP*'s "Blessing of a New Well," "Over Small Vessels," and "*Ordo* for Vases."

34. Although his thinking was out of the mainstream in regard to baptism and baptismal water, it is possible that one source of this concern was Tertullian, who was very concerned that any water used for baptism first be exorcised, owing to the potential for demonic contamination: "Without any sacred significance, unclean spirits do settle upon the waters, pretending to reproduce that primordial resting of the divine Spirit upon them: as witness shady springs and all sorts of unfrequented streams, pools in bathing places, and channels or storage tanks in houses, and these wells called snatching wells—obviously they snatch by the violent action of a malignant spirit." Tertullian, "De baptismo," 5.4, in *Tertullian's Homily on Baptism*, ed. Ernest Evans (London: S.P.C.K., 1964), 12–13.

thought to make it less vulnerable to demons than wells and vessels outside churches. Also, the ritual is designed for a font that has suffered human neglect, not one that has been attacked by demons. The concerns about pollution contracted from the human world, as expressed in these blessings, supports this idea. Three of the four rituals that cast out demonic powers also expel physical pollution, a threat all the greater for wells and containers exposed to the natural elements but of less concern for a font sheltered inside a church.[35] That such dirt required a ritual cleansing in rites that cast out demonic powers shows that the medieval notion of pollution embraced both physical and spiritual elements; although the natural world and its elements were often thought of as vessels of divine power, they could also be bearers of pollution.

The blessings of wells fall into two general categories: blessings for new wells and blessings for reconsecration of polluted wells. For the former category, the first Latin blessing (discussed below) is found in the Bobbio missal.[36] This Gallican ritual for new wells appears also in Benedict of Aniane's supplement to the Gregorian sacramentary, but in shortened form.[37] Altogether, I have chosen five rituals to demonstrate the themes of this genre of blessings: a "Blessing Where Anything Unclean Shall Have Fallen into a Vessel," from the *Liber ordinum* of Silos;[38] a "Blessing of a New Well," from the RGP;[39] a "Blessing over Small Vessels Found in Old Places," also from

35. See the Old Spanish "Blessing of an Unclean Vessel" and the *RGP*'s "Over Small Vessels Found in Old Places" and "*Ordo* for Vases." Another possible explanation for the lack of emphasis on physical pollution in the blessing of the font is the conviction that it was in greater danger from the demonic. Evidence from the Italian communes shows a universal belief among citizens in Satan's special hatred of the baptismal font, and that he was more likely to attack the font than any other sacred object. In response, communal churches enacted regulations requiring locked covers to be placed over the water, to protect it from theft by sorcerers who were believed to use it in diabolical rites. See Thompson, *Cities of God*, 28.

36. Paris, Bibl. Nat. lat. 13246; Lowe, *Bobbio Missal*.

37. Franz, 1:610; Deshusses, *Sacramentaire grégorien*, 1:476–77 (*ordo* 1461). The formulas of the supplement omit earlier references to Old Testament history. The Greek church practiced a solemn dedication at the digging of a new well: a ritual of the tenth century invokes the waters of the Jordan and Siloh to make a remedy for illness and against the powers of the Devil (Franz, 1:611).

38. Franz, 1:622.

39. *RGP* 2:374 (*ordo* 231). This *ordo* has three alternative formulas: the first formula is the same blessing as is found in the supplement (no. 1461) noted above; the second and third alternative formulas are from the Gellone sacramentary (Ge 2855, 2856), a Gelasian sacramentary of the eighth century.

the RGP;[40] a "Blessing of Whatsoever Vases You Please," from a manuscript of Augsburg dated to some time between the twelfth and fourteenth
centuries;[41] and a "Blessing of a Font Which Has Been Neglected," from the
same Augsburg manuscript.[42]

The first Gallican formula of the RGP, a "Blessing of a New Well," ex-
tracted from the supplement, draws a strong connection between pollution
and the powers of the demonic: "We entreat the mercy of your goodness,
Lord, that with your heavenly blessing you might sanctify and distribute the
water of this well for a healthy communal life, and thus shall you deign to
drive away from it all the incursions of diabolical temptation." The third formula, drawn from the Gelasians of the eighth century, presents similar concerns: "through the office of our prayers, with spectral tricks and diabolical
deceits repulsed from here through the office of our prayers, may this well
remain purified and cleansed."[43] Diabolical temptation, which would seem
to have power equal to the divine's to infiltrate and suffuse natural elements,
is depicted here as a form of pollution, a spiritual part of the physical filth
that is made "pure and cleansed" by the sacred.

This power of the divine to dispose of the unclean is also evident within
early blessings for drinking vessels. In the alternative prayer of a "Blessing
over Vessels Found in Old Places," taken from the Gelasian sacramentary of
the eighth century and designed for the cleansing of drinking and storage
vessels found in heathen ruins or buried in the earth, the celebrant speaks

40. *RGP* 2:375 (*ordo* 233). The first formula of this *ordo* is from the supplement (Deshusses, *Sacramentaire grégorien*, 1:476, no. 1460) and is found in the Gellone sacramentary (Ge
2851). The second alternative formula of *RGP* 233 is found in the Gellone sacramentary (Ge
2851), though not in the supplement; the Gellone sacramentary continues with two additional alternatives.

41. Franz, 1:622; the ritual is drawn from Clm 3908, fol. 197. The first half of this blessing is the same as *RGP* 2:375 (*ordo* 234); the blessing is also found in the Gellone sacramentary (Ge 2854).

42. Franz, 1:620. The blessing is closely related to *RGP ordo* 232.2 (*RGP* 2:375), "Blessing
of a Font Which Has Been Neglected," which is an alternative formula. The same formulas are
found in the Gellone sacramentary (Ge 2857–58).

43. *RGP* 2:374 (*ordo* 231.1) (= suppl. 1461, from Gallican sources, e.g. the Bobbio missal).
These two selections are a melange of two separate blessings, the second being an alternate for
the first: Deprecamur, domine, clementiam tuae pietatis, ut aquam putei huius caelisti benedictione sanctifices et ad communem vitam concedas salubrem, et ita ex eo fugare digneris
omnem diabolicae temptationis incursum [231.3 (= Ge 2856)] per nostrae offitium orationis,
repulsis hinc fantasmaticis calliditatibus atque insidiis diabolicis, purificatus atque emunda-
tus hic puteus perseveret.

thus: "God, who in the advent of your son our Lord cleansed the faithful, be favorably present by means of our invocations, and by the bounty of your grace cleanse these vessels, which by the indulgence of your kindness brought forth from the chasm of the earth after a space of time you returned to human use."[44] Grace here gives humans the power to cleanse and expel pollution by means of ritual. By excluding the unclean from this dish, the blessing excludes it also from the human community that uses the dish, simultaneously protecting the members of that community and binding them closer to the sacred power that maintains the integrity of the community.

The same connection between filth and satanic delusion is found in other rituals, for example, the "Blessing of Whatsoever Vases You Please," from the manuscript of Augsburg, dated to some time during the twelfth to fourteenth centuries:

God, protector of the faithful, inhabitant of the vessels of those subject to you, we ask that you might deign to illuminate these your vessels with the serene eyes of your godliness, so that the abundant blessing of your grace might descend upon them and using them with health may these selfsame ones merit vessels made clean for you through your grace, in order that the enemy of the human race might retire far from here at your command, that the deceits of the Devil be driven far away; every expelled pollution from evil might disappear far away.[45]

44. *RGP* 2:375 (*ordo* 233.2): Deus, qui in adventu filii tui domini nostri omnia tuis mundasti fidelibus, adesto propitius invocationibus nostris, et haec vascula, quae tuae indulgentia pietatis post spacia temporum a voragine terrae abstracta humanis usibus reddidisti, gratiae tuae largitate emunda. In rituals designed to purify contaminated wells and vessels, God is cast as a purifier and cleanser of the polluted. This attribution appears in four of the five rituals studied, dating from the tenth to the eleventh century and originating in the Old Spanish liturgy and in the *RGP* (see the Old Spanish "Blessing of Unclean Vessels," the *RGP*'s "Blessing of a New Well," "Over Small Vessels Found in Old Places," and "*Ordo* for a Neglected Font").

45. Franz, 1:622: Protector fidelium, deus, subditorum tibi corporum habitator, quesumus, serenis oculis tue pietatis hec vascula tua illustrare digneris, ut descendat super ea gratie tue benedictio larga et cum salubritate utentes eisdem ipsi per gratiam tuam tibi mereantur vasa effici munda, ut procul tuo imperio hinc humani generis hostis abscedat, procul diaboli fraudes absistant, procul omnis pollutio nequitie abstera vanescat. A shorter version of this prayer also appears in the *RGP* and is very close to a blessing from the Gellone sacramentary; see *RGP* 2:375 (*ordo* 234) and Ge no. 2854. The MS Franz employs is Clm 3908, fol. 197r. This and the previous rite are old Germanic ones, used for containers found in moors or dug up, which, having been in contact with paganism, had to be purified of all impurity and demonic taint (Franz, 1:620). Such rituals designed for ancient vessels are found in most early medieval collections, notably in Benedict of Aniane's supplement to the Gregorian sacramentary,

This passage presents us with a number of fascinating points. First, the nature of God as protector is asserted, a theme developed further as the rite shows how God's power was thought able to inhabit material objects, protecting them and their users from evil and pollution.[46] Second, we can see how this ritual prayer created community by expelling the unacceptable (in this case, the "enemy of the human race," who will "retire far away") and protecting the acceptable. Third, the spiritual quality of evil or iniquity is linked by this prayer with demonic pollution and (implicitly) with the physical pollution within the unconsecrated vessel, connecting the material world with the immaterial vices so beloved by the enemies of the faithful. Finally, we see how God's mere attention was thought to act as a purifying force in the reference to God's eyes' "illuminating" the vessel.

The idea of the eyes' providing the light by which we see was transmitted through Plato's *Timaeus*, the singular systematic treatment of light and optics available in the West during much of the early Middle Ages.[47] Plato argued that visual fire emanated from the observer's eye and coalesced with daylight to form an optical medium capable of transmitting images to the soul. This theory of emanation was picked up by later Neoplatonic authors, most notably Pseudo-Dionysius the Areopagite (d. 500), whose metaphysics of light was transmitted to the Latin West through the writings of John Scottus Eriugena (c. 810 to c. 877).[48] Eriugena fused the thought of St. Au-

---

but become rarer from the fourteenth century onward. They were intentionally omitted from copies made of older manuscripts during this period and were almost extinct by the fifteenth century (Franz, 1:620–21).

46. Complementing this aspect is the familiar notion of God as protector, which is elaborated with the idea that the divine also inhabits the bodies of the faithful. This quality appears in only one ritual of the five studied, namely, the *ordo* for vases that appears first in the Gellone sacramentary and later in the *RGP*, but that it is present in recensions of the *RGP* means that it experienced wider use in the areas under the influence of the Franco-Roman liturgy than its singular appearance suggests. Finally, the *RGP*'s one blessing of a well characterizes God as the commander of water. This essential quality resonates with previously discussed blessings that explicitly connect the elements with their Creator and command those elements to obey the requests made by the faithful through ritual performance.

47. The image of God's eyes' providing illumination within our body of texts is confined to this single blessing. Ferial and Mass blessings, however, often make reference to God's illuminating those suffering from both physical and spiritual blindness, often mentioning the divine illuminating the "inner eye" of the person. For examples, see *CB* nos. 1405a, 973a, 2038a, and 1374b.

48. For a detailed survey of Eriugena and his thought, see Dermot Moran, *The Philosophy of John Scottus Eriugena: A Study in Idealism in the Middle Ages* (Cambridge: Cambridge University

gustine, Pseudo-Dionysius, Gregory of Nyssa, and Maximus the Confessor to produce his own theory of illumination. From Augustine, John Scottus adapted the definition of God as the *lux mentium*, the light of the mind, or "the Light which illuminates Itself," and the characterization of light as good, salvation, life, and knowledge, and darkness as sin, evil, death, and ignorance.[49] These definitions were common to Augustine's and Pseudo-Dionysius's thought, but Pseudo-Dionysius expanded Augustine's theory by portraying God as the source of light, from whom innumerable beams of light spread out to form and touch all creation; he argued that while we can symbolically associate God with light, we can also associate God with darkness, since God is neither light nor darkness but beyond them.[50] The darkness of God for Dionysius and Eriugena was symbolic of the transcendent nature of the divine: God's "light" is so bright to human eyes as to appear as an impenetrable darkness.

Eriugena's presentation of Pseudo-Dionysius's metaphysics of light was the dominant influence in optics in the later Carolingian era and remained influential into the high Middle Ages.[51] Perhaps the best known example of Pseudo-Dionysius's popularity and impact on Western spirituality is found in the personal metaphysic of Abbot Suger of St. Denis, whose abbey church initiated the Gothic style and its love of windows, which let in the "true light to which Christ is the door" so as to instruct the worshipper that there was a reality beyond that perceived by the senses.[52] This brief summary of the metaphysics of optics and light is relevant to our own study of a high medieval blessing of a vase in several ways. In the first place, the dating of this

---

Press, 1989). For his theory and metaphysics of light, see ibid., 79–80, 111, 116–17, and 267; and Dierdre Carabine, "Eriugena's Use of the Symbolism of Light, Cloud and Darkness in the *Periphyseon*," in *Eriugena: East and West: Papers of the 8th International Colloquium of the Society for the Promotion of Eriugenan Studies, Chicago and Notre Dame, 18–20 October 1991*, ed. Bernard McGinn and Willemien Otten (Notre Dame: University of Notre Dame Press, 1994), 141–52.

49. Moran, *Philosophy of Eriugena*, 79, 111, 116–17; Carabine, "Eriugena's Use of Symbolism," 143.

50. Moran, *Philosophy of Eriugena*, 117–18; Carabine, "Eriugena's Use of Symbolism," 145.

51. Eriugena's metaphysics of light was elaborated by St. Thomas Aquinas and Robert Grosseteste, who began the scientific study of light as a physical phenomenon. Although challenged by ancient and Islamic scientific treatises that became known to the West in the thirteenth century, this theory remained influential in the study of optics. See David C. Lindberg, "Optics, Western European," *DMA* 9:247–53.

52. David B. Evans, "Pesudo-Dionysius the Aeropagite," *DMA* 10:203–4; Gabrielle M. Spiegel, "Suger of St. Denis," *DMA* 11:502–4.

blessing to the twelfth to fourteenth centuries places it in roughly the same period that witnessed the Gothic translation of Dionysian light metaphysics into architectural theology, as well as revolutionary developments in optics. This strongly suggests that, rather than being calcified liturgical expressions of belief, blessings could be responsive to contemporary religious influences. In the second place, this blessing's use of light imagery and metaphysics demonstrates the medieval belief, found throughout these rituals, in a deep and abiding connection between the realm of the spirit and the material world, in which light expressed the essential nature of God reaching out to cleanse the polluted.

In addition to blessing new wells and vessels, the church also presented various liturgical rituals for the reclamation of springs and containers that had been defiled. The prerequisite for such a ritual was corruption of a well by carrion or impure animals, a category defined by the canonical term *morticinum*.[53] Any animal could foul a well or vessel by drowning or dying by some other means in its waters, while certain animals—cats, dogs, mice, weasels, crows, chickens, and pigs (if they shed human blood)—were considered inherently impure and corrupting. These definitions are consistent with the blood prohibition contained in God's commandments to Noah (Gn 9:4), the Mosaic food laws (Lv 11 and Dt 14) and apostolic decree (Acts 15:29).[54] While this view of *morticinum* was well known in the Greek East, in the Latin West up until the fifth century the apostolic decree on this subject was referred to in only one text and was missing in the ban on drowned animals, applying the blood ban only when murder fouled a well or vessel.[55] The major early medieval influences on the Western understanding of impurity were the Irish and Anglo-Saxon penitentials, especially those dealing with food prohibitions promoted through the influence of the easterner Theodore, archbishop of Canterbury (d. 690). The Old Gelasian sacramentary does not contain a specific ritual for the cleansing of a polluted well or vessel, as this work was compiled before the food prohibitions en-

---

53. For a discussion of this term and its application, see Franz, 1:612–14.

54. Ibid., 1:613.

55. Ibid., 1:616. St. Augustine lent clearest expression to this freer interpretation of *morticinum:* while Augustine's writings on the subject were gradually lost to the early Middle Ages, they received de facto support from the Levitical commands and apostolic decrees found in the Vulgate Bible (which were used as the justification for Western penitential texts' application of punishment for pollution). See K. Böckenhoff, *Das apostolische Speisegesetz in den ersten fünf Jahrhunderten* (Paderborn: Ferdinand Schoningh, 1903), 98, 108ff.

tered into continental penitentials.[56] The enforcement of penance for those violating *morticinum* figured, however, in many Carolingian legislators' efforts at reform and in the writings of contemporary ecclesiastical leaders.[57] In practice, Western blessings of polluted wells relied upon the sprinkling of holy water in the well, the washing of the well with holy water, and ritual consecration to reconcile the well to human use. Such prayers were available in the Gelasians of the eighth century (notably the Gellone sacramentary, whose prayer was later copied into the RGP), and later witnesses such as the Augsburg manuscript (discussed above). These blessings appear as late as the fifteenth and sixteenth centuries in printed rituals.[58]

Blessings as a shield against pollution and evil employ common motifs and icons of the Christian cosmos to effect the cleansing of the tainted. In the *Liber ordinum*'s "Blessing Where Anything Unclean Shall Have Fallen into a Vessel," the author invokes the words of Jesus to assure the recipients of the blessing that they need fear no pollution from this physical vessel:

> Your mercy, Lord, we humbly entreating beseech . . . so that your blessing might descend on the pollution of these vessels: may he, who said "Anything

56. Franz, 1:618. The text cognizant of the apostolic decree was Canon 14 of Adamnan, in F. G. A. Wasserschleben, ed., *Reginonis abbatis Prumiensis libri duo de synodalibus causis* (Leipzig: G. Engelmann, 1840), 122. Franz believed that the occasional need for a ritual for cleansing was met by recourse to the rites of reconciliation of repentant heretics, and he cites as evidence the Leofric missal's prayer *Oratio super eos qui morticinum comederint*, which duplicates the Gelasian sacramentary's first alternate prayer to the ritual *Reconciliatio rebaptizati ab heredicis*. See Warren, *Leofric Missal*, 229; Mohlberg, *Liber sacramentorum*, ordo 87. This prayer postdates the primary prayer of the ritual. Franz considers the author clearly ignorant of the ritual's full purpose. The *Liber ordinum* of Silos contains a more specific prayer (Mon. Liturg. 5:172). Franz does point out, however, that enforcement of the prohibitions varied according to region; England, for example, under Eastern influences, in practice held mild views on *morticina*. The excommunication of consumers of *morticina* called for by the penitentials was moderated there, although the penitential statutes survived, and some compilers demanded a ritual reconciliation of the guilty party. See Franz, 1:617, and H. J. Schmitz, *Die Bussbücher und die Bussdisziplin* (Mainz, 1883), 2:24: Qui manducat carnem inmundam et a feris consumptam XL peniteat, si necessitas cogit, nihil est.

57. Franz, 1:616–18. For example, the *Dicta* of St. Pirmin, founder of the monastery of Reichenau (d. 753), forbade the enjoyment of *morticina;* Regino of Prüm wanted special attention given to enforcing the bans of *morticina* in episcopal inspections; yet Burchard of Worms accepted only a few of the restrictions proposed by the penitentials. See Burchard, *Decretorum liber*, book 19, chaps. 85, 87–92 (*PL* 140:1002–3).

58. Franz, 1:619; Ge 2857; *RGP* 2:375 (*ordo* 232); see above for the Augsburg MS. These later *ordines* appear to include psalms and rubrics, which the earlier rituals do not.

which enters into them, does not defile" [Mt 15:11] cleanse either the wine or oil, mead or water, so that we may perceive no stain. We your humble servants, poor priests . . . expel all filth by means of your Cross.[59]

The words of Christ on pollution remind the reader and audience of Jesus' emphasis on the heart and mind as the source of sin and serve as a form of incantational protection.[60] By speaking aloud these numinous words, the celebrant makes them real, invalidating the power of the physical to corrupt the spiritual, reminding God of his promises, and actualizing the beliefs of Christian faith in the present. The reference to the Cross serves as another source of cleansing power because the Cross was deeply associated with the mission and nature of Christ as Redeemer.

Blessings of vessels were extended beyond items of daily use to church fonts that contained holy water. The "Blessing of a Font Which Has Been Neglected," from the Augsburg manuscript (also found in RGP *ordo* 232, with variants), provides a ritual cleansing of vessels tainted by some pollution, a ritual that draws heavily on the sacred history of the Christian cosmos for its power of purification.[61] The ritual begins with the singing of the antiphon *Hic accipiet* (drawn from Ps 24:5) and three psalms: Psalm 23, *Dominus regit me;* Psalm 51, *Miserere mei Deus;* and Psalm 148, *Laudate dominum de celis.*[62]

59. Franz, 1:622: Misericordiam tuam, domine, supplices deprecamur . . . ut descendat benedictio tua in horum vasorum pollutionem: emundet sive vinum sive oleum, mela aut aquam, ut nullam inquinationem sentiamus, qui dixit: omne, quod intrat in eos, non coinquinat [incomplete citation of Mt 15:11] nos humiles servi tui, exigui sacerdotes . . . cruce tua expellimus sordes omnes. Franz believes that rituals dealing exclusively with containers rather than wells were probably confined to the monasteries in whose *rituales* the texts are found (1:620). I am not convinced that this is necessarily the case but have been unable to find rituals for cleansing containers occuring outside of monastic texts.

60. While this prayer does emphasize the dependence of humans on God, it does not emphasize the contractual nature of the relationship. Blessings of wells and vessels display the theme of contract relations in two early Spanish and German rituals of the tenth and eleventh centuries (see this "Blessing of an Unclean Vessel" and the *RGP*'s "Blessing of a New Well"). It may be that the emphasis on grace in these rituals reflects the author's conception of the rite as simple entreaty, a request for the gift of grace, and not a negotiation.

61. This blessing of a font could be said to be more sacramental in nature than the other blessings studied, as its subject is a baptismal font, but the richness of the blessing itself and the fact that it focuses on a polluted object, not the sacrament itself, makes an examination of the ritual beneficial to the larger purposes of this study.

62. The Psalms are rarely used in maritime blessings or those of wells and vessels, appearing only in this ritual, which is probably due to its liturgical context. Antiphons are even rarer than psalms in blessings of sacred objects and events. There are no antiphons specified

The antiphon is a general invocation suitable to blessings: "He will receive blessing from the Lord, and vindication from the God of their salvation."[63] The first psalm is a grateful praising of Jehovah as the Good Shepherd and a bountiful host: "beside restful waters he leads me; he refreshes my soul . . . you anoint my head with oil; my cup overflows."[64] This psalm emphasizes the qualities of refreshment and bounty to be found in the divine and has a sympathetic resonance with the subject of the rite: the "still waters" represent the ideal state of purity the blessing is attempting to restore to the polluted font, while the refreshment and anointing call to mind the cleansing that is to follow. The final psalm, a "Hymn of All Creation to the Almighty Creator," reminds the participants of the ties of the created world to the will of the divine: "Praise him, sun and moon; praise him, all you shining stars. Praise him, you highest heavens, and you waters above the heavens. Let him praise the name of the Lord, for he commanded and they were created; He established them for ever and ever; He gave them a duty which shall not pass away."[65] The scriptural description of the elements' obligations to their Creator acts as a stimulus to the polluted waters of the font to heed the ritual celebrant's invocation and be reconverted to a pure state. By the selection of Psalm 148, the author demonstrates the conviction we have seen throughout the blessings that the natural world is intimately linked to the divine, and that the performance of ritual can activate this link for the service of the human community.

> Salt is then mingled with the water as a cleansing agent, and a prayer follows:
> God, who came down to the bed of the Jordan in order to sanctify the waters
> for this one [font] . . . as you sanctified these waters at the touch of the holy
> body in its bathing, may you deign to recall these waters by the inflowing
> grace of your Holy Spirit to cleanliness through the gift by which you in Cana,
> Galilee, deigned to change water into wine with the mystery of your strength

---

in maritime blessings, while only this blessing of a font includes an antiphon. Antiphons are used in ordeal rituals, but much more infrequently than psalms are. Swiss and German ordeal rituals of the eleventh century are the only blessings to use antiphonal song (see Geneva's "Blessing of Iron" and "Exorcism of Water," the Gondekar pontifical's "Blessing of Frigid Water," and the York manual's "Judicial Duel," discussed in the following section).

63. The antiphon *Hic accipiet* does not appear per se in Hesbert's collection but does correspond to this psalm's text and bears strong resemblance to *CAO* no. 3047 (also drawn from Ps 24:5), so I have tentatively identified *Hic accipiet* as drawn from this psalm.

64. Ps 23:2–3, 5.

65. Ps 148:3–6.

shown as the beginning of your signs, and just as Elisha restored the bitter waters in the font by praying, thus through the prayers of your faithful may you mercifully blot out from these waters the horror of pollution.[66]

The engagement of divinity with water throughout sacred history is revivified through this ritual invocation, which aptly emphasizes the transformative power of the divine in acting on the elements of the physical world. By this conjuring of sacred paradigms, the celebrant prods God to remain consistent and act in the present as he did in the beginning times of the Christian faith. Through ritualized gesture, word, and object, this blessing and others like it helped not only to keep alive the history of the Christian cosmos but to infuse that history into objects that, once blessed, served the human congregation as vessels of the power that preserves.

ORDEALS AND TRIALS

The history of the judicial ordeal in the Latin West can be divided into two phases. Before the year 800 there are few sources, but after this date there is an explosion of sources dealing with the ordeal, ranging from liturgical texts to commentaries by noted theologians and liturgists, as well as by laity, on the nature and validity of the ordeal.[67] The first era shows evidence only of the ordeal of the cauldron or hot water, which was a custom probably Frankish in origin in which an object was plucked from boiling water, but this ordeal also appears in seventh-century Irish laws, although these texts

66. Franz, 1:620–21: Deus, qui ad hoc in alueum Iordanis sanctificaturus aquas descendisti . . . dum has aquas attactu sancti corporis sanctificasti per lauacrum, has aquas influente gratia tui sancti spiritus digneris ad mundiciam reuocare per donum, quo in Chana Galilee initio signorum tuorum ostenso virtutis tue mysterio aquas mutare dignatus es in vinum, et sicut Heliseus amaras orando sanavit aquas in latice, ita ad preces fidelium tuorum clementer abstergas ab his aquis pollutionis horrorem. Two of the five rituals studied here use sacred scripture, as this one does, but none of the four allusions in these blessings appears in more than one ritual. The allusions that are used deal exclusively with miracles involving water, the elements of consecration and consumption for the wells and vessels, and the issue of pollution and purification. The authors of these rituals favored the New Testament as their source, which may have been due to the Gospel's focus on redemption, salvation, and purification through obedience to the new law of Christ (three New Testament and one Old Testament references are found in these blessings). Apart from this there is again no visible chronological or regional pattern in the presence of scriptural allusion; it seems to have been drawn upon at the need and will of the author.

67. Robert Bartlett, *Trial by Fire and Water: The Medieval Judicial Ordeal* (Oxford: Clarendon Press, 1986), 4–5.

had no appreciable influence on the development of the ordeal on the continent or on its popularity.[68] Trial by cauldron in the Frankish lands was used in cases of theft, false witness, and contempt of court, and during the Carolingian era (especially after 800) three main developments occurred within this ritual's tradition: the dissemination of the practice into new regions, the multiplication of different types of ordeals, and a new governmental emphasis on the use of the ordeal.[69] Charlemagne's reign marks the invention of the trial by cold water, and his son Louis the Pious continued to support such innovation by employing a trial by hot iron, first mentioned reliably by Agobard of Lyons in the ninth century.[70]

By the ninth century the ordeal had entered its heyday, a period of popularity that lasted roughly until the beginning of the thirteenth century. During this period, the ordeal was used by all manner of authorities, from kings, who used it to question the sexual purity of queens and heiresses, to the Gregorian reformers, who employed it against simoniacs and other ecclesiastical enemies.[71] The ordeal was held to be unsurpassed as a means of eliciting truth in matters where certainty seemed impossible to determine beyond the word of one party against another. Belief in the validity of the ordeal can be seen in the writings of many ecclesiastical authors of these times; Guibert of Nogent, for example, made the comment in the twelfth century that picking up a burning brand in the name of Jesus was an argument "more powerful than any clash of words."[72] Fire in particular was thought to be efficacious in the ordeal owing to its natural ability to purify and concentrate matter, as can be seen in the case of the Gregorian reformers' efforts to wipe out the Mozarabic liturgy in eleventh-century Spain; there they cast books of the suspect liturgy into fire to test the orthodoxy of the ideas contained therein, a practice also used against the writings of the Cathars in southern France a century later.[73]

---

68. Ibid., 6.

69. Ibid., 9.

70. Ibid., 10–11.

71. Ibid., 16; see also Colin Morris, "Judicium dei: The Social and Political Significance of the Ordeal in the Eleventh Century," *Studies in Church History* 12 (1975): 95–112, esp. 103 and 108. Lechery and adultery were two of the most common offenses that came under the jurisdiction of ordeals; others were disputed paternity cases and the testing of orthodoxy (Bartlett, *Trial by Fire and Water,* 19–21).

72. Bartlett, *Trial by Fire and Water,* 21; see Guibert of Nogent, *Tractatus de Incarnatione contra Judaecos* 3.11 (*PL* 156:528).

73. Bartlett, *Trial by Fire and Water,* 22. For a successful defense in a Mozarabic trial by fire,

The twelfth century saw the regular use of the ordeal as a tool of the ecclesiastical establishment against heresy, a crime thought admirably suited to the ordeal because it involved an inner, hidden religious crime that made necessary the judgment of the only power able to discern such truth: God.[74] Ordeals were turned to only when other means of discovering the truth were unavailable, but they remained popular because of just this ability to determine hidden truth, as well as dissatisfaction with contemporary forms of determining guilt.[75] The ordeal as a form of judicial trial continued in use by the church until it was banned by the Fourth Lateran Council of 1215 and by secular authorities even later in the period, although with sharply declining frequency after 1200.[76]

The reasons for the decline of the ordeal lie in objections voiced over many years by clerics and laity alike, which can be reduced to two central concerns: do the ordeals give a just result, and are they licit? Ever since the early Middle Ages, critics had expressed concern that the results of ordeals could be manipulated by magic or deceit, but also that the ordeal itself was of questionable merit because it tried to place a human institution in a position to compel God inexorably to reveal truth.[77] The earliest critic to voice such objections, and also the one whose criticism was the most extensive, was the Carolingian Agobard of Lyons, who called the ordeal "an invention of men," a "proof which God never ordered and never wished and which, as

see A. A. Ubieto Arteta, ed., "Crónica nájerense," 3.49, Textos Medievales 15 (Valencia: La Real Academia de la Historia, 1966), 116; for the Cathar case, see Jordan of Saxony, "Libellus de principis ordinis praedicatorum," chaps. 24–25 of *Monumenta ordinis fratrum praedicatorum historica* 16, ed. H. C. Sheeben (Rome: In Domo Generalita, 1935), 38.

74. Bartlett, *Trial by Fire and Water,* 22–24.

75. Ibid., 53. In particular, dissatisfaction with the compurgation and uncorroborated oaths as a means of proof in cases involving heresy increased the ordeal's popularity. Laws and legal prescriptions of the later eleventh and twelfth centuries indicate that trial by ordeal continued to be "an important and frequent mode of proof" in most regions of Europe.

76. Ibid. Bartlett uses canon law collections and case histories to demonstrate that churchmen saw ordeals as proof into the mid-eleventh century, but in 1063 Pope Alexander II ruled that a priest accused of murder could undergo compurgation and forbade the use of trial by ordeal for clerics, thus effectively imposing a papal ban on ordeals. Despite this ban, it took some time for opposition to ordeals to become widely accepted. For the papal ruling, see ibid., 82–85; *PL* 146:1406).

77. For example, Peter the Chanter attacked the ordeals for demanding a miracle from God, which was considered sinful for it tempted God to intervene for the sake of the law. See Peter the Chanter, *Verbum abbreviatum, PL* 205:226–33, 542. See also J. W. Baldwin, "The Intellectual Preparation for the Canon of 1215 against Ordeals," *Speculum* 36 (1961): 613–36.

can be demonstrated, was not introduced through the example of the saints or any of the faithful."[78] The lack of historical sanction was a key objection of ecclesiastical opponents of the ordeal, as were demonstrations of internal inconsistencies within ordeals and the claim that ordeals sought knowledge inappropriate to human beings: "God's judgments are secret and impenetrable. . . . If all future events are unknown, what astonishing fatuousness it is to try to make uncertain things certain through detestable combats."[79]

Despite a wide and forceful range of arguments against the ordeal, such critics as Agobard had little influence in the early Middle Ages. Only in the period from 1050 to 1200 did such criticism attain a significant level of influence, when several key factors came into play that mitigated against the acceptance of judicial rituals: a belief that the judicial function of the ordeal might be overturned by God's mercy, regardless of whether the offender was guilty in the case at issue;[80] the absence of strong biblical sanction for the ordeal; and the absence of the ordeal from Roman law.[81] Owing especially to this last factor, the ordeal became a target of the wider twelfth-century campaign against customary law in the name of Roman and canon law, a campaign supported by the Scholastic movement's insistence on an increasingly strong distinction between nature and the supernatural.[82] This distinction was expressed in many ways, most particularly in the growing specificity of what constituted a miracle and what a sacrament, and Scholastics of the twelfth and thirteenth centuries found ordeals to be a troublesome problem for this new system. Since ordeals required the natural elements to behave in an unusual or unnatural way (for example, hot iron or water would not burn the innocent but would scorch the guilty), they would logically have to

78. Bartlett, *Trial by Fire and Water*, 72. See Agobard, "Liber adversus legem Gundobadi," chap. 2 of *Opera omnia*, ed. L. van Acker, Corpus Christianorum Continuatio Medievalis 52 (Turnhout: Brepols, 1981), 32.

79. Agobard, "Liber adversus legem Gundobadi," chap. 6:43, 47.

80. For example, a French collection of miracles of the Virgin tells two stories of how the Virgin reversed the outcome of trial by battle in an act of mercy, and one story about a princess who, praying to the Virgin, had the outcome of her ordeal by water changed in her favor, despite her guilt. See *Miracles de Notre Dame de Rocamadour* 1.36, pp. 132–35, quoted in Ward, *Miracles and the Medieval Mind*, 149.

81. Bartlett, *Trial by Fire and Water*, 75–85. Confession during this period came to be seen as a possible guarantee of safety in ordeals, which made it difficult for clerics to countenance the ordeal (ibid., 80–81).

82. Ibid., 85–88.

be regarded a miracle, but if so they were very improper miracles, for ordeals demanded a miraculous effect. Such a demand was considered of dubious veracity, if not outright hubris on the part of the participants. If the ordeal was more like a sacrament, the success of which God guaranteed if the proper rituals were performed, then it did not meet the high medieval criterion for sacraments that they be scripturally instituted.[83] These objections contributed to the decline in popularity of the ordeal among churchmen of the twelfth century and led to the prohibition of clerical participation in ordeals in 1215. The end of priestly involvement was also part of the larger attempt of the Gregorian and later reformers to draw sharper lines between the clerical and lay parts of Christian life. While certain forms of ordeals continued to be employed until the end of the Middle Ages, this coordinated attack on them relegated them to the position of quaint, often barbaric customs not worthy of the law courts of laity or clergy.[84]

The one form of the ordeal that did retain some respect following the ecclesiastical crackdown of the thirteenth century was the judicial duel. Trial by battle is found in the early law codes of many Germanic peoples and was employed in a wide variety of cases, but (as with other ordeals) most often in clandestine cases in which no other reliable means of determination was available.[85] It was limited to challenges between individuals of equal social class, although no class was excluded, and only in the later Middle Ages did it become a distinctly aristocratic activity.[86] Like other ordeals, the judicial duel was a process designed to produce proof by the direct verdict of God, but unlike most ordeals it involved the violent shedding of Christian blood. Because of this it was often criticized, and it attracted the condemnation of the Carolingian Agobard of Lyons:

> Can it really be that the highest justice requires spears and swords to judge cases? We often see that the rightful tenant or claimant fighting in battle is

83. Ibid.

84. Ibid., 99. This exclusion of ordeals from the courts can be seen in the Legatine Council of Paris, which ruled in 1213 that "Duels and Ordeals should not take place in holy sites or churchyards or in the presence of bishops."

85. Ibid., 106–9.

86. Trial by battle was still used, for example, by Italian communal governments well into the thirteenth century, as can be seen in a book of the Benedictine nuns of Sant'Alessandro at Parma, which has rituals of battle pasted onto a well-used flyleaf. See Thompson, *Cities of God*, 127–28.

overcome by the superior strength or some underhanded trick of the unjust party. We do not deny that God's Providence sometimes clears the innocent and condemns the guilty, but it is in no wise ordained by God that this should happen in every case, except at the Last Judgment.[87]

Bartlett argues that another source of criticism of the ordeal was that trial by battle was "a ritual form of an activity that men frequently saw around them in a non-ritual form," and so people legitimately wondered why the result of ritualized violence should be determined by "forces [i.e., God and justice] so irrelevant to the non-ritual form [of violence]."[88] This point is debatable. It is a truism to say that human beings have long believed that victory on the battlefield depended (at least in part) on the favor of God, both in medieval and in modern times, so it seems unlikely that individuals accustomed to violence would question the credibility of trial by battle. It seems more likely that elements of the clergy may have opposed the duel not out of experience but on the basis of theology and because of the repugnance of such violent spectacles. The criticism it received notwithstanding, trial by battle continued to be practiced until the end of the Middle Ages and disappeared more because of the hostility of townsmen and monarchs than the opposition of bishops and popes.[89]

One fundamental difference between judicial combat and other forms of the ordeal can be found in the issue of priestly involvement. While numerous liturgical manuscripts show how essential priestly blessing and supervision were to ordeals, trial by battle, despite its ritual solemnity, occurred with minimal priestly involvement, although William of Rennes, in his gloss of Raymond of Peñaforte's *Summa on the Decretals*, mentions that "according to the custom of some places, priests make blessings and imprecations over the champions, just as there used to be adjurations over the hot iron or cold water."[90] Only one Latin blessing for the weapons of a duel exists, however, and the relative unimportance of liturgical ritual and priestly involvement, coupled with the fact that judicial combat did not claim or require miraculous intervention in the physical elements, made it, in one

87. Bartlett, *Trial by Fire and Water*, 117; see Agobard, "Liber adversus legem Gundobadi," chaps. 13, 27.

88. Bartlett, *Trial by Fire and Water*, 116–18.

89. Ibid., 120.

90. Ibid., 121; Raymond de Peñaforte, *De ordaliis*, ed. Peter Browe, 2 vols. (Rome: Pontificalis Universitatis Gregorianne, 1932–33), vol. 2, no. 108.

scholar's judgment, the "most natural as well as the least liturgical" of the ordeals, since it did not require a miraculous alteration in a natural element but merely the victory of a weak just man over a strong unjust man.[91] While it may stand alone, the text of this solitary ritual can still be fitted into the wider pattern of ordeal rituals, and it is with this rite that we shall begin our study of blessings of ordeals. In all, I have selected seven rituals for analysis, each demonstrating the variety of themes found within the different genres of ordeal blessings: a "Blessing of Iron [Test of Hot Iron]," from an eleventh-century manuscript of Geneva;[92] a "Blessing of Frigid Water for Making a Judgment," from the eleventh-century Pontifical of Gondekar II (1057 to 1075);[93] an "Exorcism of Hot Water for Judgment," from the eleventh-century Geneva manuscript noted above;[94] a "Judgment of Bread and Cheese," from an eleventh-century pontifical of Bamberg;[95] a "Judgment of Burning [Hot Iron]," from the twelfth-century *rituale* of St. Florian;[96] a "Judgment of Bread of the Ordeal," from the fourteenth-century Codex Lucemburgensis;[97] and a "Blessing of a Buckler and Staff for Men Advancing to a Duel," from the York manual, printed in the early sixteenth century from manuscript

91. Bartlett, *Trial by Fire and Water*, 121–22. This nature of the duel was also recognized by St. Thomas Aquinas in his *Summa theologica*, who, in discussing lots, observed that while trials by fire and water resembled lots in that they sought to discover the unknown by human actions, they were different in that "they anticipate a miraculous effect. The same point applies also to trial by battle, except that they function more like lots, since they do not anticipate a miraculous effect; except in the case where the champions are extremely unequal in strength or skill." Aquinas, *Summa theologica*, 2.2.95.8, quoted in ibid., 122.

92. Franz, 2:366; see Geneva, Bibliothèque Publique et Universitaire, 28, fols. 113b–116b.

93. Franz, 2:380–84. The ritual is also edited in the *RGP* 2:393–94 (*ordo* 248); from Eichstätt, Bistumsarchiv, pontifical of Gondekar II (1057 to 1075); for other MSS containing the *ordo*, see Michel Andrieu, *Les ordines romani du haut Moyen Âge*, 6 vols. (Louvain: Spicilegium Sacrum Louvaniensis, 1931–61), 1:59.

94. Franz, 2:374.

95. Ibid., 2:385–88. Franz drew the ritual from Bamberg, Staatsibibliothek, lit. 54, fols. 120r–121v; it also appears in *RGP* 2:394–97 (*ordo* 249); see also Andrieu, *Ordines romani*, 1:63–73, at 71 (the same or a similar *ordo* is found in Bamberg 53, fol. 139v; see Andrieu, *Ordines romani*, 1:59, listing other MSS containing the same *ordo*, including the pontifical of Gondekar II, Lucca 607, and Wolfenbüttel 4099).

96. Franz, 2:369–72. The ritual is drawn from Sankt Florian, Stiftsbibliothek, 467, fols. 128r–132v.

97. Franz, 2:388. The manuscript, Luxembourg, Bibl. Nat. 50, is from the fourteenth century; see K. Zeumer, *Formulae merovingici et karolini aevi*, *MGH SRM* Legg., section 5 (Hanover: Impensis Bibliopoli Hahniani, 1882), 691.

sources dating from the end of the fourteenth century to the beginning of the fifteenth.[98] Seven other rituals will provide corroborating evidence for the conclusions drawn from these rituals; for a listing of these supporting blessings and their content, see the index.

The blessing for the weapons of a judicial duel introduces the first common theme in ordeal blessings, emphasis on the martial virtues of God. The late medieval "Blessing of a Buckler and Staff for Men Advancing to a Duel," from the York manual, begins with the singing of several psalms and a simple blessing of two martial instruments, a buckler and a staff. The first psalm is Psalm 70, *Deus in adiutorium,* an urgent call for help from the divine.[99] The second is Psalm 34, *Benedicam dominum in omne tempore,* a song of praise of Jehovah's care for those who fear him. Of particular interest in this psalm is the confidence expressed in the security God gives to the godly:

> The angel of the Lord encamps around those who fear him, and delivers them. O taste and see that the Lord is good. . . . When the righteous cry for help, the Lord hears, and rescues them from all their troubles. The Lord is near to the brokenhearted, and saves the crushed in spirit. Many are the afflictions of the righteous, but the Lord rescues them from them all.[100]

Such words reaffirm the protective power of divinity but also emphasize saving those unjustly afflicted. In a judicial duel one party was assumed to be innocent, and this affirmation could both comfort him and remind God of his obligation to act with consistent benefaction toward the righteous.

---

98. Bartlett, *Trial by Fire and Water,* 120–21. This ritual also appears in the *Manuale ad usum insignis ecclesiae Sarum,* 31; and the pontifical of Glasgow (c. 1180), 211.

99. Ordeals frequently specify the use of particular psalms: eight of the fourteen studied and supporting rituals include psalms that emphasize God's judgment and dominion and the beatitude of the faithful (see Geneva's "Blessing of Iron," the Gondekar pontifical's "Blessing of Frigid Water," Geneva's "Exorcism of Water," St. Florian's "Judgment of Hot Iron," Luxembourg's "Ordeal of Bread," the York manual's "Judicial Duel," the Parisian "Psalter Ordeal," and Vyssi Brod's "Remedy versus Theft"). This usage, however, shows no discernible pattern of change over time, suggesting that psalmody was included or excluded at the will and taste of the author or scribe. The reason for the strong presence of psalmody in ordeals is unclear. Perhaps a need for the power and authority of scripture was felt most acutely in rituals that call for a miraculous intervention of God to change the elements. It is also possible that the uncanonical status of ordeals, their greatest flaw in the eyes of ecclesiastical critics, encouraged the authors of these blessings to point out God's role as judge and savior in scripture, implicitly validating the appeal and his willingness to intercede on behalf of truth and justice.

100. Ps 34:7–8, 17–19.

The third psalm of the rite, Psalm 91, is also familiar. The early passages are especially relevant to the subject of the blessing:

> You who live in the shelter of the Most High, who abide in the shadow of the Almighty, will say to the Lord, "My refuge and my fortress; my God, in whom I trust." For he will deliver you from the snare of the fowler and from the deadly pestilence; he will cover you with his pinions, and under his wings you will find refuge; his faithfulness is a shield and buckler.[101]

The items of the blessing become a direct reflection of sacred scripture, linking the present reality of the duelists with the salvific promises of God that permeate the Psalter. The duel thereby gains validity by association, putting God's promises to the test with the very symbols used to embody them. This confident reading is followed with the antiphon *Ne reminiscaris* discussed in the previous chapter, which implores God to forget the sins of the supplicant.[102] As before, this antiphon can be interpreted as an expression of the uncertainty of medieval humans in regard to God's good nature, but it may also be seen as a kind of insurance, imploring God not to use the coming duel to judge the participants for some other sin they may have committed apart from the issue that led to the duel. Given that high medieval commentators expressed concern that God might show his mercy by allowing a guilty party to survive an ordeal unscathed, it does not seem unreasonable that he might do the opposite as well.

These psalms are followed by a lengthy prayer, offered up by the priest while kneeling and holding the staff and shield:

> Adonay, strengthener and fortifier and sustainer of your faithful, unfailing, unending, unerring Father, eternal God, who destroyed great peoples and strong kings on behalf of your people of Israel, and who allowed your child David to triumph over the giant blaspheming you and also trusting in his own power: we humbly implore you, that you might deign to bless, help, protect, strengthen and preserve, and enclose with the fortress of the holy angels this your servant, believing in you.[103]

---

101. Ps 91:1–4.   102. Franz, 2:364–65.

103. Ibid., 2:365: Confortator et corroborator sustentamentumque tuorum fidelium, Adonay, indeficiens, interminabilis, inenarrabilis pater, aeterne deus, qui gentes magnas regesque fortes coram populo tuo Israel destruxisti, quique puero tuo David de gigante te blasphemante atque in sua virtute confidente triumphare concessisti: te supplices exoramus, ut hunc famulum tuum in te confidentem benedicere, adiuvare, protegere, confortare et conservare atque sanctorum angelorum praesidio vallare digneris.

The warlike character of Jehovah of the Old Testament, not the peaceful face of the Lamb of God depicted in the Gospels, is conjured here to serve the combatant. The distinction between God's aspects highlights the highly adaptable and fluid nature medieval people attributed to sacred power. God's personal involvement in battles involving righteousness versus wickedness in the sacred past serves as a paradigm for the judicial process, and confirms the human world's necessary reliance on divine power. Scriptural allusion such as this is vital and ubiquitous in the blessings for ordeals and duels. Nine of the rituals examined contain such allusions, with the Old Testament being slightly more favored by the authors of the blessings: fifteen events or individuals are drawn from the Old Testament as compared to eleven from the New Testament. The former appear in eight rituals, while the New Testament is used in only five.[104] Scripture appears in ordeals from every region included in our study, but Swiss blessings make the most use of these sacred stories.[105] Although there does not seem to have been much innovation or expansion of scriptural allusion over time, there are distinctive qualities to ordeal allusions: they are numerous, many appear in more than one blessing, and those common allusions appear in all subcategories of these rituals, unlike (for example) the use of scripture in blessings for health and recovery, which have common themes but in which the common allusions are clustered in single subcategories.

To return to the ritual in question, God's martial virtues are imparted to the prostrate duelist by the subsequent prayer:

> "Grant to him, Lord, right faith, firm hope, steadfastness of heart, strength of body, health in every limb, so that through your help he may merit to seize victory and may he return both thanks and praise for you, sole omnipotent God." . . . Then let him [the duelist] rise up and again let this be said to him: "Strengthen and be robust, hope in the Lord and do good and refuse to forget all his retributions. May He himself give you life eternal and victory and blessing in the world without end."[106]

104. See the *RGP*'s "Judgment of Bread and Cheese," the Gondekar pontifical's "Blessing of Frigid Water," Geneva 28's "Exorcism of Hot Water" and "Blessing of Iron," the Luxembourg "Ordeal of Bread," the York manual's "Judicial Duel," Clm 14508's "[Ordeal] of Boiling Water," Clm 100's "Psalter Ordeal," and Vyssi Brod's "Remedy versus Theft."

105. See the index.

106. Franz, 2:365: "Praesta ei, domine, fidem rectam, spem firmam, cordis fiduciam, corporis fortitudinem, omnium membrorum valetudinem, quatinus te adiuvante victoriam

Thus the power, indeed the nature, of the historical divinity is transferred from God to humanity through this ritual blessing, which binds these two actors closer together through its contractual promises of mutual gain.

While the martial virtues of God are stressed in prayers for judicial combat, the elements of judgment and justice in less aggressive forms of examination, such as the ordeal by hot iron, emphasize the sacred as that which arbitrates. Their prayers correspond to the legal institution of the ordeal, appealing to the omnipotence, justice, and discernment of God.[107] In a "Blessing of Iron [Test of Hot Iron]," from an eleventh-century manuscript of Geneva, God's capacity as judge is stressed: "God, the just and strong and patient judge, you who are the author and lover of justice and often merciful, who determines justice . . ."[108] Such references to the judgment of God are near universal among the ordeal rites, appearing in seven examined rituals.[109] While his justice is tempered with mercy, God is appealed to here as the one force that can uncover the truth and judge accordingly: "Omnipotent eternal God, who knows the concealed things of our hearts, who made known everything unknown not only to the foolish, but even to the wise

capessere mereatur tibique, deo soli omnipotenti, et gratias et laudes referat." . . . Tunc surgat et iterum dicatur ei: "Confortare et esto robustus, spera in domino et fac bonitatem et noli oblivisci omnes retributiones eius. Ipse det tibi vitam aeternam et victoriam et benedictionem in saeculum saeculi."

107. Ibid., 2:393. In all these rituals, scriptural allusions to the Old Testament predominate, which is unsurprising given the emphasis that it places on the role of Yahweh as a just judge of the law. Many of these references also appear in ancient Christian exorcism formulas (ibid., 2:394). Franz points out that the formulas he presents are generally older than the MSS that contain them, the oldest belonging to the ninth century. More complex rites were also in use, he notes, which used extensive biblical allusion (2:398).

108. Ibid., 2:366: Deus iudex iustus et fortis et patiens, qui es auctor et amator iusticie multumque misericors, qui iudicas equitatem . . . The MS is Codex Genevensis, Staatsbibliothek, lat. 28, fols. 117–188a, the missal of Moustier in Tarantaise.

109. The most common characteristic of God mentioned in these blessings is judgment, specifically of God as a just judge. This aspect of God's nature is found in seven of the blessings examined. Appearing in rites of the ninth, eleventh, twelfth, and fifteenth centuries, the majority (four rituals) date from the eleventh century (see Geneva's "Blessing of Iron" and "Exorcism of Water," the Gondekar pontifical's "Blessing of Frigid Water," St. Florian's "Judgment of Hot Iron," Clm 14508's "Blessing of Boiling Water," the Bamberg pontifical's "Blessing of a Small Jug," and the Vyssi Brod (formerly Hohenfurt) Cistercian "Remedy against Theft"). Four of these rituals are from German manuscripts, two from Swiss, and one from Austrian, so it seems clear that this notion of God found wide acceptance in the performance of ordeals in German-speaking regions. For further information, see the index.

. . ."[110] God is portrayed in numerous rituals as the knower of secrets, the one who can look into the private minds and hearts of human beings and determine the truth. Given that the use of ordeals was intended for cases in which there was no other means of arriving at a sound judgment, as the truth was hidden in the hearts of the innocent and guilty, this attribution makes sense. This quality of God appears in four rituals of the tenth, eleventh, and twelfth centuries, the apogee of ordeals' popularity in the medieval West, and can be found in manuscripts of Swiss, German, and Austrian origin and provenance, also suggesting widespread use (at least in German-speaking areas).[111] As the knower of all secrets, God is called upon in these rituals to adjudicate human disputes, in much the same manner as he protects and strengthens the faithful who live in accordance with the negotiated relationship of blessings for praise we have seen elsewhere.

The request for judgment arises not only from the belief in the mutually beneficial relationship between God and humans but also from the conviction that God is perfectly capable of rendering a just judgment:

> God, who presented a great sign through fire, who saved your child Abraham from the flame of the Chaldeans with others dying; God, who let the bush burn before the sight of Moses and not be all consumed by the flames; God, who led the three youths unharmed from the fire of the fully lit furnace of the Chaldeans, God, who incinerating by fire the people of Sodom and Gomorrah granted safety to your servant Lot with his family; God, who before the advent of your spirit in the likeness of fire decreed that the faithful be parted from the unfaithful . . .[112]

The allusions to biblical events focus on the theme of God as judge, and all of them use the element of fire in association with heated iron as God's instrument in saving the just and condemning the wicked. By this means the

110. Franz, 2:367: Omnipotens sempiterne deus, qui occulta cordium nosti, qui omnia non solum insipientibus, sed etiam prudentibus ignota prodidisti . . .

111. See Geneva's "Blessing of Iron" and "Exorcism of Water," the *RGP*'s "Judgment of Bread and Cheese," and St. Florian's "Judgment of Hot Iron."

112. Franz, 2:367–68: Deus, qui per ignem signa magna ostendisti, qui Abraham, puerum tuum, de incendio Caldeorum quibusdam pereuntibus salvasti; deus, qui rubum ardere ante conspectum Moisi et minime comburi permisisti; deus, qui ab incendio fornacis Caldeorum plenius succensi tres pueros illesos eduxisti; deus, qui incendente igne populum Sodome et Gomorre Loth, famulo tuo, cum suis salutem donasti; deus, qui ante adventum spiritus tui illustratione ignis fideles tuos ab infidelibus decrevisti . . . The scriptural allusions are to Gn 11:31, 15:7, Dt 3:20–27, Gn 19:24–29, 1 Kgs 18, Ex 14, 19, and 20.

ordeal itself is indirectly legitimized by sacred precedent at the same time that it pressures God to act consistently and follow his own example of benevolence toward the righteous.[113] In this context, God is seen as the light of truth that dispels the darkness of deceit in this blessing of the iron:

> Our Lord God, Father omnipotent, light unfailing, hear us. . . . Holy Lord, Father omnipotent, eternal God, the light which in your name . . . we bless and we sanctify, we ask that it [the iron bar] might be blessed and sanctified by you . . . who saved the three children Shadrach, Meshach, and Abednego sent by order of the king of Babylon into a furnace of burning fire, and led them out unharmed: you, most clement ruler, grant that if someone who is innocent shall place his hand on this hot iron may he abide safe and unharmed with you present, Lord, and just as you freed from the fiery furnace the three above mentioned boys and saved Susanna from a false criminal charge, thus may you, God omnipotent, deign to preserve unharmed the hand of the innocent.[114]

113. As a whole, the allusions common to ordeal blessings focus on the power of God to affect the natural world, illuminate human beings, and save the righteous: God's guidance of Abraham through Chaldea; the fire of the burning bush, which did not consume the bush; the salvation of the three Hebrew children from the fiery furnace; the baptism of Jesus and salvation of Peter from drowning in the Sea of Galilee; the miracle of Elijah causing an iron to float on water; the salvation of Susanna from her false accusers; Jesus' illumination of the blind; the salvation of Daniel from the lion; the rescue of Jonah from the belly of the whale; and the salvation of St. Paul from flood. The salvation of the three children and of Susanna are the most common of these allusions, often appearing linked in the texts (for examples, see Clm 14508's "Ordeal of Boiling Water," the *RGP*'s "Judgment of Bread and Cheese," and the Geneva "Exorcism of Hot Water"). The popularity of scripture in these particular rituals is intriguing; I would argue that it means that these blessings drew on scripture not only to contextualize themselves within the sacred history of God's miracles, but also because the uncanonical nature of ordeals created enough uncertainty about their validity that authors felt compelled to give scriptural precedents for God's miraculous intervention on behalf of the righteous. Scripture, then, affirmed the blessing's ability to work miracles and justified the practice of the ordeal for the meting out of justice.

114. Franz, 2:366: Domine deus noster, pater omnipotens, exaudi nos, lumen indeficiens. . . . Domine sancte, pater omnipotens, eterne deus, lumen, quod in nomine tuo . . . benedicimus et sanctificamus, quesumus, ut a te benedictum et sanctificatum sit . . . qui tres pueros Sidrac, Misac et Abdenago iussu regis Babilonis in caminum ignis accensi missos salvasti et illesos eduxisti: tu, clementissime dominator, presta, ut, si quis innocens in hoc ferrum calidum miserit manum suam, salva et illesa te, domine, prestante permaneat, et sicut tres pueros supradictos Ananiam, Azariam, Misahelem de camino ignis liberasti et Susannam de falso crimine salvasti, sic manum innocentis, deus omnipotens, salvare digneris illesam, qui vivis. See *RGP* 2:385, 387 (*ordo* 247.13, 18). God is cast as light embodied in ritual blessings of hot iron from Switzerland and Austria of the eleventh and twelfth centuries (see Geneva's "Blessing of Iron" and

The power of the divine to illuminate and liberate flows from this invocation, making these events live again in the minds of those present for the ordeal as it affirms God's nature as a just and reliable judge of the human heart.

The final element of this ritual is a conjuration of the iron itself, which reveals the medieval understanding of the nature of God and the relationship between this creative power and the cosmos which he created.

> I adjure you, creature of iron, through God the Father omnipotent and the Son, the Holy Spirit and through the awesome day of judgment and through the twelve apostles and through the seventy-two disciples and through the twelve prophets . . . through every being you have created and their teachers . . . that you might be exorcised and confirmed against the deceptions of the Enemy and against this your man, if he is the deceiver in this crime, hence guilty . . . may you [the iron bar] make him [the defendant] be consumed in demonstration of his opposition and may you not take pity on him nor may you find rest for him, who is the adversary of your Creator.[115]

This conjuration is fascinating on several levels. First, it provides us with another example of blessings addressing the physical elements of creation (in this case, iron) as something intimately linked to the social life and regulation of the human community.[116] This is a common theme in ordeal blessings; it appears in various forms in both the ordeals studied here and supporting rites. Second, in the invocation of "every being you have created" we have another demonstration of the medieval belief that anything created by

---

St. Florian's "Judgment of Hot Iron"). This attribution associates God with both the metaphorical light that reveals things hidden in the darkness of ignorance and doubt and with the literal, physical glow given off by irons heated in a forge. God is present, then, in both the exterior and interior process of the ordeal, as both judge and revealer of truth.

115. Franz, 2:368: Adiuro te, creatura ferri, per deum patrem omnipotentem et filium et spiritum sanctum et per tremendum diem iudicii et per XII apostolos et per LXXII discipulos et per XII prophetas . . . et per omnes quos tu creasti ac doctores eorum . . . ut facias exorcizatum et confirmatum adversus inimici insidias et adversus hominem istum, si seductor est istius criminis, unde culpatur . . . efficias eum combustum esse ad contrarietatis sue ostensionem neque misereris eius nec adquiescas ei, qui adversarius est creatori tuo.

116. The notion of elements responding to the sins of humans could even be used for political ends, such as when King Philip IV of France pressed false accusations of heresy, sodomy, denial of Christ, and desecration of the Cross against the Knights Templar in the early fourteenth century. These offenses were so heinous that Philip's summons to the estates general to deal with the Templars claimed that "Heaven and Earth are agitated by the breadth of so great a crime, and the elements are disturbed. . . . Against so criminal a plague everything must rise up: laws and arms, every living thing, the four elements." Cohn, *Europe's Inner Demons*, 96.

God, for that reason alone, can convey the power of the sacred.[117] This was not merely an acknowledgment of the power of God but a way to command the elements of the natural world on which the ordeal relied, whether hot water, cold water, hot iron, earth, air, fire, or water. The connection of the divine with the natural world, and the connection of human beings to these powers, was affirmed by these blessings as they called upon that bond to determine truth and remove uncertainty from the community of the faithful. Third, we see how not only the figures of sacred history but also the events of that history—here its end, the day of judgment—can bring God's power into the created world, stretching into the past and present through the power that binds the cosmos. Fourth, the conjuration extends the human belief in a cosmic struggle between the divine and the demonic to the reality of the natural world and its elements. This is evident in the prayer's final command to the iron bar to show no mercy to the guilty who is the "adversary of your Creator."[118] This vocative address connects the struggles of human society against the forces of darkness to the essence of the created world itself, uniting both through their opposition to a common foe. The parallel between the goals of human beings and created things is unexpected if we accept the limited concept of the Middle Ages as a religious culture that rejected the world as unsuitable matter for the Christian mind and soul. But if we accept that a more positive view of the physical world was present in medieval culture than a strictly Augustinian perspective allows, than this appeal makes sense. Finally, compare this adjuration with a Celtic *Lorica*, the *Breastplate of Laidcenn,* and the devotional text *The Broom of Devotion*:

> Help me, Unity in Trinity . . . I beseech the Thrones, Virtues, Archangels, Principalities, Powers and Angels to defend me with their massed ranks and to scatter my enemies. Then I beseech the other champions, the Patriarchs and the sixteen Prophets, the Apostles, pilots of the ship of Christ, and all the martyrs, athletes of God . . . Oh, God, defend me everywhere with your impregnable power and protection. Deliver all my mortal limbs, guarding each with your protective shield, so the foul demons shall not hurl their darts into my side, as is their wont.[119]

117. Four studied rituals and one supporting blessing stress this aspect of the divine, and all but the blessing of a duel originate in Germany and Austria in the tenth, eleventh, and twelfth centuries.

118. Franz, 2:368.

119. Davies, "The Breastplate of Laidcenn," in his *Celtic Spirituality,* 289–90.

I beseech you by your four chief prophets who foretold your Incarnation: Daniel and Jeremiah and Isaiah and Ezekiel. I beseech you by the nine orders of the Church on earth, from psalm-singer to episcopate . . . I beseech you by the nine orders of the Church in heaven, that is, Angels and Archangels, Virtues, Powers, Principalities, Dominations, Thrones, Cherubim, Seraphim . . . I beseech you by all the lawfully wedded couples, with suffering Job who faced many trials . . . I beseech you by all the holy bishops who founded the ecclesiastical city in Jerusalem . . . that you will take me under your protection, defense and care, to preserve me and protect me from devils and all their promptings.[120]

These two texts clearly share a common adjurational formula with the adjuration of the iron in our ordeal blessing, a formula that calls upon not only heavenly but also earthly powers to accomplish the end of divining truth and healing the community.

The last ordeal of iron of interest to this study demonstrates several of the themes we have already discussed and adds a new perspective on how communities used the power of the holy to identify themselves and to discipline and regulate the conduct of their members. The "Judgment of Burning [Hot Iron]," from the twelfth–century *rituale* of St. Florian, includes adjurations aimed at terrifying a guilty party into confessing his guilt:

I adjure you, men, through the Father, Son and Holy Spirit, and through the Holy Trinity and through the invocation of the only begotten Son of God and through your Christianity, which you received, and through the Holy Gospel and relics, which are contained within this very church, that you might not presume by any means to communicate or approach the altar if you did or consented to this thing or knew who did it.[121]

120. Davies, "The Broom of Devotion," in ibid., 292–95.

121. Franz, 2:369–72: Adiuro vos, homines, per patrum et filium et spiritum sanctum et per sanctam trinitatem et per invocationem unigeniti filii dei et per vestram christianitatem, quam suscepistis, et per sanctum evangelium et per reliquis, que in ista continentur ecclesia: ut non presumatis ullo modo communicare neque ad altare accedere si hoc fecistis aut consensistis aut scitis, qui fecerint. The ritual is found in the twelfth-century *rituale* of St. Florian (Sankt Florian, Stiftsbibliothek 467, fols. 128–132v). Franz notes great uniformity in the *topos* of New and Old Testament allusions throughout the ordeal rituals he presents, some of which were clearly influenced by two well-known Latin prayers known under the name of Cyprian, which originate from the Gallician literary adaptation of Cyprian, c. 400 to 500 (although Franz doubts earlier scholarship that attested that Cyprian was the original author). For the prayers; see St. Cyprian, *S. Thasci Caecili Cypriani opera omnia*, Corpus Scriptorum Ecclesiasticorum Latinorum (Vindobonae, 1868–71), 3:145, 147–49. For previous scholarship,

When reading this passage, we must keep in mind the mortal dread that separation from the church and its saving sacraments inspired. To be denied communion, especially in the high and later Middle Ages, with its devotion to the Eucharist and its powers of salvation, was to be bereft of protection from the demonic forces that roamed the dark corners of the world searching for mortals to torment and lead into damnation. This adjuration turns the power of the divine against the sinners, casting them out of the human community. The next step would have been confession, penance, and absolution, which appear in five of the rites I examine here.[122] Ritual blessing, then, could be turned against individuals if it served the need of the Christian community, which could not afford to allow sinners to remain within the community if it was to maintain the positive relationship with God upon which its safety depended. The pollution of criminal guilt was thus excluded by means of ritual for the good of the collective.

This lengthy blessing provides us with further examples of the association of God with light and fire, and these elements' power to divine the truth. This prayer was said above the fire in which the iron would be placed, following a Mass and the ritual purification of the priest:

> Our Lord God, Father omnipotent, who is the light and who appeared to Moses through the fire in the bush, and freed the people of Israel from the darkness of Egypt with a light preceding and also inflamed the heart of the apostles with the fire of the Holy Spirit: may you bless this light, so that whatever shall have burned from its heat may be free from inciting by diabolical warmth.[123]

---

see Adolf von Harnak, *Medizinisches aus der ältesten Kirchengeschichte* (Leipzig: K. F. Pfau, 1892). These prayers provide the first identifiable source for the use of stories of Sarah and Tobias, the fiery furnace and the three youths saved by God, the salvation of Daniel, Peter, and Paul, and some of the miracles of Jesus as paradigms for ordeals (Franz, 2:395).

122. The prayers spoken before ordeals also emphasize the necessity of penance, suffering, and confession for a full reconciliation between the guilty and God and the community (see Geneva's "Blessing of Iron" and "Exorcism of Water," the Gondekar pontifical's "Blessing of Frigid Water," St. Florian's "Judgment of Hot Iron," and Luxembourg's "Ordeal of Bread"). The texts that contain this theme originate in Germany, Austria, Switzerland, and Luxembourg, and four of them were created during the eleventh and twelfth centuries, the period in which confession was increasingly viewed as an obligation of the pious Christian.

123. Franz, 2:370–71: Domine deus noster, pater omnipotens, qui es lumen quique per ignem Moysi in rubo apparuisti et populum Israel de Egyptiaca caligine liberasti celesti lumine precedente atque corda apostolorum igne sancti spiritus inflammasti: tu benedic hoc lumen, ut quidquid per calorem eius flagraverit, diabolici tepore careat incitamenti.

There is an interesting parallel here between the intense heat of divine fire and the lukewarm flame of the demonic, two forces that were thought to compete strongly in the heart of the guilty, as can be seen in a later prayer of the blessing:

> Omnipotent eternal God, who is the searcher of the hidden things of the heart: we humbly ask you, that if this man is guilty concerning the afore-done acts and, with the devil weighing on his heart, he shall have presumed to place his hand on this heated iron, may your most just truth give pain to his body, so that his soul may be saved in the final examination.[124]

In the final lengthy prayer of the ritual there is hope that the blessing will undermine the confidence of the wicked:

> so that you may not presume to accept today this iron into your hand at the Devil's prompting, but through the power of our Lord Jesus Christ and through the sign of the holy cross may you depart disordered and conquered. If, however, you are secure and innocent in yourself concerning this crime, through the name of our Lord Jesus Christ, and through the sign of the holy cross, may you have leave to approach and accept this iron without concern for yourself.[125]

The first of these prayers reveals a belief in the role played by the demonic in deceit and crime, and a conviction that salvation was possible through penitential suffering, a common *topos* of medieval religious belief that appears numerous times in ordeal rituals. While the acceptance of the physical suffering caused by ordeals as a tolerable remedy to unsolvable crimes reflects a belief in the secondary importance of the body in comparison with the soul, it is important to recall that it is *through* the suffering of the body that the soul can be saved.

In addition to assuming the essential unity of body and soul, this blessing of burning iron manifests the contractual understanding of blessing we

124. Ibid., 2:371: Omnipotens sempiterne deus, qui es scrutator occultorum cordium: te supplices exoramus, ut si homo iste culpabilis sit de rebus prefatis et diabolo cor eius ingravante manum suam in hoc ferrum ignitum mittere presumpserit, tua iustissima veritas det penam in corpore, ut anima eius salvetur in extremo examine.

125. Ibid., 2:372: ut suadente diabolo hoc ferrum hodie in manum accipere non presumas, sed per virtutem domini nostri Iesu Christi et per signum sancte crucis victus et confusus abscedas. Si autem in temet ipso securs et innocens de hoc crimine sis, per nomen domini nostri Iesu Christi et per signem sancte crucis licentiam habeas accedere et tibi ad securitatem hoc ferrum accipere.

have seen so many times before. This is evident in the blessing prayer spoken over the iron before it is placed in the forge:

> Bless, Lord, through the strength of your power this species of metal, so that in it on account of your holy name, with every deceit of demons removed far away and every enchantment and fallacy of the unfaithful restrained, the truth of your most true judgment may be made open to your faithful in order that your praiseworthy and glorious name may always be glorified in your holy church.[126]

This prayer shows how the continuance of human worship depends upon divine faithfulness, and also expels from the community that which is unacceptable or antithetical to both humans and God. Thus cleansed, the hot iron may reveal the true culprit and help purge the community of its pollution.[127]

A litany and psalms, which continue the theme of communal purity, then follow. Psalm 29, *Afferte domino*—"Ascribe to the Lord, O heavenly beings, ascribe to the Lord glory and strength"—confirms the power of God and the rightness of his role as judge by placing all creation under his dominion, echoing feudal notions of the connection between governance and justice exercised by seigniorial and royal courts.[128] Psalm 68, *Exurgat deus*, calls for the enemies of God, in this instance the deceitful guilty, to be scattered and undone. A selection from the Psalm 119, *Beati immaculati*, next presents a clear concern for strict observance of God's law: "Your decrees are wonderful; therefore my soul keeps them."[129] This verse concludes the chants, all of

126. Ibid., 2:371: Benedic, domine, per potentie tue virtutem hoc genus metalli, ut in eo propter nomen sanctum tuum omni demonum falsitate procul remota omnique fascinatione ac fallacia infidelium sublata verissimi iudicii tui fidelibus tuis veritas patefiat, quatinus laudabile et gloriosum nomen tuum in sancta ecclesia semper glorificetur.

127. The concern with pollution and the demonic was a common theme in the blessings of ordeals. Expulsion of demons occurs in five of the rituals studied, which are found in German, Austrian, and Swiss manuscripts of the ninth, tenth, eleventh, and twelfth centuries (the Gondekar pontifical's "Blessing of Frigid Water," Geneva's "Exorcism of Water," the *RGP*'s "Judgment of Bread and Cheese," St. Florian's "Judgment of Hot Iron," and Clm 14508's "Ordeal of Boiling Water"). This theme occurs most frequently (three out of the four rituals) in blessings of water to be used in the ordeals, which is appropriate given the use of blessed water as a cleansing agent in so many different kinds of blessings. Indeed, one of these four rituals makes use of aspersion in such a capacity, as does the blessing of neglected fonts.

128. Kirkpatrick, *Book of Psalms*, 147.

129. Ps 119:1–5, 7–8.

which stress the need for both individual and communal righteousness in maintaining a harmonious relationship with the divine.

Concern for the purity and unity of the community is expressed in the prayer that follows, wherein the celebrant seeks to establish, through the power of the sacred, a truly fair judgment: "And may you not suffer us to be disturbers of justice, you who highly prize justice, so that ignorance may not drag us into evil, nor favor divert us, nor the receipt of gifts or personal consideration corrupt us, but in effect join us to you by the gift of your grace alone."[130] The ways in which truth may be perverted are opposed in this prayer by the power of grace, the spiritual means to make the human community one with God in the love of justice. It is interesting to note how those seeking justice are perceived to be working on the behalf of the divine, an excellent incentive for God to lend his assistance in the internal regulation of the Christian congregation.

Blessings of water also could protect and define the Christian community. The "Blessing of Frigid Water for Making a Judgment," from the eleventh-century pontifical of Gondekar II, opens with a Mass and the singing of antiphons and psalms.[131] The first antiphon, *Iustus es, domine*, is drawn from Psalm 119:137—"You are righteous, Lord, and your judgments are just"—which asserts the validity of turning to God for justice in matters of doubt. Following this, the familiar Psalm 119:1, *Beati immaculati*, is chanted; its emphasis on the law of God suits well the determination of a case of human law. The gradual *In deo speravit* places the outcome of the ordeal squarely on God's shoulders, as it affirms the justice of trusting in God's judgment in cases of doubt, and the offertory *Sperent in te* confirms this sentiment.[132] The Communion service is Psalm 5:2, *Intellige*—"Listen to the sound of my cry, my King and my God, for to you I pray"—which again invokes the divine as judge and ruler, imploring God to be adjudicator in the coming ordeal.[133]

130. Franz, 2:372: Non nos patiaris perturbatores esse iusticie, qui summe diligis equitatem, ut in sinistrum nos ignorantia non trahat, non inflectet favor, non adeptio muneris vel persone consideratio corrumpat, sed iunge nos tibi efficaciter solius tue gratie dono.

131. Ibid., 380–84. The same *ordo*, drawn from the same MS, appears in *RGP* 2:400–414 (*ordo* 252) under the siglum G. Franz notes that the blessings of water from ordeal *ordos* borrowed heavily from the consecration formulas for baptismal water (2:397).

132. Franz inaccurately identifies the gradual as Ps 56:11 and the offertory as Ps 10:11 (2:380).

133. This psalm is a morning prayer, spoken by one who is in danger from the plots of unscrupulous and hypocritical enemies. This seems a particularly appropriate text for an

The Mass is followed by the blessing of holy water and a lengthy prayer spoken above it.[134] The prayer particularly seeks to safeguard the human world:

> Furthermore, we humbly ask that you deign to protect us by your right hand from the deceptions of men and demons, and from all falsity and fraud. Moreover, we humbly ask you, Lord, that you deign to bless and sanctify us and to manifest for us that which we seek and which is hidden from us, so that we may recognize your truth working in us.[135]

The invocation seeks to exclude the demonic from human affairs, and to make the Christian congregation aware of the divine at work in their lives. This concern for the protection of the congregation is voiced in three rituals from German, Austrian, and Swiss manuscripts of the eleventh and twelfth centuries.[136] Such awareness, and the benefits that arise from the discovery of truth in criminal affairs, could only deepen the gratitude of the human world to the divine, and would thereby deepen the bond between the two upon which human life depends.[137] This protection of the faithful was even

---

ordeal, where undoubtedly the subjected party had declared his innocence and the duplicity of his accusers; see Kirkpatrick, *Book of Psalms,* 20. God's role as king is supported, of course, by scripture, but it is also in keeping with the legal practice of the ritual's time, since one of the primary functions of kings in medieval society was the administration of justice and the settling of disputes.

134. Franz, 2:380–84.

135. Ibid., 2:380–81: Suppliciter etiam quaesumus, domine, ut nos protegere digneris dextera tua ab insidiis hominum et daemonum et ab omni falsitate et fraude. Insuper humiliter te quaesumus, domine, ut benedicere et sanctificare digneris nos et nobis manifestare ea, quae querimus et quae abscondita sunt nobis, ut cognoscamus tuam veritatem operantem in nobis. This is also the second half of *RGP* 2:403–4 (*ordo 2.20*).

136. See the Gondekar pontifical's "Blessing of Frigid Water," Geneva's "Exorcism of Water," and St. Florian's "Judgment of Hot Iron." A concern with the expulsion of spiritual pollution, namely, sin and sinners, calls to mind Mary Douglas's work on purity and pollution, most especially in the analogous relationship between the "dirt" of pollution and sin and the sinner and rituals that cast this dirt off and out of the community; see Douglas, *Purity and Danger,* 36–37. Ritual blessings of the Middle Ages serve the same purpose of cleansing the community as do the rituals of Third World cultures studied by Douglas, which suggests that her paradigm has merit in explaining the meaning of medieval blessings for their recipients.

137. The theme of such a bond or contractual relationship between the human and divine appears frequently in ordeal blessings. Four eleventh-, twelfth-, and fifteenth-century ordeals from Germany, Austria, Switzerland, and England all contain this theme. See the Gondekar pontifical's "Blessing of Frigid Water," Geneva's "Exorcism of Hot Water," St. Florian's "Judgment of Hot Iron," and the York manual's "Judicial Duel." It is tempting to suppose that the

extended to the guilty: "if guilty, may you the accused not come to this trial presumptuously, and may the water not receive you, and by this sign of the cross of Christ may your evil deed shine forth and the power of omnipotent God be made manifest."[138] This, I suggest, represents an attempt to frighten the guilty into confessing and avoiding the ordeal, and a desire on the part of the clerical author for salvation over punishment.

Belief in the efficacy of this ritual rested on the conception of God as a divine judge. Divinity is address thus: "Omnipotent and merciful God, founder of the world, in whom true judgments stand, you who judge everything and know every hidden thing . . ."[139] The belief in the power of the divine to judge thus adds its power to those possessed by the human community for self-governance, enhancing the social order with the power of the sacred. This ritual calls upon the sacred history of God's interaction with water to ensure an efficacious performance of this ordeal by water. Examples of this appear in the fourth and sixth prayers of the rite:

> Lord omnipotent God, who ordered baptism to be made in water and who deigned through the bath of regeneration to give remission of sins to the human race . . . who deigned to renew our nature in the river Jordan and commanded the wind and sea on behalf of his sinking disciples and stretched out the right hand for Peter, may you deign to bless and sanctify this frigid water.[140]

---

legal nature of ordeals encouraged thinking in contractual terms, especially in later rituals, the authors of which may have been influenced by the systematization of canon law and the presence of Roman law in the later medieval schools. But whereas the first proposition has some merit in its simple elegance, the second is untenable. Roman law contained no provision for ordeals, and the absence of these rituals from a body of law experiencing the youthful vigor of its glamour and prestige has traditionally been interpreted as one of the principal causes of ordeals' condemnation by the Fourth Lateran Council of 1215. Thus ordeal texts represent more a persistence of customary law and practice than a response to new forms of law evolving in the high and late Middle Ages.

138. Franz, 2:382–83: ad hoc iudicum non praesumptuosus accedas, et aqua te non suscipiat, et hoc signo crucis Christi tua malitia appareat et virtus omnipotentis dei manifestetur.

139. Ibid., 2:381: Omnipotens et misericors deus, mundi conditor, in quo sunt vera iudicia, qui cuncta iudicas et abscondita cuncta nosti . . .

140. Ibid.: Domine deus omnipotens, qui baptismum in aqua fieri iussisti et per lavacrum regenerationis humano generi remissionem peccatorum donare dignatus es . . . qui in Jordane flumine nostram innovare dignatus es naturam et discipulis suis mergentibus ventis et mari imperavit et Petro dextram porrexit, hanc aquam frigidam benedicere et sanctificare digneris. These prayers are from *RGP* 2:405–6 (*ordo* 252.22 and 24); both are alternatives for

Water's power as a regenerative agent in baptism and its submission to its creator are reaffirmed by this recollection of sacred paradigms, drawing ever more clearly the intimate connection between the holy and the natural world. This is complemented by the seventh prayer, which retells the history of water:

> I adjure you, water, in the name of God the Father omnipotent, who created you in the beginning and commanded you to minister to human needs, who also ordered you to be segregated from the waters above. I adjure you also through the ineffable name of Jesus Christ, son of omnipotent God, under whose feet the element of the sea offered itself as something to be walked on, who furthermore desired to be baptized in you. . . . I adjure you through the name of the holy and individual Trinity, by the will of which the element of waters was divided and the people of Israel crossed on dry footways, at whose invocation also Elias made iron, which had slipped from its haft, swim over the water, so that by no means may you receive this man N. if he is in any way culpable concerning this affair.[141]

The name of God is invoked as an artifact of power here, much as it was in the blessings of cemeteries, the dubbing of knights, and the benedictions to end illness and speed recovery. In ordeals this theme appears in this German manuscript and in a Swiss text, both from the eleventh century, that involve water as the instrument of the ordeal.[142]

While the prayers of this ritual are offered in God's presence and were undoubtedly believed to be heard by God, they are directed at the supposedly insensible pool in which the ordeal is to be conducted. Through Christ the celebrant subjugates the natural world to human needs and attributes

---

the prayer discussed in note 122, above. There is also a reference in this rite's adjurations to the prototypical paradigm of God saving those unjustly accused, the freeing of the three Israelite boys from the furnace (see Franz, 2:383).

141. Franz, 2:382: Adiuro te, aqua, in nomine dei patris omnipotentis, qui te in principio creavit et te iussit ministrare humanis necessitatibus, qui etiam te iussit segregari ab aquis superioribus. Adiuro te etiam per ineffabile nomen Iesu Christi, filii dei omnipotentis, sub cuius pedibus elementum maris se calcabile praebuit, qui in te etiam baptizari voluit. . . . Adiuro te per nomen sanctae et individuae trinitatis, cuius voluntate aquarum elementum divisum est et populus Israhel per illud siccis vestigiis transiit, ad cuius etiam invocationem Helias ferrum, quod de manubrio exierat, super aquam natare fecit, ut nullo modo suscipias hominem hunc N, si in aliquo est culpabilis de eo. The prayer is *RGP* 2:407 (*ordo* 252.27). The scriptural references are to Gn 1:7 and 2 Kgs 6:5–7.

142. See the Gondekar pontifical's "Blessing of Frigid Water" and Geneva's "Exorcism of Water."

human characteristics to the natural elements, further proof of belief in the deep connection between nature and humans. This approach to water is seen in the ninth prayer of the rite, in which the celebrant says, "I adjure you, water, through the name of Christ, and I instruct you that you might give ear to us through the name of him, whom every creature serves."[143] This retelling of water's relationship with God is an encouragement and a reminder to the waters of ordeal of their true nature, as in earlier blessings involving the natural world's forces. It is also an affirmation to the audience and participants in the rite that this is a sensible operation with precedents in God's other acts involving water. Thus both actor and acted upon are empowered by the ritual to arrive at truth, and to regulate the internal life of the community through faith and the power of God.[144]

The protection of the community invoking the ordeal is also found in exorcisms of water for use in judicial trials. The first prayer of an "Exorcism of Hot Water for Judgment," from the eleventh-century Geneva collection, helps to establish security for the community: "I exorcise you, creature of water, in the name of the Father . . . so that you might be made exorcised water for driving out all the power of the Enemy and every phantasm of the Devil . . . in order that every man shall fear and tremble at the holy name of the glory of the Lord."[145] The awe and fearful trembling before the divine is turned by this ritual into a tool by which to control crime and disorder. Dread of the boiling water, and the divinity that inflicts it upon the guilty, serve as a deterrent to theft, which in turn keeps the Christian community untainted by those acts that might distance it from the protection of God's power.

The nature and history of God are invoked by this ritual to enhance its power to discern truth in uncertainty. God is once again cast as a judge who uncovers hidden things:

143. Franz, 2:383: Adiuro te, aqua, per nomen Christi et praecipio tibi, ut nobis oboedias per nomen eius, cui omnis creatura servit.

144. This ritual also contains the appeal to the water to expel the guilty, another example of how medieval people accepted the existence of a powerful connection between the natural world and the interior world of human morality.

145. Franz, 2:374: Exorcizo te, creatura aquae, in nomine dei patris . . . ut fias aqua exorcizata ad effugandam omnem potestatem inimici et omne fantasma diaboli . . . ut omnis homo timeat et contremiscat nomen sanctum glorie domini nostri. This curious phrase appears to be unique to this blessing; while the name of the Lord can be invoked to elicit fear (as in the *ordinarium* of Valencia's *"Ordo* for Blessing and Exorcizing Fruits" [Franz, 2:166]), the fear and glory of God's name are never linked outside of this blessing.

I beseech you, Lord, illuminator of all things, who sees and knows the covered and the concealed and the private, the thoughts and loins of all . . . Lord Jesus Christ, you who are a judge just and strong and patient and very merciful, through whom all things were made, God of gods and Lord of lords, who on account of us humans and our salvation descended from the bosom of the Father and deigned to assume flesh from out of the Virgin Mary, and through your Passion redeemed the world and descended into hell and collected the Devil in the outer darkness and liberated all the just . . .[146]

The emphasis on the saving acts of the divine judge in this prayer, a close adaptation of the text of the Apostle's Creed, would have been quite appropriate in a human juridical affair believed to offer salvation to the recalcitrant or deceitful. The potential to save souls through confession and penitence was expressed by the recollection of other events in salvation history:

We humbly entreat you, Lord God, who in Cana, Galilee, in a wonderful sign, through your power made wine from out of water, and led out three boys, Shadrach, Meshach, and Abednego, unharmed from the furnace of burning fire and freed Susanna from a false accusation, and opened the eyes of the man born blind, raised four-day-dead Lazarus from the tomb and stretched forth your right hand for the sinking Peter: do not consider our sin in this prayer, but may you deign to manifest your true and holy judgment to all men in this . . . so that both he himself, doing penance, may come to correction through true confession, and your holy and true judgment may be declared in all the races, through you, redeemer of the world, who will come.[147]

---

146. Ibid., 2:375–76: Deprecor te, illuminator domine omnium rerum, qui et occulta abditaque et secreta, cogitationes et renes omnium nosti et vides . . . Domine Iesu Christe, qui es iudex iustus et fortis et paciens et multum misericors, per quem facta sunt omnia; deus deorum et dominus dominantium, qui propter nos homines et propter nostram salutem de sinu patris descendisti et ex virgine Marie carnem assumere dignatus es, et per passionem tuam mundum redemisti et ad inferos descendisti et diabolum in tenebris exterioribus colligasti et omnes iustos liberasti . . . The scriptural allusions are to Jn 2:7; Dt 3, 13; Jn 9:6, 11:43; and Mt 14:31.

147. Ibid., 2:375: Te, domine deus, supplices deprecamur, qui in Chana Galilee signo admirabili tua virtute ex aqua vinum fecisti et tres pueros, Sidrac, Misac et Abdenago, de camino ignis ardentis illesos eduxisti et Sussanam de falso crimine liberasti, ceco nato oculos aperuisti, Lazarum quatriduanum a monumento suscitasti et Petro mergenti dextram porrexisti: ne respicias peccata nostra in hoc oratione, sed tuum verum et sanctum iudicium coram omnibus hominibus in hoc manifestare digneris . . . ut et ipse deinceps per verum confessionem penitentiam agens ad emendationem perveniat, et iudicum tuum sanctum et verum in omnibus declaretur gentibus, per te, redemptor mundi, qui venturus.

By focusing the power of the divine on one suspect, this ordeal provides an example to the community of God's justice and reaffirms the rightness of the Christian world view. The scriptural allusions are orientated toward asserting the power of the divine to save the righteous, as in the case of the chastised Peter sinking in the sea, and revealing that which is hidden in darkness, as in Lazarus's arising from the shadows of the tomb and the illumination of the blind man. These events lend their numinous power to the ritual's purpose, which in turn actualizes the events' reality by making them live again and reassume all their power and wonder.

Other incidents, paradigms of divine truth and justice, are invoked to lend power to the ritual: "We confess to you, Lord, God of our Fathers, and we give thanks and praise you and also bless and beseech you, that you might show us the truth of this matter just as you did between the women before Solomon and between the false judges and Susanna and before Daniel and among the apostles in electing an apostle."[148] The wisdom of Solomon, which of course sprang from a divine source, is brought into these medieval proceedings by this conjuration because it connects the ordeal both with the sacred evolution of the Christian Church following the death of Jesus and with the contractual nature of that relationship when judgments are called for. The blessing ends with an abjuration of the man suspected, which is offered "humbly" by the priest:

> I adjure you, man, through the Father, Son and the Holy Spirit, and through your Christianity, which you accepted in baptism, and the male and female saints of God, that you not presume to approach the altar or to eat the body and the blood of the Son of God, if you did or consented to any role in these things which are charged to you.[149]

Communion is then distributed, and the priest says a closing prayer beseeching truth from the ordeal.[150] The invocation of all the saints marks it

---

148. Ibid., 2:376: Tibi, domine, deus patrum nostrorum confitemur teque laudamus atque benedicimus precamurque, ut veritatem istius rei manifestes nobis sicut fecisti inter mulieres apud Salomonem et inter falsos iudices et Susannam apud Danielem et apud apostolos in eligendo apostolum. The scriptural allusions are to 1 Kgs 3:16–27; Dt 13:45–64; and Acts 1:15–26.

149. Ibid., 2:377: Adiuro te, homo, per patrem et filium et spiritum sanctum et per tuam christianitatem, quam in baptismo accepisti, et per omnes sanctos et sanctas dei, ut non presumas accedere ad altare neque corpus et sanguinem fillii deo sumere, si aliquam causam de his, que tibi obiciuntur, fecisti aut consensisti.

150. Ibid.

as typical, for as only two rituals call on specific intercessors by name, litanies and invocations of "all the saints" are quite common in ordeals that include adjurations, occurring in all the blessings examined except the judicial
duel.[151] In all these rituals the saints are used as conjuring tools to drive out
demons and their power to conceal the truth and harden the hearts of the
guilty, preventing the latter's salvation.

While the ordeals of iron and water are the most familiar to students
of this era, there is a significant body of other ordeals that can shed further
light on the understanding and use of blessings in ordeals. One of the most
common of these alternative ordeals employed bread as a means of divining the truth in disputed cases.[152] The "Judgment of Bread of the Ordeal,"
from the fourteenth-century Luxembourg collection, provides an elaborate
series of steps in which the priest blesses holy water while the deacon ritually bakes a loaf of bread. During the baking, the choir sings an antiphon and
incipit (exhorting God to rise up, judge, and assist the celebrant), the seven
penitential psalms, and a litany.[153] The priest then says several short prayers
and the entirety of Psalm 123, a supplication for mercy that also complains
of persecution, a plaint that would ring familiar in the ears of an innocent
candidate for the ordeal: "Have mercy upon us, O Lord, have mercy upon us,
for we have had more than enough contempt. Our soul has had more than
its fill of the scorn of those who are at ease, of the contempt of the proud."[154]
Here the lament of the psalmist is spoken for the benefit of the believer, reminding God of the injustice of the wicked and the suffering of the just,
in the hopes that this blessing and ordeal will inspire God to protect those

151. The two rituals are Bamberg's "Blessing of a Small Jug" and "Psalter Ordeal." Other
blessings in which litanies and invocations of all the saints are present include the Parisian
"Psalter Ordeal."

152. Franz notes that authors of ordeal rituals often took liturgical elements and adapted
them for less orthodox means of examination, which included the addition of nonecclesias-
tical elements such as unusual names of angels, kabbalistic words, etc. (see the *Iudicium panis
pendentis* and *Iudicium offae*) (Franz, 2:397).

153. The antiphon is *Iudica, domine, nocentes me*, drawn from Ps 35:1–2, and the incipit *Exurge, domine, adiuva nos*.

154. Franz, 2:388: In primis preparet se sacerdos cum dyacono, et presbiter faciat aquam
benedictam, et dyaconus preparet farinam ordeaceam, quam et ipse pistret cum benedicta
aqua et coquat, cantantibus ambobus interim septem penitentiales psalmos cum letania et
precibus istis: "Non nobis. Iustus es. Iudica, domine, nocentes me, expunga impugnantes me,
apprehende arma et scutum et exurge in adiutorium michi. Exurge, domine, adiuva nos." Et
psalmum istum: "Levavi oculos meos, qui habitas in celis" usque ad finem.

who love and serve him. A short prayer requesting that God's power permeate the bread follows: "God, who on Mount Calvary displayed the wood of the Holy Cross and was seized through Judas, who through Judas surrendered his Son, demonstrate for us through this judgment of the ordeal bread whatever we ask in your name."[155] This invocation is a good example of the medieval belief in the versatility of the sacred, which was accessible by human agency as long as the intention and performance of the ritual followed the accepted form.

The ritual continues with the priest placing the bread behind the altar and saying a Mass, followed by his inscribing a cross in the middle of the loaf and placing a spindle in the middle of the cross.[156] This is done so that "when indeed anyone is accused in a case of theft or fornication or murder and shall have come before the priest, let the priest take the blessed bread and give it to two faithful men, so that through spinning it hangs between those two judges."[157] This remarkable ritual is another example of the medieval belief in the power of the divine to work through mundane physical objects for the betterment of the faithful community. It also demonstrates that the laity (in this case, the "two faithful men") could play a significant role in such blessings, which is especially notable in the subsequent prayers.

A typical conjuration of the bread follows, with the notable call for intercession through "the mother of Our Lord, and through the prophets Hosea and Jonah who prophesied Nineveh, and through Lazarus, whom God raised from the tomb, and through the blind man, whom the Lord enlightened, and through all the monks and all the canons and all the laity."[158]

155. Ibid.: Deus, qui in monte calvarie lignum sancte crucis ostendisti et per Iudam deprehensus es, qui per Iudam tradidit filium suum, demonstra nobis per hoc iudicium panis ordeacei, quidquid in nomine tuo querimus.

156. Ibid.: Cocto autem pane, accipiat presbiter et ponat retro altare et celebrat missam, que illo die fuerit. Finita missa, faciat crucem in medio panis et in medietate crucis mittat fusum et in summitate fusi vertiginem, et reponat presbiter apud se, quamdiu panis inputribilis sit.

157. Ibid.: Cum vero aliquis accusatur in crimine furti vel fornicationis vel homicidii et venerit coram sacerdote, accipiat sacerdos benedictum panem et det duobus fidelibus viris, ut per vertiginem pendet inter duos illos iudices.

158. Ibid., 2:389: per matrem domini, et per Ozee prophetam et Ionam prophetam, qui Ninive prophetavit, et per Lazaram, quem deus suscitavit de monumento, et per cecum, quem dominus illuminavit, et per omnes monachos et omnes canonicos et omnes laicos. The scriptural allusions are to Hos 7:9, Jon 1:2, and Jn 11 (esp. 11:21–27), and Jn 9:1–12. The last allusion is particularly interesting, since in Jesus' reply to his disciples concerning the cause of

While the inclusion of the prophets, the sanctioned bearers of divine truth, is not surprising, it is interesting that, in the case of Lazarus and the blind man, the idea is expressed that the subjects of a blessing can themselves be transmitters of further blessings. They serve as examples of the capacity of the divine to provide miracles and therefore act as an indirect confirmation of the validity of rituals such as the ordeal of bread. Such historical individuals may have been perceived as human links to the divine, demonstrations of how divine power intersected with human and could benefit all humanity through individual experience. The inclusion of the laity as a conjuring power is remarkable, as it implicitly asserts the active role the laity could play in the successful completion of blessings. It also presents us with the idea of the divine working through the corporate body of the living church to the latter's benefit.

The physical act of eating blessed food was also used as a method of ordeal. The "Judgment of Bread and Cheese," from the eleventh-century recension of the RGP, instructs priests to take dry bread and dry goat cheese and inscribe the initials "PN" on both sides of each food item, and to inscribe in small script the things stolen and the names of those accused.[159] This inscription could serve a double purpose: on the one hand, the inscription of "PN," the initials of *Pater noster,* would intimately associate the physical foodstuff with the identity and essence of the divine; on the other, the inscription of the stolen property and the suspects' names forms another link to the human, material elements of the dispute.[160] These ritualized items become a bridge between all parties involved in the ordeal, allowing the power of the sacred to touch all and thereby divine truth. This inscription is followed by an unremarkable blessing of the bread and cheese, but the subsequent alternative blessing makes interesting use of scriptural stories to ensure the ordeal's success:

the blind man's disability, Jesus says, "We must work the works of him who sent me while it is day; night is coming when no one can work" (Jn 9:4–5). The "work" of Christ can be seen as a parallel to the "work" of the ordeal, i.e., as accomplishing God's purpose by ferreting out the guilty and vindicating the righteous. Thus the ordeal gains another level of legitimacy by connecting it not only to the words but also to the work of Jesus.

159. Franz, 2:385; this ritual is from the *RGP* 2:394–97 (*ordo* 249); the MS used by Franz is the eleventh-century pontifical, Bamberg, lit. 54.

160. *RGP* 2:394 (*ordo* 249.1) expands the *PN* of Franz's edition to *Pater Noster.*

God, who freed Moses and Aaron from the land of Egypt, David from the hand of King Saul, Jonah from the belly of the whale, Peter from chains, Paul from the flood, Susanna from a false accusation, the three boys from the furnace of burning fire, Daniel from the mouth of a lion, one stricken with palsy from the bed, Lazarus from the tomb, stretch forth your mercy so that you may not permit this bread or cheese to enter the mouth of the one who committed the theft.[161]

The allusions are to the moments in sacred history when God granted freedom to the faithful and innocent, whether freedom from accusation (Susanna and the three Israelite children), physical danger (Jonah, Daniel, and Paul), illness and death (the palsiac and Lazarus), or the hostility of superiors (the young David). Through these allusions, frequent elements of other ordeal blessings, sacred history is embodied anew in the performance of this ritual of blessing, keeping the Christian community's past alive and real as it serves the daily needs of justice.

A second alternative exorcism in the ritual reveals the belief, noted above, in the power of blessings to control physical elements, in this case the mixture of elements that form the human body: "And may you, Lord Jesus Christ, not permit this bread or cheese to be eaten by the man who committed this theft, and if he was ignorant of the crime may he eat healthily, and if he was conscious of it, made trembling may he then vomit it forth on account of your holy name."[162] Such an acceptance of God's power to influence the matter he created was essential to the belief in the validity and efficacy of ordeals, which serves as another example of how important even liturgical authors considered the material world to be, for it could serve as the instrument for distinguishing the righteous from the sinner, a discrimination

161. Ibid., 2:394–95 (*ordo* 249.4): Deus, qui liberasti Moysen et Aaron de terra Aegypti, David de manu Saul regis, Ionam de ventre ceti, Petrum de vinculis, Paulum de fluctibus, Susannam de falso crimine, tres pueros de camino ignis ardentis, Danielem de lacu leonum, paraliticum de grabato, Lazarum de monumento, ostende tuam misericordiam, ut, qui hoc furtum commisit, panem vel caseum istum eius fauces intrare non permittas (see also Franz, 2:385–86). The palsiac reference is to Mk 2:11.

162. Franz, 2:386; *RGP* 2:395 (*ordo* 249.5), lines 11–15: Et tu, domine Iesu Christe, non permittas panem vel caseum hunc isti homini manducare, qui istud furtum commisit, et si criminis nescius est, salubriter manducet, et si de eo conscius est, factus tremebundus evomat illud propter nomen sanctum tuum. This is also another example of the likely influence of, and certainly the similarity to, the prayer *Libera domine* from the Gellone death ritual. The only incident not common to both prayers is the recollection of Lazarus. See Paxton, *Christianizing Death*, 118–20.

at the heart of how Christians identified themselves and their community.

In conclusion, the blessings of vessels, objects, and events display themes common to blessings of places and persons: contract relations, the invocation of scripture to actualize sacred history in the present, the use of God's name as an artifact of divine power, and the employment of saints as intercessors. These shared themes demarcate the essential nature and character of the ritual blessings studied here. The concluding chapter elaborates on this part of the medieval liturgy and offers some thoughts on future research in this area.

CONCLUSION

The tradition of Christian blessing was a rich, complex, and pervasive component of the culture and religion of the medieval West. From its origin in ancient Israel, blessing spread to all parts of Latin Christendom through the agency of the Roman liturgy of late antiquity, developing both within and apart from the Mass. Blessing was further developed and elaborated in the early Middle Ages through the Roman Catholic Church's contact with Germanic peoples, who enthusiastically adopted ritual blessing as they adapted it to meet local ritual needs. This Franco-Roman tradition was first fully realized in the tenth-century Romano-Germanic pontifical, upon which the later pontificals and benedictionals of the high and late Middle Ages built. Careful analysis of these rituals can tell the historian much about medieval people's understanding of ritual, the sacred, and the divine power to which blessings appealed. Blessings also show us how medieval Christians, both lay and clerical, conceived of their cosmos and their relationship to the powers of their cosmology. Let us conclude with a summary of the medieval conceptions of the sacred and divine as seen in blessings as a window into medieval cosmology, and examine the blessings' relationship to the piety of the age.

THE NATURE OF THE SACRED IN THE MIDDLE AGES

The nature of the sacred is a subject that every culture addresses in some form or other. The culture of the medieval Latin West is no exception. There are many commonalities between our age's understanding of the sacred and divine and the medieval understanding. God's qualities of omnipotence, omniscience, goodness, mercy, wrath, and justice are familiar to medieval and modern pulpits alike. But the ritual blessings of the Latin church offer a much richer picture of the divine than these absolutes alone. Blessings portray God as a force characterized above all by his adaptability and utility. As a farmer in agricultural blessings, a purifier in reconciliations of violated cemeteries, a militant defender in blessings of knights, a doctor in blessings against illness, and a just judge in ordeal blessings, God was nothing if not versatile. The divine manifested whatever "face" was necessary to meet the needs and expectations of the individual and the community.

God is in fact so adaptable in these blessings that one wonders if his chameleonlike nature is simply a function of his omnipotence. While this notion has some merit, it ignores subtleties in this adaptive process that present a more complex image of God. The presence of distinct personae of God within the blessings raises the question why such elements would be included in a ritual if there was universal acceptance of God as an abstract omnipotence. In that case, why not simply declare God omnipotent and move on to the request of the blessing? I believe the answer is that the medieval conception of God was much too rich and nuanced for such familiar abstractions to be sufficient. Not only is God described in many different terms and roles in the blessings, but he is often cast in contrary ways within a single blessing: the God who demands service to selfless ideals of knighthood also bestows personal glory and worldly renown; the God who heals communities of sin punishes individual sinners; the God who mercifully protects the faithful from harm mercilessly annihilates the unfaithful. The divine was thought able to change his nature at will, and the blessings suggest that medieval people were more concerned about how and when God's power manifested itself than about the scope of that power as a theological principle.

The second notable trait of divinity in blessings is its ambivalence and ambiguity. This trait is implicit in the constant qualification and contextualization of God that we see in pilgrim blessings that stress God's guidance and salvation of the wandering Tobias, or when God was made to recall his assistance to the Israelites in crossing the Red Sea, or in the blessing of a cemetery, when the celebrant implores God's intervention: "just as you blessed the earth of the graves through the hand of the first fathers, namely Abraham, Isaac, and Jacob."[1] Why would this process of contextualization be necessary if God's presence and action were assured? It could be that these

---

1. *RP12th* 287 (*ordo* 52b.12).

allusions and exhortations were included as a way to honor God for his past deeds, but I believe this is insufficient explanation for the prevalence of such allusions in the blessings. Rather, I contend that these allusions were included because medieval people's conception of God had much more room for doubt and uncertainty than we might be inclined to believe from reading traditional historical and theological sources.

The blessings' exhortations and invocations of God strongly suggest that confidence in God's intervention was not at all solid. Instead, the constant use of scriptural allusion implies that medieval authors believed it necessary to "remind" God of his past beneficence, to ensure that he would act again in the same manner to save his followers. If author and recipient of a blessing were confident that the ritual would work, this would not have been necessary. These activities would be redundant in the minds of those certain of God's beneficent intention. But if there was ambivalence about God's reliability, if medieval people were anxious about God's good will and protection, then the call for repeated blessings becomes meaningful. It is the effort of uncertain minds to extinguish uncertainty, to cover all bases and hedge all bets, to ensure that a God who could be forgetful would not let his attention wander and his people suffer for it. For medieval believers God was a force of tremendous power, but that power was not entirely reliable. Prayer, praise, and ritual performance were necessary to ensure continued good relations between humanity and divinity to ensure the survival of the faithful.

Medieval conceptions of the sacred are further characterized by a belief in the deep engagement of the sacred with the natural world. Blessings of all kinds make mention of God as creator of, and participant in, the natural world and its elements: as the creator of water, God's name is invoked when celebrants sought to purify waters for aspersion and for ordeals; as the creator of nature, God is associated with all growing things in blessings for fields and crops; as the founder of light and light embodied, God is invoked to illuminate homes, forges, and places of ordeals with light that casts out darkness and reveals hidden things.[2] And in rituals dealing direct-

2. The importance of God's name as a verbal artifact of sacred power is evident throughout the blessings and is best examined in Lester Little's study of the history of cursing in the ancient world and Christian West. Little points out that the ancient Hebrews understood names to hold power: the eradication of a person's name was a standard element in Hebrew curses because they believed that one's name expressed the essential nature of the individual, and so to have no name denied both one's essence and one's existence (Little, *Benedictine*

ly with natural elements, blessings exhort the elements to "remember" their creation and the authority of the divine. All of these examples demonstrate belief in a substantial and meaningful interrelationship between the sacred and the natural worlds. They also are powerful evidence for understanding medieval religion as a faith that did not wholly reject the visible world beset by sin, a world ignored or decried in a strict Neoplatonic or Augustinian perspective, but that saw and valued the presence of divinity in nature. Medieval piety used the divinity within nature through rituals that tied human and God into a negotiated web of worship, service, and protection.

The connection between humanity and divinity is the third major aspect of medieval peoples' understanding of the sacred. The blessings, like scripture, contain different perceptions and interpretations of the bond between human beings and the divine: as a covenant, as an unequal relationship in which God assists an undeserving people, as a freely given gift of grace and salvation by God to the faithful. But the most pervasive and powerful presentation of the human-divine relationship is that of contract. We have seen how often blessings of all categories negotiate the terms of this relationship, promising moral probity and worship in exchange for divine power and protection, especially from the demonic and all the pollutions associated with it. It was this contract that scriptural allusion and song reaffirmed as having precedent in sacred history and therefore validity and legitimacy in the present. Blessings' contractual language suggests that medieval people conceived of their lives and cosmos as being founded not merely on the obligation of thanksgiving to the Creator but on an essential interdependence that inextricably bound the faithful to divinity as it brought mutual benefits to both.

The performance of God's good will is another important component of the medieval idea of the sacred, and in these rituals it is thought to be done most often not by the direct intervention of God or the saints but by angels and archangels. Echoing Flint's description of angels in popular religion as the "chosen activators" of God's will, angels appear in all categories of blessings, although they are most commonly found in blessings of space and persons. Although saints are the most commonly invoked intercessors

---

Maledictions, 68–69). The use of the name of God as an instrument of power in the blessings can be understood as an extension of this ancient belief, inherited by the West through the maledictions of the early Middle Ages. As the essence of the divine, the name of God would be a potent tool for protection and succor from the afflictions of life.

when physical harm threatened recipients of blessings, angels appear more frequently in the blessings as a whole, and in more types of blessings than saints do. This predominance may mean that medieval authors and audiences understood angelic protection to be a more rapid and efficacious type of assistance than that offered by saints; or it could be due to angels' lack of a specific pattern of patronage, such as those possessed by patron saints. Angels, then, represent a "generic" form of sacred power that God could dispatch as needed to protect the faithful.[3] The strong presence of angels in blessings of space suggests that these beings were seen as better long-term guardians than saints, in as much as the angelic protection invoked by such blessings was designed to last for all time.

The final major element of medieval understandings of God and the sacred is their relationship to their opposites, the demonic and profane. Distinguishing between the demonic and the profane can be problematic, as they are often linked in blessings. In such cases pollution is defined both as the general ill will of sinners and other forces abroad in the world and as the evil action of Satan and his demonic host. Blessings present a traditional image of the inimical and incompatible nature of divine and demonic in rituals that purge the demonic through the application of divine power. The deep connection of the sacred with the natural world is indirectly attested to by the diversity of things vulnerable to pollution. Belief that so many things were vulnerable implies that these things could also be inhabited by the power of the divine, and indeed the restoration of that inhabitation is explicitly sought in some blessings. In short, the blessings provide a clear picture of belief in the fundamental opposition between the demonic and the divine, which define each other through both that opposition and through the similarities of their choices of dwelling places.

THE BLESSINGS AND LAY PIETY

The blessings of the medieval church were the products of their times, and as such reflected contemporary religious interests and both lay and clerical attitudes. Furthermore, although blessings were products of their time and therefore reflected common religious concerns, they continued to be

3. Although guardian angels figure in medieval religion from its earliest origins, they were increasingly a part of popular devotion from the fourteenth century onward. There is no evidence, however, that this increase in popularity caused an increase in angels' presence in the blessings. For a full list of blessings in which they appear, see the index.

performed over a long period, and it is likely that changes in piety caused the meaning of blessings to be reinterpreted over time. The piety of the clergy and ecclesiastical hierarchy might be assumed to have been the dominant influence in the composition of liturgical rituals of blessing, but such an assumption ignores the significant elements of the blessings that clearly were inspired by the needs, aspirations, and beliefs of the laity. First, the blessings' use of scripture mirrors both clerical and lay piety's use of scripture and Christian legend as a tool of contextualization by which to identify, empower, and make meaningful the lives of individuals and communities.[4] The same process has been discerned in the study of saints, whose cults and *vitae* have been interpreted as means of making the sacred past of the saints live within believers.[5] The popular cults and legends of particular saints could help craft communal identity, as blessings located the faithful within the shared identity of the chosen people.[6] Conviction in the continuity of this sacred history is evident in the studies of medieval historians who have found in popular notions of time and space beliefs in the eternal presence of

4. Jean-Claude Schmitt, in his superb study of the legend and cult of the holy greyhound, Guinefort, has shown how the rituals and cult of this "saint" could legitimize the existence of the local community by grounding it in the memory of the supernatural events of the greyhound's legend. See Jean-Claude Schmitt, *The Holy Greyhound: Guinefort, Healer of Children since the Thirteenth Century,* trans. Martin Thom (Cambridge: Cambridge University Press, 1983), 1–8. Peter Brown's work on the cult of the saints further supports this idea of Christian scripture and legend as a means of making real and meaningful the sacred stories medieval believers heard. Brown shows how the *Passio* read at saints' feasts could "abolish" time and return worshippers to the time of the martyrs (Brown, *Cult of the Saints,* 80–84). My own interpretation of the importance of scripture and legend in the blessings complements these scholars' understanding of the function of scripture and myth in ritual.

5. Scholars of hagiography, such as Thomas Head and Richard Kieckhefer, have explored how authors of *vitae* sought to connect their communities with the sacred past by associating them with the sacred lives of saints, strengthening the community through that association, and how saints and their believers understood the liturgy to make real and present the sufferings of Christ. See Thomas Head, *Hagiography and the Cult of the Saints: The Diocese of Orleans, 800–1200* (Cambridge: Cambridge University Press, 1990), 100–101; Kieckhefer, *Unquiet Souls,* 89–121. Miri Rubin's study of the liturgical feast of Corpus Christi supports this view, especially in her assertion that this particular feast took its participants back to the time of Christ and made it live again. This is especially clear in her portrait of the ritual reenactment of Christ's burial and resurrection during Holy Week, which grew in popularity as the importance of the Corpus Christi feast waxed. See Rubin, *Corpus Christi,* 334–42, 294.

6. This is supported by Augustine Thompson's study of the rituals and piety of the Italian communes of the twelfth through the fourteenth century.

sacred time within the life of the community—not surprising considering that the church portrayed itself as timeless, embracing all Christians, living and dead, in the past, present, and future.[7] These popular beliefs strongly suggest that the process of contextualization we have observed in blessings is an explication of implicit and accepted lay beliefs about time and the sacred, arguing for the influence of the laity and their piety on these clerically composed rituals.

The view of the relationship between God and the faithful as a contract finds parallels in popular piety. Similar relationships have been found between saints and supplicants in the increasingly popular late medieval practice of death masses and votive prayer, and in late medieval developments in the use and exploitation of sacred power through eucharistic celebration.[8] The contractual exchange of worship and moral rectitude for divine aid could serve many purposes, from healing of the individual to protection

7. Swanson, *Religion and Devotion in Europe*, 15. Emmanuel Le Roy Ladurie's work on the religious life of the village of Montaillou, for example, argues strongly that the laity of this village conceived of their own world as being intimately connected with the time of the saints and scripture, since they saw no disjuncture between the world of the sacred past and the world of their present. Le Roy Ladurie, *Montaillou: The Promised Land of Error*, trans. Barbara Bray (New York: Vintage Books, 1979), 277–88. These notions of sacred time reenacted, or eternally present, mirror my own conclusions, and the blessings' use of scripture appears to fit naturally into the era's use and popular understanding of scripture and liturgy, complementing the other forms of worship and service that kept the human community alive and meaningful.

8. Thomas Head has explored the contractual bond between saints and their petitioning servants, demonstrating the lay expectation that service to the saint would result in divine aid for the faithful, who sincerely prayed to and honored their patron saint. Head, "I Vow Myself to Be Your Servant," 226–27. A similar contractual relationship has been found within the late medieval Christian community, as can be observed in Eamon Duffy's excellent study of late medieval English popular piety. Duffy shows that this form of exchange drove the popular practice of giving of alms to the poor, who were in turn expected to offer up prayers for the benefactor, or for a deceased loved one. Duffy, *Stripping of the Altars*, 360. Miri Rubin presents another example of contract; Rubin draws attention to the creation of the "Charter of Christ," an "articulation of the Passion through Eucharistic symbolism" that used the metaphor of a legal contract to inscribe a parchment with the promise made by Christ's suffering body. In Rubin's words, this metaphorical contract "establishes an exchange of Christ's sacrificed body which brought the hope of redemption for Man's love" (*Corpus Christi*, 306). Rubin also shows how, in the feast, sacred power could become negotiable and exchangeable for worldly power (243–71). Thus the picture of human-divine relations painted in my analysis of blessings of space confirms scholarship in other areas of popular medieval religious experience, and we can see how blessings reflect the piety of both the laity and clerical authors.

of the community. This practice had many parallels in other aspects of medieval devotion: for example, the Third Orders, guilds, and confraternities, which developed as part of the high medieval trend toward a more penitential spirituality, provided for their members mutual support and a contractual exchange of reciprocal benefits, that is, prayer and donations in exchange for a good funeral, postmortem prayers, and remembrance.[9] Indeed, in the words of one scholar, this element of contract was built into the medieval religious paradigm:

> For most people, hope of ultimate success [of salvation] had to lie in some degree of free will, of being able to strike a bargain with God. Here again the emphasis lay on action, on personal commitment—but with some dangers. Too much stress on personal responsibility, or on the possibility of a contractual relationship between the individual and God based on the former's actions and obligating God to grant salvation smacked of the heresy of the Pelagians: yet some suggestion of such Pelagianism was all but unavoidable in a spiritual climate which emphasized works as a means to salvation.[10]

This argument finds support in a charming story of a contract seemingly broken, told in a recent study of the piety of citizens of the Italian communes: "When Sibyllina Biscossi got no results from her prayers to Saint Dominic to restore her eyesight, she berated the saint: 'Give me back those prayers and praises I offered to you for no purpose!' The saint got the message and restored Sibyllina's sight posthaste."[11] One wonders what a contemporary theologian would make of such a story, but clearly it would have struck a chord with all who labored in hope of a cure from a pilgrimage or shrine, especially for those who left disappointed.

Blessings, unlike the above exchange or the practice of magic, did not claim to be able to compel God to act, except, perhaps, in the controversial field of ordeals. The contract in blessings is based on sincerity, service, worship, and devotion, all of which fit perfectly into orthodox Christian doctrine and what Eamon Duffy has cogently dubbed "lay Christianity," and Augus-

9. Swanson, *Religion and Devotion in Europe*, 113–14. Similar arrangements existed, for example, between the growing number of hermits in the high and late Middle Ages and local communities that supported them in exchange for the holy person's prayers. Ibid., 130.

10. Ibid., 30.

11. Thompson, *Cities of God*, 202, quoting Tomasso of Bossolasco, *Vita* [*B. Sibyllinae Papaiensis*], *AS* 9 (March 3), 1.3, p. 68: Resititue mihi orations meas et laudes aliaque quae tibi obtuli frusta!

tine Thompson has persuasively argued for the everyday piety of ordinary Christians from all levels of society. And, finally, the blessings' emphasis on protecting the community complements previous scholars' description of the liturgy of the Mass as a means of regulating social relations, effecting reconciliation, defining communal identity, and protecting that identity and communal integrity.[12]

As a contractual understanding of blessings is clearly supported by the historiography of popular piety, so too is characterizing these rituals as responsive to lay needs, beliefs, fears, and desires. Festal liturgies such as Corpus Christi, the cult of saints, and collections of miracle stories have been presented convincingly as ways that the church met the needs and concerns of the laity.[13] The more questionable elements of blessings find parallels in a wide variety of purely popular, apotropaic gestures and incantations that recent scholarship has rescued from the condemnation of early studies, which judged such activities as quasi-pagan or worse, by effectively presenting them as flowing from traditional, legitimate Christian belief and practice.[14] The same may be said for blessings, especially for those featuring ad-

12. John Bossy has argued convincingly that the medieval Mass served numerous social functions for its participants, two of the most significant being the division of the community from its enemies and the binding of that community through social reconciliation and ties of shared belief and experience. Bossy, "Mass as a Social Institution," 37–50. The blessings of ordeals are a prime example of this process at work outside the Mass, for they serve the same purpose of creating community identity and solidarity, much like blessings in times of war and blessings of agriculture. Blessings seeking to divine truth through ritualized miracles drew the faithful together to vindicate the innocent, draw forth confession and penitence from the guilty, and cast out the unrepentant sinner.

13. Rubin, *Corpus Christi,* 215, 219, 223–24; Thomas, *Decline of Magic,* 29–32. Other scholars have demonstrated that medieval saints and their miracles were prized for their practical utilitarian value in meeting the needs of communities and individuals. In the words of Augustine Thompson, for the laity, "the surest holiness was ordinary and useful" (*Cities of God,* 191–93). See also Aviad Kleinberg, *Prophets in Their Own Country* (Chicago: University of Chicago Press, 1992), 126–48; Ronald Finucane, *Miracles and Pilgrims: Popular Beliefs in Medieval England* (Totowa, N.J.: Palgrave Macmillan, 1977), 59–99; and Thomas, *Decline of Magic,* 29–32.

14. Duffy, *Stripping of the Altars,* 260–98, esp. 283. The blessings for healing and recovery are a good example of this process, for while they incorporate adjurations that read like a conjuring spell, these adjurations all invoke beings or elements that fit perfectly into the hierarchy of the Christian cosmos. These adjurations are accompanied by aspersion, an ancient and acceptable ritual method for purifying people, places, and things for Christian use. And even the most thaumaturgical activity found in the blessings, the ritualized imitation of the healing of the blind man at Siloh, is nothing but a reenactment of sacred history, drawing its power not from the gestures and words in and of themselves (as in the case of magical spells), but from

jurations and conjurations, which draw extensively on Christian images and cosmology to effect their purpose. Thus blessings fit well into the economy of sacred power found throughout medieval religion, a faith that responded to the needs and beliefs of the laity with ritual, story, and worship.

Blessings were important in the religious lives of the laity, and their development in the twelfth through fourteenth centuries suggests that they gained in popularity alongside the rise of "personalized religion" in this era. Peter the Chanter could suggest in the twelfth century that standing devoutly and attentively was the limit for the laity in terms of participating in the liturgical life of the church, but such a suggestion was out of touch with a laity who sought to deepen their experience of religion.[15] This trend was driven by increasing lay desires to associate with the monastic spiritual elites within the church, an increasing desire for a personal experience in this world of "authentic" Christian life, and a drive to achieve the *vita apostolica* through preaching and poverty.[16] The new definition of the search for Christ in *this* world reduced the significance of retreat from the world as a benchmark of piety.[17] Blessings, especially those of persons, harmonize with this trend toward personalized religion; indeed, the increasing popularity of formal re-

---

the numinous power of Jesus, the original author of this miracle and the font and origin of all medieval blessings' power. The laity knew, for example, that Christ's words could put Satan to flight, and that the Ave Maria could sanctify even a drink in the local tavern, and this was not considered magic. See Trexler, *Christian at Prayer*, 35, and Thompson, *Cities of God*, 352–54.

15. Thompson, *Cities of God*, 244, citing Peter the Chanter, *De oratione et specibus illius;* Trexler, *Christian at Prayer*, 185. Other conclusions than that the laity were and should be passive and inert in liturgical activities can be seen as valid through their power to demand votive masses from the clergy, who were obligated to provide them, and in examples of pious laymen such as Ranieri of Pisa, who had learned to read and who during Mass read from a Psalter and even designed his own custom litany of saints to recite during the service. Thompson, *Cities of God*, 244–48.

16. Vauchez, *Spirituality of the Medieval West*, 65–74. Vauchez argues that the eleventh- and twelfth-century laity embraced the flowering of personalized religion, such as pilgrimage, crusading, lay brotherhood, and confraternities, as a way to experience the sacred in this world and in their subordinate station within the church. Thompson's study of the communes also shows that laypeople's prayerbooks from the later thirteenth and early fourteenth centuries had general characteristics in line with this new impulse in religion: prayers that tend toward the penitential, focusing especially on the Cross and repentance of sin; prayers and hymns to the Virgin, especially in women's books; litanies of saints; and very occasionally prayers for special protection or against evils. All of these, despite their lay associations, are very theologically "correct." Thompson, *Cities of God*, 363–67.

17. Swanson, *Religion and Devotion in Europe*, 11.

ligious rituals of dubbing knights and making pilgrims is one of the main points of evidence cited by scholars as proof of the movement of the laity toward experiencing the religious life in their own station, and thus we can conclude that the composition of these blessings was influenced, if not solely controlled, by trends in the lay piety of the era.[18]

Blessings fit into the laity's desire for spiritual empowerment, as they provided the ritual vehicle by which an individual could move closer to God without leaving the secular world deplored by traditional monastic spirituality, and (especially in the case of ordeals) could encourage the saving grace of confession and penance in those guilty of crimes against the Christian community.[19] The positive view of life in the world inherent in lay move-

18. Vauchez in particular argues that from the late eleventh century to the early thirteenth the laity strove most vigorously toward experiencing "authentic Christianity" in this world, and it is also during this period that the greatest number of dubbing rituals and pilgrim blessings were composed (see index, and Vauchez, *Spirituality of the Medieval West*, 75–81). The laity were also elevated in status by the ruling of the Fourth Lateran Council of 1215, which stated that even married layperson could merit salvation and eternal life: "For not only virgins and the continent but also married persons find favor with God by right faith and good actions and deserve to attain to eternal blessedness" (Norman P. Tanner, ed. and trans., "Fourth Lateran—1215," in *Decrees of the Ecumenical Councils* [Washington, D.C.: The Catholic University of America Press, 1990], 1:231). This was a major turning point for a group that had previously been seen as hopelessly mired in superstition and doomed to damnation by the "carnal" life from which the exalted monastic orders had turned away (Swanson, *Religion and Devotion in Europe*, 23). Despite this commendation of married life, there was no significant change in the number of blessings for the married home and wedding bed of newlyweds after the Fourth Lateran, probably because such rituals were already well established in the canon of medieval blessings and needed no promotion or expansion.

19. This is a surprising parallel to nearly contemporaneous beliefs of the high medieval penitential movement. That movement, typically represented by the fourteenth-century Italian Bianchi, stressed communal and public confession and penitence as essential in the process of salvation. See Vauchez, *Spirituality of the Medieval West*, 75–80, 88–100; Swanson, *Religion and Devotion in Europe*, 102–6, 108–16; and Daniel Ethan Bornstein, *The Bianchi of 1399: Popular Devotion in Late Medieval Italy* (Ithaca: Cornell University Press, 1993), 144–46. But the historiography of ordeals has usually regarded the penitential movement as typical of the post–Fourth Lateran church, which rejected clerical performance of ordeals and mandated annual confession and penance for the laity. The argument is best represented by Bartlett, who asserts that faith in confession and penance proved incompatible with faith in the ordeal, for if a contrite person confessed and did penance, then the ordeal could not determine her guilt for the crime in question, as God had already forgiven the sinner. Bartlett argues that the disappearance of the ordeal in twelfth- and thirteenth-century courts was in part the result of an increasingly fine distinction made between sin and crime, the former being interior and considered God's concern, the latter including visible offenses punishable by human justice.

ments is present in blessings whose positive perspective on the natural and social world diverges sharply from the Augustinian perspective of the monastic orders, which devalued life in this world in favor of renunciation and preparation for the next life. This perspective had a strong influence on medieval religious movements, both elite and popular. The most noticeable in the high and late Middle Ages are the monastic reform movements of the tenth through twelfth centuries and the penitential movement of the twelfth and later centuries. The Cluniac monastic order that flowered in the tenth and eleventh centuries placed heavy emphasis on contempt for the world, that is, for traditional secular values and a life not exclusively dedicated to God.[20] This movement was, according to Vauchez, a major factor in marginalizing the laity, whose occupations and social status forbade them active participation in the ascetic renunciation of monks.[21] Despite this marginalization, Vauchez argues that the laity vigorously attempted to associate themselves with the "angelic" monks of Cluny, and later Cîteaux, through service and lay brotherhood. The penitential movement of the twelfth and thirteenth centuries was another lay attempt to arrive at greater contact with God through imitation of his chosen monks. Taking the vows of a crusader, joining the military orders, belonging to lay confraternities, and adopting mendicancy all were ways the laity sought the pious, ascetic renunciation of worldly values while living in the world outside the monastery.

While the blessings demonstrate a concern with the spirit characteristic of the Augustinian perspective treasured by monks and penitents, they also clearly prize domestic prosperity, happiness, material comfort, and earthly

This created an attitude in many clerics that made it difficult to allow ordeals to be performed: "God's verdict was heard in confession and absolution, supervised by the priest, alone with the sinner in the church, not in the secular publicity of the courts. One form of priestly power, the management of the ordeal, would have to be sacrificed to another form, the authority of the confessional" (Bartlett, *Trial by Fire and Water*, 80–81). Blessings composed for ordeals, however, do not support such a sharp break between faith in confession and faith in the ordeal. Ordeal blessings as early as the eleventh and twelfth centuries sought to elicit sincere confession and penance from the guilty so that both the body and the soul of the criminal might be saved from death and damnation; in this, they reflect both the spiritual concerns of liturgical authors and the material concerns of the lay community, while ignoring the 1215 prohibition.

20. Rafaello Morghen, "Monastic Reform and Cluniac Spirituality," in *Cluniac Monasticism in the Central Middle Ages,* ed. Noreen Hunt (London: Macmillan, 1971), 18, 20, 28. Late medieval hagiography also shared this perspective. See Kieckhefer, *Unquiet Souls,* 1–15.

21. Vauchez, *Spirituality of Medieval West,* 38–43.

renown, worldly values that are not shunned but rather are sought by the invocation of divine power through ritual and prayer. As these rituals were composed for the benefit of both clergy and laity, it is reasonable to conclude that the Augustinian perspective of a segment of the regular and secular clergy does not tell the whole story of popular piety in the high and late Middle Ages. Rather, the blessings suggest that the lay piety of this era had a more positive understanding of the life of the Christian in this world, embracing elements of both secular and sacred life to produce a meaningful spiritual existence. Blessings sought the rewards of worldly life, namely, material prosperity and domestic happiness, and in this they reflect priorities and values more familiar to the medieval laity than to the monastic and ecclesiastical hierarchy of the medieval church.

While the blessings are replete with traditional images of God as father, light, and lord over a celestial court, they also raise questions about medieval understandings of the divine.[22] Scholars are divided over the conviction

22. Medieval literature and liturgy are replete with traditional images of divinity. For some examples of the blessings' congruence with these images, see Paschal Baumstein, "Benedict's God and the Monk's God," *Cistercian Studies* 22 (1987): 304–15. Baumstein shows how St. Benedict and his later followers perceived God as both father and a source of light. Both images appear in the blessings of persons, places, and things, which suggests that these rituals drew not only on popular images of the divine but also on perceptions fostered by the elite spirituality of the cloister. The perception of God as lord and monarch finds support, too, among period documents and in modern historiography. The ordeal's portrayal of God as king of kings, for example, which appears in tenth- and eleventh-century texts, and as a just judge in ninth-, eleventh-, and twelfth-century texts, harmonizes with Vauchez's argument that God was understood through feudal modalities during the tenth and eleventh centuries, i.e., God was depicted as a lord and justice giver, a mirror of the functions and status of the feudal landlord (Vauchez, *Laity in the Middle Ages*, 3–26; *Spirituality of the Medieval West*, 38–61). A similar connection between secular forms of governance and divinity is found in Cistercian monastic writings of the eleventh and twelfth centuries studied by Martha Newman. Inverting Vauchez's argument, Newman argues that the Cistercians used the idea that secular power has a divine source to advocate merciful rule by secular lords and kings and to stress that good rulers should use their power to serve the needs of the church. A comparable transformation was sought by Cistercian authors who desired to reform the knightly order into warriors who served the church, and who employed war against the enemies of the church to achieve a personal transformation into penitent servants of Christ (Newman, *Boundaries of Charity*, 177–80, 182). Cluniac monks in the tenth century pursued a similar strategy, presenting images of ideal rulers and knights who served the will of churchmen and fought only to protect the poor and powerless as a defense against rapacious feudal strongmen who threatened their survival and independence. See Barbara Rosenwein, *Rhinoceros Bound: Cluny in the Tenth Century* (Philadelphia: University of Pennsylvania Press, 1982), 57–83. The blessings' portrait of God, while

and certitude of the faith of the period. Vauchez argues that medieval faith, especially of the thirteenth and early fourteenth centuries, was a faith without doubt, founded on unshakeable confidence in the goodness and power of God to protect his faithful.[23] But Richard Swanson presents a convincing image of the faith in which "medieval Christianity was incessantly fluid and evolving, often uncertain, unwilling to be certain, and plagued with doctrinal pluralism approaching individualism."[24] Studies of festal liturgies and saints' *vitae* have shown how the miracle stories and other elements of these sources stress the reliability of God, and the validity of trust in God to work miracles for the righteous.[25] On the surface this emphasis on divine reliability appears to be a sign of steadfast belief, but upon closer examination it appears more likely to be a deliberate attempt to correct the errant and affirm the doubtful in their faith, another manifestation of the ambiguity and anxiety about God's benevolence that we see in the blessings. These admonitions and assurances would be unnecessary for authors convinced of their audiences' unswerving faith, but for authors who saw doubt in their congregations or themselves, such assurances would be comforting and necessary.

The ambiguous vision of God as a divinity who must incessantly be reminded of his past beneficence to the faithful, and encouraged to continue that beneficence in the present, is found in blessings of all kinds and periods, and is supported by outside studies of village communities and their *mentalité*, which was often uncertain that God had control over natural events, seeing many events as springing from Satan or his demonic minions.[26] That blessings diverge from orthodox piety's understanding of divinity as omnipotent but fall neatly into place beside known popular beliefs and popular

---

reflecting images known to a medieval audience, is nevertheless a part of the same process of depicting divinity as the font and archetype of good lordship, structuring and garbing the ineffable divine in terms familiar to medieval audiences of all ranks.

23. Vauchez, *Laity in the Middle Ages*, 85–93, esp. 90.

24. Swanson, *Religion and Devotion in Europe*, 18. Swanson's point is well taken, especially when we consider the increase in lay involvement in devotional activities, and the active role Thompson has shown that the laity played in the liturgy itself, at least in the Italian communes. See Thompson, *Cities of God*, 239–40, 343–79.

25. Rubin, *Corpus Christi*, 112–13. Rubin argues in particular that divine intervention was eminently reliable when it involved the Eucharist, the most holy of the Christian sacraments.

26. Le Roy Ladurie, *Montaillou*, 277–88. This uncertainty about God's control over the natural world, and thus over people's lives, and God's possible inability to prevent disaster, parallels the uncertainty of the blessings, which could not fully entrust the survival of their recipients to God without ritually prompting God to do his duty.

forms of devotional liturgy and literature is a powerful argument for the significant influence of lay piety on shaping the content and aims of these clerically composed rituals.

Some substantial characteristics of high and late medieval popular piety, however, do not appear to have affected the content of these blessings. One such characteristic is the image of Christ. Scholars such as Vauchez and Swanson have pointed out how high medieval images of Christ, both textual and artistic, focused on Christ's glorious humanity, but in the wake of the disturbances of the fourteenth century this emphasis shifted to depicting Christ as a "man of sorrows" and stressing the agonies of Jesus in the Passion. A similar shift in the blessings' descriptions of Christ would be a strong indicator of the responsiveness of these rituals to popular piety. But no such trend presents itself clearly. Only rituals of the thirteenth century or later mention Christ's humanity, and only three of all the rituals we have examined. Blessings that stress the Passion of Christ appear as early as the ninth century; only two of the twelve blessings that specifically mention Christ's Passion date to the thirteenth century or later. Therefore, we must conclude that popular devotional images and ideas of Christ played only a limited role at most in shaping the texts of these rituals. Blessings seem rather to have relied heavily on addressing God the Father in his role as Creator, Lord, Healer, and Savior, with the actual life and person of Christ playing an essential but secondary role.

We can also use the increasing popularity of Marian devotions in the high and later Middle Ages to measure the responsiveness of the blessings to lay piety. Mary as blessed Virgin and mother of God appears in blessings of the eighth to twelfth centuries and fourteenth to sixteenth centuries. The evidence does not, however, clearly demonstrate the growing importance of Mary as an intercessor. Of the thirteen blessings that mention Mary, six of them occur in or before the eleventh century, two belong to the twelfth, one to the fourteenth, three to the fifteenth, and one to the sixteenth century. While fifteenth-century rituals show a markedly greater use of Mary, the increase does not seem significant enough to ignore the even greater presence of the Virgin in the tenth and eleventh centuries. From this evidence we may only confirm with certainty the obvious importance of Mary as an intercessor and conclude that changes in Marian devotions played only a minor role in the composition and content of blessings.

While the preceding two issues suggest the limitations of lay piety's influence on the blessings, the survival of these blessings does indicate that they continued to be both a significant and sought-after form of ritual. This is evident from a brief examination of the number of blessings produced throughout our period. A survey of critical editions of early sacramentaries, pontificals, benedictionals, and missals shows that there could be great variety in how many blessings were included in early and high medieval liturgical texts. The Egbert pontifical (mid-tenth century) contains eleven extrasacramental blessings, its contemporary the Leofric missal has twenty-four such blessings, the benedictional of Archbishop Robert of Jumièges (late tenth century) has only two blessings, and the Romano-Germanic pontifical has fifty-five blessings.[27] This brief quantitative survey shows the popularity of blessings, and further analysis is useful for judging the effect of ecclesiastical theology on these rituals. If we posit that an Augustinian spirituality and theology of the ecclesiastical hierarchy was dominant in influencing blessings' content, then the concern of twelfth- and thirteenth-century sacramental theology to distinguish the canonical seven sacraments from noncanonical benedictions, and to assign to the latter the inferior status of sacramentals, can reasonably be expected to have had an impact on the popularity of such rituals in liturgical books of the period. But the evidence of quantitative analysis argues against this assumption: as we showed above, early texts varied wildly in the number of blessings included, peaking in number in the Romano-Germanic pontifical and then undergoing a decline in eleventh-century books such as the missal of Robert of Jumièges (thirteen blessings) and the Canterbury benedictional (five rituals), and in the RP12th (twelve blessings). Thus, if a pattern of decline can be found, it predates the revolution in sacramental theology. Indeed, although only six extrasacramental blessings were included in the thirteenth-century PRC, the later PWD expands the twelfth-century Roman pontifical's twelve relevant blessings to nineteen. This survey suggests that the popularity of blessings among liturgical authors and lay audiences was little touched by the fine theological distinctions of monastic and clerical theologians, and although such blessings decline in number after the early Middle Ages, they nonetheless remain a vibrant part of popular devotion until the end of the medieval period.

The thematic elements and quantitative production of blessings do not,

---

27. For all of these texts, see chapter 1 and the discussions of their rituals in chapters 2 through 4, and the bibliography.

however, tell the whole story of the relationship between blessings and lay piety. Blessings were inescapably the product of their times, but the meaning of those rituals from one generation to the next assuredly changed as the historical and religious context changed. A brief survey of the various categories of blessing studied in the preceding chapters reveals that change over time was real and significant in interpreting blessings. The first notable change is found in blessings for houses and the wedding bed. Blessings for domestic space throughout our period focused on the physical protection of the inhabitants, but little attention was paid to questions of salvation in the earliest of rites. Following the decree of Fourth Lateran Council on the possibility of salvation for the married, however, we can detect a slow change in attitudes toward the meaning of domestic space and the blessings used to consecrate it. This is most evident in a fifteenth-century blessing of a wedding bed in which the bed is no longer described as simply a safe haven for the couple but as a place in which salvation could legitimately be sought: God is implored to "guard your servants resting in this bed from all the fantastic illusions of demons; guard them while they pass the night, so that sleeping they might meditate on your precepts and they might perceive you through sleep."[28] While a desire that prayers be heard had appeared in early blessings of such space, this later ritual clearly defines the nuptial bed, the central space for the pursuit of righteous Christian union, as properly reserved to the service of God. This change, I would argue, reflects a fundamental shift in the laity's self-image, so that a ritual once orientated toward survival and prosperity now confirmed the possibility of salvation within marriage for the laity.

The reinterpretation of blessings is also evident in the later ritual consecrations of cemeteries. The blessings of the eleventh and twelfth centuries were concerned primarily with creating a pure and safe haven in which the dead could await judgment and paradise. From the time in which these blessings were composed until the time of William Durandus's ritual for blessing a cemetery, however, lay religion began to transform its notion of death, the dead, and judgment. The clearest signs of this transformation

---

28. Franz, 2:182: custodi famulos tuos in hoc lecto quiescentes ab omnibus fantasticis demonum illusionibus; custodi eos vigilantes, ut in preceptis tuis meditentur dormientes et te per soporem senciant. This text is from BAV Pal. lat. 501. Earlier blessings that display concern for the answering of prayers include the *RGP*'s "Another Blessing of a House" and the *PWD*'s "Concerning the Blessing of a House."

come with the evolution, during the thirteenth century, of purgatory as a real and fearsome place within the Christian cosmos and the dramatic rise in popularity of postmortem prayer, designed to erase the dead's sins and speed them on their way through purgatory. Sin is a minor element in early cemetery blessings, mentioned only in terms of the remission of sin earned through Jesus' sacrifice on the Cross. But at the end of the thirteenth century William Durandus's blessing expands this issue enormously by focusing thrice upon the absolution of sin for those interred in the cemetery:

> absolved from the bonds of sins and returned into eternal felicity and numbered in the assemblage of saints, may they find you, who are eternal life, good and merciful . . . Lord, appoint your holy angel a guardian for this cemetery and absolve the souls of them whose bodies are buried here in you from all the chains of sins, so that they may be happy without end in you always with your saints. . . . Give, we ask, the pardon of sins for the souls of your faithful resting here in you, so that this host of salvation may be the remedy and rest of their souls and bodies.[29]

This new emphasis on absolution from sins that would entangle one in purgatory, I contend, reflects the growing anxiety of the laity to save themselves and their loved ones from the pains of that dim place. Blessings of cemeteries now meant more than simple protection from roving demons and other dangers; now these rituals were another means by which to escape punishment in the next life, a change that undoubtedly contributed to the persistence of such rituals down to the end of the Middle Ages.

We have already seen how the content and meaning of reconciliations of violated churches and cemeteries responded to the rise of heretical movements that attacked belief in sacred ground and ritual, but such an evolving relationship of meaning and context is not unique to spatial blessings. Blessings of crusaders manifest changes over time that suggest that the meaning of the blessing changed for audience and celebrant. Early crusade blessings stress the granting of bodily protection and victory to recipients of the Cross, but as the centuries passed this emphasis was joined by a concern

29. *PWD (ordo 2.5.21, 24, 25):* a peccatorum nexibus absoluti et eterne felicitati redditi et sanctorum cetibus annumerati, te, qui es vita eterna, benignum et misericordem . . . domine, angelum tuum sanctum deputa custodem et quorum quarumque corpora in te hic sepelientur animas eorum ab omnibus absolve vinculis delictorum, ut in te semper cum sanctis tuis sine fine letentur. . . . Da, quesumus, fidelium tuorum animabus hic in te quiescentibus veniam peccatorum, ut hec salutaris hostia sit remedium et requies animarum eorum et corporum.

with the health of the soul. The pontifical of Durandus requests safety and defense for bodies and souls, but it also requests the multiplication of "spiritual gifts," the granting of absolution for sins and the imparting of grace, so that "after the completed journey, you [the crusader] may be able to return to us safe and corrected."[30] These benefits, along with an emphasis on service to and sacrifice for the church, appear later in the fifteenth-century blessing "For Those Crossing over [the Sea] against the Turk," from Kremsmünster, which also explicitly requests avoidance of the pains of purgatory.[31]

This change in crusade blessings, especially concerning purgatory, parallels the change of meaning we first perceived in the blessings of cemeteries from the late thirteenth century: rituals first intended for protection from hostile forces and dangers metamorphose into rituals for personal salvation and spiritual growth, a change brought about by a change in lay religion that increasingly concerned itself with personal spirituality and penitence.[32] The blessings of crusaders from the end of the medieval period, notably Meissen's "[Blessing] Made for Affixing the Sign of the Cross," from the sixteenth century, add to this new meaning a new foe—heretics who threaten the unity of the church and the survival of the true faith—which further changes the meaning of these rituals. Aimed outward, early crusade blessings targeted infidels, thrusting outward the boundaries of Christendom; later blessings aimed inward and thus became a tool not of expansion but of consolidation, control, and defense. The effect of such a change in orientation on the meaning of crusader blessings is debatable. I would argue that it probably contributed to a greater sense among the laity that crusader blessings were understood as yet another weapon in the arsenal of rituals that protected the Christian community from its enemies, both natural and supernatural.

A related category of blessings, the ritual dubbing of knights, further demonstrates that changing contexts meant changing meaning for blessings and their participants. As discussed in chapter 3, the earliest blessings for knights and their equipment were probably designed for kings or powerful local nobles. These early rituals emphasized the importance for rulers of protecting the weak and powerless, notably widows and orphans, and the

30. *PWD* (*ordo* 2.30.3).

31. Franz, 2:306.

32. This also can be seen as the success of efforts by eleventh- and twelfth-century Cistercian writers to promote war in the service of the church as a process of penitence and spiritual growth. See Newman, *Boundaries of Charity*, 183–90.

church at large from external enemies, such as the pagan Viking raiders of the ninth and tenth centuries.[33] There was also, naturally, a strong desire for victory for the defenders of the church. But this somewhat worldly agenda began to change subtly in the rituals of the thirteenth century, when the emphasis on communal protection began to include a concern for more spiritual issues, notably the salvation of the individual knight.[34] This is most evident in Durandus's pontifical, in which the celebrant commands, "Knight, be peaceful, steadfast, faithful, and devoted to God. . . . You will have awakened from the sleep of evil and stay awake in the faith of Christ and worthy renown."[35] This change is noteworthy in that it parallels the goal, described by Martha Newman, of Cistercian authors of the twelfth century who sought to convert war in the service of the church into "a form of penance through which warriors learned to control their wills and progress toward their salvation."[36] These monks argued that church-sanctioned warfare's goal was more inward than outward, part of a process of personal penitence that focused the individual's attention on the humanity and sacrifice of Christ and encouraged the warrior to undergo the same interior changes in secular life that he could achieve (albeit in a higher form) if he joined a monastery.[37] That knightly blessings manifest a similar attitude toward the purpose and practice of knighthood indicates that, rather than being merely a tool by which clerics sought to control the knightly class, dubbing blessings became to aspiring knights both a rite of passage into a new social status and a means by which to convert their profession into their salvation. As the knightly class evolved in the high Middle Ages, so too did their rituals, shifting from nominally Christian rituals for victory and defense into rituals that meant the beginning of both knighthood and the knight's quest for salvation.

Finally, blessings for ordeals reveal that changes in lay religion continued to influence the content and meaning of rituals, even when those rituals were condemned by the ecclesiastical hierarchy. Three ordeal blessings, two involving bread and cheese and a third a judicial duel, demonstrate that in the ab-

33. For example, see the *RGP*'s "Blessing of a Newly Girded Sword" and the Besançon pontifical's "Blessing of a Sword." A similar emphasis can be found in the *PWD*'s "Blessing of Armor."

34. See the thirteenth-century "*Ordo* for Arming the Defenders of the Church."

35. *PWD* 449–50 (*ordo* 1.28.10–11).

36. Newman, *Boundaries of Charity,* 182.

37. Ibid., 183.

sence of official sanction such rituals were adapted to fit in with independent developments in lay piety. As I demonstrated in the preceding chapter, ordeal blessings often expressed a desire for confession and penitence from the guilty. Ordeals composed after the 1215 ban on clerical participation express a desire for the spiritual rectitude and personal salvation of the accused: for example, prior to a duel the priest called on God to grant the fighter "right faith, firm hope, steadfastness of heart, strength of body," and encouraged the fighter to "hope in the Lord and do good and refuse to forget all his retributions."[38] Although a concern for salvation was always expressed in some form in early ordeals, it is only in these late rituals that this desire for proper faith and good deeds is clearly present. This suggests that the changes in late medieval lay religion, namely, the rise of postmortem prayer and masses, and the value placed upon confession and good works in atoning for venial sin, influenced the understanding of ordeals. Condemned by the ecclesiastical hierarchy, ordeal blessings continued to be composed, but they seem to have been understood in a new light by authors and perhaps audiences as well: rather than a mere display of civic justice, the ordeal and duel became a devotional opportunity to advance along one's own path to righteousness and salvation. In this, the ordeals and the duel surpass the ecclesiastical restriction set by the Fourth Lateran Council, proving that blessings continued to be adopted and adapted by late medieval people whose need determined the both the content and the meaning of their rituals.

ANTHROPOLOGICAL THEORY OF RITUAL
AND THE MEDIEVAL BLESSING

Throughout this study I have made occasional recourse to the theorists and paradigms of anthropology, particular the evolving discipline of ritual theory, to make sense of the meanings behind the blessings. In this conclusion I would like to highlight the relevance of several theorists' paradigms of ritual as particularly helpful in analyzing these often formulaic liturgical texts. The first is the early phenomenologist Rudolph Otto. His structured

38. See the York manual's "Blessing of a Buckler and Staff for Those Advancing to a Duel" and Vyssi Brod's "Remedy against Theft," both fifteenth-century blessings; Franz, 2:364–65, 389–90. It is interesting that later ordeals seem to embrace more martial imagery to express their purpose than earlier rituals did. This may be a sign that, following the Fourth Lateran Council, nonviolent ordeals adopted the language of the more acceptable judicial duels, which were not addressed by the council.

schema of how human beings relate to the sacred situates many isolated elements of medieval Christian blessings in a context of universal human experience, making it a valuable tool for grasping the meaning that lies buried under the *topos* and formulas of medieval liturgical texts.[39] Otto's collection of sensations felt in the presence of the numinous and the attributes ascribed to the divine find many parallels in the blessings. The most obvious is found in blessing prayers addressed to God in which the unworthiness and dependence of humanity upon God is stressed, a relationship thoughtfully described by Otto's "dependence sense."[40] This perception is not original to medieval Christianity, being found in both the Old and New Testaments, but is nevertheless an important element of the medieval understanding of divinity. The role of the *numen*, as Otto dubbed it, as creator of all nature and living things is also found repeatedly throughout blessings, from blessings of crops to ordeal blessings, a manifestation of the "creature consciousness" that Otto describes.[41]

The second theorist of relevance is Ronald Grimes, whose nuanced definition of ritual includes the elements of ceremony and liturgy, which I see as essential to understanding medieval blessings. For Grimes, ceremony was a symbolic drama that creates communal and individual identity (and often does so in competitive opposition to outsiders), holds power, and often masks social contradictions and ambiguities. Medieval blessings exhibit many of these qualities. Symbolic drama may be seen, for example, in eye blessings' imitation of the healing of the blind by Jesus, a potent dramatic and symbolic act. Blessings of pilgrims and knights are also symbolic dramas, complete with items and insignia, performed not only for the recipients but also for the community, which must now accept the new social status of the blessed. We have seen, too, how blessings of knights, war, and ordeals create an "us-versus-them" mindset by opposing the Christian community to both enemy outsiders and renegade community members. The very nature of blessings as rituals that seek access to divine power for the purpose of addressing daily needs meets the third qualification required by Grimes's definition of ceremony.[42]

Liturgy, another component of ritual as defined by Grimes, has three essential qualities, according to Grimes: liturgy performs an act of cosmic ne-

---

39. For a full discussion of Otto's theory, see the introduction.
40. Otto, *Idea of the Holy*, 8–11.   41. Ibid.
42. Grimes, *Beginnings in Ritual Studies*, 48.

cessity, guaranteeing the continuance of the cosmos accepted by the partici-pants in a ritual; liturgy emphasizes the connection of people to a higher reality, to "things as they really are" and not simply as they appear to be; and liturgy serves as an essential element in making the sacred history of a peo-ple endure and remain meaningful. The second and the third qualities clear-ly derive from previous ritual theory discussed in the notes to this work, so I will confine my comments here to discussing liturgy as an act of cosmic necessity. While no blessing warns that its absence will bring about some catastrophic or apocalyptic punishment of the church, the process of ritu-al negotiation we have observed in blessings contains within itself a neces-sity born of its own failure: improper worship or insincerity doomed these rituals to failure, and their failure exposed the individual and community to natural and supernatural dangers. That these dangers were considered real and widespread is obvious from the variety and complexity of blessings; the perceived necessity of blessings to the survival of the Christian community is equally evident from the frequency with which they were demanded by the laity. As part of the medieval liturgy, blessings were definitely of cosmic *im-portance* for the bond they created between humanity and God, but we can-not wholeheartedly embrace Grimes's assertion that all liturgy is cosmically *necessary* unless we view the cosmos in terms of the community itself—un-less, that is, we see the community *as* the cosmos.

Otto and Mircea Eliade's work provides a sound structure by which to understand blessings as rituals that tapped into God's immanent power within the created world and used that power to enrich and validate the lives of individuals and communities by connecting them with the "true being" so prominent in Eliade's explanation of myth and ritual.[43] Eliade's stress on the re-creation of mythic stories as the heart of rituals, and the means by which people connect their own lives to sacred history and all its power, laid the groundwork for the theories of later scholars such as Mary Douglas and Clifford Geertz on the sacred past in ritual. The importance of this theme, which manifests itself throughout the blessings' use of scripture and Chris-tian legend, to various scholars of ritual theory demonstrates two things: first, that the similarities between modern and medieval religion are real, and that the study of modern ritual theory, particularly phenomenology, can help us to use these similarities to expand our understanding of Christian

43. Eliade, *Sacred and Profane*, 8–65.

blessing; and second, that this theory provides a good way for historians to understand seemingly rote recitations of scripture and Christian legend as distinctly meaningful efforts to connect the needs of this world, of this life, to the greater story of God's redemption of the human race.

FINAL THOUGHTS

Throughout the course of this study, I have endeavored to demonstrate that the liturgical blessings of the medieval church were rituals complex in both content and meaning, and that although they were composed by clerical authors, they responded to and reflected the piety of the laypeople who frequently received such blessings. In the course of this demonstration we have seen how the blessings present a distinct and sometimes controversial perception of the divine, the sacred, and humanity's relationship to divine power. Founded on a deep conviction of the importance of divinity in *this* life, and the profound connection of *this* world to the sacred world, medieval blessings sought the divine as a source of power, protection, solace, and certainty for a laity more concerned with survival than with theological abstractions. The texts of these rituals show how desperate the laity and celebrants were to ensure God's protection, and how anxious they were that the divine not forget them in their times of need.

But, as we have also seen, even such "utilitarian" rituals reveal much about larger issues of medieval people's cosmology, their perceived role in the cosmos, and the connection between themselves and the powers of that cosmos. Blessings represent the active negotiation of that connection, mingling speech, song, gesture, and motion to affirm a contractual relationship that provided divine protection and sacred power in exchange for human worship, veneration, and moral probity. I have examined this relationship, and the piety in which it is embedded, with historical methodology, aided at points by the theoretical paradigms of anthropology. This examination has consistently shown the relevance and virtue of using such theories to illuminate rites that hide their distinct meaning and importance in the shroud of formula and *topos*. This study has also shown that, while these theories are useful, the historian must resist the temptation to embrace them without reservation. When handled circumspectly, however, even theory considered dated by anthropologists can breath new life into modern historians' efforts at understanding the meaning of extrasacramental liturgy and its importance in the religion and culture of the medieval West.

Finally, the study of these rituals of blessing makes an important contribution in its own right to the history of medieval spirituality. Taken as a whole, blessings represent a spiritual alternative to the renunciation and contempt for the world espoused (if not always practiced) by the ecclesiastical establishment and the monastic orders of the period. This spirituality, while utilitarian and worldly in its emphasis on survival and material prosperity, is nonetheless integral in any attempt to create an accurate portrait of the "lay" Christianity of the high and late Middle Ages. Not solely creations of clerical piety and theology, liturgical blessings were like a mirror held up to the needs, desires, fears, and hopes of the laypeople who received them. Although the image is at times partial and imperfect, the reflection gives us a rare glimpse into the elusive world of the medieval laity, where daily life was made bearable by the protections offered by the church's blessings and the power of God, the only shelter in a seemingly chaotic world filled with hostile powers and natural dangers.

BIBLIOGRAPHY

PRIMARY SOURCES

Acta sanctorum quotquot toto orbe coluntur: Vel a catholicis scriptoribus celebrantur. Edited by Johannes Bolland et al. 68 vols. Antwerp: Jacob Meursium et al., 1643–.

Adomnan. *Adomnan's Life of Columba.* Edited by Marjorie Anderson. Oxford: Clarendon Press, 1990.

Agobard of Lyons, St. *"Liber adversus legem Gundobadi."* Chapter 2 of *Opera omnia.* Edited by L. van Acker. Corpus Christianorum Continuatio Medievalis 52. Turnhout: Brepols, 1981.

Alcvino. *Vita Willibrordi archiepiscopi Traiectensis. MGH SRM* 7:81–141.

Amalarius of Metz. *Amalarii episcopi opera liturgica omnia.* Edited by Johanne M. Hanssens. Studi e Testi 138–40. Vatican City: Biblioteca Apostolica Vaticana, 1948.

Ambrosiaster. *Quaestiones veteris et Novi Testamenti. PL* 35:2213–417.

Amiet, Robert. *The Benedictionals of Freising [Munich Bayerische Staatsbibliothek codex lat. 6430].* Henry Bradshaw Society 88. Maidstone, Kent: British Legion Press, 1974.

Andrieu, Michel, ed. *Les ordines romani du haut Moyen Âge.* 6 vols. Louvain: Spicilegium Sacrum Louvaniensis, 1931–61.

———. *Le pontifical romain au Moyen Âge.* 4 vols. Studi e Testi 86–89. Vatican City: Biblioteca Apostolica Vaticana, 1938–41.

Aquinas, St. Thomas. *Summa theologica.* Edited by T. Gilby. 60 vols. London: Eyre and Spottiswoode, 1963–76.

Arnold of Villanova. *Medicina salernitana, id est conservandae bonae valetudinis pracepta cum luculenta et succincta Arnold Villanovani in singula capitula exegesi per Iohannem Curionem recognita et purgata.* Erfurt: Jacobus Stoer, 1591.

Arteta, A. A. Ubieto, ed. *Crónica nájerense.* Textos Medievales 15. Valencia: La Real Academia de la Historia, 1966.

Ashmole, Elias. *The Institution, Laws and Ceremonies of the Most Noble Order of the Garter.* London: T. Dring, 1693.

Athanasius. *Vita Sancti Anthony. PG* 26:835–978.

Augustine. *De actis cum Felice Manichaeo libri duo*. PL 42:517–51.

———. *De civitate dei*. PL 41:13–806.

———. *De ordine libre duo*. PL 32:977–1020.

———. *Corpus scriptorum ecclesiasticorum latinorum* 40. 2 vols. Edited by Emanuel Hoffmann. Vienna: F. Tempsky, 1899–1900.

———. *The Catholic and Manichaean Ways of Life* (*De moribus ecclesiae Catholicae et de moribus Manichaeorum*). The Fathers of the Church: A New Translation, vol. 56. Translated by Donald A. Gallagher and Idella Gallagher. Washington, D.C.: The Catholic University of America Press, 1966.

———. *Sermons: Volume I on the Old Testament*. Edited by Edmund Hill. Vol. 1 of *The Works of St. Augustine: A Translation for the Twenty-First Century*, ed. John E. Rotelle. New York: New City Press, 1979.

Balbo, Barnardo. *Vita S. Lanfranci*. AS 25 (June 5).

Bannister, H. M., ed. *Missale gothicum*. Henry Bradshaw Society 52 and 54. London: Henry Bradshaw Society, 1917–19.

Banting, H. M. J., ed. *Two Anglo-Saxon Pontificals: The Egbert and Sydney Sussex Pontificals*. London: Boydell Press, 1989.

Basil, St. *Contra Eunomium libri quinque*. PG 29:463–774.

Bede, The Venerable. *Historia ecclesiastica gentis anglorum*. Edited by B. Colgrave and R. Mynors. Oxford: Clarendon Press, 1969.

Benedict, St., Abbot of Monte Cassino. *The Rule of Saint Benedict, in Latin and English*. Edited by Justin McCann. Westminster, Md.: Newman Press, 1952.

Benedictus Levita. *Capitularum collectio*. PL 97:697–913.

Biagio of Faenza. *Vita* [*S. Humilitatis Abbatissae*]. AS 18 (May 5): 207–13.

Birch, Walter de Gray. *The Book of Nunnaminster, i.e., the British Museum MS Harley 2965*. Hampshire, UK: Hampshire Record Society, 1889.

Blamires, Alcuin, with Karen Pratt and C. W. Marx, eds. *Women Defamed and Women Defended: An Anthology of Medieval Texts*. Oxford: Clarendon Press, 1992.

Boccaccio, Giovanni. *The Decameron*. Translated by G. H. McWilliam. London: Penguin, 1972.

Boenig, Robert, ed. *Anglo-Saxon Spirituality: Selected Writings*. Classics of Western Spirituality. New York: Pastoral Press, 2000.

Boethius. *The Consolation of Philosophy*. Translated by V. E. Watts. New York: Penguin, 1969.

Bonet, R. A., and M. Bonet, eds. *Acta apostolorum apocrypha*. Vol. 1. Darmstadt: Wissenschaftliche Buchgesellschaft, 1959.

Bruno of Segni. *De sacramentis ecclesiae*. PL 165:1089–110.

Burchard of Worms. *Decretorum liber*. PL 140:537–1090.

Caesarius of Arles, St. *Saint Caesarius of Arles, Sermons*. Edited by M. M. Mueller. 3 vols. Washington, D.C.: The Catholic University of America Press, 1956–73.

Cagin, Paul, ed. *Le sacramentaire gélasien d'Angoulême.* Angoulême: Societe Historique et Archéologique de la Charente, 1919.

Chevalier, Ulysse, ed. *Sacramentaire et martyrologe de l'Abbaye de Saint-Rémy.* Bibliothèque Liturgique 7. Paris: A. Picard, 1900.

Cilia, Gelasius di. *Thesaurus locupletissimus continens varias et selectissimas benedictiones, coniurationes, exorcismos, absolutiones, ritus, administrationem sacramentorum, aliorumque munerum pastoralium, ad utilitatem Christi fidelium, et commodiorum usum parachorum, omniumque sacerdotum, tam saecularium, quam religiosum curam habentium: Ex diversis ritualibus et probatissimis authoribus locupletior et redditus a Gelasio di Cilia.* 7th ed. Paedeponti: State and City, 1750.

Combaluzier, Fernand, ed. "Un bénédictionnaire épiscopal du Xe siècle." *Sacris Erudiri* 14 (1963): 286–342.

———. "Un pontifical du Mont St-Michel." In *Millénaire monastique du Mont Saint-Michel T.I.: Histoire et vie monastique, sous la direction de J. Laporte, O.S.B- Coll. Bibliothèque d'Histoire et d'Archéologie chrétiennes,* ed. J. Laporte, 383–98. Paris: P. Lethielleux, 1967.

Cyprian, St. *S. Thasci Caecili Cypriani opera omnia.* Corpus Scriptorum Ecclesiasticorum Latinorum. Edited by Wilhelm A. Hartel. 3 vols. Vindobonae, 1868–1871.

Damian, Peter. *Sermon 69. PL* 144:897–904.

———. *Opuscula. PL* 145:20–857.

———. "De perfectione monachorum." In *De divina omnipotentia, e altri opuscoli,* ed. Paolo Brezzi, 203–331. Florence: Vallechi, 1943.

Dante. *Dante's Purgatory.* Translated and edited by Mark Musa. Bloomington: Indiana University Press, 1981.

Davies, Oliver, ed. *Celtic Spirituality.* Classics of Western Spirituality. New York: Paulist Press, 1999.

De Cilia, Gelasius. *Thesaurus locupletissimus continens varias et selectissimas benedictiones, coniurationes, exorcismos . . . redditus a Gelasio di Cilia.* 7th ed. Paedeponti, 1750.

Decréaux, Joseph, ed. *Le sacramentaire de Marmoutier dans l'histoire des sacramentaires Carolingiens du IXesiècle.* 2 vols. Vatican City: Pontifical Institute of Christian Archaeology, 1985.

Deferrari, Roy J., ed. *Hugh of St. Victor: On the Sacraments of the Christian Faith (De sacramentis).* Cambridge, Mass.: Medieval Academy of America, 1951.

Dell'Oro, F., ed. "Le 'benedictiones episcopales' del codice Warmondiano." *Archiv für Liturgiewissenschaft* 12 (1970): 148–254.

Deshusses, Jean, ed. *La sacramentaire grégorien, ses principales formes d'après les plus anciens manuscrits.* Spicilegium Friburgense 16, 24, 28. Fribourg: Editiones Universitaires, 1971, 1979, 1982.

Deutsches Institut für Erforschung des Mittelalters. *Monumenta germaniae historica: Scriptores rerum merovingicarum.* 7 vols. Edited by Bruno Krusch and W. Levison. Hanover: Impensis Bibliopoli Hahniani, 1885, 1913, 1920.

Doble, G. H., ed. *Pontifical Lanalatense: A Pontifical Formerly in Use at St. Germans, Cornwall.* Henry Bradshaw Society 74. London: Harrison and Sons, 1937.

Duchesne, Louis, ed. *Liber pontificalis: Texte, introduction et commentaire par l'abbé L. Duchesne.* 3 vols. Paris: E. Thorin, 1955–57.

Dumas, Antoine, and Jean Deshusses, eds. *Liber sacramentorum gellonensis.* Corpus Christianorum Series Latina 159–159a. Turnhout: Brepols, 1981.

Durandus, William. *The Symbolism of Churches and Church Ornaments: A Translation of the First Book of the Rationales divinorum officiorum.* Translated by John Mason Neale and Benjamin Webb. London: T. W. Green, 1906.

Eadmer's History of Recent Events in England. Edited by Geoffrey Bosanquet. London: Cresset Press, 1964.

Elliott, J. K., ed. *The Apocryphal New Testament: A Collection of Apocryphal Christian Literature in an English Translation.* Oxford: Clarendon Press, 1993.

Expositio super missam. PL 138:1163–86.

Farsit, Hugh. *Libellus de miraculis Beatae Mariae. PL* 179:3.

Férotin, Marius, ed. *Le liber ordinum en usage dans l'église wisigothique et mozarabe d'Espagne du cinquième au onzième siècle.* Monumenta Ecclesiae Liturgica 5. Paris: Firmin-Didot, 1904.

———. *"Liber mozarabicus sacramentorum" et les manuscrits mozarabes.* Monumenta Ecclesiae Liturgica 6. Paris: Firmin-Didot, 1904.

Fischer, Ludwig, ed. *Bernhardi et lateranensis ecclesiae prioris ordo officiorum ecclesiae lateranensis.* Munich: F. P. Datterer, 1916. Reprint, 1985.

Franz, Adolph, ed. *Das Rituale von St Florian aus dem 12. Jahrhundert.* Freiberg: Herder, 1904.

———. *Die kirchlichen Benediktionen des Mittelalter.* 2 vols. Freiberg im Breisgau: M. Herder, 1909. Reprint, Graz: Akademische Druck-Verlagsanstalt, 1961.

Friedberg, Emil, ed. *Concordia discordantium canonum.* Leipzig: B. Tauchnitz, 1879. Reprint, 1959.

Gamber, Klaus. *Codices liturgici latini antiquiores.* 2d ed. Freiberg: Universitätsverlag Schweiz, 1968.

Grassus, Beneventus. *The Wonderful Art of the Eye: A Critical Edition of the Middle English Translation of His "De probatissima arte oculorum."* Edited by L. M. Eldredge. East Lansing: Michigan State University Press, 1996.

Gratian. *Decretum.* Corpus Christianorum Series Latinorum 187. Turnhout: Brepols, 1978. Reprint of Migne's 1855 edition.

Gregory of Nyssa. *De vita Moysis. PG* 44:298–433.

Gregory of Tours. *De virtibus [virtute] Sancti Martini* 1:42. *MGH SRM* 1 (2):364.

———. *In gloria martyrum* 23. *MGH SRM* 1 (2):51–52.

———. *Glory of the Confessors.* Translated by Raymond van Dam. Liverpool: Liverpool University Press, 1988.

Gregory the Great. *Pastoral Care.* Translated by Henry Davis. New York: Newman Press, 1950.

Guibert of Nogent. *Tractatus de incarnatione contra Judaecos.* PL 156:489–527.

Heraid of Tours. *Capitularia.* PL 121:763–73.

Hesbert, René-Jean, ed. *Corpus antiphonalium officii III: Invitatoria et antiphonae.* Rome: Herder, 1968.

Hildegarde of Bingen. *Holistic Healing.* Translated by Manfred Pawlik, Patrick Madigan, and John Kulas, with Mary Palmquist. Collegeville, Minn.: Liturgical Press, 1994.

Hincmar of Rheims. *Capitula synodica.* PL 125:773–803.

⸺. *De divortio lotharii regis et tetbergae reginae.* PL 125:620–733.

Hittorp, Melichor. *De divinis catholicae ecclesiae officiis ac mysteries.* Paris, 1610.

Honorius of Autun. *Gemma animae.* PL 172:541–737.

Isidore of Seville. *Etymologiae.* Scriptorum Classicorum Bibliotheca Oxoniensis. Edited by Wallace Martin Lindsay. 2 vols. Oxford: Clarendon Press, 1911. Reprint, 1971.

Jacob Pameli of Bruges. *Micrologus.* PL 151:974–1022.

John of Marmoutier. "Historia Gaufredi ducis normannorum et comitis Andegavorum." In *Chroniques des comtes d'Anjou et des seigneurs d'Amboise,* ed. Louis Halphen and Rene Poupardin, 172–231. Paris: A. Picard, 1913.

Jonas. *Vita Columbani abbatis discipulorumque eius. MGH SRM* 4:1–156.

Jordan of Saxony. "Libellus de principis ordinis praedicatorum." In *Monumenta ordinis fratrum praedicatorum historica* 16, ed. H. C. Sheeben. Rome: In Domo Generalitia, 1935.

Lawlor, Henry J., ed. *The Rossyln Missal.* Henry Bradshaw Society 15. London: Harrison, 1899.

Legg, John Wickham, ed. *The Sarum Missal.* Oxford: Clarendon Press, 1916.

Lowe, E. A., ed. *The Bobbio Missal.* Henry Bradshaw Society 58. London: Boydell Press, 1920. Reprint, 1991.

Lüdtke, Willy. "Bischöfliche Benediktionen aus Magdeburg und Braunschweig." *Jahrbuch für Liturgiewissenschaft* 5 (1925): 97–122.

Lull, Ramon. *The Book of the Ordre of Chyvalry.* Early English Text Society 168. Translated by William Caxton. Edited by Albert T. P. Byles. Oxford: Oxford University Press, 1926.

Mansi, Joannes D., ed. *Sanctorum conciliorum nova et amplissima collection cuius Joannes Dominicus Mansi et post ipsius mortem florentinus et venetianus editores ab anno 1758 ad annum 1798.* 53 vols. Paris: H. Welter, 1901–27.

Martène, Edmond, ed. *De antiquis Ecclesiae ritibus.* 3 vols. Rouen: Sumtibus Guillemli Behourt, 1700–1702.

Mignes, Jacques-Paul, ed. *Patrologiae cursus completus, series latina.* 222 vols. Paris: Parisiis, 1844–64.

⸺. *Patrologiae cursus completus, series graeca.* 161 vols. Paris: Parisiis, 1857–66.

Moeller, Edmund, ed. "Les bénédictionnaires d'Augsbourg et de Berlin." *Questions Liturgiques et Paroissiales* 50 (1969): 123–39.

———. *Corpus benedictionum pontificalium.* 3 vols. Rome: Turnhout, 1971–73.

Mohlberg, Leo Cunibert, ed. *Sacramentarium Veronense.* Rome: Casa Editrice Herder, 1956.

Mohlberg, Leo Cunibert, Leo Eizenhöfer, and Peter Siffrin, eds. *Liber sacramentorum Romanae Aeclesiae ordinis anni circuli: Cod. Vat. Reg. Lat. 216; Paris Bibl. nat. 7193, 41/56: Sacramentarium Gelasianum.* Rerum Ecclesiasticarum Documenta, Series Maior Fontes 4. Rome: Casa Editrice Herder, 1960.

Morin, German, ed. *Sermones ex integro a Caesario compuisti vel ex aliis fontibus hausti.* Corpus Christianorum Series Latina 103–4. Turnhout: Brepols, 1991.

Orderic Vitalis. *Ecclesiastical History.* Vol. 6. Edited by Marjorie Chibnall. Oxford: Clarendon Press, 1999.

Origen. *Contra celsum.* Edited by Henry Chadwick. New York: Cambridge University Press, 1965. Reprint, 1980.

The Passion of St. Bartholomew the Apostle. Vol. 1 of *The Homilies of the Anglo-Saxon Church* 1, ed. B. Thorpe. London: Aelfric Society, 1844–46.

Peter the Chanter. *Verbum abbreviatum. PL* 205: cols. 021–528.

Pichéry, Eugène, ed. *Jean Cassien Conferences, Volume I, i–vii.* Paris: Editiones du Cerf, 1955.

Plato. *The Dialogues of Plato.* Translated by B. Jowett. Vol. 3. Oxford: Clarendon Press, 1964.

Pseudo-Bede. *"De mundi celestis terrestrisque constitutione": A Treatise on the Universe and the Soul.* Edited by Charles Burnett. London: Warburg Institute, University of London, 1985.

Quasten, Johannes, ed. *Monumenta eucharistica et liturgica vetustissima.* Florilegium Patristicum 7. Bonn: Petri Hanstein, 1935–36.

Rabanus Maurus. *Commentaria in Exodum. PL* 108:9–246.

———. *De magicis artibus. PL* 110:1095–110.

Ratherius of Verona. *Sermo VII: De ascensione domini. PL* 136:734–40.

Raymond de Peñaforte. *De ordaliis.* Edited by Peter Browe. 2 vols. Rome: Pontificalis Universitatis Gregorianae, 1932–33.

Richter, Gregor, and Albert Schönfelder, eds. *Sacramentarium Fuldense: Saeculi X.* Henry Bradshaw Society 101. Fulda: Druck der Fulder Actiendruckerei, 1912. Reprint, 1980.

Rule, Martin, ed. *The Missal of St. Augustine's Abbey, Canterbury.* Cambridge: Cambridge University Press, 1896.

Schroeder, H. J., ed. *Disciplinary Decrees of the General Councils: Text, Translation and Commentary.* St. Louis, Mo.: B. Herder, 1937.

Serapion of Thimus, St. *Bishop Sarapion's Prayerbook: An Egyptian Pontifical Dated Probably about 350–56.* London: S.P.C.K., 1899. Reprint, Hamden, Conn.: Archon Books, 1964.

Serra, J. Rius, ed. "Benediciones episcopales en un manuscrito de Roda." *Hispana Sacra* 10 (1957): 161–210.

Sicard of Cremona. *Mitrale. PL* 213:9–347.

Simpson, J. A., and E. S. C. Weiner, eds. *The Oxford English Dictionary.* 20 vols. Oxford: Clarendon Press, 1989.

Stokes, Whitley. *The Tripartite Life of Patrick with Other Documents Relating to the Saint.* 2 vols. Rolls Series 89. London: Eyre and Spottiswoode, 1887.

Tanner, Norman P., ed. and trans. "Fourth Lateran—1215." In *Decrees of the Ecumenical Councils,* 1:236–96. Washington, D.C.: The Catholic University of America Press, 1990.

Tertullian. *De testimonio animae.* Corpus Scriptorum Ecclesiasticorum Latinorum 20. Edited by August Reifferscheid and Georg Wissowa. Vindobonae: F. Tempsky, 1890.

———. *De Corona militis. PL* 2:73–101.

———. *Tertullian: Disciplinary, Moral and Ascetical Works.* Edited by Rudolph Arbesmann, Emily Joseph Daly, and Edwin Quain. The Fathers of the Church 40. Washington, D.C.: The Catholic University of America Press, 1959.

Trexler, Richard C. *The Christian at Prayer: An Illustrated Manual Attributed to Peter the Chanter.* Binghamton, N.Y.: Medieval and Renaissance Texts and Studies, 1987.

Turner, Derek, ed. *The Claudius Pontificals (from Cotton MS. Claudius A. iii in the British Museum).* Henry Bradshaw Society 97. Chichester, UK: Henry Bradshaw Society, 1971.

Urich, St. *Antiquoires consuetudines cluniacensis monasterii. PL* 149:643–779.

Vidal, J. M. *Bullaire de l'inquisition francaise au XIV sieclé.* Document 72. Paris: Librairie Letouzey et Ané, 1913.

Vita Ursmari episcopi et abbatis Lobbiensis. MGH SRM 6:445–70.

Vogel, Cyrille. *Medieval Liturgy: An Introduction to the Sources.* Translated by William G. Storey and Neils Krogh Rasmussen. Washington, D.C.: Pastoral Press, 1986.

Vogel, Cyrille, and Reihard Elze, eds. *Le pontifical romano-germanique du dixième siècle.* 3 vols. Studi e Testi 226–27. Vatican City: Biblioteca Apostolica Vaticana, 1963, 1972.

Wakefield, Walter, and Austin Evans, eds. *Heresies of the High Middle Ages.* New York: Columbia University Press, 1991.

Warren, F. E., ed. *The Leofric Missal.* Oxford: Clarendon Press, 1883.

Wasserschleben, F. G. A., ed. *Reginonis abbatis Prumiensis libri duo de synodalibus causis.* Leipzig: G. Engelmann, 1840.

William of Malmesbury. *De gestis regnum anglorum.* Book 5, *Historiae novellae libre* 3. Edited by William Stubbs. London: Eyre and Spottiswoode, 1887.

Wilson, H. A., ed. *The Benedictional of Archbishop Robert.* Henry Bradshaw Society 24. London: Henry Bradshaw Society, 1903.

———. *The Pontifical of Magdalen College, with an Appendix of Extracts from [7] Other English*

Manuscripts of the Twelfth Century. Henry Bradshaw Society 39. London: Harrison and Sons, 1910.

———. *The Gregorian Sacramentary under Charles the Great.* Henry Bradshaw Society 49. London: Henry Bradshaw Society, 1915.

Wooley, Reginald M., ed. *The Canterbury Benedictional (Brit. Mus., Harley ms. 2892).* Henry Bradshaw Society 51. London: Boydell, 1917. Reprint, 1995.

———. *The Benedictional of John Longlonde, Bishop of Lincoln.* Henry Bradshaw Society 64. London: Harrison and Sons, 1927.

Zeumer, Karl, ed. *Formulae merovingici et karolini aevi. MGH,* sec. 5. Hanover: Impensis Bibliopoli Hahniani, 1882.

SECONDARY SOURCES

Amundsen, Darrel W. *Medicine, Society and Faith in the Ancient and Medieval Worlds.* Baltimore: Johns Hopkins University Press, 1996.

Ariés, Phillipe. *The Hour of Our Death.* Translated by H. Weaver. New York: Knopf, 1981.

Arrington, George E., Jr. *A History of Ophthalmology.* New York: MD Publications, 1959.

Ashley, Kathleen, ed. *Victor Turner and the Construction of Cultural Criticism: Between Literature and Anthropology.* Bloomington: Indiana University Press, 1990.

Austin, J. L. *How to Do Things with Words.* 2d ed. Edited by J. O. Urmson and Marina Sbisà. Cambridge, Mass.: Harvard University Press, 1975.

Avitabile, L., M. C. Di Franco, V. Jemolo, and A. Petrucci. "Censimento dei codici dei secoli xi–xii." *Studi Medievali,* 3d ser., 11 (1970): 1127–28.

Baldwin, J. W. "The Intellectual Preparation for the Canon of 1215 against Ordeals." *Speculum* 36 (1961): 613–36.

Baldwin, Marshall W., ed. *The First Hundred Years.* Vol. 1 of *A History of the Crusades,* ed. Kenneth Setton. Madison: University of Wisconsin Press, 1969.

Barber, Richard. *Pilgrimages.* Woodbridge, UK: Boydell Press, 1991.

Baring-Gould, Reverend Sabine. *The Lives of the Saints, with an introduction and additional lives of English Martyrs, Cornish, Scottish and Welsh Saints, and a full index to the entire work.* 16 vols. Edinburgh: John Grant, 1914.

Barrow, Julia. "Urban Cemetery Location in the High Middle Ages." In *Death in Towns: Urban Responses to the Dying and the Dead, 100–1600,* ed. Steven Bassett, 94–100. London: Leicester University Press, 1992.

Bartlett, Robert. *Trial by Fire and Water: The Medieval Judicial Ordeal.* Oxford: Clarendon Press, 1986.

Baumstein, Paschal. "Benedict's God and the Monk's God." *Cistercian Studies* 22 (1987): 304–15.

Bauschatz, Paul C. *The Well and the Tree: World and Time in Early Germanic Culture.* Amherst: University of Massachusetts Press, 1982.

Bayard, Jean Pierre. *Le sacre des rois.* Paris, 1964.

Bell, Catherine. *Ritual: Perspectives and Dimensions.* New York: Oxford University Press, 1997.

Blake, E. O. "The Formation of the 'Crusade Idea.'" *Journal of Ecclesiastical History* 21 (1970): 11–31.

Bliese, John R. E. "The Just War as Concept and Motive in the Central Middle Ages." *Medievalia et Humanistica,* new ser., 17 (1991): 1–26.

Böckenhoff, Karl. *Das apostolische Speisegesetz in den ersten fünf Jahrhunderten.* Paderborn: Ferdinand Schoningh, 1903.

Bornstein, Daniel Ethan. *The Bianchi of 1399: Popular Devotion in Late Medieval Italy.* Ithaca: Cornell University Press, 1993.

Bornstein, Diane. "Family, Western European." *DMA* 4:599–605.

Bossy, John. "The Mass as a Social Institution, 1200–1700." *Past and Present* 100 (1983): 29–61.

Bouman, Cornelius A. *Sacring and Crowning: The Development of the Latin Ritual for the Anointing of Kings and the Coronation of an Emperor before the Eleventh Century.* Groningen: J. B. Wolters, 1957.

Bouyer, Louis. *Rite and Man: Natural Sacredness and Christian Liturgy.* Translated by M. Joseph Costelloe. Notre Dame: University of Notre Dame Press, 1963.

Bowman, Leonard J. "Itinerarium: The Shape of the Metaphor." In *Itinerarium: The Idea of Journey,* ed. Leonard J. Bowman, 3–33. Salzburg: Institut für Anglistik und Amerikanistik, Universität Salzburg, 1983.

Bozóky, Edina. "Mythic Mediation in Healing Incantations." In *Health, Disease and Healing in Medieval Culture,* ed. Sheila Campbell, Bert Hall, and David Klausner, 84–92. New York: St. Martin's Press, 1992.

Brett, Laurence F. X. *Redeemed Creation: Sacramentals Today.* Wilmington, Del.: Michael Glazier, 1984.

Browe, Peter. "Der Segen mit Reliquien, der Patene und Euchariste." *Ephemerides Liturgicae* 45 (1931): 383–91.

Brown, A. R. "Death and the Human Body in the Later Middle Ages: The Legislation of Boniface VIII on the Division of the Corpse." *Viator* 12 (1981): 59–82.

Brown, Elizabeth A. R. *"Franks, Burgundians and Aquitanians" and the Royal Coronation Ceremony in France.* Philadelphia: American Philosophical Society, 1992.

Brown, Peter. *The Cult of the Saints: Its Rise and Function in Latin Christianity.* Chicago: University of Chicago Press, 1981.

Brown, Virginia. "A Second New List of Beneventan Manuscripts." *Mediaeval Studies* 40 (1978): 269.

———. "Origine et provenance des manuscrits bénéventains conservés à la bibliothèque capitulaire." In *La Cathédrale de Bénévent,* ed. Thomas Forrest Kelly, 149–65. Ghent: Ludion, 1999.

Brundage, John A. "Cruce signari: The Rite for Taking the Sign of the Cross in England." *Traditio* 22 (1966): 289–310.

———. "Holy War and the Medieval Lawyers." In *The Holy War*, ed. Thomas Patrick Murphy, 99–140. Columbus: Ohio State University Press, 1976.

Bruni, J. P. "Sacred Humanity, Devotion to the." *NCE* 12:828–30.

———. "Wounds of Our Lord, Devotion to." *NCE* 13:1035–36.

Buc, Phillipe. *The Dangers of Ritual: Between Early Medieval Texts and Social Scientific Theory*. Princeton: Princeton University Press, 2001.

Burke, Peter. "Death in the Renaissance." In *Dies illa: Death in the Middle Ages*, ed. Jane H. Taylor, 59–66. Liverpool: Cairns, 1984.

Butler, Elizabeth M. *Ritual Magic*. Magic in History Series. University Park: Pennsylvania State University Press, 1998.

Bynum, Caroline Walker. "Women's Stories, Women's Symbols: A Critique of Victor Turner's Theory of Liminality." In *Anthropology and the Study of Religion*, ed. Frank Reynolds and Robert Moore, 105–25. Chicago: Center for the Scientific Study of Religion, 1984.

———. *Holy Feast, Holy Fast: The Religious Significance of Food to Medieval Women*. Berkeley and Los Angeles: University of California Press, 1987.

Callewaert, C. "Qu'est-ce que l'oratio super populum?" *Ephemerides Liturgicae* 51 (1937): 310–18.

Camille, Michael. "Signs of the City." In *Medieval Practices of Space*, ed. Barbara Hanawalt and Michal Kobialka, 1–36. Minneapolis: University of Minnesota Press, 2000.

Carabine, Dierdre. "Eriugena's Use of the Symbolism of Light, Cloud and Darkness in the *Periphyseon*." In *Eriugena, East and West: Papers of the 8th International Colloquium of the Society for the Promotion of Eriugenan Studies, Chicago and Notre Dame, 18–20 October 1991*, ed. Bernard McGinn and Willemien Otten, 141–52. Notre Dame: University of Notre Dame Press, 1994.

Caraffa, Filippo, and Giuseppe Morelli, eds. *Bibliotheca sanctorum*. 12 vols. Rome: Citta Nuova, 1960–70.

Chavasse, Antoine. *Le sacramentaire gélasien*. Tournai: Desclée, 1958.

Cohn, Norman. *Europe's Inner Demons: The Demonization of Christians in Medieval Christendom*. Rev. ed. Chicago: University of Chicago Press, 2001.

Cohn, Samuel K., Jr. "The Place of the Dead in Flanders and Tuscany: Towards a Comparative History of the Black Death." In *The Place of the Dead: Death and Remembrance in Late Medieval and Early Modern Europe*, ed. Bruce Gordon and Peter Marshall, 17–43. New York: Cambridge University Press, 2000.

Constable, Giles. "Opposition to Pilgrimage in the Middle Ages." *Studia Gratiana* 19 (1976): 125–46.

———. "The Commemoration of the Dead in the Early Middle Ages." In *Early Medi-*

eval Rome and the Christian West: Essays in Honor of Donald A. Bullough, ed. Julia M. H. Smith, 169–95. Boston: Brill, 2000.

Cowdrey, Herbert E. J. "The Genesis of the Crusades: The Springs of Western Ideas of Holy War." In *The Holy War,* ed. Thomas Patrick Murphy, 9–32. Columbus: Ohio State University Press, 1976.

———. "Canon Law and the First Crusade." In *The Horns of Hattin: Proceedings of the Second Conference of the Society for the Study of the Crusades and the Latin East, Jerusalem and Haifa, 2–6 July 1987,* ed. Benjamin Z. Kedar, 41–48. Jerusalem: Variorum, 1992.

Crichton, J. D. *The Dedication of a Church.* Dublin: Dublin University Press, 1980.

Croon, Johan Harm. "Water." In *The Oxford Classical Encyclopedia,* ed. Simon Hornblower and Antony Spawforth, 1619. Oxford: Oxford University Press, 1996.

Daniélou, Jean. *The Angels and Their Mission According to the Fathers of the Church.* Westminster, Md.: Newman Press, 1957.

Davidson, H. R. Ellis. *Myths and Symbols in Pagan Europe: Early Scandinavian and Celtic Religions.* Syracuse: Syracuse University Press, 1988.

Davis, Natalie Zemon. "From 'Popular Religion' to Religious Cultures." In *Reformation Europe: A Guide to Research,* ed. Stephen Ozment, 321–41. St. Louis, Mo.: Center for Reformation Research, 1982.

Delumeau, Jean-Pierre. "Un dossier de bénédictions." In *Fêtes et liturgie: Actes du colloque tenu à la Casa de Velázquez, Madrid, 12–13–14 décembre 1985,* ed. Alfonso de Esteban Alonso and Jean Pierre Etienvre, 291–98. Madrid: Casa de Veláquez/Universidad Complutense, 1988.

Deshusses, Jean, and Benolt Darragon. *Concordances et tableaux por l'étude des grands sacramentaires.* Spicilegii Friburgensis Subsida, vols. 9–14. Fribourg: Éditiones Universitaires Fribourg Suisse, 1982–83.

Dix, Gregory, ed. *The Treatise on the Apostolic Tradition of St. Hippolytus of Rome.* London: S.P.C.K., 1937. Reprinted with supplement, London: Henry Chadwick, 1968.

Donnelly, Seamus, Colm Donnelly, and Eileen Murphy. "The Forgotten Dead: The *Cilliní* and Disused Burial Grounds of Ballintoy, County Antrim." *Ulster Journal of Archaeology* 3, no. 58 (1999): 109–13.

Donnison, Jean. *Midwives and Medical Men: A History of Inter-Professional Rivalries and Women's Rights.* London: Heinemann, 1977.

Douglas, Mary. *Purity and Danger: An Analysis of the Concepts of Pollution and Taboo.* London: Routledge, 1966.

———. *Natural Symbols: Explorations in Cosmology.* New York: Pantheon Books, 1982.

Duby, Georges. *The Chivalrous Society.* London: Edward Arnold, 1979.

———. *The Three Orders: Feudal Society Imagined.* Translated by Arthur Goldhammer. Chicago: University of Chicago Press, 1980.

Duffy, Eamon. *The Stripping of the Altars: Traditional Religion in England, 1480–1600.* New Haven: Yale University Press, 1992.

Durkheim, Emile. *The Elementary Forms of the Religious Life.* Translated by Joseph Ward Swain. London: George Allen and Unwin, 1976.

Eck, Diana L. "Rivers." In *The Encyclopedia of Religion,* 15th ed., ed. Mircea Eliade, 425–28. New York: Macmillan, 1987.

Eisenhöfer, Ludwig. "Untersuchungen zum Stil und Inhalt der römischen *Oratio super populum.*" *Ephemerides Liturgicae* 52 (1938): 258–311.

Eliade, Mircea. *The Sacred and the Profane: The Nature of Religion.* Translated by Willard R. Trask. New York: Harcourt Brace, 1959.

———. *Myth and Reality.* Translated by Willard R. Trask. New York: Harper and Row, 1963.

Erdmann, Carl. *The Origin of the Idea of Crusade.* Translated by Marshall W. Baldwin and Walter Goffart. Princeton: Princeton University Press, 1977.

Evans, David B. "Pseudo-Dionysius the Aeropagite." *DMA* 10:203–4.

Every, George. *The Mass.* Dublin: Gill and Macmillan, 1978.

Fabris, Rinaldo. "Blessings, Curses and Exorcisms in the Biblical Tradition." In *Blessing and Power,* ed. Mary Collins and David Power, 13–23. Edinburgh: T. and T. Clark, 1985.

Farmer, David Hugh. *The Oxford Dictionary of the Saints.* 3d ed. Oxford: Oxford University Press, 1992.

Farmer, Sharon. *Communities of St. Martin: Legend and Ritual in Medieval Tours.* Ithaca: Cornell University Press, 1991.

Finucane, Ronald. *Miracles and Pilgrims: Popular Beliefs in Medieval England.* Totowa, N.J.: Palgrave Macmillan, 1977.

Fischer, Norbert. "Topographie des Todes: Zur sozialhistorichen Bedeutung der Friedhofsverlegungen zwischen Mittelalter und Neuzeit." In *Aussenseiter zwischen Mittelalter und Neuzeit: Festschrift für Hans-Jürgen Goertz zum 60,* ed. Norbert Fischer and Marion Kobelt-Groch, 81–97. Leiden: Brill, 1997.

Fisher, J. D. C. *Christian Initiation: Baptism in the Medieval West.* London: S.P.C.K., 1965.

Flint, Valerie J. "The Early Medieval 'Medicus,' the Saint—and the Enchanter." *Social History of Medicine* 2, no. 2 (1989): 127–45.

———. *The Rise of Magic in Early Medieval Europe.* Princeton: Princeton University Press, 1991.

———. "Space and Discipline in Early Medieval Europe." In *Medieval Practices of Space,* ed. Barbara Hanawalt and Michal Kobialka, 149–66. Minneapolis: University of Minnesota Press, 2000.

Flori, Jean. "Les origines de l'adoubement chevaleresue: Étude des remises d'armes et du vocabulaire qui les exprime." *Traditio* 35 (1979): 209–72.

Forbes, Thomas Rogers. *The Midwife and the Witch.* New Haven: Yale University Press, 1966.

Fossier, Robert. *Peasant Life in the Medieval West.* Translated by Juliet Vale. Oxford: Basil Blackwell, 1988.

Frazer, Sir James. *The Golden Bough: A Study in Magic and Religion.* 3d ed. 12 vols. New York: Macmillan, 1951.

Gaier, Claude. "Le rôle militaire des reliques et de l'étendard de Saint Lambert dans la principauté de Liège." *Le Moyen Âge* 72 (1966): 235–50.

Gautier, Léon. *La chevalerie.* Paris: Sanard and Derangeon, 1884.

Geary, Patrick J. *Furta sacra: Thefts of Relics in the Central Middle Ages.* Princeton: Princeton University Press, 1978.

Geertz, Clifford. "Religion as a Cultural System." In *Anthropological Approaches to the Study of Religion,* ed. Michael Banton, 1–46. London: Tavistock Publications, 1966.

———. *The Interpretation of Cultures.* New York: Basic Books, 1973.

Giese, Wolfgang. "Die 'lancea Domini' von Antiochia." In *Fälschungen im Mittelalter: Internationaler Kongress der Monumenta Germaniae Historica, München, 16–19 September 1986,* ed. Wolfram Setz, 5:485–504. Hanover: Hahnsche Buchhandlung, 1988.

Gluckman, Max. *Essays on the Ritual of Social Relations.* Manchester: Manchester University Press, 1962.

———. *Order and Rebellion in Tribal Africa.* New York: Free Press, 1963.

Gordon, C. H. "Leviathan: Symbol of Evil." In *Biblical Motifs,* ed. A. Altman, 1–10. Cambridge, Mass.: Harvard University Press, 1966.

Gribben, Arthur. *Holy Wells and Sacred Water Sources in Britain and Ireland: An Annotated Bibliography.* New York: Garland Publishing, 1992.

Grimes, Ronald L. *Beginnings in Ritual Studies.* Rev. ed. Columbia: University of South Carolina Press, 1995.

Gulezynski, John T. *The Desecration and Violation of Churches.* Catholic University of America CLS 159. Washington, D.C.: The Catholic University of America Press, 1942.

Gy, Pierre-Marie. "Benedictions." *DMA* 2:177–78.

———. *La liturgie dans l'histoire.* Paris: Editions Saint-Paul, Editions du Cerf, 1990.

Gyug, Richard F. "The Pontificals of Monte Cassino." In *L'età dell' abate desiderio: storia, arte e cultura; Atti del IV convegno di studi sul medioevo meridionale, Montecassino e Cassino 4–8 ottobre 1987, Miscellanea cassinese* 67, vol. 3.1, 413–39. Montecassino: Publicazioni Cassinesi, 1992.

Harnak, Adolf von. *Medizinisches aus der ältesten Kirchengeschichte.* Leipzig: K. F. Pfau, 1892.

Hass, Jeffrey D. "The Development of the Medieval Dubbing Ceremony." *Michigan Academician* 28 (1996): 123–33.

Hatchett, Marion J. *Sanctifying Life, Time and Space: An Introduction to Liturgical Study.* New York: Seabury Press, 1976.

Head, Thomas. "I Vow Myself to Be Your Servant: An Eleventh-Century Pilgrim, His Chronicler and His Saint." *Historical Reflections* 11, no. 3 (1984): 215–30.

———. *Hagiography and the Cult of the Saints: The Diocese of Orleans, 800–1200.* Cambridge: Cambridge University Press, 1990.

Hempel, Johannes. *Die israelischen Anschauungen von Segen und Fluch im Lichte altorientalischer Parallelen.* Zeitschrift der deutschen morgenländischen Gesellschaft 79. Leipzig: F. A. Brockhaus, 1925.

Hiley, David. "The Norman Chant Traditions: Normandy, Britain, Sicily." *Proceedings of the Royal Musical Association* 107 (1980–81): 1–33.

———. "Quanto c'e di Normanno nei tropari siculo-normanni?" *Rivista Italiana Musicologia* 18 (1983): 3–28.

———. "Chant of Norman Sicily." *Studia Musicologia* 30 (1988): 379–91.

Hill, Edmund, ed. *Sermons.* In vol. 1, *On the Old Testament,* part 3 of *The Works of St. Augustine: A Translation for the 21st Century,* ed. John E. Rotelle. Brooklyn, N.Y.: New City Press, 1979.

Hill, John H. "Crusades and Crusader States: To 1192." *DMA* 4:33–41.

Hirschberg, Julius. *Geschichte der Augenheilkunde.* Vols. 12–14 of *Handbuch der gesamten Augenheilkunde,* ed. A. K. Graefe and Theodor Saemisch. Leipzig: Wilhelm Engelmann, 1899–1911.

Hollister, C. Warren. "Knights and Knight Service." *DMA* 7:276–79.

Holloway, Julia B. "The Pilgrim in the Poem: Dante, Langland, and Chaucer." In *Allegoresis: The Craft of Allegory in the Middle Ages,* ed. J. S. Russell, 109–32. New York: Garland Publishing, 1988.

Houser, J. "Pilgrimage." *DMA* 9:654–61.

Iogna-Prat, Dominique. "La terre sainte disputée." *Médiévales* 41 (2001): 83–112.

Jobes, Gertrude. *Dictionary of Mythology, Folklore and Symbols.* New York: Scarecrow Press, 1962.

Johnson, E. J. "Ashes, Liturgical Use of." *NCE* 1:948–49.

Jolly, Karen Louise. *Popular Religion in Late Saxon England: Elf Charms in Context.* Chapel Hill: University of North Carolina Press, 1996.

Jungmann, Josef. *Die lateinischen Bussriten in ihrer geschichtlichen Entaic Klung.* Innsbruck: F. Rauch, 1932.

———. *The Mass of the Roman Rite.* 2 vols. New York: Benziger, 1983.

Keen, Maurice. "The Ceremony of Dubbing to Knighthood." In Keen, *Chivalry.* New Haven: Yale University Press, 1984.

Kelly, Henry Ansgar. *The Devil at Baptism: Ritual, Theology and Drama.* Ithaca: Cornell University Press, 1985.

Kieckhefer, Richard. *Unquiet Souls: 14th-Century Saints and Their Religious Milieu.* Chicago: University of Chicago Press, 1984.

———. *Magic in the Middle Ages.* New York: Cambridge University Press, 1993.

Kiernan, Thomas, ed. *Aristotle Dictionary.* London: Peter Owen, 1962.

Kirkpatrick, A. F. *The Book of Psalms.* Grand Rapids: Baker Book House, 1982.

Klaniczay, Gábor. *The Uses of Supernatural Power: The Transformation of Popular Religion in Medieval and Early Modern Europe.* Translated by Susan Singerman. Edited by Karen Margolis. Princeton: Princeton University Press, 1990.

Klauser, Theodor. *A Short History of the Western Liturgy.* Oxford: Oxford University Press, 1979.

Kleinberg, Aviad. *Prophets in Their Own Country.* Chicago: University of Chicago Press, 1992.

Kristeller, Paul. *Iter italicum: A Finding List of Uncatalogued or Incompletely Catalogued Humanistic Manuscripts of the Renaissance.* London: Warburg Institute, 1963.

Kroll, Jerome, and Bernard Bachrach. "Sin and the Etiology of Disease in Pre-Crusade Europe." *Journal of the History of Medicine and Allied Sciences* 41 (1986): 395–414.

Kuntz, Paul G. "Augustine: From Homo Erro to Homo Viator." In *Itinerarium: The Idea of Journey,* ed. L Bowman, 34–53. Salzburg: Institut für Anglisitik und Amerikanistik, Universität Salzburg, 1983.

Ladner, Gerhart B. "Homo viator: Medieval Ideas of Alienation and Order." *Speculum* 17 (1967): 233–59.

Lauwers, Michel. "Le cimetière dans le Moyen Âge latin: Lieu sacré, saint et religeux." *Annales: Histoire, Sciences Sociales* 54, no. 5 (1999): 1047–72.

Lechner, J. *Der Schlussegen des Priesters in der heiligen Messe.* In *Festschrift Eduard Eichmann zum 70. Geburtstag,* ed. William G. Joseph, Martin Grabmann, and Karl Hofmann, 651–84. Paderborn: Schöningh, 1940.

LeGoff, Jacques. *The Birth of Purgatory.* Translated by Arthur Goldhammer. Aldershot, UK: Scholar Press, 1990.

Lemay, Helen. "Women and the Literature of Obstetrics and Gynecology." In *Medieval Women and the Sources of Medieval History,* ed. Joel T. Rosenthal, 189–209. Athens: University of Georgia Press, 1990.

Leroquais, Victor. *Les pontificaux manuscrits des bibliothèques publiques de France.* 3 vols. Paris: Macon, 1937.

Le Roy Ladurie, Emmanuel. *Montaillou: Promised Land of Error.* Translated by Barbara Bray. New York: Vintage Books, 1979.

Lindberg, David C. "Optics, Western European." *DMA* 9:247–53.

Linder, Elisha. "Human Apprehension of the Sea." In *The Sea and History,* ed. E. E. Rice, 15–22. Phoenix Mill, UK: Sutton Publishing, 1996.

Little, Lester K. *Benedictine Maledictions: Liturgical Cursing in Romanesque France.* Ithaca: Cornell University Press, 1993.

Livingstone, E. A. ed. *The Oxford Dictionary of the Christian Church.* 3rd ed. Oxford: Oxford University Press, 1997.

Löhrer, Magnus. "Sakramentalien." *Sacramentum Mundi* 4 (1969): 341–47.

Lowe, Elias Avery. *The Beneventan Script: A History of the South Italian Minuscule.* 2d ed. Prepared and enlarged by Virginia Brown. 2 vols. Rome: Edizioni di Storia e letteratura, 1980.

Lukes, Steven. *Emile Durkheim: His Life and Work, a Historical and Critical Study.* New York: Penguin, 1977.

Macdonald, Allan John. *Berengar and the Reform of Sacramental Doctrine.* New York: Longmans, Green, 1930.

Manselli, Raoul. *La religion populaire au Moyen Âge: Problèmes de méthode et d'histoire.* Montréal: Institut d'Études Médiévales Albert-le-Grand, 1975.

Mansfield, Mary. *The Humiliation of Sinners: Public Penance in Thirteenth-Century France.* Ithaca: Cornell University Press, 1995.

Martimort, Aimé-Georges, ed. *The Church at Prayer: An Introduction to the Liturgy.* Translated by Austin Flannery and Vincent Ryan. New ed. Collegeville, Minn.: Liturgical Press, 1988.

Matthew, Donald. *The Norman Kingdom of Sicily.* Cambridge: Cambridge University Press, 1993.

Mauss, Marcel. *Sociologie et anthropologie.* Paris: Presses Universitaires de France, 1950.

McLaughlin, Megan. *Consorting with Saints: Prayers for the Dead in Early Medieval France.* Ithaca: Cornell University Press, 1994.

Melczer, William. *The Pilgrim's Guide to Santiago de Compostela.* New York: Italica Press, 1993.

Miller, John H. *Signs of Transformation in Christ.* Englewood Cliffs, N.J.: Prentice-Hall, 1963.

Mol, Hans. *Identity and the Sacred: A Sketch for a New Social-Scientific Theory of Religion.* New York: Free Press, 1976.

Mollat du Jourdin, Michel. *Europe and the Sea.* Oxford: Blackwell, 1993.

Moran, Dermot. *The Philosophy of John Scottus Eriugena: A Study in Idealism in the Middle Ages.* Cambridge: Cambridge University Press, 1989.

Moreton, Bernard. *The Eighth-Century Gelasian Sacramentary: A Study in Tradition.* Oxford: Oxford University Press, 1976.

Morghen, Raffaello. "Monastic Reform and Cluniac Spirituality." In *Cluniac Monasticism in the Central Middle Ages,* ed. Noreen Hunt, 11–28. London: Macmillan, 1971.

Morris, Colin. "Judicum dei: The Social and Political Significance of the Ordeal in the Eleventh Century." *Studies in Church History* 12 (1975): 95–112.

Morris, J. V. "Blessing." *NCE* 2:612–13.

Morris, Richard K. *The Church in British Archaeology.* CBA Research Report 47. London: Council for British Archaeology, 1983.

Mowinckel, Sigmund. *Psalmstudien.* 6 vols. Kristiania, Norway: In kommission bei J. Dybwad, 1921–24.

Muncey, R. W. L. *History of the Consecration of Churches and Churchyards.* Cambridge: W. Heffer and Sons, 1930.

Murray, Alexander. "Missionaries and Magic in Dark Age Europe." *Past and Present* 136 (1992): 186–205.

Neuman de Vegvar, Carol Leslie. "Images of Women in Anglo-Saxon Art, II: Midwifery in Harley 603." *Old English Newsletter* 25, no. 1 (1991): 54–56.

Newman, Martha G. *The Boundaries of Charity: Cistercian Culture and Ecclesiastical Reform, 1098–1180.* Stanford: Stanford University Press, 1996.

Nowell, Irene. "The Narrative Context of Blessing in the Old Testament." In *Blessing and Power,* ed. Mary Collins and David Power, 3–12. Edinburgh: T. and T. Clark, 1985.

Oakley, Francis. *The Western Church in the Later Middle Ages.* Ithaca: Cornell University Press, 1979.

Ohler, Norbert. *The Medieval Traveler.* Translated by Caroline Hillier. Woodbridge, UK: Boydell, 1989.

Otto, Rudolf. *The Idea of the Holy.* Translated by John W. Harvey. London: Oxford University Press, 1923.

Paxton, Frederick. *Christianizing Death: The Creation of a Ritual Process in Early Medieval Europe.* Ithaca: Cornell University Press, 1990.

———. "Liturgy and Healing in an Early Medieval Saint's Cult: The Mass *in honore sancti Sigismundi* for the Cure of Fevers." *Traditio* 49 (1994): 23–44.

Pedersen, Johannes. *Israel: Its Life and Culture.* 2 vols. London: Oxford University Press, 1926.

Pelikan, Jaroslav. *The Christian Tradition III: The Growth of Medieval Theology (600–1300).* Chicago: University of Chicago Press, 1978.

Pennick, Nigel. *Celtic Sacred Landscapes.* York, UK: Thames and Hudson, 1996.

Pierce, Joanne M. "'Green Women' and Blood Pollution: Some Medieval Rituals for the Church of Women after Childbirth." *Studia Liturgica* 29 (1999): 191–215.

Pinto, Lucille. "The Folk Practice of Obstetrics and Gynecology in the Middle Ages." *Bulletin of the History of Medicine* 47 (1973): 513–23.

Plötz, R. "'Benediction perarum et baculorum' und 'coronatio peregrinorum': Beiträge zu der Ikonographie des Hl. Jacobus im deutschen Sprachgebiet." In *Volkskultur und Heimat: Festschrift für Josef Dünninger zum 80 Geburtstag,* ed. Josef Dünninger, Dieter Harmening, and Erich Wimmer, 339–76. Würzburg: Königshausen & Neumann, 1986.

Power, Cornelius M. *The Blessing of Cemeteries.* Washington, D.C.: The Catholic University of America Press, 1943.

———. "Cemeteries, Canon Law of." *NCE* 3:386–87.

Quinn, J. R. "Blessings, Liturgical." *NCE* 2:613–15.

———. "Sacramentals." *NCE* 12:790–92.

Randel, Don Michael, ed. *The New Harvard Dictionary of Music.* Cambridge, Mass.: Belknap Press of Harvard University Press, 1986.

Reinburg, Virginia. "Liturgy and Laity in Late Medieval and Reformation France." *Sixteenth-Century Journal* 23, no. 3 (1992): 526–46.

Reynolds, Roger. "Death and Burial." *DMA* 4:118.

———. "Ordination, Clerical." *DMA* 9:263–69.

————. "Le cérémonies liturgiques de la cathédrale de Bénévent." In *La Cathédrale de Bénévent*, ed. Thomas Forrest Kelly, 167–205. Ghent: Ludion, 1999.

Richardson, Henry G. "The Coronation in Medieval England." *Traditio* 16 (1960): 111–202.

Riché, Pierre. "Spirituality in Celtic and Germanic Society." In *Christian Spirituality: Origins to the Twelfth Century*, ed. Bernard McGinn and John Myendorff, 163–76. New York: Crossroad, 1985.

Ries, Julien. "Blessing." Translated by J. C. Haight and A. S. Mahler. In *The Encyclopedia of Religion*, ed. Mircea Eliade, 16 vols., 2:247–53. New York: Macmillan, 1987.

Rivard, Derek A. *"Pro iter agentibus:* The Ritual Blessings of Pilgrims and Their Insignia in a Pontifical of Southern Italy." *Journal of Medieval History* 27 (2001): 365–98.

————. "Consecratio cymiterii: The Ritual Blessings of Cemeteries in the Central Middle Ages." *Comitatus* 35 (2004): 22–44.

Rodwell, Warwick. *Archaeology of Religious Places: Churches and Cemeteries in Britain.* Rev. ed. Philadelphia: University of Pennsylvania Press, 1989.

Rogers, Elizabeth Frances. *Peter Lombard and the Sacramental System.* Merrick, N.Y.: Richmond Publishing, 1976.

Rogers, Randall. "Peter Bartholomew and the Role of 'the Poor' in the First Crusade." In *Warriors and Churchmen in the High Middle Ages: Essays Presented to Karl Leyser*, ed. Timothy Reuter, 109–22. London: Hambledon Press, 1992.

Rosenwein, Barbara H. "Feudal War and Monastic Peace: Cluniac Liturgy as Ritual Aggression." *Viator* 2 (1971): 129–57.

————. *Rhinoceros Bound: Cluny in the Tenth Century.* Philadelphia: University of Pennsylvania Press, 1982.

Rubin, Miri. *Corpus Christi: The Eucharist in Late Medieval Culture.* Cambridge: Cambridge University Press, 1991.

Rudhardt, Jean, and Erica Meltzer. "Water." In *The Encyclopedia of Religion*, ed. Mircea Eliade, 16 vols., 15:350–58. New York: Macmillan, 1987.

Rush, A. C. *Death and Burial in Christian Antiquity.* Catholic University of America Studies in Christian Antiquity 1. Washington, D.C.: The Catholic University of America Press, 1941.

Russel, Frederick H. *The Just War in the Middle Ages.* New York: Cambridge University Press, 1975.

Russell, James C. *The Germanization of Early Medieval Christianity: A Sociohistorical Approach to Religious Transformation.* New York: Oxford University Press, 1994.

Saitta Revignas, Anna. *Catalogo dei manoscritti della biblioteca casanatense.* Vol. 6. Rome: Istituto Poligrafico dello Stato, 1984.

Saliba, John A. *"Homo religiosus" in Mircea Eliade: An Anthropological Evaluation.* Leiden: Brill, 1976.

Salmon, Pierre. *Les manuscrits liturgiques latins de la Bibliothèque Vaticane.* Studi e Testi 251, 253, 260, 267, 270. Vatican City: Biblioteca Apostolica Vaticana, 1968–72.

Schanz, J. P. "Wounds of Our Lord, Theological Significance of." *NCE* 13:1036–37.

Schmitt, Jean Claude. *The Holy Greyhound: Guinefort, Healer of Children since the Thirteenth Century.* Translated by Martin Thom. Cambridge: Cambridge University Press, 1983.

Schmitz, H. J. *Die Bussbücher und die Bussdisziplin.* 2 vols. Mainz: F. Kircheim, 1883.

Scribner, R. W. "Interpreting Religion in Early Modern Europe." *European Studies Review* 13 (1983): 89–105.

———. "Ritual and Popular Religion in Catholic Germany at the Time of the Reformation." *Journal of Ecclesiastical History* 35, no. 1 (1984): 47–77.

———. "Cosmic Order and Daily Life: Sacred and Secular in Pre-industrial German Society." In *Popular Culture and Popular Movements in Reformation Germany,* ed. R. W. Scribner, 1–16. London: Hambledon Press, 1987.

Searle, John R. *Speech Acts: An Essay in the Philosophy of Language.* Cambridge: Cambridge University Press, 1969.

Seasoltz, R. K. "Churches, Dedication of." *NCE* 3:862–64.

Sedlmayr, Hans. *Die Entstehung der Kathedrale.* Zurich: Atlantis Verlag, 1956.

Semple, Sarah. "A Fear of the Past: The Place of the Pre-Historic Burial Mound in the Ideology of Middle and Later Anglo-Saxon England." *World Archaeology* 30, no. 1 (1998): 109–26.

Sheerin, Daniel J. "The Consecration of Churches Down to the Ninth Century." In *Further Essays in Early Roman Liturgy,* ed. Geoffrey G. Willis, 133–73. London: S.P.C.K., 1968.

———. "Dedication of Churches." *DMA* 4:130–31.

Simek, Rudolf. *Heaven and Earth in the Middle Ages: The Physical World before Columbus.* Translated by Angela Hall. Woodbridge, UK: Boydell and Brewer, 1996.

Siraisi, Nancy G. *Medieval and Early Renaissance Medicine: An Introduction to Knowledge and Practice.* Chicago: University of Chicago Press, 1990.

Smith, Jonathan Z. *Imagining Religion: From Babylon to Jonestown.* Chicago: University of Chicago Press, 1982.

———. *To Take Place: Toward Theory in Ritual.* Chicago: University of Chicago Press, 1987.

Spiegel, Gabrielle M. "Suger of St. Denis." *DMA* 11:502–4.

Stallybrass, Peter. "Patriarchal Territories: The Body Enclosed." In *Rewriting the Renaissance: The Discovery of Sexual Difference in Early Modern Europe.* Edited by Margaret W. Ferguson et al. Chicago: University of Chicago Press, 1986.

Strocchia, Sharon T. "In Hallowed Ground: The Social Meaning of Burial Revenues at St. Maria del Carmine, 1350–1380." *Michigan Academician* 14, no. 4 (1982): 445–52.

———. "Death Rites and the Ritual Family in Renaissance Florence." In *Life and Death in Fifteenth-Century Florence,* ed. Marcel Tetel, 120–45. Durham: Duke University Press, 1989.

Sumption, Jonathan. *Pilgrimage: An Image of Medieval Religion.* London: Faber and Faber, 1975.

Swanson, R. N. *Religion and Devotion in Europe, c. 1215–c. 1515.* Cambridge Medieval Textbooks. Cambridge: Cambridge University Press, 1995.

Tester, S. J. *A History of Western Astrology.* Bury St. Edmunds, UK: Boydell Press, 1987.

Theilman, John M. "Communitas among Fifteenth-Century Pilgrims." *Reflexions Historiques* 311 (1984): 253–70.

———. "Medieval Pilgrims and the Origins of Tourism." *Journal of Popular Culture* 20, no. 4 (1986): 93–102.

Thibaut, J. B. *L'ancienne liturgie gallicane: Son origine et sa formation en Provence aux Ve et Vie siècles sous l'influence de Cassien et de saint Césaire d'Arles.* Paris: Maison de la Bonne Presse, 1929.

Thomas, Keith. *Religion and the Decline of Magic.* New York: Scribner, 1971.

Thompson, Augustine. *Cities of God: The Religion of Italian Communes, 1125–1325.* University Park: Pennsylvania State University Press, 2005.

Todorov, Tzvetan. "Le discours de la magie." *L'Homme* 18 (1973): 38–65.

Trexler, Richard C. *Public Life in Renaissance Florence.* New York: Academic Press, 1980.

Turner, Victor. *The Forest of Symbols: Aspects of Ndembu Ritual.* Ithaca: Cornell University Press, 1967.

———. *The Ritual Process: Structure and Anti-structure.* Chicago: Aldine, 1969.

———. "The Center Out There: Pilgrim's Goal." *History of Religions* 12, no. 3 (1973): 32–54.

———. *Drama, Fields and Metaphors: Symbolic Action in Human Society.* Ithaca: Cornell University Press, 1974.

———. "Ritual as Communication and Potency: An Ndembu Case Study." In *Symbols and Society,* ed. Carole E. Hill, 58–81. Athens: University of Georgia Press, 1975.

Turner, Victor, and Edith Turner. *Image and Pilgrimage in Christian Culture: Anthropological Perspectives.* New York: Columbia University Press, 1978.

Van Gennep, Arnold. *The Rites of Passage.* Translated by Monika B. Vizedom and Gabrielle L. Caffee. Chicago: University of Chicago Press, 1960.

Van Sylke, Daniel. "The Churching of Women: Its Introduction and Spread." *Ephemerides Liturgicae* 115 (2001): 208–38.

Vauchez, André. *La spiritualité du Moyen Âge occidental: VIIIe–XIIe siècles.* Paris: Presses Universitaires de France, 1975.

———. *The Laity in the Middle Ages: Religious Beliefs and Devotional Practices.* Translated by Margery J. Schneider. Edited by Daniel Bornstein. Notre Dame: University of Notre Dame Press, 1993.

———. *The Spirituality of the Medieval West, 700–1100.* Translated by Colette Friedlander. Kalamazoo: Cistercian Publications, 1993.

Vogel, Cyrille. *Medieval Liturgy: An Introduction to the Sources.* Translated by William G. Storey and Neils Krogh Rasmussen. Washington, D.C.: Pastoral Press, 1986.

Vorgrimler, Herbert. *Sacramental Theology.* Translated by Linda M. Maloney. Collegeville, Minn.: Liturgical Press, 1992.

Ward, Benedicta. *Miracles and the Medieval Mind.* Philadelphia: University of Pennsylvania Press, 1982.

Westermann, Claus. *Blessing in the Bible and the Life of the Church.* Translated by Keith Crim. Philadelphia: Fortress Press, 1968.

Wildiers, N. Max. *The Theologian and His Universe: Theology and Cosmology from the Middle Ages to the Present.* New York: Seabury Press, 1982.

Yoder, Don. "Toward a Definition of Folk Religion." *Western Folklore* 33 (1974): 7–14.

Zacher, C. K. *Curiosity and Pilgrimage: The Literature of Discovery in Fourteenth-Century England.* Baltimore: Johns Hopkins University Press, 1976.

Zika, Charles. "Hosts, Processions and Pilgrimages: Controlling the Sacred in Fifteenth-Century Germany." *Past and Present* 118 (1988): 25–64.

INDEX

Aaron, 35, 67

Abraham, 27, 49, 96, 97n175, 101; blessing of, 270; dagger of, 200; led out of Ur, 148; tax-collectors as sons, 127

absolution, 207, 286–87, 287–88

Agobard of Lyons, 238, 239, 241–42

agriculture: blessings of, 53–54, 55; natural hazards, 54; protection of blessings, 54; supernatural hazards, 54

alb, 107

Alexander I, Pope, 63

Alfred, King of England, 156

altar, 113, 125–26

ambiguity: social, 4, 290; of God's nature, 58, 59–60

amice, 107, 121

Andrieu, Michel, 37, 133, 223n21

angels: and the sacred in blessings, 272–73; archangel Gabriel, 181; archangel Michael, 169, 178n141, 181; archangel Raphael, 181; angelic intervention, 60; as light, 176; cemetery blessings, in, 111; defense, of, 177, 179, 244; duel blessing, in, 244; evil, 180; generic power, 273; guardian angels, 143n37, 177, 206, 210, 252; healing, in, 181, 191–92; human vulnerability, 17; invoked, 193; *lorica*, in, 251; ministers, as, 115, 116; protectors of homes, 79–80, 80n118, 81, 82; pro-

tectors of knights, 169, 177; protector of sailors, 224; protectors of travelers, 143–44; reconciliations, in, 115

anthropology, 2, 8, 135, 137; medieval blessings, and, 289–92

antiphons and verses: *Accingere [gladio tuo super femur tuum potentissime]*, 173; *Aperite mihi portas iustitiae*, 101, 102; *Asperges me*, 94, 98, 123; *Benedicamus patrem et filium cum sancto spiritu*, 210; blessing of cemeteries, in, 109; *Confirma hoc*, 121; *Deus in sancto via supra*, 128; *Domine ad te dirigatur*, 129; *Exsurgat deus et dissipentur inimici eius*, 120, 125; frequency in reconciliations, 120n261; *Haec requies mea in saeculum saeculi*, 103; *In viam pacem*, 147; *Iudica, domina, nocentes me*, 263; *Iustus es, domine*, 256; *Narrabo nomen tuam*, 121; *Ne reminiscaris*, 151, 245; *Pax huic domui*, 129; *Placebo domine*, 99; *Sanctum est verum lumen*, 130; *Signum salutis*, 18; *Specie tua*, 173; *Speciosus [forma prae filiis hominum]*, 173; *Ut obsequium servitutis nostre*, 125; *Veni creator*, 89; *Vox domini super aquas*, 61

Antony, St., 36

anxiety, 60, 73, 164–65

apples, 187

apostles, 250, 251

Apostle's Creed, 261

apotropaicism, 4, 11, 16; in non-sacramental

317

INDEX

comitatus, 156

communes, 178, 276

community: blessings and continuity, 47;
concern for purity and unity, 256; connection to divine, 60; as Christian cosmos, 291; of the dead, 90, 93; definition
and exclusion, 4, 166, 178, 253, 256;
God and human needs, 20, 89, 270;
healing masses, 206; living bound to
dead, 192; protected by divine, 17, 43, 56,
65, 76, 179; protection by knights, 172;
protection of homes, 80; protection
of workplaces, 89; regulation by ritual, 290; regulated by sacred power, 96;
restoration of violated places, 124, 127;
ritual separation from, 135, 136, 137; and
saints, 5; and sacred space, 46; and sacred time, 274–75

communitas: defined, 135–136; problems,
137n13; threat to order, 136

confession and penance, 288–289

Consolation of Philosophy, 58–59

Constantine, Emperor, 138

conversion, 21, 91

consciousness, 2, 9, 52, 292

contract, 56, 272. *See also* prosperity; worship

cope, 107, 121, 123

Corpus Christi, 277

corruption. *See* pollution

cosmos: Christian conception, 269, 286;
connected to divine, 250; history of,
184, 222; humans grounded in, 45; imbued with divine, 215; liturgy defends,
73–74; liturgy essential to maintain,
291; Purgatory, 286

cosmology, Christian: in adjurations,
278; of Augustine, 14; being and, 77;
and blessings, 292; construction, 23,
129; the East in, 99; and heavens, 76;
Israelite and water, 67; and knighthood, 166; the North in, 103; and piety,

5; and ritual, 4; the South in, 102;
the West in, 100; Christian place in,
269

covenant, 272

creation, 45, 61, 195

crops: corpus Christi, 43; Mass celebrated
for, 72. *See also* crop blessings

crop blessings: Blessing of a Cross on
the Road or standing above a Crop,18;
Blessing of New Fruits [RGP], 54;
Blessing of Vegetables [RGP], 54–55;
Blessing of Seed [*Liber ordinum* of Silos],
55; Blessing of Water against Vermin in
the Crops [RGP], 55, 61–67; Blessing of
Crops [*rituale* of St. Florian], 55, 60–61;
Blessing against the Worms Which Af-
flict Vegetables [Clm 7021], 55, 74–
77; Exorcism of Blessed Water Versus
Whatever Worms and against Whatever
Animal Is Destroying the Fruit of the
Earth [*manuale* of Lausanne], 55, 67–69;
Ordo for the Blessing and Exorcising of
Fruits against Locusts, Grasshoppers,
and Other Corrosive Animals [*Ordinari-
um* of Valencia], 55, 67–74

cross: in blessings, 18–21; and church
structure, 48; creates sacred space, 72,
106–12; in Crusade blessings, 286; and
crusaders, 141, 153; immersion of, 186;
marking graves, 92; power through
contact, 110; power against evil, 21, 71;
power to heal, 200; power versus enemies,154; as purifying pollution, 235;
sympathetic power, 107; as talisman, 72.
See also sign of the cross

Crucifixion, 141

crusaders, 153–55, 169, 280

Crusades, 141, 175, 202

culture: biblical and women, 205; Christian faithful, 95; human religious, 1, 45;
Greco-Romans and house blessings, 77;
needs of, medieval, 172; and paganism,

Virgin Mary (*cont.*)
   206, 208, 211, 261, 264; late-medieval
   devotions, 283
Vogel, Cyrille, 30n26, 37n51

wallet, 141
war: 171, 175, 176, 178, 288
water: against fevers, 187; aspersion: of armor, 166; in blessings of houses and
   reconciliations, 63; of cemeteries, 94–
   95, 97, 98, 109; of houses, 79; of polluted wells, 234; pregnant women, 210;
   ships, 223, 224; violated places, 121, 123,
   125; workplaces, 85; baptismal, 30, 259,
   262; belief in power of aspersion, 64,
   271; blessing in ordeal, 257, 263; created by God, 271; in crop blessings, 61–
   62, 74; cross-water, 186–87; in healing
   blessings, 188; holy blessed, 21; Hugh
   of St. Victor, 65; origins, 61–64, 67; and
   pre-Christian divinities, 226; purification, 227; as purification and healing,
   67–68, 69; reminded of purpose, 259,
   260; shield versus demons, 62, 63
weak, the, 166–67
wedding beds, 82–84. *See also* house blessings.
well, dish, and vessel blessings: "Blessing
   of a Font Which Has Been Neglected"
   [Augsburg], 229, 235–37; "Blessing of a
   New Well" [RGP], 228, 229; "Blessing
   over Small Vessels Found in Old Places" [RGP], 228–29, 229–30; "Blessing
   of Whatsoever Vases You Please" [Augs-
   burg], 229, 230–231; "Blessing Where

Anything Unclean Shall Have Fallen
   into a Vessel" [Silos], 228, 234–35
wells: pre-Christian, 13; as place of relief,
   47; holy, 186, 226–27; polluted, 234
west, 100, 107
widows, defense of, 157, 161, 165, 287
William Durandus, Bishop of Mende, 24,
   93, 285
William of Rennes, 242
wine, 56, 186, 187n178
witchcraft, 180
witches, 75n97. *See also tempestari*
women, 205–7
words, 12, 43, 85, 127, 155
workplaces, 85–89
world, natural: afflictions of, 192; and agriculture, 53; blessings' protection from,
   41–43; blessing saves, 166; as changing,
   59–60; chaos of, 293; elements infused
   with power, 66, 215; license to enjoy,
   130; and pilgrimage, 141–42; pilgrimage as renunciation of, 139; protected by
   baptism; 63 sacred origin, 56; as transitory, 47; profane, 84; purged by crucifixion, 117; renunciation and contempt for,
   293; social order, 162; visible and invisible, 76, 90
worship, 1, 19, 118, 127; blessed items in,
   217; in exchange for divine aid, 272,
   275–76; laity's secondary role, 134
wounds, of Christ, 162n98, 200, 202
wrath, of God, 223

York manual, 244

Blessing the World: Ritual and Lay Piety in Medieval Religion was designed and typeset in Ven-
detta by Kachergis Book Design of Pittsboro, North Carolina. It was printed on 60-pound
EB Natural and bound by Edwards Brothers of Lillington, North Carolina.